Counseling in Schools

Comprehensive Programs of Responsive Services for All Students

FIFTH EDITION

John J. Schmidt

East Carolina University, Emeritus

Boston • New York • San Francisco
Mexico City • Montreal • Toronto • London • Madrid • Munich • Paris
Hong Kong • Singapore • Tokyo • Cape Town • Sydney

Senior Sponsoring Editor: *Virginia L. Blanford*
Editorial Assistant: *Matthew Buchholz*
Marketing Manager: *Erica DeLuca*
Production Editor: *Gregory Erb*
Editorial Production Service: *Omegatype Typography, Inc.*
Composition Buyer: *Linda Cox*
Manufacturing Buyer: *Linda Morris*
Electronic Composition: *Omegatype Typography, Inc.*
Cover Designer: *Joel Gendron*

For related titles and support materials, visit our online catalog at www.ablongman.com.

Between the time website information is gathered and then published, it is not unusual for some sites to have closed. Also, the transcription of URLs can result in typographical errors. The publisher would appreciate notification where these errors occur so that they may be corrected in subsequent editions.

ISBN-10: 0-205-54040-6
ISBN-13: 978-0-205-54040-2

Library of Congress Cataloging-in-Publication Data

Schmidt, John J.
    Counseling in schools : comprehensive programs of responsive services for all students / John J. Schmidt. — 5th ed.
        p. cm.
    Includes bibliographical references and index.
    ISBN 0-205-54040-6 (pbk.)
    1. Educational counseling—United States. 2.   Student counselors—United States.
    3.   Counseling in elementary education—United States. 4.   Counseling in middle school education—United States. 5.   Counseling in secondary education—United States. I.   Title.
    LB1027.5.S2585 2008
    371.4—dc22

                                                                                2007060021

Printed in the United States of America

10 9 8 7 6 5 4 3 2 1   RRD-VA   11 10 09 08 07

*To my grandson, Aidan John Bergquist,
whose life has taught me so much about
development, relationships, and compassion.*

About the Author

Dr. John J. (Jack) Schmidt is Executive Director of the International Alliance for Invitational Education and professor emeritus of counselor education at East Carolina University, Greenville, North Carolina. From 1989 until 2002, Jack chaired the Counselor and Adult Education Department at ECU.

He completed his bachelor's and master's degrees at St. Michael's College in Vermont and earned a doctorate in counseling from the University of North Carolina at Greensboro. In addition to being a counselor educator, Jack has been a social studies teacher; an elementary, middle, and high school counselor; a school system director of counseling and testing services; and the state coordinator of school counseling with the North Carolina Department of Public Instruction from 1985 until 1989.

A popular speaker, Dr. Schmidt is also an active writer. Author of over fifty articles, professional manuals, book chapters, and book reviews, he has published more than a dozen books, including *A Survival Guide for the Elementary/Middle School Counselor* (2nd ed.); *Intentional Helping: A Philosophy for Proficient Caring Relationships; Invitational Counseling,* co-authored with Dr. William Purkey; and *Social and Cultural Foundations of Counseling and Human Services.*

Dr. Schmidt has received many awards and recognitions. Among the counseling awards are North Carolina Elementary School Counselor of the Year, North Carolina Counseling Association's Professional Writing and Research Award, The University of North Carolina at Greensboro's first Counselor Education Alumni Professional Excellence Award, the NCCA's Ella Stephens Barrett Award for leadership and service to the counseling profession, and the North Carolina School Counselor Association's Ruth C. McSwain Distinguished Professional Service Award.

He has served as President of the North Carolina Counseling Association and the North Carolina Association for Counselor Education and Supervision. He has served on editorial boards of national and international journals, including *The School Counselor* and *Counselor Education and Supervision.* In addition, Jack served two terms on the North Carolina Board of Licensed Professional Counselors, and currently is a Director on the National Board of Certified Counselors.

Jack lives with his wife, Pat, in Roaring Gap, North Carolina. They have one daughter, Dawn, a son-in-law, Eric, and three grandchildren, Evelyn, Erica, and Aidan, who live in Pennsylvania.

Contents

3   *The School Counselor and Program Leadership   53*

8 *Collaboration and Consultation   183*

9 *Student Appraisal   207*

10   *Educational and Career Development*   *235*

11   *Evaluation of School Counseling Programs*   *257*

Preface

Change has become the order of the day as the twenty-first century approaches the end of its first decade. Technology, particularly the Internet, has altered lifestyles, expanded educational opportunities, hastened the pace of life, and modified personal and professional relationships. The school counseling profession, having completed its first hundred years, has also been affected by changing attitudes and political trends regarding education and schooling. This fifth edition of *Counseling in Schools: Comprehensive Programs of Responsive Services for All Students* considers these many changes and influences while providing information about the development of the school counseling profession and the important role that professional counselors have in schools. This new edition continues to advocate for the development of comprehensive programs of services that identify the role of counselors in schools while assisting all students in the areas of academic, career, and social/personal development.

Current language and terminology, new texts, and recent articles that attempt to refocus the profession have helped me prepare this revision. In addition, recommendations from several reviewers and colleagues give the new edition a historical perspective balanced with current ideas about transforming the profession. As a result, this revision offers a professional foundation with which new school counselors can take leadership roles in advocating for comprehensive school counseling programs and responsive services for all students. In that spirit, the fifth edition of this text has a new subtitle: *Comprehensive Programs of Responsive Services for All Students.*

Professional counselors working in schools face the persistent twin challenges of clarifying their own roles and designing an appropriate program of services. Although the profession has made progress in meeting these challenges, many counselors find themselves in situations in which they are unable to provide adequate responsive services to students, parents, guardians, and teachers. Other assigned functions, often unrelated to their preparation as professional counselors, frequently prevent them from providing crucial educational, career, and personal assistance. This fifth edition continues to encourage counselors in schools to establish an appropriate professional identity through an assertive posture that conveys who they are and what they can offer to schools.

As with past editions, this edition of *Counseling in Schools* traces the development of school counseling, presents contemporary roles and functions for school counselors, and explores future possibilities for the profession. It is designed both for students who are preparing for a career in school counseling and for professionals seeking information about the nature of school counseling services.

How This Book Is Organized

Counseling in Schools includes comprehensive programs of services designed to meet the needs of students, parents, and teachers during the elementary, middle, and high school years. Thirteen chapters illustrate the common goals and various functions found in the practice of school counseling at these three levels of education as well as aspects that influence the role of counselors in schools. This book is divided into three basic sections.

• The first four chapters describe the historic development of school counseling; provide an overview of the diverse students, communities, and schools served by counselors; summarize the role of counselors in elementary, middle, and high schools; and present components of a comprehensive school counseling program.

• The second section, comprising Chapters 5 through 10, focuses on the major functions of counselors in schools and provides practical ideas for developing a program of services. Chapter 5 introduces these functions as the responsive services of the school counseling profession, and Chapter 6 provides an outline of practical strategies for planning, organizing, implementing, and evaluating a comprehensive counseling program. Chapters 7 through 9 illustrate how professional counselors incorporate each major function and responsive service into the practice of school counseling. Chapter 10 offers an overview of educational and career development, the two primary purposes of counselors working in schools. An important responsibility of school counselors is to help students with their educational and career decisions—a process that begins in the primary grades and expands in secondary schools with the involvement of parents, teachers, and counselors guiding students toward occupations, post-secondary educational opportunities, and adulthood. Three case studies close Chapter 10 and illustrate how the core services of a comprehensive program come together in a collaborative effort to assist all students.

• The last section, comprising Chapters 11, 12, and 13, presents professional issues related to the practice of school counseling. Chapter 11 explores issues related to program evaluation and reviews methods of assessing counseling services, as well as those related to performance appraisal and supervision of school counselors. Chapter 12 summarizes legal and ethical issues related to the practice of counseling in schools and presents the ethical standards of the school counseling profession as put forth by the American School Counseling Association (ASCA). Chapter 13 considers the future of school counseling, relating schools of tomorrow to students of tomorrow and examining both of these visions within the context of school counseling programs and services. Technological advances and their impact on learning and counseling are explored, as are some of the social changes expected in years to come.

A list of further readings, a section of self-check exercises, and a selection of relevant websites that may be of interest to school counselors appear at the end of each chapter. Learning about a profession's heritage and the functions and responsibilities that comprise its identity becomes more significant when students can absorb the information through practical exercises and outside reading. These added experiences often give special meaning to a person's professional development.

What Is New in This Edition

This edition of *Counseling in Schools* includes a new chapter on diversity (Chapter 2), because schools of today and tomorrow reflect an ever-increasing diversity of students, families, and communities, and this reality provides countless challenges for the professional counselor. To help the new counselor, Chapter 2 explores the terminology of multiculturalism; various aspects of diversity, such as culture, religion, rural and urban schools, and exceptionality among others; and cultural competencies expected of successful school counselors.

This revision also includes an additional case study related to middle school counseling. With this addition to Chapter 10, three cases now illustrate how programs consisting of comprehensive and responsive services might operate across all levels of school counseling—elementary, middle, and high school.

Another significant change to this fifth edition is additional information about the ASCA National Model (2003) and comparisons with other comprehensive school counseling approaches, particularly two models developed by Gysbers and Henderson (2000) and Myrick (2003). This additional material in Chapter 4 offers new professional counselors opportunities to examine similarities and differences among some of the more popular models of comprehensive school counseling programs.

Counseling in Schools continues to illustrate a divergence of professional practice. How counselors function in their schools is often determined more by state and local educational, political, and administrative decisions than by the mission promoted by the school counseling profession. Consequently, no single text can be the quintessential source for one's knowledge. This edition of *Counseling in Schools* presents a programmatic description of school counseling. As such, it touches briefly on many of the components and services of a comprehensive program, but it does not attempt to give extensive treatment to these aspects. Other courses and other texts in counselor preparation have that mission, and a school counseling internship, which culminates the preparation of professional counselors, brings this knowledge together in a realistic setting.

The components of a comprehensive school counseling program advocated here are the ideal elements and practices embraced by professional counselors in schools. In many schools, the way that school counselors function often appears light-years away from the roles and practices proposed in this text. Traditional roles and functions may no longer be relevant to meet the needs of future populations. This text embraces a futuristic, positive vision of what the school counseling profession could become tomorrow.

What Else Is Available for Students and Instructors?

- **Instructor's Manual and Test Bank.** A comprehensive Instructor's Manual is available in both print and electronic download formats to qualified adopters. Please ask your Allyn & Bacon sales representative to obtain a copy.

- **myhelpinglab** This online resource is designed to help students in counseling and psychotherapy, social work, marriage/family therapy, and human services make the transition from their academic coursework to their professional practice. It is appropriate for use in any course in which video footage of actual therapist–client sessions, case worker–client interactions, rich cases, and licensing/career preparation is important. Student access to MyHelpingLab can be packaged with new copies of any Allyn & Bacon counseling textbook at no additional cost.

Acknowledgments

This revision is the product of the efforts of many people. I sincerely appreciate the direction of Virginia Lanigan, my editor at Allyn and Bacon, and her assistant, Matthew Buchholz, who guided this project. I also am grateful to the reviewers of the proposal for this fifth edition: Laurie Carlson, Colorado State University; Charlotte R. Hamilton, South Carolina State University; Virginia Magnus, University of Tennessee, Chattanooga; Michael Nystul, Colorado State University; David Olguin, University of New Mexico; Delila Owens, Wayne State University; and Edward Wierzalis, University of North Carolina, Charlotte. Their reactions and suggestions were most helpful. As with all of my projects, this revision would not have been possible without the support of my wife, Pat. It is impossible to overstate her support and affection over the many years of our partnership.

—JJS

1

The School Counseling Profession

More than a hundred years ago an emerging new profession in the United States began primarily in educational settings. Known as the *guidance* profession for the first half of its existence, this relatively new field of study and practice has evolved into a growing *counseling* profession with members working in a variety of educational and clinical settings.

Today, professional counselors work in hospitals, mental-health centers, industries, family centers, schools, and other settings. Although they practice their profession in different settings with dissimilar missions, these counselors are united by their understanding and command of basic communication and helping skills; a common knowledge base of psychological, sociological, and human development theories; and similar goals that identify them as colleagues in the counseling profession. The work settings of these counselors may differ, but their professional practices are founded in related theories of counseling and human development, an appreciation of the power of the human spirit, and a commitment to changing systems and relationships for the betterment of all concerned. School counseling is a specialty area of this extended helping profession called *counseling* (Gladding, 2004; Nugent, 2000; Vacc & Loesch, 2000).

At the start of each new school year, children and adolescents across the United States enroll in classes, learn information, and acquire new skills to expand their personal, social, and career development. This is true for students in elementary schools through universities. In all of these educational settings, students relate to many different professionals who assist them in pursuing and achieving their educational goals. School counselors in elementary, middle, and high schools are among the professionals who assist students with developmental tasks. They also help parents and teachers who are challenged by the countless needs of children and adolescents in today's society. These counselors provide program leadership and offer services to students, parents, and teachers so that students have equal opportunity to reach their educational goals, choose an appropriate career direction, and develop as fully functioning members of a democratic society.

In this book, you will learn about the practice of professional counseling in schools. When compared with other notable vocations such as medicine, law, and teaching, school counseling is a relatively young profession; however, its growth was remarkable during the twentieth century, particularly in the United States. In this twenty-first century, the growth has continued and includes the emergence of counseling in schools in several countries across the globe. To fully appreciate the role of school counselors in U.S. education during this period and the role that these counselors will have in the twenty-first century, it is appropriate to begin with an understanding of the counseling profession as a whole. What is this field called counseling, and who are these professionals called counselors?

Counseling as a Profession

Throughout history many different people and professionals have become confidants and helpers for persons who have sought assistance, who have been less fortunate than others, or who have simply needed the comfort of a friend. Literary and historical accounts are filled with references to philosophers, wizards, fortune-tellers, medicine men, and others who in their unique and sometimes mythic ways were the pioneers of the helping professions. It is likely that the ancestors of professional counselors were the elders of ancient tribes who advised their youthful members, guiding them toward responsible decisions and behaviors. In ancient times, helping relationships among tribal members probably focused on learning basic survival skills. As civilizations progressed, these relationships developed into processes for encouraging youth to acquire proficiency in personal, social, and survival skills.

History shows that a variety of helping relationships have been formed within cultures and among people. In all human encounters and relationships, people have sought the wisdom and advice of others, including friends and professionals whom they respected. It is basic human nature to reach out to people to be helped or to help others.

In most instances, people who seek assistance are concerned with issues that revolve around relationships with themselves and others. Often these relationships involve questions of personal acceptance, social belonging, and future goals. People ask: "Who am I?" "Where do I belong?" "What should I being doing with my life?" In assisting with these and other questions, helpers create a caring atmosphere where desired goals can be explored and a plan for achieving these goals can be forged. This helping process of gathering information, becoming aware of oneself, exploring options and goals, and choosing a direction is, in essence, a description of professional counseling.

Professional counseling is the process of establishing a relationship to identify people's needs, design strategies and services to satisfy these needs, and actively assist in carrying out plans to help people make decisions, solve problems, develop self-awareness, and lead healthier lives. At times, counseling relationships help people avoid negative events and prevent harmful circumstances from impeding their growth and development. Other times, these relationships help people assess the progress they are making in life and plan strategies to ensure continued development. A third type of counseling relationship is appropriate when people experience difficulties and cannot remedy problems without support and intervention by others. In summary, different types of helping relationships are established by counselors to prevent problems, develop human potential, and remedy difficult situations.

The first type of helping process, prevention, can be understood in historical terms. Early civilizations worked to protect their camps and villages from natural disasters and human or other animal encroachment. Survival and expansion of the tribe were predicated on security measures that the members put in place. In a similar way, human survival and development relate to preventive plans that individuals and groups make and carry out for their own protection. Professional counselors, in schools and other settings, assist people and organizations in preventing losses, avoiding crises, and thwarting other calamities that impede progress in education and life.

Adequate prevention allows for optimal development. Counselors in schools and other institutions provide services that encourage people to develop their fullest potential. In schools, these services include, as you will see in this book, a variety of interventional, instructional, and informational services. When combined into a logical plan that addresses the needs of all students in a school, these services form a comprehensive school counseling program. A comprehensive program allows students to experience many developmental activities as part of a broad curriculum. It also offers direct counseling relationships between students and their school counselors, as well as other responsive services to meet the needs of all students.

Preventive and developmental services have the potential to enhance the lives of most people, including students in school, but there are times when children, adolescents, and adults have difficulties that warrant direct counseling. For example, today's students are challenged by an array of concerns that affect their educational progress. Child abuse, family dysfunction, addictive behaviors, society's fascination with violence, the impact of advancing technology, and other factors influence children's lives every day. In schools and other agencies, professional counselors assist students in meeting and resolving these challenges through individual counseling, group procedures, consultations with parents and teachers, and referrals to appropriate community agencies and private practitioners. Such responsiveness by counselors and the referrals that they coordinate address critical needs of children, adolescents, and adults and, therefore, are part of their comprehensive program. In summary, the services of counselors are aimed at preventing problems, focusing on developmental issues, and addressing critical concerns that pose an immediate threat to an individual's emotional, social, and psychological well-being.

Historical Background

The ancient Greeks are credited with creating a philosophy of living that focused on the nature of human development. The writings of Plato and Aristotle, in particular, contributed three foundations of the counselor profession to our contemporary fields of education, psychology, and human development. Plato's speculation about the nature of humankind began the exploration of individual development and our journey into the science of human behavior. Later, Aristotle added to this learning process by studying the environmental influence and discovering the importance of individual perception.

Following ancient Greek civilization, Hebrews and Christians of the post-Roman period proposed concepts regarding free will, self-determination, and human value that have contributed to the development of democratic ideals cherished by most contemporary societies. In many ways, these democratic principles parallel those that are central to effective counseling relationships. These beliefs assume that people have the right to be free, can make choices to benefit their development, want to be accepted as equal members of the group, and can learn to be responsible members of society.

As Western civilization continued through the Middle Ages, the spread of Christianity formalized educational opportunities and helping relationships through the work of priests, monks, and other clergy. For example, in the Catholic church, the sacrament of penance, in years past commonly called "confession," created a type of helping relationship. While the sacrament of penance placed people in a subservient relationship to God, this relationship also encouraged the confession of sins, their absolution, the forgiveness of transgressions, and the act of assuming responsibility for one's misdeeds. The priest, acting as an agent of God, helped the individual through this process of confession and renewal of faith. Interestingly, the priest maintained a vow of silence in much the same way that today's counselor honors the confidential nature of relationships with clients.

During the Middle Ages, priests and other clergy were among the few who were able to read and interpret scholarly works to the common person. As a result, they informed people not only about church doctrine but also about developmental issues such as career choices. In a historical review of early occupational literature, Zytowski (1972) noted that most writings of this time probably placed priests in the role of counselors because what was written was intended for scholarly consumption and not practical application. Interestingly, the spiritual relationship that many people have with the rabbis, ministers, priests, mullahs, or other clergy today often includes a counseling component. The emerging field of pastoral counseling in the United States is evidence of this.

Toward the beginning of the seventeenth century, books about vocational development and occupational choice began to appear. A major work by Tomasco Garzoni of Italy provided detailed descriptions of a number of occupations and professions of the times. This work, translated as *The Universal Plaza of All the Professions of the World,* was published in twenty-five Italian editions and in several other languages. In 1631, Powell published *Tom of All Trades; Or the Plain Pathways to Preferment,* a picture book of different occupations with information about how to enter these vocations and what education was necessary. This was the first career information book published in English. In the eighteenth century, authors such as Joseph Collyer, Edmund Carter, Denis Diderot, and R. Campbell continued the focus on occupational choice and career development. Campbell's book, *The London Tradesman,* was promoted in 1747 as "a compendious view of all the trades, professions, arts, both liberal and mechanic, now practiced in the cities of London and Westminster . . . for the information of parents, and instruction of youth in their choice of business" (Zytowski, 1972, p. 446). These and other publications provided the first information services related to vocational development and were the precursors of what was to become career guidance and counseling.

Many other writers, philosophers, and leaders through the ages have added to the legacy that contributed to the development of the counseling profession. René Descartes' *Principles of Philosophy,* in which he explored the territory of human thought, Jean-Jacques Rousseau's emphasis on the freedom of natural development, Immanuel Kant's rational view of man, and later Paul Tillich and Martin Heidegger's existential teachings are among the efforts that helped build a foundation for much of what we call counseling, psychology, and human development today.

The birth of psychology as a field of study at the end of the nineteenth century began the systematic inquiry into human behavior and development. When Wilheim Wundt began his Psychological Institute at the University of Leipzig in 1879, psychology became an acceptable area of study (Gibson & Mitchell, 1999). An event that paralleled the development of psychology as a scientific field was the psychiatric movement in the medical profession, which gave an organic focus to the treatment of seriously disturbed patients. In 1908, Clifford Beers published *A Mind That Found Itself,* an exposé of the horrible conditions in mental institutions of the times. Beers himself was hospitalized as a schizophrenic patient on and off during his lifetime, and with this book he aroused public attention and concern about the treatment of mental illnesses. With impetus from Beers's book and the efforts of a few psychologists, the mental-health movement began in the United States. This movement encouraged the establishment of local psychopathic hospitals, the forerunners of today's community mental-health programs and the mental-health counseling profession.

A related movement in the development of the counseling profession was the establishment of child guidance clinics in Chicago by William and Mary Healy in 1909. The clinic emerged from their work with physically ill children in the slums of Chicago. With philanthropic funding, the Healys established the Juvenile Psychopathic Institute, a clinic designed to serve juvenile delinquents (Nugent, 2000). Their approach was to view the physical and psychological problems of children as related elements of a total picture. The clinic begun by the Healys was the first of over one hundred child guidance clinics established in the United States at the start of the twentieth century. It was later administered by the state of Illinois and became the Institute of Juvenile Research.

Combined, these early events led to the emergence of several professions that helped people with social, personal, and vocational concerns. Social workers, psychologists, and counselors who practice in today's mental-health clinics, rehabilitation centers, and schools find their roots in these historical moments. The theories of practice and helping skills of the counseling profession are founded in many of the beliefs and discoveries presented by scholars and practitioners of these early times. As a result, the counseling profession relies on a broad knowledge of human development, psychology, sociology, and education. At the same time, it incorporates effective communication and leadership skills with the essential human qualities of caring, genuineness, regard, and respect for others.

Identity

All counselors, regardless of the professional setting in which they work, have this broad knowledge base and use similar helping processes. What distinguishes them from one another and gives them a particular identity are the specific needs and developmental concerns of the clients who seek their help. For this reason, mental-health counselors practice their profession in slightly different ways than career counselors, family counselors, or school counselors do. Though the breadth of their services and nature of their activities may differ, however, their essential goals and purposes are similar. A similar comparison can be made among school counselors who serve different levels of educational practice in elementary, middle, and high schools. The nature of specific activities at these levels may differ as a result of the developmental needs of students, but the broad goals and general processes used in comprehensive school counseling programs are similar across all three levels.

Because professional counselors are trained in a broad spectrum of theory and knowledge in the fields of psychology, education, and human development, and at the same time practice their professions in a range of settings, they often use titles that reflect their work environment. For example, we find mental-health counselors in psychiatric hospitals and mental-health centers and sometimes in the employee assistance programs of business and industry. Their training generally takes place in college or university counselor education programs. In contrast, school counselors work in elementary, middle, or high schools. They are trained in counselor education programs with an emphasis on human development, learning, and school environments. Nevertheless, a fundamental knowledge of human development and a command of helping processes and skills are essential for both mental-health and school counselors. This common background is what links them and other counselors as colleagues in the counseling profession.

Many different types of counseling professionals function in a variety of settings. At the same time, other helping professionals also use counseling processes in their roles. Clinical social workers, psychiatric nurses, and counseling psychologists are among those who use counseling and consulting processes similar to those used by counselors in hospitals, mental-health centers, prisons, industries, and schools. In some instances, these individuals consider themselves members of both professions. For example, some members of the American Counseling Association (ACA) also belong to the American Psychological Association (APA). They consider themselves counselors and psychologists, which is not uncommon among professionals who are trained in both counseling and psychology. In fact, the APA has a division for counseling and development.

The proliferation of these overlapping professions has been particularly noticeable in the United States. Perhaps this is because, as this country developed during the eighteenth and nineteenth centuries and accelerated through the Industrial Revolution into the twentieth century, personal, social, career, and educational issues became increasingly important. These factors, combined with the multicultural realities of the United States, have contributed to the complexity of living a productive, well-adjusted life in this country. Because the United States prides itself on democratic principles, equal opportunity, and human service, it is understandable how so many related helping professions could emerge. In particular, it is especially clear why counselors have had such an important role in our schools, which themselves incorporate principles of democracy, equity, and opportunity for all students. It is within this context that we now examine the development of the school counseling profession.

Development of School Counseling

The counseling profession entered the U.S. schoolhouse in the early twentieth century. Up to that time, classroom teachers provided whatever social, personal, or career assistance students needed. Perhaps the delay of the profession's entry into U.S. schools occurred because the earliest schools were highly selective in admitting students. They were exclusive academies, selecting only the wealthiest of students. The curricula of these schools prepared young men for professions, such as law or medicine, or for the religious ministry. As the country expanded and progressed, the selectivity of schools decreased and equal opportunity in education became a reality for men and women. At least this was true for white men and women. The beginning of publicly supported schools opened educational doors to women as well as men from all economic levels of society. Thus, an increasingly divergent population began entering schools, and teachers alone could no longer meet the broad spectrum of needs expressed by these students.

The school counseling profession began as a vocational guidance movement that emerged from the Industrial Revolution at the beginning of the twentieth century. Some negative by-products of the tremendous industrial growth of this period were city slums, ethnic ghettos, and apparent neglect of individual rights and integrity. In response to these conditions, proponents of the Progressive Movement, a reaction to the negative effects of industrial growth, advocated for social reform. Vocational guidance was one aspect of this response. For example, in 1895 George Merrill began experimental efforts in vocational guidance at the California School of Mechanical Arts in San Francisco (Miller, 1968). Merrill's program offered exploratory experiences for students in the occupational trades taught at the California school, and these experiences were accompanied by counseling, job placement, and follow-up services.

Generally, the guidance movement of this period instructed school children, adolescents, and young adults about their moral development, interpersonal relationships, and the world of work. Jesse B. Davis is thought to be the first person to implement a systematic guidance program in the public schools (Gladding, 2004; Wittmer & Clark, 2007). From 1898 to 1907, he was a class counselor at Central High School in Detroit, Michigan, and was responsible for educational and vocational counseling with eleventh-grade boys and girls. Davis became principal of a high school in Grand Rapids, Michigan, in 1907 and at that time began a schoolwide guidance program. He encouraged his English teachers to include guidance lessons in their composition classes to help students develop character, avoid problem behaviors, and relate vocational interests to curriculum subjects.

The work of Jesse B. Davis was complemented by programs in other parts of the country. Frank Goodwin organized a systemwide guidance program for the Cincinnati, Ohio, schools in 1911, and, in 1908, Eli Weaver at the Boys High School of Brooklyn gained national recognition for his efforts in organizing guidance services in New York City (Miller, 1968). About this time, Anna Y. Reed developed guidance programs in the Seattle school system that focused on the employability of students and incorporated business ethics and concepts about the free enterprise system (Gibson & Mitchell, 1999). These and other efforts in guidance established the beginnings of what was to become the school counseling profession.

These facts notwithstanding, Frank Parsons is often mentioned as the "Father of Guidance" and is credited by most historians as the person who began the guidance movement in the United States. In 1908, Parsons organized the Boston Vocational Bureau to provide assistance for young people. The bureau was established by philanthropist Mrs. Quincy Agassiz Shaw and was based on Parsons's ideas and plans for vocational guidance, which stressed a scientific approach to selecting a career (Gysbers & Henderson, 2000). According to Parsons, "No step in life, unless it may be the choice of a husband or wife, is more important than the choice of a vocation" (1909, p. 3).

Parsons's attention to vocational development was framed by his concern about society's failure to develop resources and services for human growth and development. At the same time, he was concerned about helping young men make the transition from their school years into the world of work. In his book *Choosing a Vocation,* which was published after his death, Parsons (1909) highlighted three essential factors for choosing an appropriate vocation: (1) clear self-understanding of one's aptitudes, abilities, interests, resources, and limitations; (2) knowledge of the requirements, advantages, disadvantages, and compensation for different types of employment; and (3) an understanding of the relationship between these two groups of facts. This conceptualization of successful career development still holds credence today. Self-understanding, knowledge of one's career interests, and general knowledge about careers go hand in hand for a person to be successful in life.

Parsons's plan also included training counselors to help young students with vocational development. Nine months after establishing the Vocational Bureau, he began a program designed to train young men to become vocational counselors and managers of vocational bureaus for YMCAs, schools, colleges, and businesses throughout the country (Miller, 1968). A few years later, the School Committee of Boston created the first counselor certification program. Requirements for this school counselor's certificate included study of education and experience in a vocational school or a vocational service. This certification program was eventually adopted by Harvard University as the first college-based counselor education program.

Frank Parsons's work had a significant impact on the vocational guidance movement. In Boston, the superintendent of schools designated over one hundred elementary and secondary teachers to become vocational counselors (Nugent, 2000). As noted earlier, the guidance movement spread to many other parts of the country, including New York City, Grand Rapids, and Cincinnati. Within a few years, city school systems across the country had developed guidance programs.

Early developments in the guidance movement were complemented by the creation of the National Vocational Guidance Association (NVGA) in 1913. This organization began publishing the *National Vocational Guidance Bulletin* on a regular basis in 1921. Over the next several decades this publication underwent several name changes, eventually becoming the *Career Development Quarterly*. In 1952, when NVGA joined with the American Personnel and Guidance Association (APGA), the *Personnel and Guidance Journal* became the major publication of this national association of counselors. Later, this publication was renamed the *Journal of Counseling and Development* of the American Association for Counseling and Development (AACD). The creation of the NVGA is significant because it began the unification and identification of what has become the counseling profession of today. This is especially true for the school counseling profession.

Emergence of Guidance and Counseling in Schools

The work of Jesse Davis, Anna Reed, Eli Weaver, Frank Parsons, and a host of other pioneers created the momentum for the development of a school counseling profession. From the 1920s through the 1940s, many events occurred that gave impetus, clarity, and direction to this emerging profession. Coincidentally, many of these developments, with their roots founded in the vocational guidance movement, raised questions about the profession's narrow focus on vocational development. Eventually, some leaders of the counseling movement began to encourage a broader focus that included issues of personality and human development beyond vocational guidance. This broader view laid the groundwork for many of the counseling theories and approaches that were created in the years that followed. Some of these were developed in the years before World War II and helped to define school guidance and counseling of that period.

Before World War II. After the vocational guidance movement of the early 1900s, World War I was the next major event that had an impact on the developing counseling profession. During the First World War, the United States military began using group-training procedures to screen and classify draftees. Intelligence testing, developed in the beginning of the decade, was the catalyst for this movement. In particular, work begun by French psychologist Alfred Binet, and later expanded by Lewis Terman and Arthur Otis, was adapted by the military. Arthur Otis developed an intelligence test that could be given to large groups and administered by unskilled examiners. This test became the basis for the military's *Army Alpha Examination,* a paper-and-pencil test, along with a second test, the *Army Beta Examination,* developed as a performance test (Baker & Gerler, 2004).

During this time and in the decade immediately following the war, a great number of tests were developed and marketed, but many were inadequately designed and inappropriately standardized. Nevertheless, the military's interest in using group measurement techniques was embraced by schools and the education profession when the war ended. The potential for applying testing and other measurement techniques to pupil assessment helped catapult the development and expansion of standardized testing in U.S. schools.

The 1920s also saw the rise of progressive education in the schools. This movement, introduced by John Dewey, emphasized the school's role in guiding students in their personal, social, and moral development (Nugent, 2000). As a result, schools began incorporating guidance activities into the curriculum for the purpose of developing skills for living (Brewer, 1932). This movement was short-lived and was criticized by parents, teachers, and others as being too permissive and anti-educational. These critics wanted to focus on fundamentals of education and claimed that moral development was in the purview of the home and church. This criticism, in addition to declining public funds brought on by the Great Depression, all but caused the abandonment of support for guidance activities and counseling services in the schools.

One by-product of the emphasis on data collection through group testing used by the military during this period was the development of counseling approaches that stressed the measurement of students' traits and characteristics. The late 1930s saw the first theory of guidance and counseling, called Trait and Factor Theory, developed by E. G. Williamson at the University of Minnesota. Using Parsons's vocational program as a springboard, Williamson and his colleagues became leading advocates for what became known as the *directive* or *counselor-centered* approach to school counseling. In his book *How to Counsel Students,* Williamson (1939) wrote that counselors should state their "point of view with definiteness, attempting through exposition to enlighten the student" (p. 136). In this direct approach, counselors were expected to dispense information and gather data to influence and motivate students.

Later, Williamson softened this view to some degree. In 1958, he wrote that the counselor is responsible for helping "the student become more sophisticated, more matured in understanding the value option that he faces and to identify clearly those that he prefers. The search is the important educational experience—not a control of a behavior, a rigging in favor of one choice or the other, even though the counselor may have his personal preference" (Dugan, 1958, p. 3). At the same time, the directive approach maintained that counselors could not give complete freedom of choice to students who were not capable of making the best decisions for themselves. According to this view, counselors were obliged to protect the interests of society, the school as an institution, and the student. Williamson believed that the development of individuality on the part of students must be balanced with concern for self-destructive and antisocial behaviors. He declared that people achieve individual freedom through effective group membership, interdependence, and adherence to high social ideals.

In his approach to counseling, Williamson (1950) developed six steps for assisting students:

1. *Analysis*—the gathering of data about the student and the student's environment
2. *Synthesis*—the selection of relevant data and the summary and organization of these data to understand the strengths and weaknesses of the student
3. *Diagnosis*—the development of a rationale regarding the nature and etiology of the student's problems
4. *Prognosis*—a prediction of outcomes based on the actions chosen by the student
5. *Treatment*—various approaches and techniques selected for the counseling relationship
6. *Follow-up*—an evaluation of the effectiveness of the counseling relationship and the student's plan of action

About the time that Williamson and his colleagues were developing their directive counseling approach, others continued to question the narrow focus of the vocational guidance movement. Counselors and psychologists alike echoed this concern and stressed that vocational choice is simply one of many developmental issues with which counselors should assist students. These views began to broaden the goals of guidance and counseling in education. As a result, a resurgence in school counseling began.

World War II to the Space Age.   The 1940s saw major changes in the counseling profession, and these developments had significant impact on the practice of counseling in schools. Among the influences during this period, three major events seem to have shaped these developments: (1) the popularity of the client-centered approach to counseling developed by Carl Rogers; (2) the onset and impact of World War II on U.S. society; and (3) government involvement in the counseling and education professions after the war. In addition, organizational changes within the profession and emerging theoretical models of counseling were significant influences during this period. Each of these events had an impact on the developing identity and direction of the counseling profession.

The Rogerian Influence.   Carl Rogers probably had more influence on the counseling profession and the development of counseling approaches than any other individual. Two of his books, *Counseling and Psychotherapy: New Concepts in Practice* (1942) and *Client-Centered Therapy: Its Current Practice, Implications, and Theory* (1951), had a significant impact on counseling in both school and nonschool settings. Most important, Rogers gave new direction to the profession by focusing on the helping relationships established between counselors and their clients and by recognizing the importance of personal development in these relationships. This focus moved the profession away from the counselor-centered perspectives of earlier times and emphasized a growth-oriented counseling relationship as opposed to an informational and problem-solving one.

This new vision for the profession challenged both the trait-factor approaches that emerged from vocational guidance and the testing movement following World War I and the therapist-centered views embraced by Freudian psychoanalysts of the early 1900s. At the same time, Rogers's acceptance of self-concept theory as a foundation for effective therapeutic relationships disputed the strict behavioral views of the psychological movement in the United States, which was gaining prominence during this period. His works marked the beginning of a debate that continues today in discussions within the counseling and psychology professions. Ironically, both counseling and psychology identify Carl Rogers as a significant contributor to each profession's development.

For nearly fifty years, Rogers's contributions to the development of counseling theory and practice helped strengthen and identify the emerging counseling profession. Most important, he encouraged counselors to attend to the person in the process. This view was highlighted by Rogers and his followers in the 1970s and 1980s as they gradually changed from a "client-centered" approach to a "person-centered" one.

Rogers not only developed a theory of counseling, he also researched, tested, and revised it during his lifetime. He also encouraged other theorists and researchers to do likewise. The now classic works of Carkhuff and Berenson (1967) and Truax and Carkhuff (1967) validated the variables of empathy, respect, and genuineness espoused by Rogers and his disciples as essential characteristics of all therapeutic relationships. In addition, early studies of client-centered counseling reported evidence of psychological adjustment, improved tolerance, accelerated learning, and other benefits of this approach (Axline, 1947; Grummon & John, 1954; Thetford, 1952).

Opinions about Rogers's influence on the school counseling profession are not uniformly favorable. Wittmer and Clark (2007) noted that inordinate attention placed on the individual by the client-centered approach "somehow took us off-track in school counselor preparation and may have contributed to the inappropriate training of many school counselors" (p. 3). In particular, the emphasis on individual counseling processes tended to neglect preventive and developmental interventions needed in school environments. Nevertheless, the impact of Rogers's work on counseling practices both in and out of schools was remarkable.

World War II and Government Influence.   Two other events that influenced the counseling profession during this period were World War II and increased government involvement in the counseling and psychology professions. As the United States entered the war, the government requested assistance from counselors and psychologists to help in screening, selecting, and training military and industrial specialists. This emphasis gave impetus to another area related to the counseling profession—personnel work in business and industry. After the war, the Veterans Administration (VA) provided funds for graduate students to become trained as counselors and psychologists. About this time, the term *counseling psychologist* emerged in VA specifications, further distinguishing psychology from vocational guidance (Gladding, 2004).

Another example of governmental influence in the counseling profession was the George-Barden Act of 1946. This legislation provided funds to develop and support guidance and counseling activities in schools and other settings. For the first time in history, school counselors and state and local supervisors received resource, leadership, and financial support from the government. This action fueled the start of a period of rapid growth for guidance and counseling services in schools.

One governmental change that occurred in the 1950s was the reorganization of the Guidance and Personnel Branch of the U.S. Office of Education (Gysbers & Henderson, 2000). In 1952, this office was disbanded under the Division of Vocational Education, and from 1953 to 1954 a Pupil Personnel Services Section operated in the Division of State and Local School Systems. In 1955, a Guidance and Personnel Services Section was reestablished. The development of this office helped to move the school counseling profession further away from its original vocational emphasis to a broader student services perspective. This trend continued through the 1950s and into the 1960s.

In 1957, the Soviet Union lofted the world into the space age with its successful launching of *Sputnik I*, the first earth satellite. This single event rang a tremendous national alarm about the capability of the United States to stay ahead of the Russians in the space program, with industrial and technological advancements, and in military strength. Gibson and Mitchell (1999) wrote that an "indirect but nevertheless significant result of [Sputnik] . . . was the 'lift off' of the counseling and guidance movement in the United States" (p. 12). The ensuing public outcry and criticism of educational institutions eventually led to the passage of Public Law 85-864, entitled the National Defense Education Act of 1958 (NDEA).

The NDEA was preceded by several national studies sponsored by the Office of Education, the National Science Foundation, and the Committee on Financing Higher Education during the early 1950s. These studies concluded that

1. Schools needed to improve their testing of student aptitude and to design systems to identify students' potential earlier in their educational careers.
2. Counselors were needed to encourage students to stay in school, concentrate on academic courses, and enter college.
3. Scholarships were needed to assist talented students who were financially unable to attend college after high school.

These findings and conclusions set the stage for the immediate action that followed the launching of Soviet *Sputnik I*. As a result, public opinion was amenable to the swift passage of the National Defense Education Act to

- Provide loans to students in colleges and universities.
- Offer financial incentives to secondary schools to improve mathematics, science, and foreign language instruction.
- Create National Defense Fellowships for graduate students interested in teaching at the college level.
- Support the improvement of guidance and counseling programs in secondary schools.
- Establish language institutes and research centers to improve the teaching of foreign languages.
- Encourage research to develop the effective use of television and related media for improved instruction.
- Establish vocational education programs.
- Create a Science Information Services and a Science Information Council.
- Improve statistical services for state educational agencies. (Miller, 1968)

Title V of the NDEA focused specifically on school counseling and guidance services in two important ways. First, it provided funds to help states establish and maintain school counseling, testing, and other guidance-related services. Second, it authorized the establishment of counseling institutes and training programs in colleges and universities to improve the skills of those who were working with students in secondary schools or of persons who were training to become school counselors. These special institutes began during the summer of 1959 at fifty colleges and universities where over 2,200 counselors were trained (Miller, 1968). Title V, section A, of the NDEA provided $15 million a year to assist local school systems in developing and strengthening guidance and counseling services, and section B provided approximately $7 million a year for universities and colleges to establish training institutes to prepare school counselors (Shertzer & Stone, 1966).

As a result of the NDEA, Title V, all the states, the District of Columbia, and three territories expanded school counseling services during the late 1950s and early 1960s. The Counseling and Guidance Branch of the U.S. Office of Education added consultants to its staff, thereby increasing its leadership role in the development of programs at the state level. The following changes occurred in the years immediately following the passage of the NDEA (1958–1963):

1. The number of full-time counselors increased 126 percent from 12,000 to 27,180, and the ratio of counselors to students dropped from 1:960 to 1:530.
2. The number of state guidance consultants increased from 99 to 257.
3. Over 400 counseling institutes were funded by government with more than 13,000 counselors trained.
4. Local school district expenditures for guidance and counseling services rose from $5.6 million to over $127 million. (Miller, 1968, p. 37)

Organizational Changes and Professional Influences. As a result of these national initiatives, the 1950s saw a continued acceleration of the school counseling profession. This development was marked by particular events that altered the national counseling associations spearheading this professional movement. The first of these events was the establishment of the American Personnel and Guidance Association (APGA) in 1952. The APGA grew out of an alliance of organizations called the American Council of Guidance and Personnel Associations (ACGPA), which began in 1935. This group of organizations aligned with each other to share concerns about educational issues, vocational guidance, and other personnel matters. Initially, the four organizations that formed the APGA were the American College Personnel Association, the National Association of Guidance Supervisors, the National Vocational Guidance Association, and the Student Personnel Association for Teacher Education. Shortly afterward, APGA began a fifth association, the American School Counselor Association, which became Division 5 of APGA. In the years that followed, many more divisions emerged and joined the larger parent association.

Another phenomenon that influenced the development of the counseling profession during this time was the introduction of several new theories of counseling. As noted earlier, Carl Rogers opened the debate between the directive and nondirective schools of thought in the 1940s. The 1950s continued this dialogue and witnessed the emergence of several new theories including behavioral approaches and a host of other counseling and developmental theories began during this period. The humanistic and existential movements, illustrated in the writings of Combs (1962), Jourard (1964), May (1966), and Maslow (1957), and the emergence of group counseling also influenced the profession.

Although there was much overlap among the concepts of some of these theories, there were enough differences in terminology and philosophy to create an array of counseling models, methods, and strategies. In 1976, Parloff identified more than 130 counseling theories and approaches, and since that time the number has continued to grow. Generally, these theories can be classified under one of five categories: psychoanalytic (including psychodynamic), person-centered, cognitive, behavioral, and affective (Vacc & Loesch, 2000). Some approaches to counseling, such as Reality Therapy (Glasser, 1965), multimodal counseling (Gerler, 1990), Adlerian counseling (Sweeney, 1998), and invitational counseling (Purkey & Schmidt, 1990, 1996), are more popular and compatible with school counseling programs.

Expansion of School Counseling

The 1960s saw continued development and expansion of the counseling profession. This was, in part, a result of legislation to increase services and enhance existing programs and the refinement and clarification of the role of the school counselor. Expansion of the profession coincided with a shift toward the developmental role of counselors, as illustrated by C. Gilbert Wrenn's now classic book, *The Counselor in a Changing World* (1962), which set the stage for a broader focus for counseling programs and services.

The 1960s. The United States and other developed countries were moving from the industrialization of the early part of the twentieth century to the technological advances of the twenty-first century. Among these technological changes would be a host of social, economic, educational, and career adjustments that would encourage people to seek the assistance of counselors in solving personal and social difficulties or in locating information to make career decisions. Automation in industry would affect employment and career counseling for adults as well as for students in schools. Changing roles of women would affect family structures, and the accelerated pace of society would increase daily stress in most people's lives. A number of other developments, including altered sex roles and sexual preferences, a wider economic gap between lower and upper classes, an increased fear of nuclear war, and astonishing medical discoveries that promised to lengthen the life span, all contributed to human challenges and critical decisions for which counselors were needed.

Federal legislation during this period continued to have an impact on the counseling profession and the role of counselors, particularly school counselors. For example, the Elementary and Secondary Education Act of 1965 (Public Law 89-10) provided funds and supported special programs to help schools improve educational opportunities for students of low-income families. This bill also provided funds for services that would not normally be available in most schools.

The 1960s saw a new, expanded role for school counselors, with movement away from an emphasis on guidance programs. The counseling literature of this time, particularly *The School Counselor* journal and a few major texts, began to delineate the role and functions of counselors in schools. Books such as C. H. Patterson's *Counseling and Guidance in Schools* (1962) and E. C. Roeber's *The School Counselor* (1963) gave impetus to the development of a clear professional role and defined specific functions of counselors in schools. These descriptions and definitions complemented the emerging roles of other student services workers such as school social workers, school psychologists, attendance officers, and health workers. During this period, the term *guidance* was targeted by some authors as a vague and sometimes confusing label for counselors, teachers, and other people who attempted to define the role and functions of counselors in schools. In 1966, Shertzer and Stone wrote

> Guidance has been defined in many ways. An examination of the plethora of books and articles . . . indicates that the word . . . has been used to convey each author's opinions and biases. Indeed, a major criticism . . . is that the word "guidance" has been rendered relatively meaningless by the variety of ways . . . it is used. (1966, p. 30)

Nearly five decades later, the discussion about the terms *guidance* and *counseling*, and the choice of an appropriate language to identify the school counselor's role and functions continue to be important professional issues. The confusion over the terms *guidance* and *counseling* is compounded by the absence of a theoretical foundation for guidance as a professional function. Muro and Kottman (1995) noted, "While there is some theory available to guide counseling practice, formal guidance theory still needs elaboration and definition" (p. 49). It is difficult to comprehend how any profession could establish a credible identity on a nonexistent theoretical foundation.

In the period following 1960, the role and functions of school counselors emphasized in the professional literature included programmatic and process functions. Programmatic functions emphasized strategies to develop comprehensive programs of services, such as defining goals and objectives, assessing students' needs, aligning services with the school's curriculum, coordinating student services, and evaluating results. In addition, educational and vocational planning, student placement, and referral systems frequently were included in this category. Process functions described specific activities by which counselors provided direct services to students, parents, and teachers. These functions included individual and group counseling, student assessment, parent assistance, and consultation with teachers and parents. In many respects, these components, as you will see in later chapters of this book, remain as important functions of counselors in today's schools.

Clarification of the school counselor's role and functions during the 1960s paved the way toward a broader professional perspective on programs of services offered by counselors in schools. Many writers at this time emphasized comprehensive guidance and counseling programs as essential aspects of the school curriculum. The intent of these programs was for school counselors and classroom teachers to play a vital, collaborative role.

In 1968, Miller wrote that an "effective guidance program requires the cooperative effort of every teacher in the school" (p. 75). Yet, this cooperative role for administrators and teachers remained unclear because of several factors. For one, guidance continued to be associated strictly with the role of the school counselor. To this day, this perception endures in many schools where the mere mention of the word *guidance* has teachers and administrators turning their heads toward the counselor's office.

A second factor that made it difficult for teachers to embrace a guidance role was a narrow focus on the subject matter that they were responsible for teaching. This is true in today's schools as well. Sometimes teachers, particularly in secondary schools, place so much emphasis on the instruction of English, mathematics, science, and other subjects that they forget the broader, developmental concerns of students. Although many attempts have been made, the U.S. schools have not infused guidance—that is, lessons of self-development and social skills—into the curriculum and daily instruction.

Expansion into New Areas.   Emphasis on the role of teachers in guidance in the 1960s and 1970s highlighted specific functions for establishing a foundation of collaboration between school counselors and teachers. This collaboration continues to be an essential ingredient of today's comprehensive school counseling programs. Some of the functions mentioned for teachers in the late 1960s and early 1970s included the development of helpful cooperative classroom environments, assessment of students, orientation of students to classroom procedures, establishment of helping relationships, integration of educational and career information, promotion of social and personal development, encouragement of healthy study habits, development of effective referral procedures, and cooperation with schoolwide guidance activities (Miller, 1968; Shertzer & Stone, 1966, 1981). Many of these elements were also found in research on excellent teaching and effective schools (Hoy, Tarter, & Kottkamp, 1991; Purkey & Smith, 1983).

Counseling in Elementary Schools.   This reexamination of guidance and counseling occurred at a time when the expansion of counseling services into elementary schools began. Though some elementary counselors were employed in the Boston schools in the early 1900s, and a few elementary child consultants were found in other metropolitan areas during this time, educational and vocational development at the secondary level overwhelmed serious efforts in the primary and intermediate grades until the early 1960s. The introduction of the elementary counselor during this period influenced the development of the school counseling profession and the expansion of services in schools.

During the initial decades of school counseling's development and growth, little was written or designed to help elementary counselors define and describe their role in schools. There is some indication that counseling in elementary schools was advanced by the work of William Burnham in the 1920s and 1930s (Faust, 1968a). Burnham emphasized the vital role of classroom teachers in ensuring the mental health of children. However, there were few notable elementary counseling programs established at this time (Gibson, Mitchell, & Basile, 1993). As a result, no clear model for elementary counseling existed.

For the most part, traditional secondary guidance views and approaches were borrowed by the few elementary counselors who were employed before 1950. According to Faust (1968a), the first signs of the contemporary elementary counselor appeared in the late 1950s and early 1960s. A national survey in 1963 reported that elementary counselors performed the following activities (McKellar, 1964):

- Counseling with individual children
- Conferring with teachers to assist them with understanding of children's needs and developmental characteristics
- Conferring with parents about student development and progress
- Referring children and families to agencies

In 1964, the government expanded NDEA to include elementary school counseling as well as counseling in junior colleges and technical schools (Gibson et al., 1993). As a result, NDEA training institutes added a focus on counseling in elementary schools. Despite this added emphasis, elementary counseling was slowly accepted by school systems and by the public in general. In part, this is because of uncertainty about the counselor's role in elementary education. One event that helped elementary counselors identify their distinct role in the schools was a 1966 report by the Joint Committee on the Elementary School Counselor (ACES-ASCA, 1966). This report outlined the role and functions of elementary school counselors under the headings of "Counseling, Consulting, and Coordinating." Subsequent writings in the 1960s and 1970s differentiated and expanded these three major functions (Brown & Srebalus, 1972; Hill & Luckey, 1969).

In 1967, Greene surveyed a large sample of elementary counselors with an inventory of 104 counselor functions. Over 1,100 counselors across the country responded; 65 percent of the sample were full-time certified counselors. Greene's study found a large difference in the functions performed at the upper elementary grades when compared with those at the lower grades. Counselors at the intermediate grades seemed to have more direct contact with children, whereas primary counselors spent more time consulting with parents and teachers. The most common services in both intermediate and primary grades were referral services. Another study at this time surveyed the role and functions of elementary counselors as perceived by teachers, principals, counselors, and counselor educators (Foster, 1967). An *Elementary School Counselor Questionnaire,* consisting of eighty-four items, found that all five groups ranked counseling types of activities as most important to the role of the elementary counselor.

The proliferation of these types of studies gave visibility to elementary school counseling. As a result, more counselors were employed to work in elementary schools. In 1967, a national survey found almost 4,000 elementary counselors employed in forty-eight states (Van Hoose & Vafakas, 1968). Four years later, in 1971, elementary counseling continued its growth with the total number of elementary school counselors reaching almost 8,000 (Myrick & Moni, 1976). This growth was complemented by the publication of the *Elementary School Guidance and Counseling Journal* by the American School Counselor Association in the late 1960s.

Early studies of elementary school counselors' functions not only gave clarity to the emerging role of elementary school counselors but also contributed in a larger sense to the direction of contemporary school counseling. In particular, the elementary movement gave a clearer identity to the school counseling profession as a developmental force in the education of children and adolescents. The elementary counseling movement in combination with national legislative action broadened the scope of school counseling services. This expanded perspective included a role for counselors to provide services to audiences beyond students in the school. In particular, it encouraged counselors to assist parents and teachers with the challenge of ensuring optimal development of all children. This challenge was instrumental in moving school counselors into consulting roles: providing in-service help to teachers, offering parent counseling and education programs, and being team members with other student services professionals (Faust, 1968b).

Counseling for Special Needs.   The Education Act for All Handicapped Children of 1975, which we will discuss in Chapter 2, was a catalyst to the realization of this consulting role. This bill, commonly referred to as Public Law 94-142, mandated that schools provide free public education for all children, and it established a formula for distributing financial aid from the federal government to the states and local school districts. Although the role of school counselors was not specified, this law addressed special education and related support services. Today, the school counselor's role with exceptional students generally consists of a range of services that include

1. Participating in school-based meetings to determine appropriate services and programs for exceptional students
2. Assisting with the development of the Individual Education Plan (IEP) required for
   every student who has an identified exceptionality
3. Providing direct counseling services for students
4. Counseling and consulting with parents
5. Consulting with classroom and special education teachers
6. Planning, coordinating, and presenting in-service programs for teachers
7. Planning extracurricular involvement for special education students
8. Keeping appropriate records of services to students

The involvement of counselors in special education has been a mixed blessing in helping them decipher a clear role with appropriate functions. The inclusion of exceptional children in public education has expanded the role of school counselors by involving them in
program planning, parent counseling and consulting, and curriculum monitoring. At the
same time, however, clerical and administrative tasks required to ensure proper placement
and protection of children's rights are cumbersome and time-consuming. A combination of
federal, state, and local regulations has contributed to a maze of paperwork, hearings, and
meetings. Where counselors are delegated the responsibility for these procedures, they find
themselves removed from the expanded role of serving all students in comprehensive programs of services and, instead, relegated to the role of coordinator or administrator of special services. By contrast, in schools where counselors are not responsible for procedural
aspects of special education, they are more likely to establish and implement counseling
programs that offer a wide range of services to a larger portion of student populations. With
regard to exceptional students, these counselors are able to provide direct counseling and
consulting services, which is the intent of Public Law 94-142.

Legislative and Governmental Influence.   Other legislation of the 1960s and later years
has influenced the changing and emerging role of school counselors. For example, various
vocational education acts stimulated career guidance projects and refocused the school's
role in vocational development. Also, the Family Educational Rights and Privacy Act of
1974, commonly known as the Buckley Amendment, gave students access to records about
themselves, requiring counselors to form closer relationships with students and parents.
Since the late 1970s, several bills have been in the federal legislature to support comprehensive programs in elementary school counseling. Although all these initiatives have not
become law, they have inspired a nationwide movement to address the need for services to
elementary children.

Another national event that influenced school counseling was the publication of *A
Nation At Risk* in 1983 by the National Commission of Excellence in Education. This report focused on the purported decline in achievement of United States students and alarmed
the country in much the same way that the launching of Soviet *Sputnik I* did in 1957. Not
everyone, however, viewed this report as a credible assessment of U.S. education. Berliner
and Biddle (1995) are two researchers who questioned the efficacy of *A Nation at Risk*.
They maintained that the report was part of a "disinformation campaign" (p. 3) and provided little evidence about the failure of U.S. schools.

Nevertheless, *A Nation at Risk* had a tremendous impact on what was reported in
the media, and this subsequently led to a plethora of reform initiatives in public education.

Although no specific references to, or recommendations for, school counseling were found in this report, the emphasis on developing "effective schools" became synonymous with a call for accountability in the classroom and in special services such as school counseling programs.

Accountability received attention somewhat earlier in the counseling literature of the 1970s and 1980s (Krumboltz, 1974; Myrick, 1984; Wheeler & Loesch, 1981). During this period, counselors were encouraged to design methods to assess how they spent their time and whether the effects of counseling and related services made a difference in student development and performance. This focus was particularly sharp at the high school level where Myrick (2003) noted that counselors were criticized for not providing organized services to address the needs of adolescents. In the 1980s, the attack on high school counseling continued and positions were eliminated in some school districts (Herr, 1986).

At the same time, counselors were being placed in elementary schools without a clear definition, description, and focus on what their role should be at this level of education. In spite of the literature that attempted to describe a comprehensive role of these new counselors, local school systems and states seemed unable to create consistent expectations of the counselor's role and function. On one hand, elementary counselors attempted to create programs that replicated the one-to-one models of senior high school counselors, and on the other, they adapted the role of guidance teachers, traveling from classroom to classroom presenting lessons in affective education. Neither of these models delivered a comprehensive program of integrated services.

Counseling in Middle Schools.　A similar dilemma existed in the early middle schools that evolved from the junior high schools of the 1960s. Again, the counseling literature during this time attempted to describe a comprehensive role for middle school counselors (Stamm & Nissman, 1979; Thornburg, 1986), but in many instances counselors struggled to find an identity and define their purpose. During the 1980s and 1990s, the need for school counselors to develop a clear identity and describe their role and functions at the various levels of school practice became paramount. Today, this need to establish a clear professional identity for counseling in schools continues (Baker & Gerler, 2004).

The Twenty-First Century

The most influential event to impact U.S. schools during the early part of this century has been the reauthorization of the elementary and secondary education act by the federal government under the No Child Left Behind Act of 2001 (U.S. Department of Education, 2002). The passage and implementation of this act has not been without controversy, both among school counseling professionals and the greater education profession (Thomas, 2005; Houston, 2005). Counselors who work in schools have demonstrated both positive and negative perceptions of No Child Left Behind (NCLB) (Dollarhide & Lemberger, 2006). Among the positive aspects are the emphasis placed on accountability processes for schools to demonstrate overall effectiveness as well as counselors to show that the programs and services they develop and deliver make a difference in student learning. This includes the use of data to make programmatic decisions for all students, and particularly those who are at-risk.

Linked to this emphasis on accountability and use of data to make educational decisions, however, is the negative perception about high-stakes testing that has put great and perhaps inappropriate pressure on students, parents, and teachers to perform simply for test results. Although assessment processes are necessary to measure academic progress, this undue weight placed on testing by NCLB may ignore the importance of individual differences, developmental stages, and issues of diversity that are foundational to determining appropriate curriculum, instructional methods, and other services for the broad audience of students attending schools today (Comer, 2005; Stone & Dahir, 2006).

Notwithstanding the positive and negative perceptions of NCLB by counselors and other school professionals, it is clear that the legislation helped propel the movement toward comprehensive programs of services in the school counseling profession in recent years (Stone & Dahir, 2006). That result has contributed to the evolving professional identity of counselors that work in schools.

A Professional Identity

The counseling literature in general and the school counseling literature specifically continue to stress the importance of clear professional identity. Many achievements and decisions by the counseling profession in recent years have helped create and solidify such an identity. Among these are the more consistent use of the terms *counseling* and *school counseling,* such as in the names of the professional associations: American Counseling Association (ACA) and the American School Counselor Association (ASCA). Today the ACA has a membership of approximately 60,000 and consists of the following divisions:

American Mental Health Counselors Association (AMHCA, chartered in 1978)

American Rehabilitation Counseling Association (ARCA, chartered in 1958)

American School Counselor Association (ASCA, chartered in 1953)

Association for Adult Development and Aging (AADA, chartered in 1986)

Association for Assessment in Counseling (AAC, chartered in 1965)

Association for Creativity in Counseling (ACC), chartered in 2004

American College Counseling Association (ACCA, chartered in 1991)

Association for Counselors and Educators in Government (ACEG, chartered in 1984)

Association for Counselor Education and Supervision (ACES, chartered in 1952)

Association for Gay, Lesbian and Bisexual Issues in Counseling (AGLBIC, chartered in 1997)

Association for Multicultural Counseling and Development (AMCD, chartered in 1972)

Association for Specialists in Group Work (ASGW, chartered in 1973)

Association for Spiritual, Ethical, and Religious Value Issues in Counseling (ASERVIC, chartered in 1974).

Counseling Association for Humanistic Education and Development (AHEAD, chartered in 1952)

Counselors for Social Justice (CSJ)

International Association of Addiction and Offender Counselors (IAAOC, chartered in 1972)

International Association of Marriage and Family Counselors (IAMFC, chartered in 1989)

National Career Development Association (NCDA, chartered in 1952)

National Employment Counseling Association (NECA, chartered in 1962)

Each of these associations represent a portion of the thousands of professional counselors practicing in the United States as well as in other countries. While they practice in diverse professional settings, all these counselors adhere to the same ethical standards, come from similar training programs, and have common professional goals. What differentiates them, as noted earlier in this chapter, is the focus of their professional setting—the clients and counselees they serve.

Among the organizations representing professional counselors, the American School Counselor Association has one of the largest memberships—over 17,000 members. While impressive, this membership represents only a portion of the professional counselors who work in elementary, middle, and high schools across the United States. This is a matter of concern. Stronger professional collegiality on the part of school counselors across the country will help create a clear identity in the future.

Professional Development and Accreditation

Another factor that has contributed to an identity for school counselors is improved preparation programs that place them on equal footing with counselors in other work settings. The Council for Accreditation of Counseling and Related Educational Programs (CACREP) has been instrumental in creating standards of counselor preparation. In addition, the profession's national certification process, under the direction of the National Board for Certified Counselors (NBCC), has elevated professional identity, including a specialty certification for school counselors (NCSC).

School counselors historically have been thought of as different from counselors in clinical settings such as mental-health and family counseling centers. In part, this is because the licensure and certification requirements for school counselors vary from state to state. For instance, only recently have most states required a minimum of a master's degree to enter the school counseling profession (Randolph & Masker, 1997). Admittedly, this lack of consistent criteria for professionals who call themselves school counselors has challenged the effort to bring consensus to their role and function.

Inconsistent perceptions by administrators and teachers have added to the confusion about the school counselor's role. In some cases, administrators view counselors as "special" classroom teachers and require schedules and assignments that prevent the establishment of comprehensive counseling programs. For example, in some elementary schools, counselors are required to spend a majority of their time presenting classroom guidance as a means of giving teachers breaks or planning periods. Classroom guidance is important and appropriate for both counselors and teachers to integrate in the school's curriculum, but assigning counselors sole responsibility for this activity leaves little time for other equally important aspects of a comprehensive school counseling program. In contrast, other schools view their counselors as therapists and "magicians" who have mystical powers, and therefore keep them apart from teachers and other school personnel. These counselors are shielded from every-day responsibilities and functions of school life and are not asked to account for their role in the educational program. Because what they do is so mysterious, such counselors are not held accountable or expected to measure the value of their services in the school. This myth and others like it contribute to the challenge counselors have faced in creating beneficial programs with clear goals, realistic expectations, and measurable outcomes that enable them to become integral members of elementary, middle, and high school environments.

Neither view of school counselors as "special teachers" or "magicians" facilitates the development of effective services for students, parents, and teachers. What is needed is an understanding that school counselors are highly prepared professionals who offer specific skills and services to help students with their educational development. This is the primary role of counselors in schools. While their role and function may be different from counselors who practice in clinics, hospitals, and other settings, this difference is not due to a lack of training or level of expertise. Rather, it is a reflection of the educational and developmental focus of their programs and services. and developmental focus of their programs and services. This focus on a programmatic planning, organizing, implementing, and evaluating of services, interventions, and activities of guidance and counseling in schools has fueled the development of a fresh identity for the school counseling profession (Lambie & Williamson, 2004).

Comprehensive School Counseling Programs

As the twentieth century drew to a close, several proponents of the school counseling profession began to emphasize a programmatic focus with more attention given to developmental approaches and group processes than to therapeutic, one-on-one counseling models. This movement was spirited by the work of Norman Gysbers and others as a response, in part, to the educational reforms of the 1980s (Gysbers & Moore, 1981; Gysbers & Henderson, 2000). The thrust of this movement highlighted an important difference between professional counselors that chose to practice in schools and those who chose to work in mental-health or other clinical settings. That difference is found in the design and implementation of comprehensive school counseling programs and use of developmental approaches to address the academic, social/personal, and career needs of all students. Several school counseling texts of this period gave added impetus to this movement (Gysbers & Henderson, 2000; Myrick, 1993; Schmidt, 1993; VanZandt & Hayslip, 1994).

The twenty-first century continues the focus on comprehensive programs with increased interest in re-examining and transforming the role of school counselors (Education Trust, 1997, 1998, 2003; Erford, 2003; Stone & Dahir, 2006). Supported by the Wallace-Reader's Digest Fund, The Education Trust identified six universities in 1996 to participate in the first redesign of school counselor preparation programs. Essentially, these reconfigured school counseling programs intend to prepare professional counselors to work in schools as leaders and student advocates that focus their energy on student academic success. Since the identification of the initial six universities, another twenty-six companion universities have been selected to redesign their preparation programs according to the Transforming School Counseling Initiative (TSCI) of the Education Trust (2003).

This transformation movement gained favor, in part, because of recognition that many students were not being served under traditional models of school counseling, which some authorities believe placed too much emphasis on one-to-one helping relationships while neglecting the power of group processes to meet the needs of a larger population. Such proponents advocate for a more proactive leadership role by counselors in schools to include teachers and other professionals in advising students and providing other services in concert with those individual and group processes delivered by professional counselors.

Combined with the interest and initiative to transform school counselor preparation has been the development of the National Model for school counseling programs by the American School Counselor Association (2003). This model proposes that school counselors develop comprehensive programs of services around four themes that include leadership, advocacy, collaboration and teaming, and systemic change. Through a programmatic implementation of these four themes, school counselors move beyond delivery of specific services to a leadership, collaborative, and change agent role to help schools address the academic, social, personal, and career needs of every student.

In this book, you are introduced to the scope and breadth of a comprehensive school counseling program and to the professional preparation and knowledge needed to become an effective school counselor. This text is an overview of the elements and ingredients that give an identity to the school counseling profession and enhance the credibility of practicing school counselors. The following suggestions offer a framework for counselors to create a clear identity and purpose for working in schools. I present them here as a summary of the professional themes and issues addressed in this text. To develop a clear professional identity, school counselors:

1. Understand the history of school counseling and appreciate the significant events that led to its development and expansion. A knowledge of one's professional roots and the events that have contributed to the profession's growth gives clarity to future goals. *Without knowing where we have been, it is difficult to know where we are going.*

2. Establish consistent preparation standards on a par with professional counselors who practice in other settings. If the nature and level of training are inconsistent between different types of counselors and among counselors in the same groups, misunderstanding and misinterpretations about these counselors' roles will persist, increasing public uncertainty and contributing to less-than-adequate programs of services.

3. Expect consistent certification standards. Counseling is a profession that begins study at the graduate level of training. Specific standards and guidelines developed by the Council for Accreditation of Counseling and Related Educational Programs (CACREP) have the potential to generate nationwide standards for school counselor training and certification. Certification standards should be associated with roles and functions stressed in the professional literature and research about effective counselor performance. Criteria that are unrelated to counselor performance should be discarded. For example, some states continue to require teaching experience for counselors to be certified as school counselors (Randolph & Masker, 1997) even though research has failed to show any correlation between school counselor effectiveness and teaching experience. Baker (1994) echoed this conclusion in his review that noted, "Research findings do not support suppositions that counselors with teaching experience are superior to those without it" (p. 322). More recently, a study of school counseling interns found that candidates with teaching experience "appeared to have had no less difficulty in adjusting to their new roles than those without teaching experience" (Peterson, Goodman, Keller, & McCauley, 2004, p. 254).

Certification standards that lack evidence of research support detract from the uniqueness of the counselor's role and his or her potential contribution to the school's mission.

4. Follow national guidelines for comprehensive school counseling programs at the high school, middle school, and elementary school levels. School counseling continues to be an emerging field, and, as such, its overall purpose needs to be regularly assessed and adjusted. The American School Counselor Association (ASCA) developed national standards for school counseling programs (Campbell & Dahir, 1997), which establish "goals, expectations, opportunities, and experiences for all students" (p. 4). An ASCA manual for implementing comprehensive school counseling programs followed the publication of these standards (Dahir, Sheldon, & Valiga, 1998). These two publications provide a starting point for the profession to identify, promote, and evaluate services that are essential in helping students attain these objectives. At the same time, the national standards will help inform educational organizations of school administrators and teachers about the role and function of professional school counselors. However, as Schmidt and Ciechalski (2001) noted, additional standards that focus on professional preparation and practices for school counselors are needed.

The historical perspective in this chapter is intended to enhance your understanding and appreciation of contemporary school counseling practices and trends. School counseling, as with many aspects of life, might appear to be cyclical in its development. Some events and ideas that contributed to its early development are seen again in current professional literature. For example, in recent years Myrick (2003) and others have encouraged a developmental approach in which counselors move their work out of their offices onto playgrounds and into classrooms, hallways, and other arenas to have better access to more students. This theme is similar to an earlier view expressed by C. Gilbert Wrenn (1973), who wrote, "I believe that the counselor must accept the responsibility for helping teachers and other staff members as well as directly helping students. . . . Counselors who appear indifferent to school improvement or incompetent to contribute to such improvement will be vulnerable" (p. 261). Today's counseling literature emphasizes strong teacher involvement in counseling programs similar to the position taken in 1955 by the Association for Supervision and Curriculum Development (ASCD) in its annual yearbook, *Guidance in the Curriculum.* That publication viewed guidance not as a separate, supplementary service in the school, but rather as an essential part of the curriculum, integrated every day by teachers and counselors. All these positions are consistent with the philosophy of ASCA's national Model for School Counseling, which we will explore later in this text.

The 1970s were marked by action in many states to develop guidelines for comprehensive school counseling programs. California, Missouri, North Carolina, Oklahoma, and Wisconsin are among the states that contributed to this movement. Today, the school counseling literature continues to emphasize the comprehensive nature of school counseling services (Baker & Gerler, 2004; Gysbers & Henderson, 2000; Lapan, Gysbers, & Petroski, 2001; Myrick, 2003; Sink & Yillik-Downer, 2001). More importantly, research has begun to demonstrate a relationship between the implementation of comprehensive programs by school counselors and students' perceptions of school safety, relationships with their teachers and others, the relevance of education, and attaining higher grades (Lapan et al., 2001).

In the remaining chapters of this book you will learn about the nature of comprehensive school counseling programs; the necessary facilities and resources in counseling centers at elementary, middle, and high school levels; the responsive services offered by school counselors; the background and preparation of counselors; the importance of collaboration with teachers and student services personnel; and professional issues related to school counseling practices.

The future of school counseling as a profession depends on the ability of counselors to become an integral part of the school setting while maintaining their unique role and contribution to student welfare and development. To accomplish this goal, successful counselors identify their role; select appropriate functions; plan programs of services for students, parents, and teachers; strengthen their professional development; and evaluate their effectiveness in schools. All these tasks and role developments are performed by professional counselors in schools that today reflect an increasingly diverse society. Student populations and school communities in the United States no longer reflect audiences that existed when the profession began in the late nineteenth and early twentieth centuries. The challenge and necessity of creating comprehensive programs of school counseling services is dictated by the reality of increasingly diverse student populations and ever-changing school communities. The second chapter of this text examines this notion of diversity and explores what it means for developing comprehensive school counseling programs.

Additional Readings

Baker, S. B., & Gerler, E. R. (2004). *School Counseling for the Twenty-First Century* (4th ed.) (Upper Saddle River, NJ: Prentice Hall). Chapter Two: "A Balanced Approach to School Counseling."
This chapter introduces the notion of balancing a comprehensive program of services so that remedial and developmental goals for all students are met.

Wrenn, C. G. (1973). *The World of the Contemporary Counselor* (Boston: Houghton Mifflin).
Written over thirty years ago, this classic book has withstood the test of time remarkably well. Wrenn's message to counselors then still holds true today.

Websites

As technology has enhanced the way we communicate with students, parents, teachers, and others, so too has it enabled us to find abundant resources of information at our fingertips. In addition to the suggested readings, lists of websites at the end of each chapter offer ways to access information over the Internet. By listing these websites, neither the author nor publisher makes an endorsement of any product, material, or information presented on these or other locations on the Internet. Sites are listed only as examples of how counselors can access information. Every counselor who uses the Internet has professional and ethical responsibility to ensure the accuracy and appropriateness of information obtained when offering it as a resource to clients.

American Counseling Association
www.counseling.org
American School Counselor Association
www.schoolcounselor.org
Council for Accreditation of Counseling and Related
Educational Programs (CACREP)
www.cacrep.org
National Board of Certified Counselors (NBCC)
www.nbcc.org
Occupational Outlook Handbook: Counselors
http://stats.bls.gov/oco/ocos067.htm

Exercises

School counseling is an action-oriented profession. For this reason, the end of each chapter of this book includes a few activities and exercises that may help the information come alive and take on additional meaning. Some of the activities are suggested for small groups in your class. Others are designed for additional exploration of professional issues and for you to share your findings with the class.

1. In this introductory chapter you learned that the school counseling profession began as a reaction to social and political forces in the early 1900s. Over the next several decades the profession grew and changed as a response to other significant events in the United States and around the world. What relationship, if any, do you see with this heritage and the role of counselors in the school? Discuss this in a small group and ask someone to record the highlights of your discussion to share with the class.

2. This chapter presented major events that contributed to the development of school counseling across this country. On your own or with a small group, research the development of school counseling in your state. What were major events, legislative action, or other occurrences that influenced the profession? What role does teaching experience play in the employment of school counselors in your state? What is your belief about teaching experience and being a successful school counselor?

3. Professional identity is an important issue presented in this chapter? If you were hired by a school tomorrow as its new counselor, what five actions would you take to begin establishing a professional identity? Discuss and compare your actions with a group of your classmates.

4. What action do you think individual counselors and their professional associations should take to help clarify the identity and role of school counselors?

2

Diverse Students, Communities, and Schools

From the beginning of the school counseling profession in the late nineteenth century, students, communities, and schools have been changing. A shifting culture has been a constant in U.S. society, resulting from such dramatic changes as the abolition of slavery during the Civil War and the waves of immigrants from around the globe that were attracted to this country in hopes of finding a better life. Historically, however, these abundant attempts by culturally diverse groups to join the bountiful life offered in America were too frequently greeted by discriminatory laws, harsh immigration procedures, blatant racism, dismissive school policies, and other acts of oppression or indifference that caused conflict rather than coalition, dissension rather than collaboration. These realities challenge communities and institutions across society, especially within the helping profession.

The counseling profession, and school counseling in particular, has not readily adjusted to this influx of diverse cultures. Nor have U.S. public schools been particularly efficient in creating curricular choices to meet the needs of diverse learners, including students with exceptionalities. Some authorities have been critical of the lack of motivation by schools and school systems to make appropriate adjustments to serve a broader population of students and of the school counseling profession to do likewise (Pederson & Carey, 2003). Instead, critics maintain that schools and counselors have taken a reactive posture, relying on state and federal intervention to pass laws and set guidelines to address the learning needs of the steadily changing population they serve.

Today, the school counseling profession is attempting to formulate a more proactive stance. It is moving from the reactive posture of past decades to a more programmatic stance for the future. By implementing comprehensive programs of services, future counselors in schools will be better able to address the learning needs of a wider audience of students, embrace the diversity of families and communities, and accept the variety of communities within rural, suburban, and urban settings in which schools exist and function (Erford, 2003; Schmidt, 2004; Stone & Dahir, 2006). It is an awesome challenge, but counselors can no longer focus on a limited number of students, whether it is those of greatest emotional, social, or educational need or students of academic promise. Today's professional counselors who choose to work in schools design programs that are inclusive of all students and create collaborative relationships with teachers, parents, and other professionals to ensure this reality.

This chapter provides an overview of diversity issues that challenge contemporary counselors in their effort to design, implement, and evaluate comprehensive programs of services for schools. It briefly summarizes current issues of diversity that impact schools and counseling practices, necessary competencies required by professional counselors in schools, and practical ideas to help counselors in addressing issues of diversity through their comprehensive programs. Because of its brevity, readers are encouraged to move beyond this chapter and examine the cited references to expand understanding and learning about this topic.

Increased Diversity

The changing face of U.S. society and culture and its impact on the practice of professional counseling has been widely reported (Holcomb-McCoy, 2003; Pedersen & Carey, 2003; Schmidt, 2006). The 2000 U.S. census indicated the continuing progression and alteration of the country's population landscape. For example, the population of Asian Americans grew from approximately 3 million in 1980 to more than 10 million in 2000 (U.S. Bureau of the Census, 2003). At the same time, the Latino population outpaced the growth of the African American community, becoming the largest minority group in the country. During this period, white membership slowed and the Census Bureau predicts that by 2040 the white population in the United States will comprise less than 50 percent of the total population as compared to nearly 70 percent in the year 2000 (U.S. Bureau or Census, 2003). Given these changes, it is clear that school counselors, today and in the future, will need to become increasingly diligent in designing programs of services to reach a more diverse population of learners. These students will bring varied cultural and ethnic perspectives, different languages, valued family traditions, and an array of other traits and characteristics through the schoolhouse door.

In this chapter, we consider a few of these factors including race, ethnicity, immigration, sex, gender, spiritual and religious beliefs, family influence, and socioeconomic status. We also briefly examine regional considerations such as rural and urban schools and their influence on programmatic decisions. We begin by presenting a brief discussion of culture.

Culture

Several authorities have defined culture in terms of its meaning for professional counseling (Holcomb-McCoy, 2003; Locke, 2003; Schmidt, 2006). In the counseling and other helping professions, the term *culture* receives a broad definition and interpretation. Locke (2003) noted more than 150 definitions of culture in the literature. For the purpose of this section, culture consists of common behaviors, traditions, and beliefs demonstrated, followed, and valued by societal groups. As one example from the counseling literature, Baruth and Manning (1999) defined culture as varied "institutions, languages, values, religions, genders, sexual orientations, thinking, artistic expressions, and social and inter-personal relationships" (p. 7).

Contemporary counseling literature broadens the definition of culture as a more in-clusive notion. Therefore, when considering the concept of culture in the context of coun-seling in schools, its influence on student development and decisions made by students and their families regarding educational development, academic success, career decisions, self-development, and conformity to the culture and mores of the school community are all im-portant. In addition to understanding the concept of culture, competent school counselors also comprehend processes related to culture that help them become more self-aware of their own posture and development as well as appreciating students' development, self-views, and worldviews. Among these concepts are enculturation, acculturation, assimila-tion, encapsulation, collectivism, individualism, and subculture. Each is briefly defined in the following sections.

Enculturation

Enculturation is a process of people becoming members of a particular culture (Aponte & Johnson, 2000; Schmidt, 2006). With this process, people establish relationships that en-able them to learn about a culture and immerse themselves in its language, traditions, and customs. As such, enculturation begins and continues through varied ways and relation-ships with parents, family, peer groups, and institutions of society, such as schools, that embrace a particular culture.

School counselors working with diverse populations want to be aware of their own enculturation as well as that of the students and families they serve. Some students from diverse populations may have stronger ties to their cultural beliefs than others have. That is, the strength of their enculturation has greater influence on their adjustment to a school with traditions, belief systems, and mores that these students find unfamiliar. At the same time, the enculturation of the counselor may impede her or his ability to establish genuine and empathic helping relationships with certain students and families. Such a barrier must be addressed, understood, and dismantled if the school counselor is to be successful with such clients.

Acculturation

The literature describes acculturation as the "adaptation of the beliefs, traits, and behav-iors of a dominant culture by persons of a minority group who have significant contact with the dominant group" (Schmidt, 2006, p. 6). When students of divergent cultures enroll in a new school, they face the possibility and challenge of acculturating into an unfamiliar en-vironment. They make decisions about adopting new behaviors, customs, and ways of being that often are different from, and sometimes at odds with, their culture of origin. This process of acculturation includes attempts by students and families to retain aspects of their native culture while fitting into the new school culture.

Acculturation occurs in various ways. For example, immigrants to a new country experience this process as do people who move from one region to another in a society composed of multiple cultures. Counselors in U.S. schools are familiar with these expe-riences because this country continues to accept many immigrants and, at the same time, it is common for families to relocate to any region or state of the country. When immigrant or relocated students receive help in adjusting to these moves and are successful with the acculturation process, the overall school experience improves.

As noted in another text (Schmidt, 2006), acculturation may include stressors that come from culture shock, lack of family support or resources, perceived or real threats of discrimination and rejection, and other aspects of adapting to new ways of living or to belief systems that threaten cultural and family traditions (Roysircar, 2003). Such stress can be debilitating to students, so it is imperative that counselors be sensitive, aware, and skilled in helping diverse students adjust to a new learning environment.

Assimilation

Another process related to cultural change is assimilation. From a cultural perspective, assimilation occurs when individuals or groups of people become accepted by or absorbed into a new culture. In contrast to acculturation where it is the person or group doing the decision-making, assimilation is the purview of the dominant culture that chooses to accept, absorb, and integrate diverse people. As Ivey (2000) and others have noted, assimilation is a powerful process where the dominant culture often demands, either outright and or covertly, that newcomers embrace its standards, traditions, ways, and beliefs. Even though the United States has had a long history of immigration, we see this phenomenon often in our country. For example, the hesitancy to accept other languages has been a perpetual debate.

For school counselors, an understanding of assimilation and its impact on children and families can encourage them to take an advocacy role for all students. Balance is an important concept for counselors to use when helping new students adjust and acculturate, while helping the school monitor its use of assimilation processes.

Encapsulation

When people remain unaware, disinterested, and intolerant of divergent views and behave as if only one culture exists, they encapsulate themselves from other perspectives. Successful school counselors avoid becoming encapsulated so they genuinely accept and empathically understand the views of diverse students and families. Cultural encapsulation prevents counselors from seeing all the possibilities that exist in helping students become excellent learners, socially successful peers, mentally and emotionally healthy persons, and contributing members of the larger society. Such a posture is contrary to the mission of counseling in schools.

Collectivism

Many cultures embrace and cultivate a collectivistic philosophy, which maintains a belief that the larger group takes priority over individuals within the group. As such, it is the family, tribe, or other organized group that holds greater value than any particular individual (Robinson, 2005). In addition, every individual contributes to and is indebted to the group with which he or she identifies. This collectivistic belief is foundational because each individual member of the larger group benefits, survives, and thrives because of the group's influence and resources used in contributing to the member's development (Schmidt, 2006).

School counselors who are successful in working with diverse students have a keen understanding of the influence that collectivistic philosophy has on human development. For example, students of Asian heritage who embrace a collectivistic view may struggle with the individualism sometimes promoted in American culture, folklore, and educational policies. Counselors understand that the Western views sometimes embraced by professional counseling processes, such as self-confidence, self-reliance, and independence, sometimes conflict with more socially-centered concepts that include a belief in social interest, dependence on group process, adherence to community goals, deference to group responsibility, and dependence on group authority. In schools, counselors embrace these notions of collectivism in balance with concepts related to individualism.

Individualism

Some cultures adhere to and advocate for individual development, sometimes to the extent that they may appear to ignore the importance of the larger group or organization. These cultures place enormous value on personal growth, self-fulfillment, and individual needs and desires. During its first 200 years, the United States of America became a culture that placed tremendous value on the individual's ability to persevere and become self-reliant. This belief system was to a large degree the foundation upon which the United States expanded its territory, built an industrial powerhouse, accumulated its financial wealth, and took its place as a world leader. Today, with the United States continuing to accept diverse peoples from all over the world into its community, it seems imperative that the individualistic philosophy be more in balance with collectivistic views. That challenge faces every counselor who chooses to practice in school settings.

Services, interventions, and activities of a comprehensive school counseling program need to maintain balance between collectivism and individualism. This begins with the counseling theories that school counselors rely on in using both individual and group counseling with students (Pederson, 2000). Strict adherence to theories that overemphasize individual development and neglect the power of group influence may limit a counselor's ability to help diverse students. In contrast, the counselor that uses extensive group work, values the contribution of the family, respects collectivistic beliefs, and views the individual student as part of a greater whole has the likelihood of being successful. Such school counselors maintain a healthy understanding and appreciation for individual development while respecting the important role and influence of the family, community, tribe, or other group to which the student-client belongs. In some instances, the group or groups most influential in a student's life are subgroups or subcultures of the larger society.

Subcultures

Subgroups or subcultures exist in every larger society or culture. An aspect of human development is that people build personal identities by joining particular subgroups, becoming members of subsystems, and identifying with subcultures within their larger cultural identity. People join these distinguishable groups because of particular identifications that may be related to racial, ethnic, educational, social, economic, artistic, athletic, or other ascription.

Schools as communities of students also include subgroups and subsystems. Sometimes these groups are established by school policies and procedures and other times they are established and self-selected by students. For example, schools enroll students in classes or place them in particular courses or classrooms. At times, these assigned classes and courses cause students to group according to achievement or academic ability. Counselors often play a significant role in this identification and placement process, and the consequences of such placement frequently affects student relationships and associations throughout their educational careers.

Other ways that students join subgroups in schools is through participation in organizations and programs such as athletics, cheerleaders, band, thespian society, debate club, yearbook, and newspaper staff among others. Such clubs, teams, and organizations are formal opportunities to join subgroups, which are supplemented by everyday peer groups that students join (Schmidt, 2006). Sometimes, peer groups that students join in the greater community outside the school influence, positively or negatively, their associations inside the schoolhouse. For example, religious association may encourage students to join formal or informal spiritual groups in school. Similarly, a student's affiliation with a gang outside of school may have an impact on his or her relationships inside the school. What this means for school counselors is that they not only understand the effect of a student's primary culture and its interaction with society's dominant culture on student development, but also the countless subgroups, both in school and out in the larger community, that make a difference in students' lives (Pedersen & Carey, 2003; Schmidt, 2006). Counselors also appreciate how all these influences contribute to students' development of a worldview.

Worldview

Worldview is a construct established by each person as a product of ongoing life experiences. This is a particularly private process that incorporates an array of encounters within family, society, schools, ethnic groups, religious groups, peer groups, and a multitude of other life experiences. A person's construction of a worldview is an extension of self-concept development (Schmidt, 2006), and therefore is a unique product influenced by life experiences and by a person's distinctive personality and psychological composition.

For students in schools, their unique construction of both self-concepts and related worldviews provides a particular identity with which they interact and relate with fellow students, teachers, and others. This is an important notion for counselors as they attempt to establish helping relationships with diverse students in schools. A student's worldview not only interacts with a primary cultural worldview (e.g., the family), but also with the worldview of the counselor. Similarly, the counselor faces the same challenge in attempting to establish a successful helping relationship with the student. This challenge is compounded by the multitude of diverse factors that particular students might bring to counseling relationships. These include but are not limited to issues of race, ethnicity, sex, gender, religion, and exceptionality.

Race and Ethnicity

In literature and oral communication, the words *race* and *ethnicity* often are used to mean the same thing. This sometimes contributes to confusion about multicultural definitions and issues (Schmidt, 2006). The counseling profession through its multicultural research has attempted to explain the differences between the two terms (Comstock, 2005; Robinson, 2005; Schmidt, 2006).

Race

The etymology of the word *race* suggests it may have come from French or Italian words, *razza*, meaning breed or lineage, and from early English translations during the 1500s indicating peoples of common descent, a group of people with similar occupations, and generational relationships. The modern meaning of *race* focuses on attributions related to physical traits such as skin tone, hair texture, and facial features. However, biologists, geneticists, and anthropologists have debated this meaning since the sixteenth century. Despite this debate, the U.S. Census Bureau has used the term *race* as a biological category since its inception in the nineteenth century. Nevertheless, scientists have failed to generate research that reliably identifies genetic or other biological distinctions that enable us to classify races consistently. In fact, findings from "research of biological traits has found greater within-group variation among particular group members than between supposed different groups when examining the same traits (e.g., skin tone, blood type)" (Schmidt, 2006, p. 60).

Despite the lack of scientific evidence to support the classification of people by racial characteristics, the United States and other societies commonly use the term *race* to describe particular groups of people. At the same time, researchers have found that most people from their earliest development are able to identify accurately the "racial group" to which they belong (Helms & Cook, 1999). This ability to identify with particular groups is enhanced by the process of social construction. Societies create social constructions to carry on and preserve customs, beliefs, mores, and traditions established over time. Race is one example of social construction (Schmidt, 2006). Other examples include castes and social classes.

The lack of scientific evidence to support the categorization of people according to biological differences has not deterred the United States or other countries from using race in a classification system. As agents of the U.S. system, public schools join this process of classification, which sometimes results in negative consequences for diverse students, depending on perceptions and myths held by teachers, administrators, counselors, and other personnel. Since race is a social construction, we may assume that perceptions people have about physical appearances, and the conclusions they draw from these perceptions, are also influenced and sometimes contaminated by social or personal speculation and unfounded beliefs. Competent counselors in schools are aware of these influences and examine their own unproven beliefs about racial categorization as part of their professional development.

Some authorities from the counseling profession have argued that race may no longer be useful as a social identifier (Aponte & Johnson, 2000). Jackson and Vontress (2003) encouraged professional counselors to pay greater attention to a client's culture than to supposed racial groups. They argued, "A client's race or heritage may have little or nothing to do with culture or the presenting problem. Counselors who respond stereotypically to their clients run the risk of being anti-therapeutic" (Jackson & Vontress, 2003, p. 10). This may be an important distinction for school counselors to make as well. In designing programs and selecting interventions to help diverse students, it is probably more important to understand students' perceptions of their cultural heritage and its influence on their development than it is to make assumptions about the color of their skin, hair texture, or other physical characteristic. In sum, what students believe about their cultural and ethnic heritage is more important than what society constructs about supposed identified races.

Ethnicity

The ancient Greeks used the word *ethnos* to identify non-Greeks and other groups that shared physical and cultural traits. From that Greek word, we have the English term *ethnicity*. Over time, European cultures used derivations of the Greek word to denote groups of people with similar racial and physical traits.

Today, social scientists use *ethnicity* and related identifiers to categorize cultures and people of various heritages, separate from their supposed racial characteristics. Sometimes, the words *ethnicity* and *race* appear together, implying that they are closely related. Although this relationship is true in some instances, both terms have meanings that include distinctive processes. The social construction of race does not necessarily apply to ethnic identity. Therefore, a student's racial identity may be separate and apart from her/his ethnic identity, which develops over time through many individual, family, and social experiences. For school counselors working with diverse clients, this distinction is important. Race is constructed and perpetuated by the social group and its institutions, such as schools. In contrast, ethnicity is learned and embraced (or rejected) by students through interactions with family members and social groups. As such, ethnic identity is the process of associating and connecting with a particular cultural group that exhibits distinctive beliefs, behaviors, languages, and traditions. However, not all members of a particular ethnic group embrace the same beliefs, adhere to traditions, or behave in identical ways. As noted earlier in this chapter, subgroups within larger ethnic groups form and sometimes deviate from beliefs and traditions held by the greater culture. Knowing about this phenomenon helps counselors resist the temptation of assuming all members of a particular ethnic culture believe and behave exactly the same way.

Multiple influences contribute to ethnic development and identity. The process of ethnic identity, therefore, is complex and inconsistent among people, even those from apparently similar ethnic groups. For example, some students may be passionate about their heritage and ethnicity, practicing traditions and embracing social beliefs, whereas other students from the same ethnic groups may appear disinterested or even opposed to the beliefs and traditions to which their families adhere. How counselors in schools address these differences is important to individual students as well as their families and the larger ethnic groups to which they belong.

In today's schools, counselors, teachers, administrators, and others recognize the impact of changing social conditions and personal experiences on ethnic identity. Schmidt (2006) noted, "Migration, adoption, inter-racial marriage, religious conversion, and change in financial status are a few conditions that might influence a person's ethnic choice" (p. 86). Students enter schools today from all over the country and the world, as well as from diverse families. Immigrant, relocated, and adopted children are among those who comprise school populations in the twenty-first century. These students acculturate to new environments, customs, and beliefs, and their experiences often cause stress for individual students at school and/or at home in relating to peers and family members. Understanding the complexity of this process and empathizing with both students and their families is key to forming beneficial helping relationships in schools.

Immigration has had a long history of controversy in the United States. Although the country prides itself on being open to people from across the globe, the passage of laws limiting immigration by the government, beginning with the Naturalization Law of 1790 through the 1996 Illegal Immigration Reform and Immigration Responsibility Act, has attempted to distinguish rights among foreign-born groups, restrict immigration policies, and tighten the borders. Today, although the United States has moved toward more positive and pro-immigration legislation, we witness a backlash of sentiment exemplified by attitudes toward Mexican immigrants and fears perpetuated by terrorist activity worldwide. Yet, it is important to note that "the U.S. has generally maintained lenient policies towards immigrants and refugees in comparison to other developed countries" (Schmidt, 2006, p. 233).

All expectations are for the U.S. population to continue to grow and become increasingly diverse in the coming years. To some extent, immigration will contribute to this diversity. Terrorism, political unrest, social change, and economic instability in other countries and regions will increase the likelihood of more people trying to immigrate (Bemak & Chung, 2000). The world's changing climate and natural disasters will also encourage people to search for new homelands, and the United States will receive many of these refugees.

School counselors in the twenty-first century will serve diverse students and families. Some of these clients will migrate from other parts of the country while others arrive from distant shores. Among this diverse population will be students who struggle with adjustment to new cultural beliefs and behaviors, harbor fears of violence and oppression as consequences of their former lives, suffer the effects of poverty and neglect, or in some other ways require the knowledge and skills of empathetic counselors. This diversity is increased through the additional aspects of gender, religious beliefs, disabilities, and other characteristics considered in the following sections.

Sex, Gender, Activity, and Orientation

One aspect of cultural diversity that has expanded the focus of school counselors in recent decades involves issues of sexual development and identity, gender, sexual activity, and sexual orientation (Erford, 2003; Stone & Dahir, 2006). Diversity of sexual development is an important factor at all levels of schooling because of the range of children and adolescents who attend particular schools, differences in the onset of puberty across ages and sexes, and student, family, and community attitudes toward sexual activity among youth today. Added to the certainty of sexual development and the possibility of sexual activity are realities surrounding issues of gender differences, sexism, and sexual orientation. All of these challenge professional counselors working in school settings to design comprehensive programs of services and address the diverse needs of students.

Sex

Although some private schools restrict their enrollment to males or females, public schools typically enroll students of both sexes, boys and girls. Biologically, the distinguishing trait between the sexes is a single pair of chromosomes, the twenty-third pair called the *sex chromosomes* (XY, normal male; XX, normal female) (Wachtel, 1994). During the second month of a normal pregnancy, genetic matter begins producing proteins in the sex chromosomes that leads to hormonal activity and eventually the development of either a male or a female sex chromosome. Researchers have concluded that the existence or omission of the "Y" chromosome determines the sex of a person. When this development does not follow normal patterns and fewer or additional chromosomes result, genetic aberrations occur that lead to various disorders including Turner's Syndrome and Klinefelter's Syndrome (Schmidt, 2006).

Although much more needs to be learned, genetic and other scientific research has concluded that the chromosomal differences between males and females contribute to physical and behavioral variances. Some findings that may have significance for counselors in schools include (Kimura, 2002; Kreeger, 2002):

- Variation in brain development between males and females may relate to differences in thought-processing abilities.
- Laboratory research has noted differences in how males and females perform on handling spatial tasks, targeting moving objects, solving mathematical problems, recalling words, navigating through a maze, using language, matching items, remembering objects, and completing manual tasks (Schmidt, 2006).
- Certain hormonal deficiencies or excesses may influence sexual development and related gender choices. Consequently, aberrations in hormonal activity may contribute to atypical behavioral choices by boys or girls.

The preceding list summarizes a few examples of scientific findings that *suggest* differences between the sexes based on biological development (Kimura, 2002; Kreeger, 2002). More research is needed. Nevertheless, when published, such findings influence popular opinion and public perceptions, and have an impact on how society, especially our schools, functions regarding the learning and social activities of girls and boys.

School counselors want to keep abreast of scientific discoveries in the area of sexual development. Equally important, they want to use published findings wisely, remembering that such research usually involves group data and, as with other types of group studies, there will be variances found across participants in any given study. Competent counselors are cautious not to apply research findings with absolute precision to students because of statistical variances involved. Such counselors comprehend, for example, that if spatial task abilities are found to be different between males and females, it does not mean that *all* boys and girls in their school will perform in accordance with the research. There is always room for individual differences. Generalizing research results to particular girls or boys may be a critical error that harms students.

The biological differences, particularly genetic characteristics, discussed in previous paragraphs are part of the countless factors that influence student development, behavior, and learning. These factors interact with a host of other variables including family structure and relationships, culture, and students' individual perceptions of life events among others. Interaction among all these factors leads to a determination (or selection) of gender roles.

Gender

While the sex of a person may be determined biologically, gender roles evolve as a result of the ways that family members, both immediate and extended, and society at large value males and females and how the person perceives this process of valuation over time, particularly in early development. Consequently, a baby enters a world already predisposed to certain characteristics by being either male or female—boy or girl—with cultural beliefs and traditions perpetuating this identity. Such beliefs and traditions vary according to the culture and ethnicity into which a person is born. For this reason, in a pluralistic society such as the United States, we see a range of traditions and beliefs about male and female roles across groups including African American, Latino, Native American, Asian, and among families of various Euro-American heritage.

Schools often reflect the beliefs and traditions of the dominant culture. Yet, as noted earlier in this chapter, U.S. schools enroll students from many cultural groups and different nationalities. This reality is another challenge for professional counselors who work in schools. Gender roles valued by particular cultures and groups influence choices students make regarding course selections, career pathways, social relationships, postsecondary education, and other decisions related to their educational, social, and personal development.

Successful counselors will be knowledgeable about cultural differences that influence students enrolled in their schools and how these differences relate to gender roles. At the same time, such counselors will be aware of stereotypical views they hold about gender that might impede their work with diverse students. Equally important, successful counselors understand that stereotypical views of gender roles are often culture-specific and as members of particular cultural groups, students sometimes struggle with the views of their group as they acculturate and adapt to the dominant culture of society (Schmidt, 2006).

How individual students perceive various attitudes about gender roles, include these perceptions in the construction of their self-concept, and choose behaviors that reflect their beliefs about feminine and masculine roles is a unique process of creating a gender identity. It is not a static process. As students move through various stages of development and as changes in attitudes about sex and gender occur in society, their views about sex and gender may also change (Schmidt, 2006).

Gender roles and attributes relate to *masculine* and *feminine* characteristics assigned by society. As noted earlier, these characteristics are not static conditions, nor are they absolute, definable traits. In a way, feminine and masculine characteristics exist on a continuum of behavioral traits. Therefore, male students might express feminine characteristics such as sensitivity and sincerity in some situations while demonstrating male characteristics such as competitiveness in others. Likewise, female students may exhibit a range of gender characteristics across identified masculine and feminine behaviors depending on the situation.

In the course of developing from childhood to young adulthood, a student's perception about sex, gender roles, and masculine and feminine characteristics interacts with cultural beliefs, acculturation into the school and larger society, and his or her biological structure influencing decisions about sexuality, sexual activity, and acceptance of sexual orientation. This significant process has tremendous implications for student development personally, socially, and educationally.

Sexual Orientation

The process of sexual orientation remains an unexplained part of the course of human development. Volumes of reports and numerous research studies on this topic exist, but no single explanation has emerged at this point in time. No consistent findings have yet indicated whether sexual orientation is a product of biology, environment, or a combination of both.

"Some preliminary findings suggest a possible link to genetic and hormonal factors, but these results are tentative and, similar to environmental factors, strongly debated within and outside the scientific community. Yet, continuing research seems to verify a relationship among various biological factors and sexual orientation identity" (Schmidt, 2006, p. 104).

What the studies seem to indicate early in this century is that sexual orientation is the result of a complex process through which an individual develops biologically, interacts with environmental factors, and draws conclusions about his or her sexual identity. Therefore, the process of being a heterosexual or homosexual person is not simply a matter of choice but rather is influenced by a multitude of factors, the most important of which may be biological.

Successful school counselors working with students who express confusion about their sexual development, gender identity, or sexual orientation understand current research findings, reject stereotypical thinking, and are knowledgeable of various models of sexual identity development (Schmidt, 2006). Such counselors approach gender issues and sexual identity concerns with empathy, awareness, and knowledge, and the first step in establishing the helping relationship is being aware of biases, if any, the counselor has toward gender roles and sexual identity issues. A second step is to be informed of research findings about sexual development and gender differences. School counselors, as with other professional counselors, must be able to locate recent findings, interpret them to students in an understandable manner, and offer students resources to answer additional questions about their development.

When counselors stay informed, it enables them to educate parents, teachers, administrators, and others who provide daily guidance to students. Knowledge of research findings about sexual development and sexual activity can be incorporated into comprehensive programs to provide services that inform students and others, help remove or diminish stereotypical thinking, eliminate discriminatory school policies, and otherwise make the school environment a safe place for all students regardless of their sex, gender, or orientation.

Helping students with issues of sexual orientation is a particularly sensitive area and school counselors want to first be aware of local board of education policies or state mandates that guide them in these matters (see Chapter 12). How counselors use information about sexual development, activity, and orientation in the overall school counseling program, including individual and group counseling with students, will depend in part on the policies and laws that exist about these matters. At the same time, counselors want to be aware of their beliefs and attitudes regarding heterosexual and homosexual behavior while also being in tune and comfortable with their own sexuality. In working with individual students, school counselors will want to

- Establish accepting relationships so students feel safe and willing to share intimate thoughts and feelings.
- Accept students' perceptions and understand their confusion about sexual development and identity.
- Present students with alternative perceptions as a means of helping them understand other possibilities and explanations.
- Encourage students to explore their fears and perceptions about heterosexuality and homosexuality.
- Explore with students the option of involving their parents in these discussions because family support is essential in the process of forming sexual identity.

- Encourage all students to create healthy relationships with people of different sexes and sexual orientations. (adapted from Schmidt, 2006)

Families and Communities

Since the first celebration of U.S. independence, families have been changing. These changes have occurred in part by the country's movement from an agrarian society to an industrial and now technological world leader. Modern technology, altered values, evolving gender roles, and a host of other conditions have contributed to these changes. In addition, continuous waves of immigrants have both enriched and diversified family structure in the United States. These social and cultural forces continue to influence family structure and function and similarly the meaning and importance of community in student development.

Today's students come to school from a variety of family structures and community influences. There appears to be no "normal" family in the traditional sense. What some counselors and educators might perceive as normal family structure and function may be in contrast to the views and experiences that students bring to school, and these opposing perceptions sometimes cause conflict. Successful school counselors know their cultural values regarding family structure, beliefs, and traditions and balance these views with dissimilar perceptions about family structure and function that some students may have.

The twenty-first century United States family is as diverse as the society itself (Gladding, 2002; Hetherington & Kelly, 2002; Reynolds, 2005; Robinson, 2005; Walsh, 2003). Based on current findings and anticipated trends, the expectation is that family definition and structure will continue to change:

- Dual earners comprise over two-thirds of all two-parent families. A husband as sole wage earner for the family is an image of the past.
- The divorce rate has stabilized in recent years, yet about 30 percent of families are led by single parents. Single mothers head about 25 percent of families, and more than half of African American families are led by the mother.
- Estimates are that about 75 percent of divorced people will eventually remarry. This means that remarried families, merged families, blended families, and other configurations, have become more common in U.S. society. Many students come from these diversely structured families.
- Teenage pregnancy, although declining in recent years, continues to be an important social and economic issue. "A disproportionate number of pregnant teens comes from disenfranchised, impoverished, and minority populations. About 90% of pregnant teenagers initially choose to keep their babies. Yet, the demands of parenting and harsh economic realities often prove so pressing that these young parents often are overwhelmed, and the child eventually enters a state's foster care system." (Schmidt, 2006, p. 114)
- The number of adopted children is increasing.
- Same-sex parents are also on the rise with research indicating that gay parents are more educated and produce higher incomes than the typical heterosexual couple.
- In many communities and cultures, grandparents are the primary custodians of and caretakers for children.

- Socioeconomic status has an impact on family structure. "Economically impoverished families tend to be larger, maternally led, and rely on assistance from relatives. In contrast, affluent families tend to be smaller, are led by educated and/or professional parents, and frequently rely on hired help to care for children and manage the home." (Schmidt, p. 114)

As students develop and make choices about educational goals and career pathways, family influence is an important element in the decision-making process. The degree to which particular students accept or reject their family's values and input affects the ease or difficulty with which they move through developmental processes. All students deal with these realities, but students from diverse cultures who are adapting to and acculturating into U.S. society may find this process more challenging.

School counselors who know their families and communities, accept the diversity that enriches the school environment, and appreciate the challenges faced by all students are in better position to create comprehensive programs of appropriate services to meet student and family needs. At the same time, such openness and understanding helps counselors work with diverse students to navigate through their school life while reducing stress and tension due to family and community beliefs. As noted throughout this chapter, when working with diverse students, it is especially important for counselors in schools to control their personal beliefs and resist the temptation to interject their perspective about family bonds. When counseling diverse students, therefore, the objective is to help them make appropriate decisions while remaining respectful toward family members and their cultural traditions. In many instances, the involvement of family members in the counseling process will enable the student to adhere to family and community values while assisting them with educational, career, and social/personal decisions. A major cultural factor that influences values is religion. It influences many aspects of self-development, as does the broader concept of spirituality. We consider these two cultural aspects and their relationship to school counseling programs in the next section.

Spirituality and Religion

Spirituality and religious beliefs are important aspects of a student's development and have implications for comprehensive school counseling programs (Sink, 2004). They provide pathways in life for individual students to attach meaning and purpose to their existence. Spiritual and religious beliefs become part of students' self-development through involvement with family, participation in social and cultural activities, and individual experiences. In working with students, school counselors want to be knowledgeable and sensitive to spiritual and religious foundations that guide students' behaviors. This is particularly important when working with diverse students who may have different views and beliefs than the counselor. By understanding the spiritual values and religious underpinnings that comprise a student's belief system, counselors do not compromise the edict of "separation of church and state" that guides public schools. Rather, they demonstrate recognition and acceptance of the whole person and all aspects that constitute a self-concept, the inner guidance system for making individual choices in life (Schmidt, 2006).

Some students will have spiritual values without adherence to a formal religion. They and their families may not belong to, or attend regularly, a synagogue, mosque, church, meetinghouse, or other place of worship. Nevertheless, their beliefs are as important to their development as the beliefs of students who have a strong affiliation with a particular religion. When working with diverse student populations, counselors want to understand various spiritual and religious beliefs and traditions that contribute to students' self-views, worldviews, and perspectives about a meaningful life.

Sometimes, strong religious or spiritual views might appear to interfere with counseling services provided to students in schools. In such instances, successful counselors proceed with caution, being careful not to let their professional orientation, theoretical approach, or personal views bias the helping relationship. Most traditional models of counseling have self-empowerment, self-actualization, and self-improvement as goals. As admirable as these objectives may sound, they sometimes conflict with religious beliefs that ask people to surrender their needs and desires to a higher power (Helms & Cook, 1999). Many students derive emotional and psychological strength from their spiritual beliefs or a religious doctrine. Therefore, when working with diverse students, schools might find that such beliefs are therapeutic agents rather than negative energy (Schmidt, 2006). At times, the spiritual beliefs of students may be an essential component in the counseling relationship.

Sink (2004) argued that spiritual beliefs are often the foundation for problem-solving and decision-making processes, so "school counselors need to establish coherent and helpful ways of engaging these spiritual resources" (p. 315). Furthermore, he proposed that these efforts aim at "including the spiritual dimension within existing comprehensive school counseling programs" (p. 315).

As noted, spiritual and religious development begins with interactions within the family. They are nurtured through involvement with and participation in community activities that may include attendance and worship at a religious facility. For this reason among others, family and community are two additional cultural variables to consider in working with diverse students.

Exceptionality

Not all students have the same ability to function as regular students in the school program. Because of its attempt to educate all people for the larger public good, the United States opens its school doors to a more expanded student population than most other countries. Consequently, many students enter school without the same level of physical, intellectual, or emotional capability as their peers. They are exceptional students and they comprise another element of diversity in our schools.

As mentioned in Chapter 1, the U.S. government passed The Education for All Handicapped Children Act, commonly referred to as Public Law 94-142, in 1975. This law changed the student population and culture of public schools across the country, and subsequent revisions of the law have continued this impact. Before this law, few handicapped children attended school. Now, it is commonplace to observe students with a wide range of physical and learning disabilities in special classrooms that serve their particular needs, or mainstreamed in classrooms with other students and taught, in part, by resource teachers for their particular exceptionality.

Today, the 1975 law continues as the Individuals with Disabilities Education Act (IDEA), reauthorized in 1997 (Lockhart, 2003). Schools follow this law in tandem with two other important pieces of legislation—Section 504 of the Rehabilitation Act of 1973 and the more recently passed Americans with Disabilities Act of 1990 (ADA). Of these bills, the two that have the most significance for school counseling practice are IDEA and Section 504 (Lockhart, 2003). Although the role of school counselors in the 1970s was unclear when the first bill became law, it has become more certain that exceptional students deserve the same level of attention and service that other students receive. Consequently, the importance of planning, leading, and implementing comprehensive school counseling programs has become greater as a result of the expended audience of students served by professional counselors.

Under IDEA, school programs and services address a range of exceptional needs, from intellectually disabled to gifted and talented students. These programs and services are required to ensure the "least restrictive" mandate for educating all our citizens. The least restrictive environment means that, as much as possible, students with identified disabilities receive instruction in classes with students who are not disabled. As such, the school's educational "intent is to bring the exceptional child as close to the normal classroom setting as is feasible" (Kirk, Gallagher, & Anastasiow, 1996, p. 55).

As noted, IDEA assigns schools the responsibility for providing services to address particular exceptionalities and disabilities for all identified students. In this responsibility, the government provides funds to schools to assist with the evaluation of students and the delivery of educational services to address students' educational, intellectual, physical, or behavioral challenges. In contrast, Section 504 focuses on school policies, processes, or programs that have the potential to discriminate against particular students because of learning difficulties they may be experiencing. This law receives no federal funding. The assumption of Section 504 is that the school has the authority and power to make adjustments in such policies, programs, or processes and alleviate or remove barriers to learning for certain students. As Lockhart (2003) explained, Section 504 "attempts to level the playing field for those students who can perform well academically if their disability does not limit their access to learning" (p. 361). Unlike IDEA, Section 504 does not necessarily provide specific services for students. Rather, it gives responsibility to schools to remove barriers by adjusting programs and services to better meet the educational needs of students who happen to have a diagnosed disability.

Eligibility rules for students under IDEA and Section 504 also differ. IDEA guidelines require that identified students between the ages of three and twenty must have a disability that significantly impacts learning. Schools strictly apply the rules of evaluating, identifying, and serving students under IDEA and design an Individual Educational Plan (IEP) that is agreed on by the parents or guardians of the child to be served. An IEP includes the student's current level of academic functioning, learning objectives and annual goals for student progress, and specific services that the school will provide in meeting these goals and objectives (Baker & Gerler, 2004).

Eligibility for Section 504 requires that students have a history of a physical or mental disability that significantly limits performance in a major life function such as walking, hearing, speaking, breathing, or learning. Equally important, it requires that the disability has been assessed and confirmed by a qualified professional examiner. Examples of disabilities include impairments in vision, hearing, speech, behavioral disorders such as attention deficit hyperactivity disorder (ADHD), or temporary disabilities such as an illness or broken limb (Stone & Dahir, 2006). A major difference between Section 504 and IDEA in applying the guidelines for disabled students is that eligibility under 504 means that the identified student is capable of being successful in a learning activity if obstacles to accessing and participating fully in the activity are removed.

Many counseling texts, professional journals, and other resources have presented approaches for counselors in schools to assist exceptional students as well as those identified through Section 504 (Boscardin, Brown-Chidsey, González-Martínez, 2003; Lockhart, 2003; Schmidt, 2004; Stone & Dahir, 2006). Because the laws do not spell out specific roles for counselors in schools with exceptional students or special education programs, successful counselors stay informed of changes in the law and procedures as well as state and local guidelines that might affect the school counselor's involvement and responsibilities. In brief, counselors want to

- Attain a working knowledge of the exceptional children's program and Section 504, applicable federal, state, and local regulations, and the expected role of the counselor in applying these regulations.
- Learn the characteristics of various disabling conditions and how they might fit eligibility requirements under IDEA or Section 504.
- Collaborate with classroom and special education teachers to choose and plan appropriate counseling strategies.
- Learn about community agencies that serve students with disabilities and their families. Coordinate counseling and related services with professionals in the community.
- Integrate guidance activities into the comprehensive school counseling program so that classroom teachers can use the curriculum to educate all students about exceptionalities and disabilities.
- Provide information to students, parents, and teachers about the ways cultural differences might interact with certain exceptionalities, such as retardation and giftedness.
- Include counseling and related services to assist students with disabilities to navigate the countless transitions that occur within the school, between schools, and from school to home or the community.
- Consult and collaborate with parents of exceptional students on a continuous basis, as advocates not only for the student but for parents and guardians as well.

Some literature and research suggests that a cultural implication of disability laws and exceptionality programs has been the overidentification, underidentification, and/or misplacement of diverse students (Boscardin, Brown-Chidsey, & González-Martínez, 2003). A confounding variable in the assessment and identification processes used for exceptional students' programs is socioeconomic status, another aspect of diversity that affects schools and student learning.

Socioeconomic Status

Another aspect of diversity that touches most if not all the preceding descriptions is socioeconomic status (SES). As with other variables, socioeconomic status is a socially constructed representation. Differences in financial wealth and the distribution of wealth within and across society do exist, but the meaning assigned to these differences comes from socially constructed definitions and interpretations. For students in schools, these differences create the phenomena of social classes, which are as important to identity development as are race, gender, ability, and other traits. Social class and socioeconomic status influence self-concept development (Schmidt, 2006). Therefore, school counselors want to understand their impact when working with diverse students, especially those affected by issues of classism, poverty, and affluence.

Socioeconomic status not only influences individual identity, it also has an impact on family structure and functioning (Aponte & Crouch, 2000; Gladding, 2002; Robinson, 2005). This impact is affected by and contributes to the educational and career decisions that students make, which over a lifetime lead full circle to achieving some level of socioeconomic status. All these decisions help students determine where they will stand on the social strata and subsequently assume a class identification of "lower class," "middle class," "upper class," or some other designation created by society. These class groups are representations of various levels of socioeconomic status. In all cases of identifying with particular social classes, students will face biases and prejudices common in most socially constructed systems.

Ideally, in a democracy such as the United States people aspire to a classless society. However, Langston (2001) among others has noted that the idea of a classless society is a myth perpetuated by a culture that worships the power of self-reliance, personal ambition, and individual intelligence. The belief that all people have the same opportunity and advantage to use these individualistic traits to succeed is, according to some authorities, grossly overstated. For counselors in schools, learning about students' perceptions of self-determined traits and the likelihood of using them to achieve socially and economically is important in designing programs and providing counseling services to the total school population. In constructing their self-views, students include perceptions of social class, and in doing so, some students will accept different interpretations about themselves than more commonly held beliefs about their class. School life and the activities and relationships that influence student development can have a tremendous impact on these perceptions. This explains, in part, why some members of a social class move to higher or lower levels in the course of their lifetime (Schmidt, 2006). Guidance lessons, counseling relationships, and related services of a comprehensive school counseling program have the potential to make a positive difference in the decisions made by all students. At the same time, schools must use caution to avoid perpetuating social class biases of the larger community (Herring, 1999).

Poverty is one feature of socioeconomic status that can have a devastating effect on a student's self-concept as well as the family's access to social services and educational programs. Addressing the effects of poverty is an important first step for counselors and other helpers to take in ensuring that students can stand on a level playing field and have equal opportunity in school. Without addressing the critical issue of poverty, all the counseling and related services provided may go for naught in trying to enhance student development. Research indicates that the earlier we address this issue in a child's development, the more likely social and educational services will result in positive outcomes.

In the 1990s, about 2.5 million children in the United States lived in poverty. Census figures from 2002 indicate that almost 10 percent of families were at the poverty level, about 7.2 million families. In 2004, 28.4 percent of all female-headed households were below the poverty level compared to 5.5 percent of married-couple families (Institute for Research on Poverty, 2005). Although many impoverished children and their families overcome these conditions, studies show that early childhood development, the time when home life greatly influences brain growth, is significantly enhanced and sustained by socioeconomic status

(National Center for Children in Poverty, 1999). This finding is consistent in the research (Schmidt, 2006). In addition, many other challenges correlate with poverty including health issues, racial differences, gender, marital status, and location among others. Schools witness the results of poverty firsthand and with students and their families face seemingly insurmountable challenges in creating beneficial learning environments and services.

Socioeconomic realities, particularly the impact of impoverished conditions, require that school counselors take action beyond the typical services they offer students, parents, and teachers. To address such global issues, successful counselors become agents of social change, being active in community efforts to help needy students and families. In a sense, they become advocates for social justice, which we will discuss later in this chapter. These roles are best created and acted on through comprehensive programs of services through which counselors can orchestrate the cooperation and support of many people and professionals.

As noted, geographic location sometimes has an impact on social class. It also is a variable that stands alone as an aspect of diversity. The next section considers urban and rural schools as aspects related to diversity.

Rural and Urban Schools

American schools exist across a wide range of communities, towns, and cities. The 2000 Census found 80 percent of people live in metropolitan and suburban areas with the remaining 20 percent in rural communities. The counseling literature and research has indicated differences between rural and urban schools, the issues that students face, and the significance these differences may have for planning and delivering comprehensive programs of services (Cole, 1990; Holcomb-McCoy & Mitchell, 2005; Lee, 2005; Morrissette, 1997).

Morrissette (1997) listed several themes about the practice of school counseling in rural settings. These themes may apply to students and families in rural schools as well. First are the sense of isolation and the absence of support systems, which leads to challenges of adjusting to rural community life. A second theme involves appropriate supervision and consequential role conflicts for counselors. Most rural counselors have little or no supervision other than their principal who most likely does not have a counseling background. At the same time, small schools usually lack personnel to perform all the expected tasks, so counselors "pitch in," which sometimes raises role conflicts.

Another theme in rural schools is the lack of resources in comparison to suburban and urban communities. The rural school counselor is not only a firstline helper but in many cases the only mental-health practitioner available. This reality challenges the rural counselors to design and deliver comprehensive programs. Two final themes mentioned by Morrissette (1997) are community pressures and loss of privacy and anonymity. Small communities expect school personnel to be actively involved. While such commitment is admirable and encouraged (Schmidt, 2004), it adds pressure to the counselor's job expectations. Regarding privacy, living in a small town "where everyone knows everybody" does at times detract from a person's privacy. This is true not only for school counselors, but also for the students and families they serve.

Green, Conley, and Barnett (2005) mentioned the sociological and ecological factors that influence urban life and student development. These include a high concentration of poverty, crime, and violence within a diverse and mobile population. The diversity of urban populations is characterized by a number of variables that include ethnicity, race, various lifestyles, and a high concentration of resources. These factors are sometimes complemented by and other times in conflict with available technology for rapid communication and transportation found in cities. Some of the urban challenges that Holcomb-McCoy (1998) enumerated sound similar to trends in rural communities. They include a lack of resources, poverty, family concerns, and high dropout rates. At the same time, other conditions she listed, particularly diversity of students and violence, may not have the same level of impact in rural communities, although that trend may be changing in U.S. culture as a result of immigration and people moving out of urban areas.

Lee (2005) listed several characteristics that describe urban communities. Among them are population and structural density, high concentrations of people of color and immigrants, poverty, high crime rates, complex transportation systems, air and other environmental pollutants, large and complex school systems, inequitable access to services and treatment by the legal system, and lack of connectedness with the community (p. 185). He outlined several competencies that urban counselors must bring to their role, including the skills, knowledge, and awareness to respond to the needs of an increasingly diverse student population. Lee also encouraged urban school counselors to use empowerment theory, adopt a systemic perspective for their programmatic role, embrace a posture of advocacy for all students, collaborate with parents and teachers, reach out to other professionals and key community decision-makers, and become leaders in initiating and developing appropriate changes in the school and larger community.

Examination and comparison of rural and urban schools and the unique challenges they present to professional counselors is another example of how issues of diversity will influence the practice of school counseling. For all the factors mentioned in the preceding sections, it is clear that future counselors in schools will require particular competencies to be successful. In the final two sections of this chapter, we examine some of the competencies that appear in the counseling literature and ways those competencies are demonstrated in comprehensive school counseling programs.

The School Counselor and Multicultural Competency

As discussed, expanded diversity of student populations in schools across the United States require that counselors become prepared and continually examine their practice to achieve the highest level of competency. Several authors have addressed the importance of multicultural competency in professional counseling (Arrendondo, Toporek, Brown, Jones, Locke, Sanchez, & Stadler, 1996; Locke, 2003) and, in this section, we relate these competencies to school counseling.

The Professional Standards Committee of the Association for Multicultural Counseling and Development (AMCD) first developed basic competencies and standards of practice for multicultural counseling (Schmidt, 2006). Arredondo and colleagues (1996) further explained how competencies across three areas—awareness, knowledge, and skill—related to the practice of counseling with diverse clients. In particular, they showed how these three areas of competency interacted with personal attitudes and beliefs of counselors as well as therapeutic strategies selected by counselors. Locke (2003) expanded this information for professional counseling in schools by adding the dimension of institutional change and the role counselors have in ensuring that their schools include, encourage, and support diverse student populations, their families, and their cultures. He enumerated several outlooks necessary for institutional change:

1. A strong commitment by the school and school system for the education of culturally diverse students
2. An understanding by schools of their responsibility to teach the value of cultures
3. Support by schools for persons, such as school counselors, actively seeking ways to change institutional policies and programs to better serve diverse students and their families
4. A clear effort by the school and school system to communicate that they value diversity
5. Strategic planning and ongoing evaluation of school policies, programs, and processes related to the education of all students, including those of diverse cultures (pp. 171–172)

The challenge for professional counselors working in schools is twofold. First, they must reach a level of competency in their awareness, knowledge, and skill to make a difference in the lives of all students. Second, they must achieve leadership qualities and skills to help their schools assess, adjust, and evaluate programs, policies, and procedures to better serve all students. These are not easy tasks. To begin, counselors address their competencies, which is an ongoing process of professional development across the three areas mentioned. At the same time, they use and incorporate leadership skills to design and implement comprehensive programs to serve students, parents, and teachers while helping the school address internal issues of discrimination, prejudice, neglect, and other deterrents to creating respectful and inclusive environments for learning. The three areas of awareness, knowledge, and skill are also important criteria in helping schools achieve this goal.

Awareness

Awareness of one's culture and heritage is the starting point for building awareness of other cultures. Competent counselors achieve an awareness of the impact that their culture has had on their development—positive and negative—both personally and professionally. This awareness includes an understanding of how cultural beliefs are translated into everyday thoughts, feelings, and behavior.

School counselors who reach a level of personal awareness also understand how their cultural background may limit their ability to work with diverse students across various cultures. These limitations are not necessarily permanent, but to transcend them, counselors improve their knowledge and skill. Sometimes, counselors' cultural backgrounds and subsequent beliefs might limit their ability to help diverse students because of discomfort that hinders the establishment of genuine helping relationships. Confronting these beliefs to remove the potential for discomfort is another important first step.

Culturally aware school counselors understand how their reactions toward particular students and stereotypical views about particular cultures inhibit their ability to establish effective helping relationships. Awareness of biases and stereotypic thinking allows them to refer students to better sources of assistance. When counselors are capable of being less prejudiced about different groups of students, they are better able to serve all students equitably and effectively.

Being aware of one's cultural background and its influence on beliefs, attitudes, and behavior is an important step. That awareness is complemented by a sincere effort to learn about other cultures represented in school and an appreciation of the worldviews embraced by those cultures. All aspects of becoming aware of oneself and of others relate to the attainment of knowledge about *self* and others.

Knowledge

It is important to learn about one's own culture and its influence on personal development. As a counselor, it is also essential to learn about the cultures of others, to increase awareness about the beliefs, perceptions, and behaviors of culturally diverse students. Competent counselors add to this knowledge an understanding about racism, sexism, classism, ableism, and other forms of oppression, discrimination, and stereotypic behavior and the impact that these conditions have on human development.

The knowledge a counselor needs to become culturally informed is broad-based. It includes information about cultural heritage, values, mores, and traditions. It also includes knowledge about social and political events that have helped to shape particular cultures. As noted throughout this chapter, this knowledge incorporates an appreciation of the history of oppression, racism, poverty, and other social phenomena that contribute to students' self-views and ultimately their worldviews. Such knowledge helps counselors understand how countless identity factors interact with student development, including their educational decisions, career choices, and personal/social relationships.

School counselors who become more culturally aware and achieve a level of knowledge about various cultures also seek to expand their professional skills to handle issues of diversity competently. They realize that skill development is not a single event but rather an ongoing process of learning and practice to better serve diverse students and their families. At the same time, leadership skills enhance a counselor's ability to become a change agent in the school and community.

Skill

Knowledge of culture is an initial step to developing skills required to be a competent multicultural counselor. This is an ongoing process that includes reading professional literature and research, attending workshops and conferences, and returning to graduate school. School counselors also willingly consult with colleagues and other professionals to verify their understanding of particular students and which interventions might work in diverse situations. At the same time, effective counselors know when to refer cases to ensure that students receive the best possible care. They stay up-to-date about culturally appropriate referral sources in the community.

As part of skill-building, competent school counselors consistently and genuinely seek to broaden their personal and social experiences by actively participating in school functions, forming acquaintances with new students, and joining community organizations. They also encourage bilingual practices in their school by publishing and distributing documents about counseling programs and services in languages spoken by diverse students whenever possible.

Many other skills help counselors become competent in working with diverse populations. These include the selection and use of appropriate interventions, communication styles to assist all students, leadership behaviors to mitigate school policies that inhibit or discriminate against particular students or groups, and use of appropriate assessment skills. All of these skills and others enable school counselors to assess situations appropriately, choose developmental strategies for all students, celebrate diversity, be active in situations that demand social justice, and lead the school counseling program. In the last section of this chapter, we focus on some of these aspects of counseling in schools with diverse populations.

School Counseling and Diversity

All the discussed factors, characteristics, and issues regarding diverse student populations have importance for school counseling practice. As noted throughout this chapter, they have particular significance in planning, organizing, implementing, and evaluating school counseling programs. School counseling research and literature indicates a link between comprehensive programs and multicultural education of students as well as the multicultural competency of professional counselors in schools (Holcomb-McCoy, 2003; Lee, 2001; Locke, 2003; Sink, 2001; Stone & Dahir, 2006.). In the remaining sections of this chapter, we examine some aspects of program development and leadership, developmental counseling services, and other elements related to comprehensive programs and diversity, beginning with assessment of the school environment.

Assessment of School Environment

The school counseling literature has emphasized an important role for counselors as agents of change in schools and society. To help schools realize the impact of environmental factors on student learning, counselors consult with administrators, teachers, parents, and others to examine aspects of the school that enhance or detract from educational processes. This is essential if schools intend to create healthy environments for students across diverse groups and individual identities. Schools that intentionally create beneficial environments, and counselors who actively assess school processes, programs, and policies to assure healthy climates, combine to develop effective educational opportunities for all students.

In planning healthy school climates, counselors help administrators and teachers evaluate programs to enhance learning and determine whether these programs accomplish what is intended. Sometimes schools create programs to benefit all students, but in practice, they exclude rather than include students who need services. An example of this is a senior high school that designed an extensive after-school program of extracurricular activities to benefit students, particularly disadvantaged students. Unfortunately, the school neglected to plan after-school bus transportation and, as a result, many students did not attend because they had no way of getting home. Once the school corrected this oversight, more students were able to participate and the program was successful in reaching its goal.

Counselors also ask administrators to assess physical aspects of schools, such as lighting, floor coverings, painted walls, and building cleanliness. These and other features influence students' morale and attitude about school and learning. Once, an elementary school principal turned off all the hall lights because he had heard at a workshop that when lights are dimmed, children are quieter. Soon, the counselor and teachers noticed that the incidence of school phobia, enuresis, and acting out behavior was on the rise. The counselor convinced the principal that the lights needed to be turned up again. Instead of creating a calming influence, the dark hallways were raising anxieties of the children and stressing the teachers!

In a similar way, school policies relate to a positive climate and a posture of inclusiveness. Successful counselors review school policies to determine if they are necessary and whether these rules contribute to healthy, inclusive environments. Sometimes policies exist for the convenience of a few staff members rather than for the benefit of students as a whole. When this happens, resentment toward the school is inevitable. Policies that potentially discriminate, ignore, or otherwise neglect particular students or groups are especially problematic for diverse students and their families.

School counselors have a responsibility to see that schools are designed, organized, and governed for the welfare of all students. Their ability to assess situations and make suggestions for altering programs, changing policies, renovating places, and adjusting processes affects the success of their school counseling program and services for students, parents, and teachers. Chapter 5 gives an example of a school climate assessment instrument.

Developmental Counseling

Developmental counseling has been the philosophic basis for counseling and related services in schools for several decades (Myrick, 2003; Paisley, 2001). Throughout this text, you will find references to this aspect of comprehensive programs, so here I briefly introduce developmental counseling as it pertains to diverse students as well as the greater student population.

Students at all ages face tasks that include physical, cognitive, emotional, and other developmental stages and issues. This phenomenon crosses all human groups and cultures. Likewise, multicultural learning and development considers the various stages that students navigate during their school years in creating learning activities, counseling interventions, and other strategies. Therefore, successful counselors account for developmental stages in addition to cultural differences and nuances when planning programs, selecting counseling approaches, and generally addressing the educational, career, and personal/social needs of all students.

Celebration of Diversity

One way that comprehensive programs assist in students' multicultural development is by celebrating the diverse cultures found within the school and in the larger community (Schmidt, 2004). Comprehensive school counseling programs provide the framework for such celebrations to occur. Successful counselors lead the design and delivery of programs and services such as classroom guidance (integrated by teachers into daily instruction) and special schoolwide activities (such as a Native American exhibition) that highlight cultural differences and similarities while allowing diverse students to share various aspects of their culture and heritage. Schools integrate cultural celebrations into the curriculum across all subject areas and include activities that focus on cultural history, tradition, and rituals.

In working with classroom teachers, school counselors help to design a guidance curriculum that encourages all students across diverse cultures to set academic goals, adjust to school procedures and expectations without forsaking valued cultural traditions, and attend school regularly. As noted earlier, diverse students face similar developmental concerns as other students. When counselors address these issues, all the factors considered in this chapter receive attention. However, these cultural differences should not be identified at the expense of the richness that diversity contributes to the school community. For this reason, the celebration of culture is an ongoing part of multicultural education for all students, parents, teachers, and other professionals.

Advocacy and Social Justice

In recent years, some authorities have promoted an expanded role for professional counselors as social activists who energetically advocate for clients (D'Andrea & Daniels, 2004; Helms & Cook, 1999; Thompson, 2004). Student advocacy has been an identified role for school counselors for most of the profession's history, and today, it continues as a significant role in the ASCA National Model (Baker & Gerler, 2004; Stone & Dahir, 2006). For counselors in schools, student advocacy moves them beyond common helping relationships toward more active stances to address and confront institutional policies and programs that intentionally or unintentionally discriminate against students because of their gender, socioeconomic status, ethnicity, or family structure, among other variables. Advocacy for students takes many shapes and forms. These include promoting systemic change, helping individuals and groups of students to enhance their self-development and increase feelings of empowerment, and working outside the school as part of the larger community to bring about change in legal, political, financial and other systems to promote social justice (Stone & Dahir, 2006).

In today's schools and society, the advocacy role of counselors is as important as it has ever been. For example, the achievement gap that exists between student groups across schools, systems, and the country continues to be a critical issue. How school counselors alert their schools and school systems to inherent inequities that contribute to differences in student achievement is an indication of their advocacy. As Stone and Dahir (2006) explained, counselors in schools play a significant role in advocating for students that have been "traditionally underserved" (p. 122). At the same time, counselors work with students individually and in groups to help them decrease feelings of "helplessness" and increase their feelings of empowerment by becoming more self-aware and knowledgeable about how the environment and social system can be used for self-improvement.

Advocacy, empowerment, and social justice are complex concepts and processes. They are easier to read about than to apply in real situations. This is especially true when advocating for diverse and disenfranchised students. All the more reason for school counselors who desire to take active roles to establish the awareness, knowledge, and skills necessary to become multiculturally competent. This competency helps counselors design and implement comprehensive programs that enlist the support and services of many people, programs, and other resources. Advocacy and action for social justice are tied to a counselor's willingness and ability to lead a comprehensive program.

Program Leadership

Although counselors advocate and stand up for individual students and groups of students, it is unimaginable that they can do so by themselves and make a significant difference in their schools and communities. This is one reason that comprehensive school counseling programs have emerged and gained the support of so many authorities in the school counseling profession (Baker & Gerler, 2004; Gysbers & Henderson, 2001; Myrick, 2003; Schmidt, 2003a).

To serve diverse students and their families adequately and appropriately, school counselors recognize that they cannot do it all. By designing, organizing, implementing, and evaluating comprehensive programs of services for all students, counselors place themselves in a leadership role and balance that role with the direct, responsive services they are professionally prepared to deliver. In the next chapter, we will examine more completely the role of the school counselor and particularly the leadership stance and skills required to guide a comprehensive program successfully.

Additional Readings

Pedersen, P. B., & Carey, J. C. (2003). *Multicultural counseling in schools: A practical handbook* (Boston: Allyn & Bacon).

A comprehensive volume of fifteen chapters covering a wide range of topics related to diversity and the practice of counseling in schools.

Websites

Association for Multicultural Counseling and Development (AMCD)
www.bgsu.edu/colleges/edhd/programs/AMCD

Southern Poverty Law Center: Teaching Tolerance
www.splcenter.org/center/tt/teach.jsp

Exercises

1. Take time to reflect on the factors discussed in this chapter. By yourself or with a classmate, reflect on each of them and examine your beliefs about these variables. How will these beliefs affect your functioning as a successful counselor with diverse student populations?

2. Attend and participate in a diversity experience. Check your local paper, campus announcements, or ask a classmate who has a different ethnic background and heritage than you do. Find an ethnic celebration,

religious ceremony, musical presentation, lecture, or other event that might offer you a diversity experience that you have not had before. After attending and participating in this event, examine some of the preconceived notions you had before the event and what you think about them after the event.

3. Visit a school or schools and ask the administration how they celebrate diversity. What ways, if any, did they report, and what did you learn through these visits and interviews?

3

The School Counselor and Program Leadership

A wide range of counseling, consulting, and coordinating services and activities comprise the role of counselors at all levels of practice, including elementary, middle, and high schools. In each of these settings, counselors provide responsive services in comprehensive programs designed to address the educational, career, personal, and social development of all students. In this chapter, we focus on the professional counselor who has responsibility for designing and delivering services and providing leadership for a comprehensive program. In addition, this chapter examines the various roles, training, and credentials of counselors at all levels of school service. Later, in Chapter 4, we will define and describe a comprehensive school counseling program and continue the discussion in Chapter 5 by describing counseling and related services in more detail.

As we saw in Chapter 1, school counseling is a relatively young profession that emerged from the vocational guidance movement of the early 1900s. Since that time, the counseling profession has searched for a clear identity and role for counselors in schools. In this search for identity, school counselors have sometimes been criticized for not fulfilling their obligations. Exactly what these obligations are is a basic question all school counselors ascertain in developing appropriate goals and objectives for their programs. Without clear goals and objectives, a counselor's obligations can easily be misinterpreted and misunderstood by other professionals and by the people who seek counseling services.

As indicated in Chapter 1, misunderstandings about the counselor's role are related in some measure to the confusion between the terms *guidance* and *counseling* and how these terms are used to describe what school counselors do. Successful counselors, whether in schools or other settings, are clear about the terms they use to describe and define their programs and services, and they use these terms in a consistent fashion.

To better understand the role of professional counselors in schools, a consistent language defines what counseling is, identifies who counselors are, and describes what they do. To fully comprehend these aspects, you will first learn how the terms *guidance* and *counseling* are used in this book.

Defining School Counseling

The challenge of offering a wide spectrum of services to several different audiences makes school counselors unique in their practice. Although similar skills and expertise are required of counselors in other settings, counselors in schools, as noted throughout this text, apply their knowledge beyond the limited scope of a single service because they do so in a comprehensive program of interrelated services and activities.

School counselors have training in many areas that contribute to their overall knowledge base and professional skills. Graduate courses in human development, sociology, psychology, career information and development, tests and measurement techniques, social and cultural foundations, educational research, and counseling processes and skills give school counselors a broad knowledge base and a variety of skills to practice in elementary, middle, and high school settings. Courses in theory and practice provide counselors with a framework to formulate and clarify their professional role. In sum, this training enables school counselors to create a description of the variety of services they offer to students, parents, and teachers.

To be consistent in developing program descriptions, counselors benefit from a language that is clear and understandable to students, parents, teachers, and others who need to know why professional counselors are in the school and what counselors do. In this textbook, the term *school counseling* describes both the profession and the program of services established by counselors in schools. The term *counseling,* as used here, is not limited to remedial relationships in which counselors help clients resolve problems, nor is it restricted to one-to-one relationships. As used here, *counseling* refers to a wide selection of services and activities that counselors choose to help people prevent disabling events, focus on their overall development, and remedy existing concerns. The common ground for these three service areas is that, in each, the school counselor provides direct services to students, parents, and teachers. As such, the term *school counseling* accurately describes a broad program of services provided by professionally trained counselors who practice in elementary, middle, and senior high schools.

The term *school counseling* is a more contemporary and definitive term than is *personnel services* or *guidance services,* which are vague descriptions encompassing conflicting roles and functions for school counselors. For example, *personnel services* implies record-keeping, class scheduling, attendance monitoring, and other functions that are administrative in nature and detract from direct counseling and consulting services with students, parents, and teachers. The term *guidance,* while noted for its historical significance, is not the sole responsibility of school counselors, nor is it the domain of any single professional group. Everything done in schools, whether by administrators, teachers, counselors, or others, can be related in some way to the concept of "guiding students."

For as long as schools have existed, teachers have guided children and adolescents in classroom behaviors and in their personal relationships. By the same token, school administrators have guided students with respect to policies, curriculum, discipline, and other aspects of the educational program. Student guidance is important, and everyone who works in schools and cares about children and adolescents has a role in this process. By accepting a broader application for the term *guidance,* school administrators, teachers, and counselors recognize that the "entire educational program of the school . . . is guidance oriented (or should be). For this reason, it is inaccurate to confine guidance goals and objectives to a single program such as school counseling. Because guidance permeates every facet of the school, no one person or program has ownership" (Schmidt, 2004, p. 3). In this way, guidance remains an important concept because it names an essential part of the school curriculum, a part that is integrated into the total curriculum and not isolated in a separate program.

The terms *school counselor* and *school counseling program* are compatible with the terminology used by the national professional associations, as seen in the name of the American School Counselor Association (ASCA) and its journal, *Professional School Counseling.* In addition, the National Board for Certified Counselors (NBCC) has created a specialty certification area for school counselors.

Although the terms *school counseling program* and *school counselor* are the preferred descriptions used in this book, the term *guidance* and other designations have an important place in defining and describing the school counselor's role and program of services. Here are some of the major terms with brief descriptions used in this book. In later chapters, these terms are defined and described in greater detail.

Guidance is a term used to describe a curriculum area related to affective or psychological education. The guidance curriculum generally consists of broad goals and objectives for each grade level and, ideally, is integrated into classroom instruction by teachers and counselors in a cooperative effort. Sometimes *guidance* is used to designate a particular instructional or informational service such as "classroom guidance" or "small group guidance." Other times the word *guidance* is used to label or describe a particular schoolwide activity and focus such as "career guidance."

Counseling defines ongoing helping processes that are confidential in nature and assist people in focusing on concerns, planning strategies to address specific issues, and evaluating their success in carrying out these plans. Counseling services take the form of individual or small group counseling and are primarily for students. Depending on circumstances, school counselors sometimes offer brief counseling services to parents and teachers. In these instances, their goal may be to help a parent or teacher use resources such as community agencies or services. By helping parents and teachers in short-term counseling, school counselors give indirect assistance to children and adolescents. Successful counseling relationships require a high level of knowledge about human development and behavior as well as effective and facilitative communication skills.

Developmental guidance and counseling describes activities and services that are designed to help students focus on the attainment of knowledge and skills for developing healthy life goals and acquiring behaviors to reach these goals. Sometimes these activities are delivered in large or small group guidance sessions appropriate for all students, and other times they are designed specifically for targeted audiences in small group counseling sessions. In elementary, middle, and high schools, these developmental services are aimed at helping students focus on tasks and issues appropriate for their age and stage of life. For example, a middle grade teacher might present the career implications of learning to speak fluently and write appropriately to help students see the connection between language arts in school and future vocational choices.

Consultation comprises relationships in which school counselors, as student development specialists, confer with parents, teachers, and other professionals to identify student needs and select appropriate services. Occasionally, counselors determine that the best way to help students is to provide information to parents or teachers. In these instances, consultation takes the form of parent education groups, teacher in-service workshops, or individual conferences. Counselors also consult with students by providing brief individual and group sessions to disseminate information or offer instruction about particular topics. For example, counselors assist with the guidance curriculum by presenting or co-presenting with teachers particular classroom guidance lessons and activities. Another example is high school students interested in a peer helper program and consulting with their counselor to find out what peer helpers do and how they could join this special group of students.

Schoolwide guidance identifies planned activities that help all students focus on a particular issue or topic. Such schoolwide events might be planned jointly by school counselors, administrators, and teachers. Samples of these types of activities are a "Career Day" for senior high school students, "Develop-a-New-Friendship Week" for middle-graders, and a "Most Improved" bulletin board for elementary children.

The *student services team* is a group of professionals who specialize in providing counseling, consulting, assessment, and other related services to ensure the emotional, educational, social, and healthful development of all students. Typically, a student services team consists of the school counselor, social worker, psychologist, nurse, and other related professionals.

A *counseling center* includes the office and facilities of the school counselor. These facilities consist of office space, furnishings, equipment, and materials that are needed to implement a comprehensive program. Depending on the level of the program and the size of the school and staff, the counseling center might include private offices for the counselors, a waiting or play area, a room for testing, and a conference room for group sessions.

A *teacher advising program* is designed to give every student adequate access to an adult advisor. While teacher advising programs (TAPs) are found most commonly at the middle school level (sometimes they are called advisor-advisee programs), they can be designed and implemented at all school levels (Gallassi & Gulledge, 1997; Manning & Saddlemire, 1996; Myrick, 2003; Rappaport, 2002). Basically, these programs assign groups of students to teachers for advising about academic, social, and personal needs. Teacher-advisors also present special guidance sessions for their advisees during the year. In addition, teacher-advisee programs are excellent networks by which teachers can refer students to counselors for additional services and attention.

A *peer helper program* is established to identify and train students who can assist classmates and other students (Lewis & Lewis, 1996; Scarborough, 1997; Sink, 2005). Often, school counselors work in isolation, particularly in elementary and middle schools where ratios of students to counselors are frequently high. Peer helpers can assist counselors and teachers in meeting the needs of a greater number of students. They can be trained as listeners to be first-line helpers in a school, as mediators to assist with conflict resolutions, as tutors to assist students who are experiencing learning problems, as guidance aides to help teachers present guidance activities in classes, and as office assistants to answer the counselor's phone, run errands, and do other helpful tasks. Training is essential for students who are selected as peer helpers so they can be successful in addressing the identified needs of fellow students and meeting the targeted goals of the program.

A *parent education program* is designed to provide information about child development issues, discipline strategies at home, school progress, and other related topics. Some counselors use packaged, commercially produced programs to assist parents. Two examples are *Systematic Training for Effective Parenting* [STEP] (http://lifematters.com/step.asp) and *Active Parenting* (www.activeparenting.com). Other counselors design their own programs and activities for their schools. Occasionally, these programs are a single session, such as a presentation to a meeting of the PTA, and other times they are ongoing sessions, such as a support group of single parents led by an elementary counselor.

An *advisory committee* is a volunteer group established to guide the planning and development of a comprehensive program. The scope and breadth of comprehensive school counseling programs require input from administrators, teachers, parents, and students. An advisory committee is one way that counselors enlist the assistance of these groups to determine the needs of school populations, advise the counselor about essential services to meet these needs, and plan schoolwide activities to enhance student learning, improve relationships, and create a beneficial school climate.

Many other terms are used to describe various aspects of comprehensive school counseling programs, and most of them are included in this and other chapters. A clear understanding of the language and terms counselors use to describe who they are and what they do puts you in a stronger position to outline your role and professional identity. Identifying this role is essential to your success as a school counselor.

Varying Roles of School Counselors

Although the school counseling profession began in the secondary schools, today's counselors are prepared and employed at all educational levels. The latter part of the twentieth century and beginning of the twenty-first century saw increases in the number of counselors employed at the middle and elementary school levels. In most instances, school counselors use the same basic helping processes—counseling, consulting, coordinating, and appraising— across all school years. Because children in elementary and middle schools have different developmental needs from students in high school, it follows that specific services vary according to the needs of students in a particular school. Therefore, the role and functions of school counselors are influenced by both the specific level of practice and the needs of particular school populations served. School counselors design comprehensive programs first by assessing the needs of the students, parents, and teachers whom they serve. The variance of these needs from one school to another plays a significant role in helping counselors determine the program of services and activities most appropriate for their individual schools. This is an important point to remember as you read this chapter.

Descriptions and illustrations intended to differentiate elementary, middle, and high school counseling programs are useful as general guidelines, but to be valid they must be considered within the context of specific populations that are served by schools. For example, a high school counselor who serves students from affluent families with high expectations and promise of educational success will design a program of services that is quite different from one in a school with a high percentage of impoverished students who are at risk of school failure. For this reason, the following descriptions of elementary, middle, and high school counselors are general illustrations rather than prototypes of the roles of counselors in various educational settings. Ideally, the functions chosen by particular counselors address the unique needs and characteristics of students and communities served by the school.

The Elementary School Counselor

Historically, the responsibility for student development and guidance in elementary schools rested with classroom teachers. A few guidance specialists were present in elementary schools in the early 1920s, but most of these worked in metropolitan areas (Martinson & Smallenburg, 1958; Myrick, 2003). A national survey conducted in the early 1950s indicated that over 700 elementary counselors were employed and that more than 400 of them provided counseling and guidance services half of the time or more. This movement into elementary counseling began a shift from teachers having sole responsibility for student development to a collaborative effort shared by teachers and counselors.

The 1960s saw an emergence of counseling in elementary schools brought about by events such as the publication of the journal titled *Elementary School Guidance and Counseling,* inclusion of elementary officers in the American School Counselor Association, enactment of the Elementary and Secondary Education Act of 1965 (ESEA), and the extension of the NDEA Act in 1965, which provided funds for training institutes in elementary guidance and counseling (Gibson et al., 1993). By 1969, elementary counselors were employed in all fifty states, and by the early 1970s, the number of elementary counselors had grown to nearly 8,000 (Myrick & Moni, 1976).

The 1970s and 1980s saw increased attention to services for elementary children. To some extent, we can attribute this to the passage of the Education for All Handicapped Children Act of 1975 and the *A Nation at Risk* report of 1983. *A Nation at Risk,* produced by the National Commission on Excellence in Education, became the springboard for many educational initiatives across the country during the 1980s. Included in these initiatives were recommendations for counselors to be placed in all elementary schools (Humes & Hohenshil, 1987). Understandably, this increased demand for elementary counseling brought with it the urgency to define and describe what an ideal elementary counseling program should include.

Studies of the elementary counselor's role indicate that the expected major functions are consistent with the role of counselors at other educational levels (Gibson, 1990; Morse & Russell, 1988). Elementary programs include counseling, consulting, coordinating, and appraisal services for students, parents, and teachers in much the same way as their colleagues at upper levels. At the same time, some studies suggested that the ranking and importance of specific counselor activities may differ from the other levels of school counseling. For example, Morse and Russell (1988) reported that three of the five highest-ranking activities used by elementary counselors related to consulting relationships with teachers and educational specialists. Counselors in this study emphasized the need to help teachers help students. It is noteworthy that this finding supports the position, held by authors nearly forty years ago, advocating a consulting role for elementary counselors (Eckerson & Smith, 1966; Faust, 1968b). Today, consultation remains an essential function of elementary counselors.

Interestingly, elementary counselors have reported that their preference is to do more group work with students to help them learn appropriate social skills, enhance their self-concept, and develop problem-solving skills (Morse & Russell, 1988). This accent on group services exemplifies the importance that elementary counselors place on developmental services for children. In part, this emphasis gives elementary counseling its unique focus, a focus that includes appropriate processes and approaches to counseling with children, adequate attention to developmental activities and services, and strong parent and teacher involvement in the helping process.

Counseling Children.   Since the early years of elementary counseling, experts have debated whether children can be helped through counseling. In 1967, the American

Personnel and Guidance Association (now the American Counseling Association) stated that individual counseling offered children an opportunity to establish relationships to (a) see themselves as adequate persons, learn about themselves, and use this knowledge to set life goals; and (b) be heard by others (counselors) and express their thoughts and feelings about themselves, others, and the world in which they live.

In addition to group processes, elementary counselors use individual counseling with children. Typically, counselors establish these relationships through a series of brief counseling sessions lasting from twenty to forty minutes in length, depending on the age and maturity of the child. These individual sessions usually are scheduled once or twice a week as the counselor guides the child through successive stages of a helping relationship. These stages of counseling can be summarized as: (1) an introductory phase of building rapport, (2) an exploration of concerns the child expresses by words and actions, (3) a plan of ways to cope with and remedy these concerns, and (4) closure for this particular helping relationship, while encouraging the child to move on to other areas of development.

Successful individual counseling with young children depends on an accurate assessment of the child's readiness for this type of relationship. Counselors assess a child's language development, behavior, cognitive functioning, and ability to understand the nature and purpose of a helping relationship. Because most individual counseling requires some degree of verbal interaction, children who do not have adequate language development benefit little from these "talking" relationships. In some cases in which children are essentially nonverbal, success in individual relationships can be achieved if the language of the counselor is understood by the child. This is true, for example, with shy children. Frequently, young children are shy and hesitate to speak up at the beginning of individual counseling sessions. Inasmuch as they have adequate language development and understanding, these children benefit from individual counseling when assisted by a competent therapist, such as an elementary school counselor.

Elementary counselors use play, puppetry, and other techniques to establish rapport with children whose language development is not fully ready for verbal helping relationships. Play is an important aspect of counseling with all children. As Campbell (1993) concluded, "The fluent use of play media as a means of communication between child and counselor appears to be necessary for effective counseling to take place" (p. 3). Counselors also evaluate children's behavioral development when considering individual counseling as a mode of intervention. Severe disturbance, distraction, or other behavioral dysfunction might detract from the potential outcome of individual counseling with children. The greater a child's capacity for staying on task, centering on the subject at hand, and controlling impulsive behaviors, the more likely that "talking" counseling relationships will be successful. Behavioral techniques to help children develop these abilities are appropriate precursors to effective one-on-one counseling.

Children who cannot comprehend their role and responsibility in forming helpful relationships might benefit little from individual counseling that relies heavily on talking and listening modes. Without the necessary cognitive development, young children lack the readiness to understand the perceptions of others, select goals that benefit themselves as well as their social group, and alter their views to incorporate the opinions and values of others. These abilities and characteristics are essential if verbal counseling is to help children assess themselves, make appropriate plans for change, and take action toward desired goals.

Young children, whose perceptions are limited by egocentric views of the world and who conceptually do not grasp the notions of social interest and cooperation, might not fully appreciate the benefits of individual helping relationships. For this reason, elementary school counselors rely on active techniques, such as play, psychodrama, creative arts, and bibliotherapy to stimulate ideas, explore values, and encourage children to form helping relationships.

Group work with children is an important vehicle that counselors use to facilitate children's interaction with others and to explore their perceptions within a social context. Group work in elementary schools is most often structured as group guidance or group counseling (Gladding, 2003). In Chapter 7, you will see that group guidance is primarily instructional and informational, whereas group counseling encourages active change in cognitive, affective, and behavioral aspects of children's lives. Group guidance occurs in either large or small group settings. In elementary schools, teachers and counselors use group guidance in classrooms to assist children in developing values, social skills, career awareness, and other areas of learning. Ideally, teachers integrate these lessons into the daily curriculum, so that guidance becomes an integral part of language arts, social studies, and other subject areas.

Group counseling, on the other hand, assists children in focusing on concerns that are either crisis-oriented, problem-centered, or developmentally necessary. Groups are small, with perhaps five to eight students in a group. An example of an elementary group that is crisis-oriented is one that helps abused children deal with the trauma of their experiences, recognize their own value and worth as human beings, learn about their rights, and make plans to cope in the future. Problem-centered groups help children to center on immediate, yet less critical concerns, such as getting along with peers, and they encourage children to form plans of action to resolve these conflicts. Developmental group counseling helps children learn about social and personal aspects of their development. These growth-oriented groups address topics similar to those learned in classroom guidance, but the nature of small group counseling allows children the opportunity for more interaction and intimacy in a secure, protected relationship. In many respects, developmental counseling is a primary approach used by elementary school counselors.

Developmental Counseling and Guidance Curriculum.   Though many elementary school children today suffer from critical problems in their families and society and as a result need crisis-oriented and problem-solving assistance, a greater number can benefit from services that have a developmental focus. The assumption made by elementary counselors is that children become successful when allowed to achieve sequential goals that lead them toward self-fulfillment. Developmental counseling considers the stages of child development, including important life tasks that all children must learn and accomplish in moving toward the next level of functioning.

A comprehensive developmental program emphasizes the importance of a positive self-concept and recognizes the essential role that schools play in helping children believe in their value and worth as human beings. Developmental counseling assumes that the perceptions and beliefs formed by children about themselves and the world around them are learned through countless positive and negative experiences at home, in school, and through other relationships. Children's feelings, attitudes, and behaviors are closely linked to the conclusions they draw about themselves, cultural influences, and how they are accepted or rejected by people they know. For this reason, a developmental counseling program includes everyone and every aspect of an elementary school because *everything counts* (Purkey & Schmidt, 1996); there is nothing in a school, or in its policies and programs, that is neutral. Everything planned and implemented, from the color of the paint on the walls to daily teacher-student relationships in the classroom, has an effect on someone, somehow, in the school.

Counseling programs that adopt a developmental focus include everyone in the school community helping children attain educational, social, and career goals. The school counseling literature has presented several models of comprehensive counseling and guidance programs, including the Missouri Model (Gysbers & Henderson, 1997); the Maine and New Hampshire models (VanZandt & Hayslip, 1994); and models from other states such as Connecticut, Texas, and Wisconsin (Dahir et al., 1998). In the twenty-first century, the profession now has the National Model proposed by the American School Counselor Association (2003). Each of these models provides steps for school counselors to work with administrators, teachers, and parents to create appropriate services for students. First, these programs seek to establish a strong guidance curriculum that is planned by counselors and teachers and integrated into daily instruction. Counselors assist teachers in this effort by helping them plan the integration, locating appropriate resources, and coleading special guidance units with teachers. Second, these programs include individual and group counseling services for students who require more intense assistance than that offered by classroom guidance. These counseling services aim to satisfy children's needs and help them make adequate progress in their academic, personal, and social development. In this way, a secondary objective of a school's guidance curriculum is to help teachers and counselors identify students who need additional assistance in reaching their goals.

The goals of a guidance curriculum link with the therapeutic goals of counseling. For example, if a goal of guidance is to help all children learn about self-development and appreciate who they are, then individual and group counseling for students with low self-esteem has this as a primary goal as well. Although the activities and processes used in counseling relationships differ from those found in classroom guidance, the developmental goals are essentially the same. At the same time, individual and group counseling can provide children with an opportunity to develop skills, evaluate themselves, and achieve relationships that enable them to profit more readily from large group learning experiences. As a result of counseling, these children might benefit even more from guidance lessons incorporated into daily instruction.

Another aspect of developmental counseling programs is the strong involvement of parents. This is especially true in elementary education, where parents play a vital role in their children's development.

Parental Involvement.   Elementary counselors rely heavily on parental involvement in helping children plan and achieve developmental goals. (*Note:* The terms *parent* and *parental involvement* refer to all forms of parental and guardian relationships.) Without parental support for the program and the services that counselors and teachers offer students, progress is an uphill climb. When parents support the infusion of guidance into the curriculum and the inclusion of their children in individual and group counseling experiences, a working partnership forms between the home and school. Schools that invite parental participation, keep homes informed about programs affecting their children, and encourage parents to become involved in their children's education are more likely to achieve success with their students.

Elementary counselors value parental involvement early in their counseling relationships with children. To win parents' cooperation, counselors inform them about the counseling program through brochures, presentations at parent meetings, and individual contacts. Confidentiality is a condition of counseling with children as it is with other clients, but at the same time elementary counselors appreciate the important contribution parents make in helping children resolve problems, alter behaviors, and set future goals. For this reason, elementary counselors encourage young children to permit their parents to become involved in the helping process as soon as possible. In rare instances, such as suspected child abuse, this involvement may not be possible, but in most cases elementary counselors encourage collaborative relationships with parents to help children focus on concerns and make appropriate choices.

Together, parents, teachers, and counselors become partners in the challenging task of helping children develop in a positive and healthy direction. Parental involvement has always been an essential component of elementary counseling, as illustrated years ago by Meeks (1968) when she described the role of parents as (1) helping the school to understand the child, (2) acquiring greater understanding of their children, (3) learning and appreciating what the school is doing to help children achieve, and (4) using encouragement and positive approaches to bring about constructive behavioral change. These elements of a parent's role identify the "expert" contribution that parents make in helping schools meet the individual needs of children. This expert input, inherent in the parents' role, combines with the instructional expertise of the teacher and the developmental expertise of the counselor to form an effective collaborative relationship.

Elementary counselors encourage parental involvement in ways that include participating in parent-teacher conferences; enrolling in parent education programs on topics such as positive discipline, helping with homework, handling sibling rivalry, and communicating effectively with their children; and volunteering to help with school programs. Parental involvement has the twofold purpose of assisting children with their development and enhancing the school as a vital part of the community. Because both of these purposes are important, a comprehensive elementary school counseling program includes direct services for parents through counseling and consulting, as well as creative efforts to embrace parents in the life of the school. One example of including parents in the daily functions of an elementary school is a tutoring program that is staffed by parents and coordinated by a counselor. Tutoring by parent volunteers also provides an avenue to involve teachers in a collaborative effort to deliver services to students. Of course, teacher involvement is another vital component of an elementary school counseling program.

Teacher Involvement.   Elementary counselors are colleagues of classroom teachers and other educational specialists who serve the school. To establish effective programs of services in elementary schools, counselors develop strong working relationships with teachers and other school personnel. By doing so, they seek to become integral members of the school staff and the instructional program. They realize that the success of the counseling program is influenced by personal and professional relationships established with teachers and other colleagues in their elementary school. These relationships highlight the common goals set by teachers and counselors to ensure that all children make adequate progress in their educational, social, and personal development.

Teacher involvement begins with their comments and suggestions about the nature and design of the school counseling program. This contribution is in the form of teacher surveys, advisory committee reports, and annual program evaluations. In addition, elementary teachers become actively involved in the school counseling program through the guidance activities they integrate in daily instruction. They plan these guidance lessons in conjunction with schoolwide curricular goals and objectives established for each grade level.

This view of teachers integrating classroom guidance is not uniformly accepted by counselors and counselor educators. Some believe that classroom guidance is a primary function of school counselors and is delivered tangentially to the core curriculum (Gibson et al., 1993). In contrast, this text promotes the belief that developmental guidance is best delivered through instruction that is integrated by teachers into the curriculum. As noted in Chapter 1, this was the view put forth by the Association for Supervision and Curriculum in its 1955 yearbook, *Guidance in the Curriculum.*

A rationale for giving teachers primary responsibility for integrating guidance into the curriculum is that in typical schools, where student to counselor ratios exceed 300 to 1, it seems unlikely that a single counselor will be able to provide all the guidance instruction and other vital services expected in a comprehensive program. School counselors have an important role to play in encouraging their schools and teachers to integrate guidance, and that role is addressed throughout this book. As noted earlier, counselors assist teachers in planning an appropriate integration of guidance, help them search for materials and resources, and present special guidance lessons with the teacher when appropriate to do so.

Elementary teachers also have a vital role in referral processes for children who need counseling services. Because elementary teachers have contact with students all day long and teach children all the academic subjects, they are in an ideal position to observe student development and the obstacles that prevent progress in school. Accordingly, counselors rely on teachers' observational and diagnostic skills to refer children for services. Elementary teachers who establish close relationships with their students become the first-line helpers in the school and, as a result, are able to bring critical cases to a counselor's attention.

Another area of teacher involvement in elementary counseling is in fostering parent-school relationships. Because parents of young schoolchildren are concerned about their children's welfare, communication between teachers and parents is imperative. Teachers who value the services of school counseling programs keep counselors informed about the needs that parents have expressed, indications of family dysfunction and turmoil, and other factors affecting children in school. When possible, teachers include the elementary counselor in parent-teacher conferences for the purpose of contributing information, facilitating communication, and suggesting avenues to resolve concerns.

Finally, teachers who have expertise in areas of child development and instruction are vital resources for staff development. Some elementary teachers have special knowledge and skills that are valuable to their teaching colleagues. In such instances, counselors wisely ask these teachers to present in-service workshops, because they know their teaching colleagues will accept training more readily from someone who has experience in the classroom. This is particularly true when training teachers in instructional techniques and classroom management skills. For this reason, counselors seek out teachers who are excellent presenters and respected by their fellow teachers and invite them to become workshop facilitators and presenters.

The Middle School Counselor

Typically, the range of students in middle schools includes preadolescents between the ages of nine and thirteen, usually in grades five through eight. The unique needs of this age group require special attention, particularly those related to their physical and social development. Theorists who promote the middle school curriculum advocate educational programs that appreciate and understand the energy, confusion, and uncertainty inherent in these transitional years (Alexander & George, 1981; Stamm & Nissman, 1979; Thornburg, 1979). In addition, middle school counseling in this new millennium understands the cultural diversity of students and, as noted in Chapter 2, how comprehensive programs can best serve this diversity.

In 1986, Thornburg noted that the complex development of middle-graders requires counselors who are skilled in understanding and communicating with these young people. The complexity of preadolescent development includes the onset of physical changes coupled with an awareness of and curiosity about one's own sexuality as well as relationships with the opposite sex. In preadolescence, intellectual development is illustrated by more sophisticated and higher-level thought processes. Abstract thinking is more evident and decision-making processes begin to acquire organization and rationale. Wit, humor, and satire now complement silliness, playfulness, and other childlike behaviors. Socially, the middle-grader searches for peer acceptance and approval, struggles for independence and autonomy, yet is hesitant to accept full responsibility for the consequences of his or her own behavior.

Because these developmental tasks are so complex and the pace at which preadolescents move through them is so divergent, meeting the needs of these young people is a challenge for educators who work in middle schools. As Thornburg (1986) warned:

> It would be a mistake to underestimate the complexity of such a task and an equal mistake to perceive the task as impossible. Counselors and others who influence decisions regarding education must accept the challenge to develop effective school environments for today's middle-graders. (p. 170)

A first step for counselors who accept the challenge of a middle school program is to define their counseling role with the preadolescent student. To do this, they consider information, knowledge, and skills they must have to establish effective helping relationships with these ever-changing young people.

Counseling Preadolescents.   The unique needs and developmental stages of middle-grade students require counseling approaches that reflect this divergence. Any counselor who uses one approach or a single format with all students, regardless of the nature of the concern or developmental level of the student, may become frustrated. This is particularly true at the middle school level. Counseling middle-graders requires expanded approaches that include individual helping relationships, group experiences, peer support systems, and other processes. In addition, successful middle school counselors acquire a high level of knowledge and understanding about developmental tasks expected of preadolescents and adolescents. Finally, and perhaps most important, successful counselors understand the ways in which middle-graders perceive their world, and they comprehend the conclusions that students draw from these perceptions.

Individual counseling with middle-grade students has the potential to be successful when nonthreatening, respectful relationships are formed. Of course, counselors and students form such relationships outside the individual helping relationship as well as within it. Middle school counselors who win the acceptance and respect of students are visible in their schools. They greet students in the halls, eat lunch in the cafeteria, and are readily available to students who seek assistance. It is through these kinds of interactions that middle-graders assess the credibility, dependability, and reliability of their counselors. On the basis of these evaluative processes, students determine whether to seek assistance. Counselors who are viewed as believable and reliable are likely to be sought out when students need help.

Several counseling approaches are useful in working with middle-graders. For example, Adlerian counseling is effective in helping adolescents focus on the critical life tasks of career development, love relationships, and social accomplishments (Sweeney, 1998). Rational self-counseling offers a model for teaching children to learn emotionally healthy ways of thinking to achieve emotional self-control. Accepting responsibility for one's own actions is a key element of reality therapy, also called choice theory (Glasser, 1965, 1984, 2000), which continues to be a popular approach to use with middle-graders.

Group processes are of particular value in middle school counseling programs because of the desire of this age student to be a part of a group, to belong, and to be accepted. In middle schools, group counseling helps students to focus on either developmental or problem-oriented concerns and assist one another in achieving tasks and solving problems. Counselors also use groups in structured programs, such as small group and classroom guidance, to teach new skills or share information. Middle school counselors rely heavily on processes that facilitate the sharing of new information and teaching of developmental skills in response to the transitory needs of typical preadolescents.

Group and individual relationships are also useful in establishing effective peer helper programs, which have been successful in middle schools (Bowman & Campbell, 1989; Lewis & Lewis, 1996; Scarborough, 1997). Peer helpers assist counselors by helping students who are new to the school, being first-line helpers to students in need of counseling, referring them to the school counselor, tutoring students who are having academic difficulty, and befriending students who have been excluded, ridiculed, or otherwise rejected by their peers. A strong peer helper program enables counselors to network with students and observe their development and progress through the eyes and ears of others. These programs provide a vital referral source for the middle school counselor.

Transitional Services.   Middle school counselors provide many services that enable students to make smooth transitions from their childhood years to adolescence. Included in these services are: (1) counseling students who are fearful of new surroundings, such as when moving from elementary to middle school or from middle to high school; (2) helping students learn about the physical changes in their bodies through guidance activities and counseling services; (3) teaching communication skills to help students develop friendships and relate more effectively to their peers, parents, and teachers; and (4) presenting decision-making models and skills for students to learn how to make choices and understand the consequences of their decisions.

In many school systems, middle schools are separated physically from elementary and high schools. As a result, children change schools at least twice during their school years, usually after the fifth grade and then after the eighth grade. Added to these transitions are adjustments resulting from family divorce and relocation that also initiate moves to new schools. For some students, these periods of transition are very difficult. Middle school counselors help make these periods less traumatic by providing services before students leave their elementary schools and before entering high school. Transitional services include coordinating visits of elementary students to the middle school, orienting students who are entering the middle grades, compiling packets of information to help middle-graders and their parents become familiar with the school, scheduling field trips for graduating middle-graders to the senior high school in the spring semester, and planning career exploration activities with teachers to help students relate educational plans to their career interests. Teachers and counselors create limitless activities and services to help middle-graders cross this transitional bridge toward adolescence and adulthood.

Individual counseling, group counseling, and classroom guidance provide students with information about physical development, friendships, study skills, and a multitude of developmental tasks that students face. Middle school counselors rely on teachers' observations, peer helper networks, and parental involvement to make decisions about which students will benefit from the various services they offer. All students do not benefit equally from every service of a comprehensive counseling program. For example, some middle-graders are comfortable talking about sexual awareness and bodily changes in small or large groups, while others hesitate to discuss these matters even in individual private sessions. A successful middle school counselor takes time to listen to students, parents, and teachers and uses their suggestions in making appropriate decisions about services for individual students and the school as a whole. By doing this, counselors create optimal relationships with all parties and implement effective transitional services for students. As with elementary counseling, a key to establishing successful middle school services is the involvement of teachers.

Teacher Involvement.   A comprehensive middle school counseling program reflects the ingredients and characteristics of effective middle schools. This means that counselors align their program with the mission of the school, help teachers create and deliver appropriate instruction for all students, encourage group processes such as instructional teams and advisory groups, and become part of the school's leadership team. Counselors who adopt this philosophy are receptive to teacher involvement in establishing comprehensive programs of services.

Many aspects of teacher involvement in a middle school counseling program are the same as for elementary counseling. Planning a guidance curriculum, referring students for counseling, collaborating with counselors about student placement, and including counselors in parent-teacher conferences are as appropriate for middle school counseling as they are at other levels. Counseling programs that are built around teacher involvement usually offer some type of advisor-advisee service, which is particularly helpful with middle school development. Myrick (2003; Myrick & Myrick, 1990), a leading proponent of these services, has referred to advisor-advisee services as the "teacher as advisor program" (TAP).

Teacher advising programs in middle schools respond to the need for broad-based developmental guidance. This response is similar to the emphasis placed on developmental services at the elementary school level and at the same time relates to the middle school's role in providing transitional services for students. In middle schools, where students no longer remain with the same teacher all day long as they did in elementary schools, teacher-advisee programs provide all students with consistent contacts and relationships with significant adults. In some middle schools, students are assigned to a homeroom or home-base group that is supervised by their teacher/advisor. During these regular homeroom meetings, students participate in guidance sessions or individual conferences with their advisor (Michael, 1986; Myrick, 2003).

Successful teacher advising programs usually have strong counselor involvement. Without counselor leadership, these programs might fail to win the endorsement of vital school populations—students, teachers, and parents. George (1986) noted that teacher-advisee programs can be the most desired and simultaneously the most disliked activities by middle school students, parents, and teachers. Students dislike poorly designed programs that are presented by teachers who are unprepared and unskilled in guidance-type relationships. Similarly, teachers oppose advising responsibilities when they do not comprehend the purpose and value of these relationships, or when they fear they lack the skills to be successful with students. Opposition from parents occurs when they do not have a clear understanding of the purpose behind teacher-advisee programs and are unconvinced that the time given to these programs is well spent. To avoid these rejections, counselors assume a major role in presenting information about the program, training teachers in group facilitation skills, and locating resources and materials for teachers to use in guidance sessions with their home-base advisees. In this way, coordination becomes a major function of school counselors to ensure the success of teacher-advisee programs.

Beyond providing essential developmental guidance and supportive relationships for student advisees, the teacher-advisee program creates a vital channel in the school counselor's referral network. A teacher-advisee program is not intended to replace school counseling services, but is an ancillary component that allows teachers and counselors to work together on behalf of all children. As such, the teacher/advisor is frequently the person who refers students to the counselor for more thorough assessment, in-depth counseling, placement in a group program, or referral to another school or community service.

A teacher-advisee program also provides the initial step in developing positive parental involvement with the school. Teachers who have responsibility for advising students are the persons most likely to be in touch with parents on a regular basis. These advisors also encourage their advisees to keep parents informed of school events.

Parental Involvement.   Middle-graders are entering the phase of development when they begin to assert their autonomy and seek independence from parents and family. In this transition phase of adolescent development, middle school counselors and teachers understand the importance of parental involvement. They know that children require assistance in this passage from parents who understand when and how to let go and when and how to take control. This is as much a learning process for many parents as it is an instructional, nurturing one for their children. To help, middle school counselors and teachers plan appropriate programs in which parents can learn about preadolescent development. At the same time, counselors and teachers seek parental involvement in creating school programs, developing school policies, and designing appropriate curricula.

Because parents of middle-graders struggle themselves with entry into this transitional period, programs that assist parents with their feelings and skill development are appropriate. Counselors in middle schools assume a role in parent education by presenting programs about preadolescent and adolescent issues, teaching communication skills to enhance parent-teen relationships, and sharing information about expected developmental tasks and warning signals to look for in a teen's behavior and development. Sometimes, children move through their elementary years without significant trauma, but suddenly the sky appears to fall during the preadolescent stage. Parents who have enjoyed calmness in childhood become confused, angry, frustrated, and combative when faced with an unknown terror in their midst. Educational programs and support groups led by school counselors are helpful to these parents. One of the most important benefits of these programs is that parents who attend these groups learn they are not alone. It is comforting to know that other parents are facing similar confusion, frustrations, and struggles with their children.

As in elementary schools, middle school counselors are sensitive to the feelings and rights of parents regarding counseling services for their children. Although permission for such services is not usually required, middle school counselors make every attempt to involve parents when it is appropriate to do so. Such parental involvement requires the trust of students who are receiving counseling and a willingness on the students' part to talk with parents about concerns they raise with counselors.

Middle-graders are capable of exploring more complex ideas and deeper feelings than they were as elementary students, and simultaneously they accept more responsibility for their decisions. While these two emerging traits allow these preadolescents to participate and benefit more fully in counseling relationships, their progress is enhanced immeasurably by parental participation. As a result, middle school counselors search for ways to include parents in the helping process when students are comfortable accepting this kind of involvement.

The High School Counselor

High schools were the first to employ counselors, and many people who have attended high school since the 1960s can recall their counselor. For most, the role of the high school counselor consisted of course scheduling, college placement, and academic record-keeping. Although the presentday high school counselor's role is changing, the typical secondary counselor continues to assist students by providing information about course selections, career opportunities, test results, colleges, and scholarships.

Generally, the helping processes described earlier for elementary and middle school counselors are used at the high school level as well. Again, these processes include counseling, consulting, coordinating, and appraising. The difference in how school counselors deliver these essential services is seen in the specific activities used at different levels of practice. As with elementary and middle school counselors, high school counselors select services and choose specific activities to address the unique needs of adolescents preparing to enter young adulthood.

In an early study of parents, counselors, administrators, and the business community (Ibrahim, Helms, & Thompson, 1983), all of these groups valued services but in a variety of configurations among the functions of high school counselors. The study noted statistical differences between groups on a majority of the functions, indicating that perceptions regarding the importance of these services varied significantly. Yet, there was consensus about the value of all these activities for counselors. The study listed thirty-seven functions under the following major categories: (1) program development, (2) counseling, (3) pupil appraisal, (4) educational and occupational planning, (5) referral, (6) placement, (7) parent help, (8) staff consulting, (9) research, and (10) public relations. In another study, Gibson (1990) found that teachers viewed the most important functions of high school counselors as: (1) individual counseling, (2) providing career information, (3) administering and interpreting test results, (4) college advising, and (5) group counseling and guidance. In both studies, the identified functions are compatible with the essential services of a comprehensive school counseling program suggested in this text.

As noted in the studies above, the counseling function continues to be an important service provided by high school counselors. This confirms unpublished evaluations of school counseling programs, in which students, parents, and teachers tend to consistently perceive the following services as the most important for high school counselors: (1) help students with personal problems, (2) help students make decisions about school, (3) provide college information, and (4) help with class schedule (Schmidt, 1993, 1994, 1995, 2003b).

Counseling and Guiding Adolescents. The goals and processes for counseling adolescents are similar to those used with elementary children and middle-graders. Although the goals and processes are alike, many concerns targeted in counseling relationships with adolescents are different from those of elementary children and middle-graders. For example, Miller (1988) found that secondary counselors rated career assistance and educational planning services significantly more important than did either elementary or middle school counselors. Adolescents continue to need services that are developmental in nature, focusing on educational and career planning, academic achievement, social acceptance, self-awareness, sexual development, and other factors. Yet, many of their specific concerns are more problem-centered and crisis-oriented than simply developmental in nature. School dropout, teen suicide, pregnancy, drug use, sexual abuse, and myriad other troublesome concerns face adolescents in today's high schools.

In surveys of secondary school counselors, teachers, and students, counseling services remain a priority for high school programs (Gibson, 1990; Hutchinson, Barrick, & Groves, 1986; Hutchinson & Bottorff, 1986; Tennyson et al., 1989). There are, however, some differences in perceptions about the nature of these counseling services. According to one study, counselors viewed individual personal counseling, academic counseling, group counseling, and career planning as the four most important functions (Hutchinson et al., 1986). In practice, however, these same counselors ranked only individual personal counseling and academic counseling in the top four functions they performed. Career planning and group counseling ranked ninth and eleventh, respectively, of the sixteen items listed in the survey. In actual functions they performed, these counselors ranked scheduling and testing higher than either group or career counseling. They ranked scheduling second, and testing was fourth highest of the functions they performed.

In contrast to counselors' perceptions, students in a study of twenty-one states and 152 high schools ranked career counseling, college information, personal counseling, and scheduling as the most needed services (Hutchinson & Bottorff, 1986). However, students who participated in this study were already in college. Non-college-bound students were excluded by nature of the sample. This may explain the high ranking of college information and scheduling activities among this sample of students. What is most noteworthy about the results of this study is that less than half of the students said they actually received career counseling and slightly more than 20 percent received personal counseling. This finding parallels the conclusion that high school counselors often spend a large amount of time on administrative, clerical, and other noncounseling functions (Hutchinson et al., 1986). If surveys such as this one continue to be accurate indications of today's high school counseling services, it seems that high school counselors, by their own admission and the perceptions of others, provide services that are not direct services for students. As a result, they take time away from essential functions that should be part of their counseling programs. Some examples of these nondirect services include record-keeping, special education coordination, testing, and scheduling.

Group procedures are notably infrequent in high school counseling programs for both group counseling and group guidance activities (Tennyson et al., 1989). In part, this lack of group work at the high school level is likely due to the rigidity of daily schedules and the emphasis on earning high school credits toward graduation. Secondary teachers hesitate to release students from class to receive special services unless these services have direct impact on students' academic progress. Hence, high school counselors who work closely with their teachers to design acceptable schedules for counseling services are able to establish successful group programs. Because they are successful, teachers frequently permit these counselors to work with students, individually and in groups, even at the expense of instructional time.

Career Planning and Decision-Making.   Studies of the high school counselor's role indicate that career planning is a vital component of secondary programs. This function, which is covered in more detail in Chapter 10, includes guidance and counseling processes, both individually and in groups, to help students assess their strengths, weaknesses, and interests and choose educational and career plans that are compatible with these characteristics.

Some high school counselors use individual and group conferences at each grade level so students have the opportunity to check their progress, evaluate life goals, and set new objectives in their high school careers. These conferences serve as checkpoints for counselors and students to assess what information or other services students need in planning their future. They are preventive services planned to help students stay on track and in school. These services also encourage students to seek higher goals than they may have planned initially. Sometimes, when students enter high school at 14 or 15 years of age, the information they have about themselves, the world of work, future employment patterns, and educational opportunities is limited, outdated, or simply inaccurate. Annual conferences with counselors and teachers are one way to acquire current, accurate information.

Information Services.   Beyond the major functions of counseling, consulting, and appraising performed by high school counselors, another vital service is coordinating information for students, parents, and teachers. Elementary and middle school counselors also provide information in their programs, but at the high school level this service takes on critical importance as a response to the significant decisions facing senior high students. At the end of their high school careers, these students will have completed their formative years of development and will make major decisions about their life's plans. Vocational, educational, and marital choices occur at this juncture, and the access students have to accurate information about these and other decisions is a responsibility of high school counselors.

How counselors choose to disseminate information, the processes used to ensure that all students have equal opportunity to receive accurate information, is fundamental to a comprehensive high school counseling program. In large schools where there are several counselors, these responsibilities often are divided among the staff. In smaller schools, counselors rely on student and parent volunteers, paraprofessionals, and teachers to help disseminate information. In all cases, counselors call on teachers of required subject areas, such as English and social studies, to assist by presenting guidance activities that relate to career and educational opportunities or to allow counselors class time to disseminate information. As such, teachers at this level are integral to the school counseling program.

Parent/Teacher Involvement. High school years are signified by increased independence and responsibility for most students. As a result, we might expect less involvement of parents and teachers with counselors and students of this age level. In U.S. society, however, the increasing importance of postsecondary education at technical schools, community colleges, professional schools, and four-year colleges has extended the need for parental involvement. Today in U.S. society, parents provide financial support, moral guidance, and developmental assistance throughout adolescence and into early adulthood to enhance the career and educational opportunities of their children. We can expect this role to continue in the future.

At the same time, today's high school teachers provide much more than the content of academic subjects. Frequently, teachers give first-line assistance for critical concerns facing students. To prepare for this role, teachers receive in-service training in basic helping skills and crisis information. For example, they attend workshops on substance abuse and teen suicide to learn observation and communication skills and receive training in crisis intervention to assist school counselors, psychologists, and other student services professionals. Some high schools have adapted the teacher as advisor program (TAP) and have seen positive effects on important criteria, such as school attendance, that relate to student success in school (Myrick, 2003).

What these trends tell us is that future high school counselors may need to encourage more parent and teacher involvement than has been expected in the past. If so, future comprehensive high school programs will include more parent education and support groups, increased use of guidance activities by teachers in daily instruction, and a significant role for teachers as advisors to high school students. By increasing parental and teacher involvement in high school counseling programs, counselors may find additional avenues to help students with their educational and career planning. Consequently, high school counseling will become a more collaborative program of student, parent, teacher, and counselor functions to provide services for all students.

The preceding sections outline various roles and emphases for counselors who practice at elementary, middle, and high school levels. As the profession has moved to a more programmatic focus in establishing goals, prioritizing objectives, and delivering responsive services, a counselor's leadership role has become an important topic of discussion.

Program Leadership

A premise of comprehensive school counseling programs is that they consist of planned goals and objectives, organized strategies and interventions, and intentionally selected services and activities implemented by counselors, teachers, and others in a collaborative effort. Furthermore, evaluation procedures determine the outcomes of the overall program as well as effectiveness of individual services. All these aspects of comprehensive programs are coordinated and managed through the leadership of a school counselor. This philosophy creates a new direction for the school counseling profession from earlier service-oriented models, which placed school counselors primarily in the role of providing direct services to students, parents, and teachers. Today's professional counselors working in schools have all the knowledge and skill to provide direct services, but equally important are their leadership capabilities to orchestrate an array of strategies and interventions in meeting the educational, career, and personal/social needs of all students.

Contemporary texts on school counseling emphasize this leadership role (Baker & Gerler, 2004; Brown & Trusty, 2005; DeVoss & Andrews, 2006; Pérusse & Goodnough, 2004; Sciarra, 2004; Sink, 2005; Stone & Dahir, 2006; Studer, 2005). Erford, House, and Martin (2003) summed up the transformation of the twenty-first-century school counselor by a call for change:

> [It] is critical for professional school counselors to move beyond their current roles as "helper-responders" and become proactive leaders and advocates for the success of all students. To do this, they must move out of the traditional mode of operation and begin collaborating with other school professionals to influence systemwide changes and become an integral part of their schools and educational reform. (p. 5)

Such a transformation of the school counselor's role will require several parallel changes to occur. These include but are not limited to

- How schools choose to use the counselors they employ
- The preparation that counselors who work in schools receive during their graduate study and, specifically, the knowledge future counselors will have about leadership theory, practice, and research in order to fulfill their transformed roles
- The balance counselors are able to maintain in providing a leadership role while also delivering direct, responsive services within a comprehensive program

In the remaining sections of this chapter, we will explore each of these issues as they relate to a leadership role for school counselors.

Employment by Schools

Throughout the history of the school counseling profession, there has been an attempt to investigate the multitude of ways that counselors, employed by schools, spend their time (Brown & Trusty, 2005; Myrick, 2003). In many instances, roles and responsibilities given to counselors by their respective schools hardly resemble the professional knowledge and skills for which they prepared. This phenomenon frequently has led counselors to assume many noncounseling functions that have unduly consumed their time and taken them away from either leadership or direct service roles to help students (Baker & Gerler, 2004). For counselors of the twenty-first century to take a stronger leadership role in developing, implementing, and evaluating a program of services, school will have to "want" it to happen.

If the call for change and emphasis on programmatic leadership in school counseling is serious, it may require more than simply a process of changing the philosophy and preparation of future counselors. It may require a fundamental change in perspective that school administrators, classroom teachers, students, parents, and others involved in school practice and reform have of professional counseling in schools. If the profession spends time and energy transforming itself without any change occurring in school perceptions and practices, then we might wonder if significant change is possible at all. Combined effort by the American School Counselor Association, state organizations, and state departments of education, as well as counselor and teacher education programs, among other groups is necessary to bring about such a grand perceptual change. ASCA's promotion of its National Model (2003) with other educational organizations is a positive first step, and should be followed by initiatives to influence the preparation of classroom teachers and school administrators through accrediting bodies that govern those educational programs.

Of course, the ultimate decision of what to do in a school and how to assert a leadership posture rests with the employed counselor. To optimize the transformation movement and particularly the leadership role advocated by recent literature and research, counselors will want to embrace what Stone and Dahir (2006) called the "leadership mindset." They noted, "the counselor who possesses a mindset for leadership is the school counselor who views his or her role as another person or additional set of eyes and ears looking for and identifying environmental and institutional barriers that stratify opportunities for student success" (p. 94). Development of such a mindset begins in professional preparation programs.

School Counselor Preparation

Perhaps professional preparation is the most challenging area to examine when considering the transformation of a profession. What should we change, what should we add, what should we delete in a preparation program to effect the desired change? Later in this chapter, we will examine current preparation standards and professional credentials required of counselors who work in schools. For now, we ask the question: What might be changed about these standards of preparation or the credentials that exist for school counselors?

Counselor education programs had not placed much emphasis on leadership roles and skills in their preparation programs until the transformation movement began (Baker & Gerler, 2004). Over the past few decades, graduate programs in counseling have expanded, requiring more courses and credits to complete. What impact will additional coursework or experiences to learn about leadership roles have on preparation of school counselors? More important, should some coursework formerly believed to be important to the preparation of counselors now be deleted or diminished?

Baker and Gerler (2004) proposed that competencies in leadership result from a combination of factors including a person's individual makeup as well as his or her learned behaviors. They also noted that leadership is a complex quality and not necessarily demonstrated by specific behaviors on all occasions. From the counseling literature, they generated a list of behaviors that school counselors might use in their leadership/collaborative roles. By way of summary, the behaviors they listed included program leadership, skills to conduct productive meetings, mediation skills, competencies related to cultural awareness and sensitivity, collaboration with a wide audience of participants and stakeholders, consultation skills, ability to gather and use necessary data, and being proactive in defining a role rather than waiting to be told what to do. This summary does not do justice to their list, so you are encouraged to go directly to the source (Baker & Gerler, 2004).

To incorporate all the competencies and skills that Baker and Gerler (2004) among others encourage for counselor preparation, it may not be necessary to add or eliminate a significant amount of content. Perhaps it only requires a rethinking of how current content is taught. For example, when counselors learn about consultation theory and practice, how might that knowledge be applied in terms of a leadership role? By taking this view, the same question might be applied to all the knowledge and skills in a school counseling preparation program. What relevancy does this knowledge base and/or skill have for a counselor's leadership role in a school? This is a question that counselor educators need to address in developing curricula.

In learning about leading a school counseling program, an important aspect will be the self-awareness a counselor has about her or his leadership capabilities, and most important, their ability to be in charge of themselves. One of the challenges in becoming a programmatic leader while also delivering responsive services within a program is to maintain a balance between the two roles.

Maintaining a Balance

Few school counseling texts devote much space to the challenge of balancing time and roles between being a leader of a school counseling program and being a clinician within a program of responsive services. Yet, all the contemporary texts present both roles as important to the overall function of professional school counseling. This text does likewise.

Some authorities have speculated about the distribution of time by counselors across various functions and roles (Brown & Trusty, 2005), but these are arbitrary recommendations that do not necessarily take into account the real environment in which many school counselors work. As indicated in Chapter 2, differences between rural and urban schools may require different roles and functions for school counselors. By the same token, individual schools within the same school systems often vary widely in terms of student populations and their respective needs. In such situations, school counselors may find themselves faced with quite varied challenges and subsequently the need to design and deliver different programs of services within the same school system.

Baker and Gerler (2004) have devoted some thought to this notion of balance across a comprehensive program of services. They included an entire chapter of their text on this subject. To summarize their position, they proposed that a balanced comprehensive program "is one in which importance is attributed equally to prevention *and* intervention goals" (p. 38). They claimed that many school counseling programs do not reflect this type of balance and, consequently, too much emphasis is on intervention strategies. This conclusion and their call for balance between prevention and intervention are admirable—and ideal. The question unanswered, however, is will the resources be available in *all* schools and communities to allow counselors to achieve such a balance in their programs? Essentially, if counselors assume a leadership role in designing and maintaining a balance of services, who will deliver the necessary responsive services when the counselor is devoting time to leadership and program management?

Throughout the remainder of this text, we will explore the importance of comprehensive school counseling programs, the responsive services that have historically comprised the school counseling profession, and the need to balance the time available to devote to program leadership while delivering direct services for students, parents, and teachers. The models for school counseling programs promoted by the profession (ASCA, 2003; Brown & Trusty, 2005; Gysbers & Henderson, 2000) provide excellent frameworks to establish programs, but they do not have *all* the answers for *all* counselors in *all* schools, in *all* situations. Decisions made by counselors in schools day in and day out call on their leadership skills as well as their clinical judgment to be sure that every student has the opportunity to be successful in school.

As noted above, future trends in elementary, middle, and high school counseling will be reflected in revised preparation standards for the profession and changes in existing counselor education programs. The preparation of school counselors has changed dramatically in the profession's brief history, and new developments occur every year. Continuous revision of counselor preparation standards and programs will depend on the expected growth of the profession in schools and other settings.

Preparation of School Counselors

In the 1980s, professional associations noted a decline in interest and enrollment in school counselor education programs (Cecil & Comas, 1987). Toward the end of that decade, however, a survey of all the state departments of education indicated that more than 62 percent of the states anticipated increases in school counseling positions (Paisley & Hubbard, 1989). In this same study, less than 10 percent of the states indicated an anticipated decrease in the number of school counselors. This renewed interest in school counseling in thirty-two states was not, however, complemented by increased attention to certification and training standards in all states. With no consistent guidelines for preparing counselors, we find a wide variance in requirements across the fifty states.

At the national level in recent years, the counseling profession has promoted standards through the National Board for Certified Counselors (NBCC) and the Council for the Accreditation of Counseling and Related Educational Programs (CACREP). However, Paisley and Hubbard (1989) found that over 90 percent of the states indicated that the standards for national certification (NBCC) made little or no difference in employability of school counselors, and more than 70 percent of the states indicated the same for CACREP standards. Eleven states, nevertheless, indicated some value and use of CACREP standards in employing school counselors or for setting certification guidelines.

As the school counseling profession continues to address issues related to its growth and development, the preparation standards for professional counselors will continue to need review. Although all states require certification or licensure of school counselors, the requirements for these certifications vary greatly (Paisley & Hubbard, 1989). Regardless of the requirements in particular states, the development of national certification and counselor education standards by the American Counseling Association, particularly two of its divisions, the American School Counselor Association and the Association for Counselor Education and Supervision, has encouraged training that focuses on specific areas of study. Reputable counselor education programs typically design programs of study to include coursework in counseling theory and skill training, human development theory, group procedures, assessment skills, career development theory and information, research, social and cultural foundations, and professional issues. Some of these areas of study parallel the responsive services of a comprehensive school counseling program. Here, we briefly summarize these areas to illustrate their importance in counselor education.

The Helping Relationship

One foundation of the counseling profession, regardless of the setting in which counseling is practiced, is a competent understanding of theoretical models and clinical skills used to establish, maintain, and evaluate helping relationships. These models and skills have particular importance for individual and group counseling, but they also have application in other professional services, such as consulting and appraising. The role of school counselors is influenced by the theoretical models and clinical techniques adapted and applied by counselors in their individual schools. Therefore, the preparation counselors receive in helping relationship processes sets the tone for how well they perform basic skills and how comprehensively they design programs when employed in schools.

Counseling Theories and Approaches.   The theoretical foundations learned by school counselors in their graduate programs are similar to the training received by other professional counselors. Helping relationships with students, parents, and teachers in school settings may use different theoretical perspectives that depend on the orientation of the counselor and various needs of clients. These varying perspectives might include psychodynamic, behavioral, reality-based, cognitive, existential, or other views. At the same time, a variety of counseling approaches and techniques might be observed, even in the same counseling program. Techniques and strategies, such as bibliotherapy, puppetry, lifestyle questionnaires, psychodrama, positive reinforcement, and modeling, have their roots in particular theories of counseling.

Communication Skills.   Optimal use of helping processes requires a command of basic communication skills. The training of school counselors consists of coursework and practice in listening, facilitating, and decision-making skills. Listening skills include appropriate attending behaviors, reflective listening techniques, and paraphrasing skills to let speakers know they are being heard. These skills are particularly important early in the helping relationship to establish regard and respect between the counselor and counselee. Facilitating skills include questioning, structuring, linking, clarifying, probing, and confronting, among others. By facilitating a helping relationship, counselors in schools assist students toward appropriate decisions. This final phase of the relationship requires competent use of goal setting, adequate exploration of alternatives, and the application of other decision-making skills. In most instances, this action-oriented process will be successful if counselors are objective, provide encouragement, and allow students the responsibility for the decisions they make.

The Process of Helping.   Counseling, as used here, is not advice giving. Rather, it is the process of helping students examine concerns, gather necessary information, explore possibilities, and formulate plans of action. Sometimes, especially when counseling with young children, it is difficult to hold back one's own opinions and allow students to explore, experiment, and occasionally fail. In practice, however, this is usually the best way to establish genuine, respectful helping relationships. Accepting another viewpoint, even when it opposes yours, is a first step toward setting common goals together. With some clients, such as young children, counselors must set parameters and structures that are age and developmentally appropriate. Still, counselors can establish structure in a relationship without overtly rejecting the views of another or injecting their own views into the helping process.

A key element of counseling is that it is a process. Counseling is a series of events aimed at accomplishing a specific goal or goals. Sometimes, this element of counseling is forgotten by school counselors who see students on a regular basis but fail to monitor the progress of these relationships. Occasionally, students visit with the counselor, discuss concerns, and explore possibilities but hesitate to make changes that will alleviate their problems or optimize their opportunities for development. Counseling is more than having conversations with students who need assistance. Instead, it is movement from the identification of a concern to the implementation of a strategy to address important life goals. Chapter 6 outlines four phases of a helping process, one model that counselors can adapt when helping students face a wide range of developmental, preventive, and remedial concerns.

Human Development

A second area of study for school counselors is human development. This area frequently includes courses in developmental and abnormal psychology, sociology, family relations, and learning theory. In addition, elective areas of study include substance abuse, sexual issues, violence, stress management, and other aspects of human behavior and development.

Knowledge of Behavioral Science. One area of development that is an essential knowledge base for school counselors is human behavior. Understanding different theories of behavioral development complements the various counseling approaches used in forming effective helping relationships. In addition, school counselors frequently consult with parents and teachers to help them understand and respond to children's behaviors. A strong knowledge base in the behavioral sciences gives counselors the foundation to perform competently in these consulting relationships.

A Lifespan Approach. Counselors who work in schools need an appreciation of the lifespan of human development theory. Because school counselors work with audiences from all levels, children to adults, they require an understanding of where each person is in his or her development. For example, an elementary school counselor with a background in adult development has an advantage when trying to understand parents who are struggling with their children or when assisting teachers who are bemoaning their career choices. Understanding human development across the lifespan sensitizes helping professionals to the unique needs of a broad population.

Group Processes

Because schools employ only a few counselors to meet the needs of many students, group skills are essential to provide interventional, informational, and instructional services. Most of the communication skills learned in developing individual helping relationships are also used in group processes. Listening, facilitating, and decision-making skills are as important with groups as they are in one-on-one relationships. As you read earlier, school counselors use these skills in three types of groups: group counseling, group guidance, and group consultation.

Group Counseling.   School counselors use group counseling to help selected students focus on common concerns and developmental issues in regularly scheduled sessions. As with individual counseling, group counseling forms a confidential relationship in which students explore concerns and establish plans of action. Group counseling offers the added dimension of encouraging students to help one another. In this way, group counseling replicates a social setting in which students feel secure in exploring their concerns, listening to the suggestions of their peers, and trying out suggestions before attempting them outside the group sessions.

Group Guidance.   Group skills learned in counselor education programs are useful in providing instructional and informational services. Group facilitation and interaction skills help school counselors deliver services to a large number of students and parents. As noted earlier, teachers and counselors collaborate to present guidance activities to classes. Sometimes, teachers become concerned about the sensitive nature of topics or are otherwise uncomfortable leading particular guidance lessons. In these situations, counselors often assist by co-leading class sessions. For counselors who have no large group experiences, training in instructional skills and group management is essential. Counselors need these skills for classroom presentations and use them in other educational activities such as parent education programs, financial aid workshops, and other large group activities.

Group Consultation.   Another group process that counselors use in schools is group consultation. Sometimes students can best be assisted if the counselor consults with all the adults who are relating with these students. Group consultations with teachers and other professionals requires special understanding of consulting relationships, roles, and communication skills. These skills also complement large group interaction skills and enable counselors to become effective presenters of in-service programs for teachers and other professionals.

Student Appraisal

Assessing students and environments are two more functions of school counselors that require specific knowledge in test theory, development, and application. In particular, counselors learn about standardized achievement and aptitude tests, career inventories, and personality assessment instruments. Not all school counselors place heavy emphasis on test administration in their programs, but most are responsible for interpreting and using test results and other measurement data with students, parents, and teachers. A strong background in tests and measurement ensures the appropriate use and interpretation of data-gathering instruments and processes.

Formal Assessment.   Using tests and other measurement instruments to gather data about students and their environments are types of formal assessment processes. School counselors have knowledge of the availability of these instruments, their appropriate use and interpretation of results, their selection for use in a comprehensive counseling program, and the ethical and professional standards of testing practices.

Formal use of assessment instruments and procedures includes a schoolwide testing program of achievement and ability testing at selected grade levels. By emphasizing a point made earlier, we reiterate that school counselors sometimes have responsibility for coordinating the testing program, including setting the schedule, training test administrators and monitors, securing the tests, and distributing and collecting materials. School counselors also administer individual tests and inventories to help students, parents, and teachers make appropriate educational decisions.

Informal Assessment. School counselors are also knowledgeable of informal assessment procedures, which include observation techniques, lifestyle questionnaires, and the use of art, play, or other activities to collect data and form diagnoses about situations. Caution in using any type of assessment is warranted, and this is particularly true with untested, informal processes. The conclusions that counselors draw from these types of procedures are always in conjunction with other data gathered in assessment processes.

Career Development Theory and Information

A primary purpose of school counseling is to assist students with educational and career planning. To choose appropriate strategies in helping students address career issues, school counselors receive preparation in career development theories and information services.

Understanding the different theoretical perspectives of career development gives counselors a foundation on which to build their own theory and choose compatible strategies and approaches for their programs. For example, having a broad view of the importance of career planning enables counselors to encourage teachers to incorporate career guidance into daily instruction across subject areas of the curriculum. For example, English teachers invite their students to explore careers that rely on language and communication skills. Likewise, science teachers incorporate the limitless ways that scientific discovery affects countless career choices.

Knowledge and implementation of information services are important to counselors, especially secondary counselors, in providing students with the most recent and up-to-date information about career trends and educational requirements. A current knowledge of career resources, college requirements, technical training programs, vocational interest inventories, and other materials enables counselors to guide students and parents accurately.

Educational Research

Counseling is an imprecise science. For this reason, it is essential that practicing counselors in all professional settings take time to account for the services they provide. Effective school counselors demonstrate that the services they provide to students, parents, and teachers make a difference in students' development and in the life of the school. To accept this responsibility and actively design processes for evaluating services, counselors must have a basic understanding of research techniques. This includes a knowledge of statistics and research applications. There are many ways in which school counselors evaluate their services, and Chapter 11 reviews a number of accountability procedures.

Social and Cultural Foundations

As noted in Chapter 2, schools in the United States today serve diverse populations, and every indication is that this trend will continue for years to come. To help students adjust and teachers cope, school counselors acquire an appreciation and understanding of a multitude of sociological phenomena that affect families, communities, and schools. When counselor education programs provide information about the structural, sociological, and cultural changes in society, and explore expected outcomes and trends related to these developments, they place their graduates in a stronger position to help schools deliver needed services to students, parents, and teachers.

Changing Society.   In recent decades, U.S. society has seen tremendous social changes in the family unit, educational expectations, sexual mores, and career patterns. Added to these changes are countless advances in technology, discoveries in medical science, shifts toward a world economy, and rapid movement from industrial to information services in the world market. Counselors who are familiar with these changes and their impact on human development are better equipped to help students and teachers deal with the present consequences of these events and to predict future trends.

Multicultural Populations.   Diverse cultures continue to influence educational development in our schools. Counselors who are sensitive to ethnic and racial influences and willingly celebrate the cultural diversity of their communities are able to form beneficial relationships with a broad spectrum of people. To elevate counselors' understanding and appreciation of cultural differences, and especially the unique needs of people from different cultures, counselor education programs address a range of multicultural issues. In practice, school counselors want to take a leadership role in helping their school systems value cultural diversity (Pedersen & Carey, 2003). School counselors who serve divergent student populations and are able to broaden their cultural vision beyond their own heritage claim an advantage in establishing a broad-based comprehensive counseling program for their schools.

Ethical and Legal Issues

Counseling as a profession is guided by ethical standards and, in some cases, restricted by legal precedents. School counselors must know the ethical principles put forth by their profession and balance that understanding with a clear knowledge of local policies, state statutes, and federal laws relating to the practice of counseling in schools. Counselor education programs include study of professional ethics and legal issues as they pertain to the general practice of counseling and special incidents such as child abuse, student rights, suicide, and other matters. Chapter 12 presents several aspects of legal and ethical issues related to counseling in schools.

The School Setting

In addition to the aforementioned areas of study, school counselors learn about the nature of educational institutions and, specifically, the practice of counseling in school. This is accomplished in part through courses in education, such as educational foundations, curriculum development, and philosophy of education. Students in school counseling are also expected to have practicum and internship experiences in the school setting. A practicum allows students to use newly learned helping skills with clients in a school. An internship is an expanded experience that offers graduate students an opportunity to become practicing school counselors under the combined supervision of seasoned counselors and university instructors. Internships allow students to perform all the functions expected of a professional school counselor.

The preceding areas of study are important components of a school counselor's knowledge base and skill development. Counselor education programs, including those that prepare professional counselors for schools, follow curriculum and field experiences that incorporate these areas into a complete program of study. As noted in previous sections of this chapter, the ultimate goal of these preparation programs is to give counselors a leadership knowledge base and leadership skills to complement their counseling knowledge in designing, implementing, and evaluating comprehensive programs. Preparation of professional counselors also relates to professional standards and credentials to practice, which we will now consider.

Credentials of School Counselors

Credentialing is an important process for the counseling profession. Although school counselor certification and licensure have existed in all states for many years, certification and licensure of counselors in other settings, such as mental-health centers, prisons, and family services facilities, are more recent developments.

In addition to certification and licensure, the counseling profession has worked to create accreditation processes for institutions that prepare counselors. National, regional, and state accrediting bodies review colleges and universities to determine if their programs of study meet established criteria. When institutions satisfy these criteria, they are granted "program approval" status, and their graduates benefit from having studied in an accredited program.

The National Council for Accreditation of Teacher Education (NCATE) is the most common accrediting body for teacher education and related preparation programs in departments, schools, and colleges of education at colleges and universities. As a result, NCATE is frequently the accrediting council for school counselor preparation programs, which often locate in schools or departments of education at universities and colleges. The Council for Accreditation of Counseling and Related Programs (CACREP) is another national accrediting body and one that focuses solely on preparation standards in counselor education programs. CACREP reviews and approves graduate programs of study for counselors who are being preparing to work in a variety of settings, including schools. As this text was being revised, CACREP was in final discussions with the Council on Rehabilitation Education (CARE), the accrediting body for rehabilitation counseling. The merging of these two bodies will give more visibility and strength to accrediting processes for professional counselor preparation programs.

State Certification

To practice as a school counselor, the first credential one must receive is state certification (some states call this licensure). According to Randolph and Masker (1997), all states require certification and most require a minimum of a master's degree for initial certification. In addition, some states include teaching experience as a prerequisite for school counselor certification. Of these states, a few allow alternate experiences, such as a counseling internship, to be substituted for teaching experience. It is noteworthy that several states continue to require teaching experience as a prerequisite to counselor employment, despite the absence of research showing that such experience relates to effective school counseling (Baker, 1994).

Several states allow school counselors to become certified or licensed before they complete all the necessary requirements. These states offer provisional school counselor certification, which usually means a school system can hire a person while he or she finishes the final requirements for full certification.

State certification/licensure for school counselors is a credential that usually must be renewed periodically. To renew certification, counselors obtain continuing education units (CEUs) or additional coursework in counseling or related fields of study. School counselor certification is typically handled by certification offices in state departments of education, and many states have reciprocal agreements so that candidates certified in one state are eligible for certification in another.

National Certification

In the 1980s the American Counseling Association (ACA) became active in establishing a national certification process for professional counselors. A National Board for Certified Counselors (NBCC) was established and an application review and examination process was created. The NBCC tests eight core areas of professional training on its national certification exam: the helping relationship; human growth and development; group dynamics, processing, and counseling; lifestyle and career development; social and cultural foundations; appraisal of persons; research and evaluation; and professional orientation. Note the similarity of these knowledge areas with the recommended training components for school counselors, listed earlier in this chapter.

As noted in Chapter 1, the NBCC has also established speciality exams and certifications in certain areas, including school counseling. All these certifications are renewable in five-year cycles on completion of required continuing education experiences.

The National Board for Professional Teaching Standards (NBPTS) has also established standards for national school counselor certification and this has presented a conflict for the NBCC and many school counselors who hold the National Certified School Counselor (NCSC) certificate. The American School Counselor Association (ASCA) and the National Board for Certified Counselors (NBCC) have attempted discussions with the NBPTS because the NBCC already had its specialty certification for school counselors, and several hundred counselors hold the credential. Because some states started to grant salary bonuses to teachers who held a NBPTS certification, the issue became an important economic one for school counselors (Potts, 1999). Some counselors across the country continue to question a teacher certification board's right to set standards for a counseling specialty. At this time, the debate and discussion about this issue continues.

Certification and credentialing processes at state, regional, and national levels aim at improving the identification and performance of practicing counselors. They elevate the counseling profession in the eyes of the public and in the esteem of those who join the profession. Credentials are one way for a profession to monitor itself, ensure that services being rendered are delivered by highly trained persons, and offer a clear identity for its practitioners. In this way, state, regional, and national certification processes for school counselors help define and describe what it is that counselors do in a school setting and the training required to perform these functions.

In this chapter, we examined the role of school counselors in elementary through high school settings, the leadership role that counselors in schools assume in designing and delivering comprehensive programs, and the preparation and appropriate credentials of practicing school counselors. Adequate preparation and minimum credentials attempt to ensure the delivery of effective counseling services in schools. School counselors work with a wide audience of clients and cooperate with other professionals to deliver appropriate services. The description of the school counselor's role advocated here integrates the responsive services of a comprehensive counseling program across all levels of school practice. In the next chapter, we examine the concept of comprhensive school counseling programs and follow that discussion with an overview of responsive and related services in Chapter 5.

Additional Readings

Campbell, C. A., & Dahir, C. A. (1997). *Sharing the Vision: The National Standards for School Counseling Programs* (Alexandria, VA: American School Counselor Association).
This book summarizes the national standards for school counseling programs and student competencies that were developed by the American School Counselor Association.

Hitchner, K. W., & Tifft-Hitchner, A. (1996). *Counseling Today's Secondary Students: Practical Strategies, Techniques & Materials for the School Counselor* (San Francisco: Jossey-Bass).

An excellent resource for secondary counselors, the book gives useful ideas and strategies for serving students.

Schmidt, J. J. (2004). *A Survival Guide for the Elementary/Middle School Counselor* (San Francisco: Jossey-Bass).
A practical guide for counselors in elementary and middle schools, using the structure of a comprehensive program.

Websites

Guidance online
www.home.cfl.rr.com/nwunder/guidance.html
National Board for Certified Counselors
www.nbcc.org

Peterson's Home Page—Colleges and Career Information
www.petersons.com
School Counseling Resources
www.indep.k12.mo.us/Chrisman/wmccane.html

Exercises

1. In a brief research project, investigate the historical development of another helping profession (e.g., nursing, medicine, psychology, social work) and compare your findings with the counseling profession. How did these other professions begin? What route did their credentialing processes take to reach the point where they are today?

2. In a small group, discuss the issue of integrating guidance in the school curriculum. Highlight some of the points made in this text and contrast them with other views. Have your group take a position and outline three to five reasons why you are taking this stand. Share your conclusions with the class.

3. A school principal interviews you for a high school counseling position. She was an elementary principal before coming to the high school and says that she would like the high school program to reflect the philosophy of elementary counseling. How would you respond?

4. You are a new counselor at a middle school that serves a community with diverse cultures. List some steps you would take to prepare yourself to be an effective counselor with students who come from diverse backgrounds.

4

Comprehensive School Counseling Programs

A school counseling program is a planned component of the larger school purpose and mission. As noted in Chapter 3, it is a program consisting of particular services for which the counselor has received specialized preparation. The role of the school counselor is to design a comprehensive program of services with specific goals and objectives that complement the broader mission of the school.

By designing a purposeful program, school counselors distinguish themselves from counselors in other professional settings, who either offer a limited range of services or narrowly focused services due to the specific populations they serve. For example, marriage counselors serve couples who are experiencing difficulty in their marital relationships or who are searching for meaningful ways to nourish their relationships with each other. The primary mission of a marriage counselor is to enable couples to address and enhance communication processes in their marital relationships. Marriage counselors provide services to these couples by using individual and group sessions and incorporating therapeutic, informational, and instructional strategies in their helping relationships. If no progress is made in these relationships and dysfunctional behaviors continue, marriage counselors refer their clients to other professionals who can offer additional services.

By contrast, school counselors serve three populations: students, parents, and teachers. The responsive services that school counselors provide for these three groups include individual and group counseling, consulting, testing and assessment, group instruction, and referrals. Most important, counselors deliver these services within the framework of an organized program. The design of this counseling program is guided by the overall mission of the school, the desires and needs of the local community, the profession's research and literature, and the expanded goals of the state.

Thus far, you have learned many terms that describe what counselors do in comprehensive school counselor programs. You have also learned that understanding the professional terms that school counselors use will help you identify and clarify the purpose of a school counseling program. Identifying this purpose to an audience of students, parents, teachers, administrators, and the public at large is essential to your success as a school counselor.

The Purpose of School Counseling Programs

Every school has an educational mission, and within that mission lays a purpose for special programs such as school counseling. To some extent, the struggle of the school counseling profession to develop a clear identity has contributed to the confusion about the purpose of employing counselors in school settings. Sometimes, a counselor's inability to identify a clear purpose places that counselor in clerical, administrative, and instructional roles, diminishing the counselor's value in the school. In contrast, by developing a clear understanding of their purpose, other school counselors establish a philosophical basis on which to build a credible program. To begin, successful school counselors first ask themselves, "Why am I here?"

In earlier works, I hypothesized that the essential reason counselors are employed by schools is to help people become "more able" (Schmidt, 1986, 1991). School counselors assist students in becoming "able" learners, they support parents in their supervising and nurturing roles, and they help teachers to provide effective instruction and create healthy classroom climates for all students. This hypothesis for the role and purpose of school counselors is summarized here as a mission to provide a program of services that ensures an opportunity for all students to learn and develop to their fullest potential. Although this premise seems simple enough, the task of reaching this goal may appear overwhelming in light of today's challenges brought to school by children, adolescents, and their families. For this reason, it is imperative that school counselors view their role not as a series of unrelated crisis-oriented services, but rather as an orchestrated program of responsive services and activities that complement the instructional program of the school.

In the past, school counselors have been viewed as "support personnel." According to this view, people believed that school counselors provided ancillary services to the instruction offered by teachers and the administration required of principals. This emphasis on supporting teachers and administrators, while illustrating caring and helpful aspects of a counselor's role, tended to lessen the overall value of school counseling services. At the same time, these apparent "supportive services" were more vulnerable to economic, political, and institutional changes occurring in society. Because school counselors have historically accepted a role that is "supportive," they have occasionally let others define their role, assign them functions, dictate their mission, and design their programs.

A key element in describing a comprehensive program is the notion that the leadership and responsive services of a counselor are *essential* to the school. In this book, I present the services of a school counseling program as necessary at all school levels, elementary through high school. To steal a popular term from conservative critics, school counseling programs of services are *basic* to the fundamental goals of education.

The purpose of school counseling programs is to provide an array of services that facilitate the development of all students. As Meeks wrote in 1968, "If the purpose of counseling is to facilitate development, then the counseling process must be a part of the educational process from kindergarten through the secondary school" (p. 101). Children and adolescents in contemporary U.S. society face challenges that will continue to evolve in complexity and importance for generations to come. For this reason, schools and other institutions need to address the total development of all children. We cannot separate educational goals from personal, social, physical, and other developmental processes. School counseling services are and will remain essential to the total education of our youth.

School counselors who assume an essential role in the overall school mission are able to convince administrators and teachers about how counseling, consulting, and other services in a comprehensive school counseling program contribute to the effectiveness of the school. To do this, they design programs and services that address the development of students in three essential areas: educational development, career development, and personal and social development.

The American School Counselor Association (1997; Campbell & Dahir, 1997) has developed national standards "to better define the role of school counseling programs in American educational systems" (ASCA, 1997, p. 1). These standards are based on "three widely accepted and interrelated areas: Academic Developmental; Career Development; and Personal/Social Development" (ASCA, 1997, p. 1), and together they state what the profession "believes to be the essential elements of quality and effective school counseling programs" (ASCA, 1997, p. 7). According to Dahir (2001), support and utilization of the national standards have been promising, with state departments of education and state school counselor associations promoting their implementation. In addition, she noted that research had begun "to assess the extent to which implementation of school counseling programs based on National Standards prepare students to meet the challenging and changing demands of today's and tomorrow's world" (p. 325). The results of this research will be important in measuring the impact of the standards on the educational, career, and social/personal development of future students.

In this text, we use these three areas of student development, supported by the ASCA Standards for School Counseling Programs, as the structure for designing comprehensive programs of services. I have retained the heading "Educational Development" for the first area, as opposed to "Academic Development" because I believe it has broader meaning. To me, *educational* refers to the pursuit of lifelong learning, while *academic* is more closely related to achievement in specific disciplines and coursework.

Educational Development

A fundamental belief of effective schools is that "all children can learn" (Edmonds, 1979). The challenge in U.S. society today and in the future is to see this belief become reality in all schools for all children. To do so, schools must create climates that give every student an equal opportunity to succeed academically. Counselors contribute to this goal by assessing students' abilities, guiding teachers in placing students in the instructional program, providing services for parents to learn about their children's development and progress in school, and counseling students about their goals and plans in life.

School counselors use many different strategies and interventions to focus on the educational development of students. For example, counselors and teachers use classroom guidance activities to encourage positive self-concept development and to alter behaviors for improving school success. These classroom activities are integrated with daily lessons or designed as specially planned presentations. Individual counseling and small group counseling with students who need additional or more intense attention are also part of a comprehensive program. In addition, school counselors consult with teachers, parents, and other professionals to ensure that they consider all available services in planning a student's educational program.

Educational development is not the sole responsibility of classroom teachers. In today's society, optimal educational achievement is realized when teachers receive assistance from school counselors who provide leadership and direct services to students, offer support to parents and guardians, and form collaborative relationships with teachers and other school personnel. Through this type of team effort, students' progress is adequately monitored and appropriate responsive services are designed and implemented. In this way, counselors identify and address students' learning as a main goal and purpose of comprehensive school counseling programs.

One aspect of educational development that counselors include in their counseling programs is lifelong learning. In elementary through secondary schools, the educational focus for all students should be on learning throughout one's life rather than simply moving to the next grade level or merely "finishing school." Unfortunately, the design of U.S. schools emphasizes movement through the grades and graduation from one level to the next. This structure inhibits a broader lifelong self-development focus. School counselors have a responsibility to see that their schools encourage lifelong learning as an essential objective for all students. This process of learning throughout one's life is closely related to the second purpose of school counseling programs, one that addresses career development.

Career Development

The school counseling profession, as noted in Chapter 1, has its roots in vocational guidance. Over its brief history, the profession has changed and expanded its role, but career development remains a vital part of comprehensive school counseling programs. Today and in the future, people will face challenging decisions regarding their career choices in an ever-changing world. For this reason, students at all levels of education benefit from activities that introduce the world of work, help them examine career interests, and make decisions about educational plans that align with these interests. Having the knowledge and ability to make informed choices about a career is imperative for one's self-development and fulfillment in life. School counselors have a responsibility to assist students in this endeavor.

An essential part of every person's development includes his or her success in planning, choosing, and following a satisfying career. The success people have in pursuing this goal influences many other aspects of their lives. Alfred Adler, noted theorist and therapist, wrote that three main tasks in life include contributions through work, successful sharing with others, and satisfying love relationships (Sweeney, 1998). Each of these three tasks relates to the other two, but of the three, the success people achieve in their careers most strongly influences their social achievements and loving relationships.

The social strata to which people belong, the personal relationships they establish, and the economic successes they achieve are among many factors related to the career choices made over a lifetime. For this reason, schools have the responsibility to help all students use their knowledge and skills to develop realistic and self-satisfying career goals. School counselors help with this process by (1) providing students with accurate information about the world of work and existing career opportunities, (2) assessing students' interests and abilities and sharing these findings to enable students to make appropriate career choices, (3) considering cultural influences in career development, and (4) encouraging students to broaden their options as a precaution to future changes in career opportunities and the job market.

As a lifelong process, career development is an important component of all school counseling programs from elementary through secondary schools. To some people, career information and development seem out of context with the elementary curriculum. This is particularly so considering the attention U.S. schools give to learning basic skills and nurturing personal development. In elementary schools, career development may get only minimal attention. Although children at early ages might not be exposed to occupational information or formal presentations about career choices, they nevertheless are influenced by family, community, media, and other factors that lead them toward career decisions (Super, Savickas, & Super, 1996). Counselors and teachers can help with this decision-making process by infusing career information, self-interest activities, and illustrations of the relationship between work and education into daily instruction. At the same time, the school curriculum should guard against gender stereotyping in materials, information, and activities that it presents to these young, impressionable minds.

At the secondary school level, counselors and teachers continue this integration of career guidance into the curriculum and provide services to help students narrow their career interests and choices. In middle and junior high schools, students are exposed to activities and services that enable them to explore current trends in different careers. This exploration helps preteens and young adolescents to view career choices in realistic terms. In senior high schools, counselors use an array of strategies including career interest inventories, aptitude testing, and up-to-date occupational information to help students decide about their careers. During high school years, students' decisions about career choices connect to their future educational plans about entering the job market, enrolling in vocational schools for technical training, or attending college after graduation. In summary, responsive services, in elementary through high school, aim at helping students link their educational development with career goals.

Personal and Social Development

A third purpose of comprehensive school counseling programs is to facilitate the personal and social development of all students. Achieving academically and choosing a successful career are incomplete goals unless students understand and accept themselves personally and use this understanding to successfully relate with others. Many students achieve academic success in school only to fail in their personal and social development. These failures often lead to dissatisfying lives of social isolation, broken relationships, violent retaliations, substance abuse, depression, and, most tragically, suicide. Comprehensive school counseling programs design activities to help students learn social skills and identify personal attributes that will enable them to lead more satisfying lives.

In elementary schools, counselors and teachers develop programs and services that help students learn who they are, explore the similarities they share with others, and examine the differences that make them unique and special as individuals. Classroom guidance, individual counseling, and small group activities are examples of responsive services used to reach these goals. The elementary child's world is egocentric. As a result, the role of the elementary teacher and counselor is to help children emerge from their self-centered view of the world and move toward one that is accepting of others. Activities that encourage sharing, helping, and cooperation allow children to begin this transformation process.

In middle grades, students become more interested in social groups and members of the opposite sex. Developmentally, boys lag behind girls in many respects, and this gap is noticeable to teachers and counselors who plan activities and services for these students. Middle-grade services in comprehensive counseling programs continue the self-development processes begun in the elementary school and, in addition, place stronger emphasis on physical changes, sexual development, and the importance of social belonging. In many respects, the preadolescent's adjustment to physical changes—growth spurts, body hair, and sexual development—has a tremendous influence on all other aspects of student development. At the same time, a student's social acceptance and rejection have significant implications for future educational, career, and social choices.

Personal and social development in high school is frequently a continuation of patterns that emerge in the middle grades. Students who make smooth transitions from middle school to high school usually are successful in achieving a degree of social acceptance. On the other hand, students who are unable to resolve critical developmental issues in their middle school years usually need a counselor's assistance in high school.

Even students who have had few difficulties in elementary and middle school occasionally find challenges and obstacles in the high school years that prove overwhelming. For example, relationships between boys and girls become more serious during this stage, and the success or failure of these relationships can have a significant impact on future social encounters, educational plans, and career aspirations. Failed relationships can relate to dropping out of school, depression, and, tragically, suicide, all of which are concerns of high school counselors. In addition, sexual disease, teen pregnancy, substance abuse, violence, and other social ailments jeopardize a student's social and personal development. High school counselors and teachers plan classroom and schoolwide events, individual and small group counseling, parent education programs, and referral processes to assist students with normal, healthy development. In sum, high school services ideally prevent obstacles from interfering with this developmental process, and at the same time remedy existing concerns that block students' progress.

The broad goals and general activities described above for elementary through high school counseling programs offer a comprehensive interpretation of how counselors and teachers meet the needs of students. Such a general description needs to be given with some caveats. All students are not exactly the same, with the same perspective of the world and their place in it. The United States is blessed with a multitude of cultural and ethnic perspectives, all of which are brought to school by children of diverse backgrounds. By definition, comprehensive school counseling programs are sensitive to multicultural perspectives and plan individual, group, and schoolwide services accordingly.

The services and activities used by professional counselors at elementary, middle, and high school levels are similar. What distinguish the practice of counselors at these three different levels are the developmental stages and needs indicated by the students in these schools. Because the educational, career-development, and personal and social needs of elementary children are different from those of high school students, the specific activities and services provided by counselors for these two populations are also different. Nevertheless, some common leadership processes and responsive services are used by school counselors across all the educational levels. These processes and services help define and describe the nature and scope of a comprehensive school counseling program.

A Comprehensive Program

A comprehensive school counseling program consists of counseling, consulting, coordinating, and appraisal services offered in response to the identified needs, goals, and objectives of the school and community. In a comprehensive program, goals and objectives are identified and given priority as the result of adequate assessment and analysis of students', parents', and teachers' needs. A school counselor's decision, therefore, to focus on particular issues and to select specific activities in the program is not made randomly or accidentally. Rather, it occurs as a series of processes that include planning, organizing, implementing, and evaluating procedures. The first two of these, planning and organizing, go hand in hand to define and describe a school counseling program.

Planning consists of leadership procedures and decisions that help counselors evaluate schoolwide goals; assess students', parents', and teachers' needs; and select goals and objectives for their counseling programs. Planning processes are most noticeable at the beginning of the school year when an accurate assessment of school populations is likely to occur.

Typically, at the start of a school year, decisions about district lines, school reorganizations, and other major events have been made by local boards of education, and schools in these districts are certain about the students who will enroll and the communities that will be served for the year. Having this knowledge, school counselors assess the general needs of the school and community and make appropriate decisions about preventive, developmental, and remedial services. Although most planning occurs at the beginning of each school year, it remains a continuous process as counselors, teachers, and administrators evaluate ongoing services.

Organizing is a continuation of the planning process and includes the selection of major goals and objectives and a determination of which services can best address and meet these goals. Program organization also entails assignments and timelines for carrying out specific activities. These assignments and schedules help the school identify *who* is responsible for *what* services and *when* they will be implemented. Leadership skills of the counselor are important to this process. With adequate leadership and organization, school counseling programs clearly identify annual goals and objectives; make specific assignments for counselors, teachers, administrators, and other personnel; and develop a schedule of major functions and events for the year. In this way, program organization includes all professionals and establishes each of their roles in a school counseling program.

Implementing is the action phase of a comprehensive school counseling program. In this phase, counselors, teachers, and others deliver the services that constitute the program. Included in these services are individual and small group counseling, teacher and parent consultation, classroom and small group guidance, testing, crisis intervention, and referrals. In school counseling programs where counselors fail to plan and organize adequately, implementation may be the only phase that is readily observed. These counselors are busy performing activities, but they fail to orchestrate and align services to address the major needs of students, parents, and teachers in the school. In such cases, counselors are busy "getting the job done," but the job they have identified is not one that is essential to help students reach their educational goals.

Implementing a program that is devoid of clear goals and objectives is like piloting a plane without a flight plan. The plane is airborne, all instruments are working, but the pilot has no idea where the plane is heading or why it is going in a given direction. School counselors who "take off" without clear direction tend to implement services that haphazardly "hit and miss" the real issues and needs of students, parents, and teachers. Without adequate planning and organizing, the "hits" of these counselors are mostly fortuitous and not likely to be repeated. Conversely, repetition of successful services is more likely to occur when counselors complement their plans and activities with accurate evaluations and use of existing data to support programmatic decisions.

Evaluating consists of procedures that enable counselors to determine the success of their services, identify apparent weaknesses, and recommend program changes for the future. This phase of a comprehensive school counseling program is essential to the counselor's identity and credibility.

Excellent school counseling programs consist of planned involvement of all school personnel, adequate organization, appropriate assignment of responsibilities, competent delivery of services, and accurate measurement of outcomes. A truly effective school counseling program is one that makes a difference in the lives of students, parents, and teachers. By making a difference, school counselors create a clear identity and enhance their value in elementary, middle, and high school settings.

Adequate and accurate program evaluation also enables counselors to return to the initial goals and objectives of the program and assess what changes, if any, are needed. In this way, a comprehensive school counseling program is cyclical in nature. Figure 4.1 illustrates this cycle of planning, organizing, implementing, and evaluating a counseling program. Each of these phases of a comprehensive program consists of specific elements

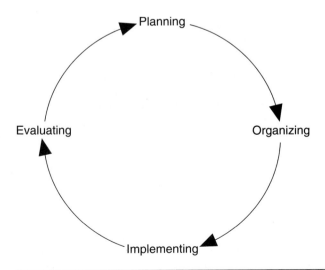

FIGURE 4.1 *Phases of a Comprehensive Program*

that will be examined more fully in Chapter 6. At this point, we examine three approaches to comprehensive programs. What follows are brief descriptions that cannot do justice to these models. I encourage you to research and review works of the original authors and other references to become more familiar with the details of these models.

The Comprehensive Guidance Program Model

Proposed and researched by Gysbers and Henderson (2000), the Comprehensive Guidance Program Model was the first clear structure to promote a programmatic approach in contrast to the traditional service-oriented approach to school counseling. This model offers three structural components: Definition, Rationale, and Assumptions. Together, these components (1) outline the mission of the program, (2) identify the professionals who deliver the program, (3) present the competencies that students will achieve through the program, (4) identify the clients of the program, (5) discuss how the program will be organized, (6) offer a rationale give direction for the program, and (7) convey the guiding principles and ethical standards upon which the comprehensive program is founded.

The Comprehensive Guidance Program Model consists of four program components including (1) a guidance curriculum, (2) individual planning, (3) responsive services, and (4) system support. Each of these components is essential to the program. The guidance curriculum provides the core for the developmental emphasis of the program. Grade level goals and competencies, K–12, focus on developmental tasks for all students, and are the basis for lessons delivered through small group or classroom guidance.

Individual planning involves strategies and activities to help students create and implement personal plans for educational, career, personal, and social development. Responsive services, as defined in this model, offer preventive or remedial assistance to students handling difficulties, facing barriers, or have other problems that impede their healthy development in one or more of the focus areas. Sometimes responsive services, such as small group counseling, might be helpful to students who are struggling with a particular developmental task. Other times, services such as individual counseling or referrals to other agencies are warranted because students are failing to resolve issues or accomplish developmental tasks.

System support has two aspects in this model. The first consists of management behaviors and activities that support the guidance curriculum, individual planning, and responsive services. The second part of system support includes efforts that support the school and the overall educational system, such as teacher consultation, parent education programs, or systemwide initiatives to improve educational opportunities for all students.

The Comprehensive Guidance Program Model (Gysbers & Henderson, 2000) encourages an assessment of current program aspects as the starting point toward developing a viable program. A next step in designing the new program is to establish priorities for delivering services. These priorities include the competencies of the counselors and other staff, parents as partners and/or as clients, identification of student clients, student competencies, and delineation of the program components (i.e., guidance curriculum, individual planning, responsive services, and system support). This delineation will identify specific activities and strategies to address the priorities for student development.

Developmental Guidance and Counseling Approach

Myrick (2003) is the primary developer of the Developmental Guidance and Counseling Approach. His model uses developmental theories as its foundation, including Erikson's (1963) stages of human development, Purkey's (1970, 1996) review of self-concept theory, and Ivey's (1986) developmental therapy, among other developmental theories.

Similar to the Comprehensive Guidance Program Model (Gysbers & Henderson, 2000), Myrick advocated for an organized curriculum to focus on eight developmental goals: (1) understanding the school environment, (2) understanding self and others, (3) understanding attitudes and behavior, (4) decision-making and problem solving, (5) interpersonal and communication skills, (6) school success skills, (7) career awareness and planning, and (8) community pride and involvement. In addition, he offered seven guiding principles for a developmental program. These principles expect that developmental guidance (1) exists for all students, (2) consists of an organized, planned curriculum, (3) is sequential and flexible, (4) is an integral part of the overall educational program, (5) involves all school personnel, (6) helps students learn efficiently and effectively, and (7) includes professional counselors who provide counseling services and interventions.

The Developmental Guidance and Counseling Approach includes similar types of services and activities as other models, but does not include a specific planning process for designing, organizing, implementing, and evaluating a program. Myrick (2003) suggested, however, that coordination of counseling and guidance services is a significant role for the school counselor, and that managing program priorities across students' developmental needs, school crises, counselor's interventions, and the time available during the school day, week, month, and year is imperative for a successful program.

ASCA National Model

As noted in an earlier chapter, the American School Counselor Association has advocated for comprehensive programs for several years and in 1997 and 1998 published its national standards for school counseling programs and suggestions for implementing these standards (Dahir, 2001; Dahir, Sheldon, & Valiga, 1998). From these publications, ASCA moved toward creating a National Model for school counseling (2003). This new model uses many of the concepts promoted by Gysbers, Henderson, Myrick, and other proponents of comprehensive, developmental programs of services. In addition, the ASCA National Model includes a focus on program accountability with an emphasis on student outcomes.

Four overarching themes surround the National Model. They are leadership, advocacy, collaboration, and systemic change. These four themes or skill areas are essential for school counselors to use in helping all students be successful in their academic, career, and personal/social development. The National Model also includes four major components: (1) Foundation, (2) Delivery System, (3) Management System, and (4) Accountability processes.

The Foundation of a comprehensive program, according to the National Model, describes the program and connects it to the school's mission and student competencies. The Delivery System outlines implementation processes and the various parts and services of the program. These include a guidance curriculum, individual student planning, responsive services, and system support, similar to those in Gysbers and Henderson's model. The Management System of the National Model offers an organizational structure and management tools for counselors to plan and deliver a comprehensive program. The Accountability aspect of this model continuously asks the question, "Did the program make a difference in student development, behavior, or achievement?" An equally important question is, "How was this difference measured?" The term *data-driven* has been associated with the National Model because of its emphasis on accountability and the need for counselors to know how to use existing data in schools to design programs of services as well as to generate data to demonstrate program effectiveness (Stone & Dahir, 2004). We will consider counselor accountability in a later chapter of this text when we explore program evaluation in more detail.

Similar to Myrick's approach, the National Model does not outline specific stages or phases of a comprehensive school counseling program. However, as Stone and Dahir (2006) noted, the model implicitly encourages implementation through the establishment of a broad-based advisory committee, setting priorities, developing student competencies, assessing current services and program activities, connecting existing services/activities to national standards and competencies, locating weak areas of the program and making appropriate adjustments, seeking commitment from all administrators, teachers, and counselors to be involved in delivering the program, and using the four major components of the ASCA National Model (p. 223).

The three models presented above have many similar components and philosophies for comprehensive school counseling programs. They complement the generic structure for comprehensive school counseling discussed in this chapter. What is important for new school counselors to remember is that some type of structure and process are necessary to design, organize, implement, and evaluate a comprehensive school counseling program, and such a program is preferred over not having any structure or process to decide who needs services, what services to deliver, and how to evaluate whether the interventions and strategies chosen were effective.

In addition to having a structure and process to establish a comprehensive program, school counselors also benefit from having an appropriate setting in which to practice. In the remaining sections of this chapter, we examine counseling facilities and resources, materials and equipment, and personnel.

Facilities

As with other institutions, schools consist of more than philosophies, programs, and services. They also are buildings, materials, equipment, finances, personnel, and other items that enable them to perform an educational function. In performing this educational function, school counselors have needs of their own. One such need is to have sufficient physical space to provide individual and small group counseling. This space is the counseling center.

The Counseling Center

To provide confidential counseling and consulting services for students, parents, and teachers, counselors need appropriate space within the school. A counseling center usually reflects the level and nature of the school counseling program. Centers in elementary schools, middle schools, and high schools vary according to the development needs of students, the size of the schools, and the types of major activities in those schools. All these factors influence the design of a counseling center.

Design. Some elementary counselors serve more than one school, and in these situations, they share space with other itinerant personnel such as speech therapists, school nurses, and special education teachers. These are not the best arrangements in which to develop comprehensive programs, but many counselors are able to create exceptional programs and provide effective services even in the most difficult circumstances.

Ideally, an elementary school counseling center includes a private office for confidential sessions with students, parents, teachers, and others and an adjoining, larger room for group sessions, play activities, and other services. This larger room might include tables and chairs; shelves for storing games, books, and other materials; a sink for cleaning up after playing with paint, clay, or similar media; and a computer center for self-awareness inventories, problem-solving activities, and interactive learning.

In middle schools, counseling centers consist of one or more offices and a larger outer space for students to use books, computers, games, and other materials for self-instruction. In some instances, middle schools assign a secretary to the counseling program and have a reception area. Also, counselors have access to a conference room to hold small group sessions with students, parents, and teachers. Because space in schools is usually at a premium, conference rooms are generally shared with administrators and teachers and scheduling their use must be carefully coordinated.

Senior high counseling centers are similar to middle school designs except that in large high schools there are more offices for counselors, and space may be designated for career materials and equipment. Senior high counseling centers usually store and display career and college materials in an area where students can have ready access to this information. In many centers, computer terminals are available to students who want to search for career and college information. Senior high counselors also have access to one or more conference rooms used for small groups, testing, departmental meetings, and other activities.

Student records should be accessible to all teachers and counselors in a school. In past years, cumulative records were frequently filed in the counseling center. While this seems a logical procedure, it also has negative aspects. For one, teachers may not have easy access to student records when folders are locked in a counselor's office and the counselor is in conference with someone. Furthermore, having student records in the counseling center perpetuates the "guidance image" of the 1940s and 1950s and the image of the counselor as keeper of the vault and manager of records. In elementary and middle schools, student records are best filed in administrative offices where appropriate school personnel can have adequate access. In high schools, where counselors may need more frequent access to student folders, a separate file room near the counseling center is suitable so that teachers can obtain student information without interrupting the services of the counseling program. As society moves rapidly toward electronic storage of records, this might not continue to be an issue in the future.

Figures 4.2, 4.3, and 4.4 illustrate counseling centers at the elementary, middle, and high school levels, respectively. These illustrations are samples of what school counseling centers might look like and by no means are intended as ideal designs.

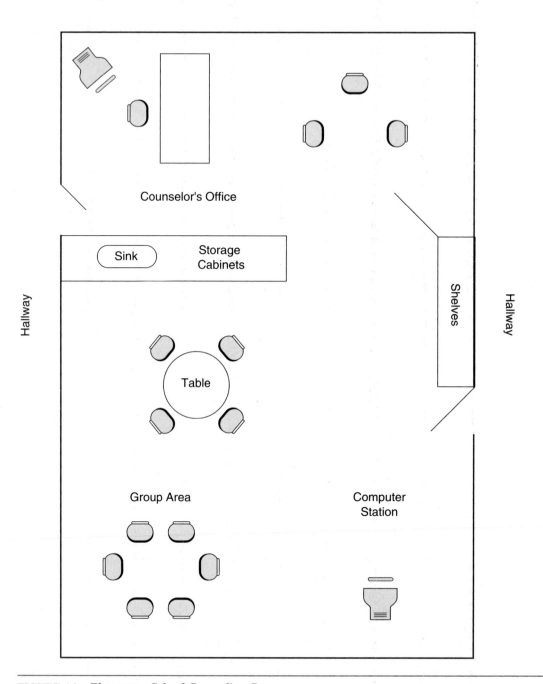

Counselor's Office

Sink

Storage
Cabinets

Hallway

Shelves

Hallway

Table

Group Area

Computer
Station

FIGURE 4.2 *Elementary School Counseling Center*

Location. Equally important to the design of a school counseling center is its location. In elementary schools, for example, if the center is located at one end of a sprawling complex away from very young children, the counselor will not be readily available to these students. Counseling centers should be located so that everyone in the school has equal

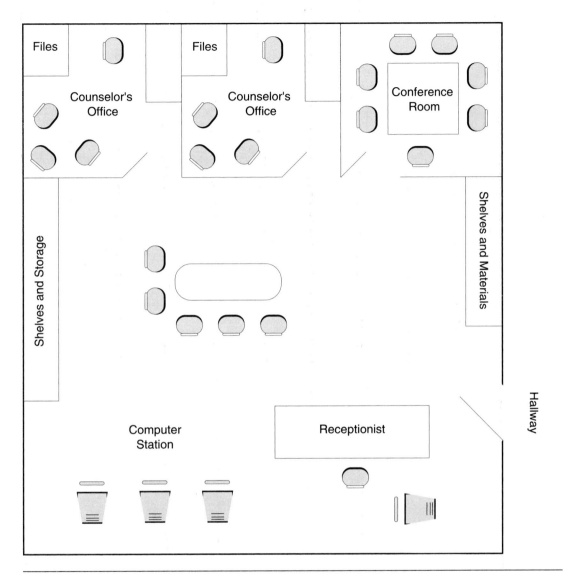

FIGURE 4.3   *Middle School Counseling Center*

access. Generally, this means placing the counseling office in a central location. Historically, the counseling office was located near the school's administration suite. Although this was advantageous in terms of communication between counselors and administrators, it sometimes was a handicap because students and teachers tended to associate counselors with the school administration. This association did not always enhance the image of counselors as advocates for all students.

The location of a counseling center should enhance its visibility, facilitate communication between all groups in the school, and invite people to enter and use its facilities. A location that accomplishes these goals places the school counselor in an optimal position to

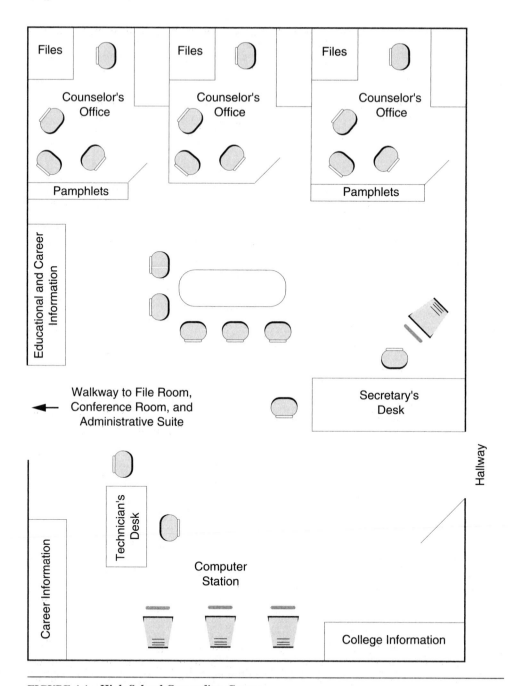

FIGURE 4.4 *High School Counseling Center*

create and deliver beneficial services to a wide audience. In this way, everyone in the school is included in the counseling program.

Materials and Equipment

A well-designed and optimally located counseling center is complete when it includes appropriate and adequate materials and equipment to deliver the intended services. In elementary centers, these materials include games and toys to use in play therapy and to establish rapport with children. Counselors use art media, computer programs, games, developmental learning kits, videos, puppets, and a variety of other items to help children express themselves, experience success, and learn social skills in a safe, nonthreatening setting.

Middle school centers have similar materials but more appropriate for preadolescents. In addition, career exploration materials, self-development resources, and high school information are included. For example, books in a middle school counseling center are available to help students address developmental needs such as adjusting to their physical changes, handling peer pressure, and preventing substance abuse.

High school centers typically have a stronger focus on career choice materials, college catalogs, test-taking skill packages, assessment inventories, and substance abuse, pregnancy, and similar materials that address critical health and social issues. As with materials found in elementary and middle school centers, information in high school programs is up-to-date and developmentally appropriate for students.

In addition to counseling and guidance materials, a school counseling center is furnished with appropriate-size tables and chairs and equipment to use with videos, computer programs, and other media. All this equipment might not be stored in the counseling center, but school counselors and teachers have access to these supplies and apparatus through the media centers of their schools. Elementary counseling centers should have tables and chairs for both young children and adults because these are the populations served. All counselors should have a telephone with a private line for consultations and referrals. Other equipment might include file cabinets, audio and video players, and computers. In summary, school counseling centers typically have

Appropriate and sufficient furnishings for students and adults

Audio and visual privacy for counselors' offices

Tables for group activities and conferences

A telephone for each counselor

A storage area for materials and equipment

Computers for self-instruction and guidance-related programs

Access to a conference room

A waiting area or activity area outside the counselor's office(s)

A secure room where student records can be stored away from the counseling center so appropriate personnel can have access

Personnel

Facilities, materials, and equipment provide the physical structure and resources for a school counseling program, but it is the people in the program who determine its true value and potential. A comprehensive counseling program includes roles for administrators, teachers, other student services specialists, student helpers, volunteers, and, of course, counselors. In addition, the program uses support staff, especially secretaries and other clerical assistants. Some high schools employ technical assistants who specialize in information management, computer scheduling, and similar services. These assistants allow counselors and teachers more time to perform the professional functions for which they were trained and employed. All these personnel contribute to the comprehensive nature of a counseling program, beginning with school counselors.

Counselors

The number of counselors hired in a school counseling program makes a difference in the quantity and quality of services offered. Usually schools employ sufficient counselors to meet the counselor-to-student ratios recommended by professional associations and accrediting organizations. Although these groups do not always have consistent guidelines for schools to follow, recommended ratios generally suggest one counselor for every 300 to 500 students enrolled, depending on the grade level of the school. Professional associations, such as the American School Counselor Association, tend to recommend lower ratios than do regional and state accreditation bodies.

It is helpful to have a sufficient number of licensed or certified counselors, but an adequate number does not supplant the need for a well-planned program of comprehensive services. Regardless of the number of counselors employed or the ratio of students to counselors, the success of a school counseling program depends on the overall design of the program, the goals and objectives selected, the leadership counselors provide, and how counselors spend their time serving students, parents, and teachers. Some schools are blessed with an ample number of qualified counselors, yet they fail to meet the needs of students because the counselors make little effort to perform an adequate assessment, seek suggestions from teachers, schedule appropriate services, and evaluate results. At the same time, some comprehensive programs are designed with limited resources and few personnel. Counselors in these poorly funded programs plan, implement, and evaluate to the best of their ability, and usually are successful in meeting the needs of many students.

Clerical Assistants

Schools receive and generate a large amount of paperwork. Sending communications to homes and other agencies; updating student records; filing report cards; preparing local, state, and federal reports; and doing a host of other paper processes contribute to a school's clerical demands. Counselors are not exempt from this burden. Schools need sufficient clerical staff to help counselors and teachers perform their respective duties in a timely fashion. Excellent secretaries and technical assistants are indispensable in today's schools, and this is true for school counseling centers as well. In elementary and middle schools, counselors do not typically have the amount of paperwork found in secondary schools. Nevertheless, any clerical task that removes elementary and middle school counselors from the essential function of providing responsive services to students, parents, and teachers should be eliminated or reassigned. To assign counselors these types of activities is not cost-effective and is a misuse of school personnel.

In high schools, counselors usually work more closely with student records, transcripts, and similar items. A secretary for the counseling center is essential, and, in large schools, a technical assistant responsible for data input and analysis is equally important. These professionals are an integral part of a secondary school's counseling center and advise counselors on efficient ways to handle data, handle the flow of communication, schedule appointments, order materials, enter schedule changes, and manage the budget. In some instances, these services might be handled by paraprofessionals or volunteers who assist in the counseling program.

Paraprofessionals and Volunteers

Paraprofessionals are persons who have some training in human services and can assist counselors with academic advising, career information, and other initial relationships. These assistants can also perform clerical tasks as the need arises, as can volunteers in the school.

Volunteers offer valuable time to assist with many school services including those of a counseling program. Parents, grandparents, guardians, retired citizens, and other people constitute a large pool of available volunteers. Some ways that school counselors use volunteers are as tutors to help students receive additional individual help, guidance assistants to assist with information in the counseling center, and clerical assistants to help secretaries keep up with communications, filing, and other responsibilities.

In all cases where schools and school counselors elect to use paraprofessionals and volunteers, adequate training and orientation to the counseling program are necessary. School counselors who accept the services of these people must take time to orient them to the school and program. In addition, counselors ensure that these paraprofessionals and volunteers have basic communication and helping skills that complement the services of the counseling program, accept the limits of their role, and understand the roles of counselors and other staff members in the school.

A comprehensive school counseling program, as defined and described in this chapter, includes a broad focus on student development goals and objectives that counselors select through a process of needs assessments and suggestions from administrators, teachers, and other school personnel. In addition, a comprehensive program is complemented by physical facilities, materials, equipment, and personnel to carry out its overall purpose. Within a comprehensive program are responsive services that define and describe the role and functions of a professional school counselor. Because counselors now function in all school organizations—elementary, middle, and high school—it is important to understand the similarities and differences in how they function at these three levels.

The next chapter describes the various services provided by school counselors in elementary, middle, and high schools as part of their comprehensive programs.

Additional Readings _____

Gysbers, N., & Henderson, P. (Eds.) (1997). *Comprehensive Guidance Programs that Work—II* (Greensboro, NC: ERIC/CASS).

This compendium of successful school counseling programs begins with a presentation about an innovative model for school counseling and ends with a chapter on program evaluation.

Myrick, R. D. (2003). *Developmental Guidance and Counseling: A Practical Approach* (4th ed.) (Minneaplis, MN: Educational Media Corporation).

Myrick's popular book offers a developmental perspective on comprehensive counseling programs. It takes a practical approach and offers helpful strategies for school counselors.

Websites _____

ASCA's National Model
   www.schoolcounselor.org/content.asp
CollegeNet
   www.collegenet.com
The Guidance Channel
   www.guidancechannel.com

Safe & Drug Free Schools Program
   www.ed.gov/about/ offices/list/osdfs/index.html
U.S. Department of Education
   www/ed/gov/offices

Exercises _____

1. Identify a school counselor in your community and make an appointment to visit and discuss the school counseling profession. During your visit, ask the counselor, "How do you plan services?" Ask the counselor if a written plan exists about the program. In class, share your observations about this counseling program. (*Note:* In sharing information about this interview, you should keep the counselor's name and the school's name confidential.)

2. Remember when you were in elementary, middle, or high school? Do you remember a counseling center? What do you recall about this place? Share your recollections in a small group and compare similarities and differences.

3. In a small group, take the four stages of a comprehensive program—planning, organizing, implementing, and evaluating—and list *specific behaviors* of the counselor that you would associate with each phase. Share these lists in class and compile a single master list.

4. Interview a classroom teacher about his or her perspectives on counseling services in schools. What degree of input should teachers have in designing a counseling program? What role does the teacher have in a comprehensive program?

5

Responsive Services of a Comprehensive Program

In past decades, school counseling programs focused primarily on the development of individual students and offered services that typically emphasized one-to-one relationships. Because many guidance and counseling services began at the senior high school level, they were heavily weighted with administrative and clerical tasks, such as scheduling classes, managing cumulative files, and recording grades on transcripts. With the expansion of school counseling into middle and elementary schools and the call for counselors to be accountable for services to students, parents, and teachers, the profession began to accept a wider focus for program development.

Earlier in this book you learned that a comprehensive school counseling program consists of a wide range of responsive services to address students', parents', and teachers' needs. Contemporary school counseling services are essential to a school's educational mission. In this chapter, you will see that these services, individually and combined, create the structure of a comprehensive school counseling program. In doing so, they illustrate how today's school counselors have moved from an emphasis on one-to-one services toward programs that advocate group processes in conjunction with individual counseling. This combination of related services enables school counselors to serve a wider audience of students. Furthermore, responsive services of a comprehensive program include activities and processes that extend beyond traditional counseling services.

Chapter 4 noted that a school counseling program consists of four major areas of service including counseling, consulting, coordinating, and appraising. Each of these areas of service is composed of specific activities. In this chapter, we explore each of these services and their unique contributions to school counseling programs. This is a broad summary of how counselors integrate these responsive services into a comprehensive program. In Chapters 7 through 9, I describe these services in greater detail.

Counseling

In helping students, parents, and teachers collect information, explore options, and make appropriate decisions, school counselors use a process commonly referred to as *counseling.*

Many texts, articles, and other sources have described and defined counseling as a helping process. Over the years, authorities have written countless definitions of counseling, with as many differences as there are similarities among them. In addition, counselors have tried to distinguish counseling processes from other therapeutic relationships, such as psychotherapy (Gladding, 2004), but these distinctions are not consistently clear (Nystul, 1993). Some theorists and practitioners believe that these efforts are fruitless because the two processes are the same, whereas others insist that psychotherapy is much more intense, in-depth, and long-term than counseling. As George and Cristiani (1995) stated, "Indeed, efforts to distinguish between the two have not met with universal approval" (p. 3).

The purpose here is not to continue this debate. Instead, it is to focus on what counseling is as a helping process and how elementary, middle, and senior high school counselors use this process in schools with students, parents, and teachers. Chapter 7 explains individual and group counseling more thoroughly. For now, we begin with a brief description of individual counseling.

Individual Counseling

School counselors frequently work with individual students to help them focus on particular concerns and make decisions about their goals, relationships, and self-development. In many instances, these helping relationships are defined as counseling because they are confidential, ongoing processes that consist of specific phases. Usually, they are founded on particular theoretical models of counseling and require a high level of helping skills. However, not all individual contacts made between counselors and students illustrate counseling relationships. Some are informational meetings where counselors share data, materials, and other information to help students make educational, career, and other types of decisions. These relationships, as we will see later, are more accurately defined as consultations.

Individual counseling can have a developmental focus by looking toward future plans and goals, but it more commonly has a remedial purpose. The counselee (also called *client*) raises a concern that is bothersome or problematic. The counselee seeks assistance to clarify a particular concern, explore options to resolve this issue, choose a plan or strategy, and be successful in remedying the situation. Individual counseling usually relies on verbal interactions between counselors and counselees. Because these relationships rely to a great extent on the verbal skills of both the counselee and the counselor, they are not an appropriate service for everyone in every situation. For example, young elementary school children with limited verbal skills probably do not benefit solely from talking relationships in individual counseling. In cases where children have limited verbal ability, counselors might use individual relationships, but the goals of these sessions are primarily to build rapport with the child and gather information through observation and play. Such information helps counselors make decisions about appropriate services to assist children, parents, and teachers with identified concerns.

Sometimes elementary school counselors can be successful with individual counseling that relies on nonverbal interactions, play therapy, and modeling techniques with young children. In these instances, counselors find that their time is well spent because these encounters help develop trust between the child and the counselor, and the information obtained in these relationships helps the counselor choose an appropriate intervention. More often, however, a child who lacks the verbal skills to interact successfully in individual counseling also lacks other developmental abilities necessary for a successful counseling relationship.

Behavioral maturity and cognitive development are two more areas that complement a student's verbal skills to make individual counseling successful (Thompson, Rudolph, & Henderson, 2004). Students who are unable to be attentive for a reasonable length of time or cannot focus on one issue at a time usually need to acquire these behavioral skills before individual counseling can be successful. At the same time, if students do not understand the relationship between their behaviors and successful development, or cannot comprehend concepts such as responsibility, self-determination, and acceptance, it is unlikely they will benefit from individual counseling as defined here. Nevertheless, school counselors frequently work with young children individually, as noted earlier, to develop helpful relationships, observe behaviors in one-on-one settings, and proactively help children learn new behaviors and coping skills.

In schools where counselors are responsible for a large number of students, the decision of whether to use individual counseling is also related to the time available. Typically, individual counseling sessions last from twenty minutes to an hour, depending on the age and developmental level of students. If a large percentage of students in the school receives individual services, this is a substantial investment of time and reduces the time available to provide other responsive services for students, parents, and teachers. For this reason, school counselors supplement individual counseling services by forming groups to meet the needs of more students.

Group Counseling

The origins of group counseling are uncertain. Most likely the earliest form of group work in schools was in group guidance, described here as instructional and informational services to assist with student development. Allen (1931) is credited with the earliest use of the term *group counseling,* but his description of the process was closer to what we know today as group guidance (Gazda, 1989). In the late 1950s and early 1960s, descriptions of group counseling were found more frequently in the counseling literature. During this time, group guidance seemed to lose status, particularly in the schools. In the late 1960s, the popularity of group counseling continued to grow with the publication of several major textbooks devoted to this process. Today, as seen in Chapter 7, group procedures that counselors use in schools include both counseling and guidance, and each form has a particular focus and purpose in comprehensive school counseling programs.

Group counseling typically consists of a few students who meet on a regular basis in confidential sessions to handle specific concerns or support each other with particular developmental goals. In these sessions, the counselor is the leader who facilitates discussions, supports all the group members, and gives direction to the helping process. Group counseling can take different forms and requires careful planning so it complements other services in a comprehensive program.

Counselors use groups to address a wide array of preventive, developmental, and remedial issues. There are also many ways that counselors form groups, choose group members, and structure group processes. Sometimes counselors form groups because certain students have similar needs, and counselors believe that by asking students to share these mutual concerns, they will benefit more from groups than through individual sessions. For instance, a middle school counselor might have several students who are referred by their parents because of family divorce. After interviewing each of the students, the counselor invites them to form a group to work through their feelings and support each other during this crisis in their lives. By establishing groups in this way, counselors use common concerns as a basis for counseling, solicit the support and assistance of each group member, ask members to focus on their major concerns, and thereby use time more efficiently to reach a greater number of students.

Although group counseling remains prominent in counseling literature, many counselors resist using this service in their schools. In part, this resistance is due to the difficulty of scheduling group sessions, especially in secondary schools with tight class schedules. Teachers are protective of their instructional time with students, and counselors struggle to create workable group schedules that cause minimal interference with class time. In comprehensive school counseling programs, group counseling is an important responsive service, and to include it counselors seek suggestions from teachers and administrators to design reasonable schedules without significantly disrupting the instructional program. Chapter 7 reviews some practical scheduling strategies used by school counselors.

Student Counseling

Of the three populations served in a school counseling program, students are the primary target group. Because students are challenged by critical issues affecting their personal, social, educational, and career development, it is essential that counselors schedule time for individual and group counseling relationships. With the ever-changing structure of the U.S. family and the desire and need for some parents to be out of the home to increase family income, many children and adolescents can be helped by someone with whom they can share concerns and receive accurate information to make appropriate decisions. To be most effective, these critical helping relationships should be private and individual in nature. At times, students may be comfortable sharing concerns with a few other students, but they still will want these discussions to remain private, and this is why group counseling is appropriate in school settings.

Because comprehensive school counseling programs have a broad focus and attempt to serve a wide range of students' needs, counselors try to keep their counseling relationships brief. For this reason, school counselors rely on other mental-health professionals, public service agencies, and private practitioners who serve as referral resources for students and families in need. The decision of when to refer a student is guided by questions such as:

1. Is sufficient progress being made with the student in the current helping relationship?
2. Does the school counselor have adequate preparation and knowledge in the area of concern to assist this student?
3. Is there a more appropriate source to whom this student could be referred?
4. Are other aspects of the counseling program being neglected due to time being devoted to this relationship?

These questions guide all counselors, whether in educational or clinical settings, in making decisions about whom to counsel and for how long. Similar questions also guide counselors when parents and teachers request counseling.

problems, family concerns, and learning disabilities are among the many issues that influence a child's progress throughout his or her school life.

As a resource in the school, the counselor is available to help parents and teachers locate information in the school system and community to assist with children's total development. For this reason, counselors find out about special programs and services in the school systems where they work, and they make every effort to learn about community resources and programs that can benefit students. Special education programs, tutoring services, child nutrition information, and other school services can be the resources to help students move smoothly through their school years. Likewise, mental-health services, recreational programs, religious-sponsored support groups, social services, and youth clubs are among the resources organized and funded by local communities to assist with human development.

Career Opportunities. School counselors are trained in career theory and development and are concerned with linking career decisions to educational progress. At the senior high school level, counselors consult with students to help them find information to make appropriate career selections. Information about career opportunities is found in local news resources, employment offices, and federal guides such as the *Dictionary of Occupational Titles* and the *Occupational Outlook Handbook.* In addition, school counselors and students use computer-based systems and the Internet to gather information about careers of interest to them.

In elementary and middle schools, counselors provide information to students and teachers about the world of work and career opportunities to help with early career exploration. Usually, counselors and teachers use this information to design career guidance experiences that they integrate with classroom instruction. For example, a middle school teacher who plans to introduce chemicals into a classroom science lesson might search for information about chemical production careers that exist in the local community and surrounding area. In this way, the teacher links career goals and objectives with science education objectives in the curriculum. The school counselor assists the teacher in planning this integration of science and career guidance. Counselors also cooperate with the school's media coordinator to suggest materials for review and purchase. At all school levels, elementary through high school, the media center is a vital resource center for a wide range of materials including career information. By cooperating with their media coordinators, school counselors ensure that career information is current, accurate, and available to students and teachers.

Educational Opportunities. Another type of informational consultation is locating educational services, programs, and opportunities that complement and support students' overall development. Facts and details about talent searches for gifted students; summer camps for enrichment activities; college and university programs for elementary, middle grade, and high school ages; and business-supported ventures in the community are a few examples of information that counselors disseminate to enhance learning opportunities for all students.

At the senior high school level, educational consultation with students becomes more visible as a responsive service of the school counseling program. High school students are narrowing their choices of career and postsecondary educational opportunities, and senior high school counselors are a primary source of information about jobs, technical schools, and colleges. Ideally, this information is also part of the teachers' role in academic advising. When this is so, information about educational opportunities is widely disseminated through the counseling program, homeroom classes, and teacher-advisor activities. Teacher-advisor services are commonly thought of as middle school programs, but high schools can also establish them to strengthen school counseling and provide more efficient services and information to students (Myrick, 2003).

Consulting with parents and students about educational opportunities raises another issue for which counselors can be a resource. Extracurricular programs and educational endeavors beyond high school cost money, and counselors frequently consult with students and parents about financial resources. The cost of sending a child to summer camp or the tuition for college is an awesome barrier for many families. Helping them find information to address these and other financial concerns is another way that school counselors act as consultants. Elementary and middle school counselors work with social service agencies, health departments, religious organizations, and other community services to find assistance for family needs. High school counselors do likewise and cooperate with colleges and universities to locate grants, loans, and scholarships for students' tuition.

Financial Assistance.   Parents want the best for their children, but often the best seems economically out of reach. In public schools, children and adolescents come from a wide spectrum of economic deprivation and affluence to study and learn side by side. Frequently this diversity separates groups of students rather than unites them. Schools attempt to provide equitable programs, services, and opportunities to disparate groups, but the wider this difference is, the greater the challenge of providing equal education for all students. Sometimes simple activities, such as eating lunch together in the cafeteria, become striking illustrations of the differences that exist among students in the same school. One child whose family does not qualify for federal assistance opens a meager lunch and sits between another student with a full plate of "free lunch" and a third student whose affluence is measured not only by the luxurious fare but also by the "space-age" container in which it is carried to school.

School counselors are frequent providers of information regarding financial resources for families and their children. In schools that are fortunate enough to have social workers, counselors share this responsibility. For some students in elementary and middle schools, financial assistance can make the difference in meeting basic clothing and nourishment needs so that students can adequately learn in school. Consulting with parents and guardians about where to seek financial assistance is essential for optimal student learning to take place.

In high schools, counselors help adolescents with resources to meet their basic needs and, as mentioned above, also help families find the funds to send students to appropriate postsecondary educational institutions. Technical schools, colleges, and universities are expensive ventures, and most of today's families need assistance in helping their children reach this goal. School counselors alone do not own this responsibility, but because of their role in academic advising, many senior high counselors assume financial assistance as one of their primary responsibilities. Secondary counselors assumed this role during the early years of school guidance and counseling. For many high school counselors it has continued, and for some it is a major function. Other secondary counselors use volunteers, such as parents, to assist students with college information and financial aid forms. In this way, counselors provide accurate financial information without allowing this single function to consume an inordinate amount of time and replace other responsive services or leadership roles in the counseling program. Volunteers receive training in current financial aid information and schedule time in the counseling center to answer questions for students and parents. They also help counselors with classroom presentations to distribute materials to students at appropriate times during the year.

As seen above, informational consultation takes many forms. School counselors use individual consultations, large group sessions, computer-based self-assessment, interest inventories, and printed media to disseminate accurate and current information. When presenting information in large group sessions, counselors often adopt another type of consulting mode; they instruct students, parents, and teachers.

Instructional Services

Contemporary school counselors include large group instruction as part of their consulting services for students, parents, and teachers. These instructional relationships are similar to classroom instruction in that they impart information or teach new skills, but they also are different because they are free of evaluation. Therefore, students who receive instruction from a counselor are typically not evaluated for their participation in these activities; students do not receive a grade. Without this element of evaluation, these instructional sessions are less inhibitive and more facilitative in encouraging students to ask questions and share opinions about important issues. These kinds of instructional consultations are usually structured as classroom guidance with students, educational programs for parents, and in-service workshops for teachers.

Classroom Guidance. As noted in Chapter 1, the school counseling profession began in the early 1900s with a focus on classroom guidance and eventually moved toward one-on-one counseling in the 1960s. Contemporary school counseling programs include large group services as well as individual counseling to meet the unique needs of all students. In these programs, guidance is an essential area of the curriculum, and teachers and counselors collaborate to plan effective educational goals and objectives and create guidance activities for daily instruction. I hold the view that classroom guidance, when delivered by counselors in schools, is a form of instructional consultation.

Counselors sometimes present guidance lessons as part of their consulting role in school. These presentations usually are the result of requests from teachers who want students to receive specific information or skills to deal with particular concerns. At times, teachers may be uncomfortable about sensitive issues, such as sexual development in adolescence, and want counselors to assist in planning and presenting guidance lessons to address these concerns. Other times, teachers feel that an "objective" presenter is more effective in achieving desired results, such as having the counselor lead classroom guidance discussions to focus on student behaviors in class.

In comprehensive programs, counselors also use guidance instruction in small group sessions. These small group guidance sessions are either one-time meetings or ongoing sessions to share information or teach coping skills to students who have a particular need. In these groups, counselors use some type of media or instructional material to help students understand and achieve the identified goals. Sometimes, the difference between ongoing small group guidance and group counseling becomes blurred. This is particularly true when working with young children for whom group counseling can be quite structured because of their maturational levels. The major difference between guidance and counseling in these instances may simply be the aspects of confidentiality and privacy, which are essential in all counseling relationships. Instructional relationships, such as small group guidance, do not necessarily include the element of privacy or the limit of confidentiality.

Parent Education.   Another type of instructional consultation used by school counselors is parent education programs. As with classroom guidance, parent education can take place in a single session, such as a counselor's presentation to a parent-teacher association meeting, or can occur in a series of meetings that focus on parental and family needs. In all these presentations, school counselors assume different roles depending on the nature of the programs they have designed. For example, in presenting information about child development to a group of elementary school parents, a counselor may take the role of an "expert consultant," sharing research and other factual data. In contrast, another counselor may lead a parent discussion group about child discipline and take a "facilitator" role to keep the discussion on target and give all participants an opportunity to share their opinions. In this second case, the counselor facilitates learning by having parents share their own "expertise" as family leaders.

By using their consulting skills and instructing parents in various aspects of child development, adolescent behavior, and communication skills, school counselors provide indirect responsive services to a larger number of students. As parents become more knowledgeable and skilled, they create beneficial relationships with their children and optimal home environments for learning. For this reason, these types of functions for school counselors are essential in comprehensive programs. When counselors are unable to provide these services directly to parents, they rely on community resources, such as private counselors, mental-health practitioners, and social workers, who are willing and able to organize and lead parent education groups.

Teacher In-Service.   A third type of instructional format used by school counselors is teacher in-service workshops. Because teachers are the first-line helpers in schools, they need information and instruction to provide initial services for students who request assistance or have a need. School counselors assist teachers by planning and presenting workshops on particular topics or skill development. As with parent education groups, when counselors are unable or unqualified to lead such training, they seek appropriate instructors or consultants to present these seminars. In many cases, teachers in schools are well qualified to present in-service assistance for their colleagues. Perceptive school counselors survey teachers at the beginning of each year to assess their needs and establish a list of potential presenters. Form 5.1 is a sample of this kind of survey.

By planning and organizing various instructional services, school counselors illustrate how they contribute to the overall school mission. They also strengthen their relationships with parents, teachers, administrators, and other school personnel, enabling counselors to establish ties that enhance their role in problem solving and mediating situations, which are other types of consultations.

FORM 5.1   *Teacher In-Service Survey*

Teachers: Please check below the topics of interest about which you would like in-service presentations this year. If you want to hear about topics not listed, please indicate so on the bottom of the form. Also, if you have expertise in a particular area and are willing to present a workshop or a session at a faculty meeting, please indicate so at the bottom of this form.

Topics for in-service this year:

___ Learning disabilities	___ Suicide prevention
___ Classroom management	___ Conferring with parents
___ Instructional techniques	___ CPR training
___ Special education regulations	___ Communication skills
___ Computers in the classroom	___ Handling crises
___ New instructional material	___ Using the media center
___ Conflict resolution	___ Peer helper programs

Other topics: _____

_____

I am willing to present on: _____

Name: _____

Problem-Solving Services

As with any large organization consisting of diverse groups, schools are sometimes challenged by threats and hazards posed by students, parents, and teachers. Students sometimes feel school rules are unfair, parents are dissatisfied with instructional procedures, and teachers want support from home and family in educating children. These and other conflicts can disable schools if not addressed openly and with genuine regard for all parties. Counselors use consulting skills and processes to assist people in resolving these conflicts, accepting the views of others, and selecting agreeable goals to move forward. In these consulting relationships, counselors use effective communication skills, support all sides involved in the conflict, and attempt to negotiate reasonable solutions.

Parent-Teacher Conferences.   One way that school counselors assume a consulting role to resolve problems is by facilitating parent-teacher conferences. These meetings are scheduled either at regular times during the year to report student progress, test results, and other educational information to parents, or when either teachers or parents become concerned about student development and behavior. The role of the school counselor in these conferences varies depending on the issues at hand and who has initiated the conference. When a teacher calls the conference and invites the counselor to attend, that teacher defines the purpose of the conference and role of the counselor. Sometimes counselors and teachers need to negotiate this role, particularly if the counselor believes the role defined by the teacher conflicts with professional or ethical guidelines. Occasionally, counselors arrange parent-teacher conferences and assume leadership roles.

When parent-teacher conferences are held for informational purposes, a counselor's involvement may simply be to share and interpret data, such as a child's test results. When conferences are scheduled to resolve differences between parents and teachers or to solicit parental support about a child's behaviors, a teacher may ask the counselor to lead the conference, mediate differences, and facilitate decision-making to assist parents and teachers in reaching an agreeable solution. On such occasions, the teacher calls on the counselor's leadership abilities.

Parent-teacher conferences, particularly those that rely on the counselor's ability to mediate and facilitate solutions, can test a counselor's leadership skills as well as his or her professional relationships with parents and teachers. Counselors want to establish helpful relationships with both parents and teachers, but sometimes the support they give to one party causes them to lose favor with the other. Ideally, counselors remain neutral in these consulting roles and draw on the expertise of parents as leaders of the family and the knowledge of teachers as instructional experts in the school. The goal in these conferences is to have all these respective experts share their views, select common goals for the good of the child, and agree on reasonable strategies to reach these goals. These types of consultations test a school counselor's preparation in communication and helping skills. It is often difficult to satisfy all parties, particularly when they do not agree on clear alternatives.

Administrative Conferences.   Another situation in which school counselors use their consulting skills is when principals and other administrators seek information about problems they are having with particular students or difficulties they observe in the school as a whole. School principals are charged with managing all aspects of the educational and extracurricular programs. This is an awesome responsibility and most principals rely on specialists, such as school counselors, to provide accurate information and use specialized training to assist with problems.

Effective counselors meet with their principals on a regular basis to report the progress of their counseling program and inform the principal about significant events that affect the school. In these conferences, counselors keep administrators up-to-date about responsive services and critical issues they are handling in the program. Although confidentiality cannot be broken in these conferences with principals, counselors can share general information about their concerns regarding situations in the school. For example, a senior high counselor who has seen a sudden rise in referrals for substance abuse may not be able to give the names of students receiving counseling but could alert the principal about the increased use of drugs and alcohol by students in general. In this way, administrators, teachers, and counselors can place themselves in a position to plan preventive services in the school, solicit community support, and involve parents as necessary in assisting students in need.

Communication between administrators and counselors is essential to provide appropriate and comprehensive services in schools. Such cooperation allows for respect and acceptance of professional roles and builds a level of trust with which the judgment of counselors and the leadership of principals is balanced to meet the needs of students. When school counselors fail to achieve this level of cooperation and trust, they become limited in the services they offer to students, parents, and teachers.

Student Services Team Conferences. Many authors of articles and books on counseling advocate a team approach for coordinating student services in schools (Gysbers & Henderson, 2000; Humes & Hohenshil, 1987; Schmidt, 2004; Stone & Dahir, 2006). Team approaches use various titles that include student services team, pupil personnel team, child study team, and others. Although these names may differ, their purposes and goals are similar. Generally, these teams include the school counselor, a psychologist, a social worker, a nurse, an administrator, and teachers. Special education teachers are usually represented. Occasionally, these teams include professionals from agencies outside the school, such as mental-health counselors, case workers from social services, and pediatricians from medical centers. Involvement of these professionals widens the range of expertise on the team and opens more options and alternatives to help with student development.

The main purpose of student services teams is to follow cases of children and adolescents who are experiencing particular learning and behavioral difficulties. The teams coordinate services and see that each student receives adequate attention to meet his or her needs. Sometimes, teams include agency representatives to coordinate services between the school and community. In the most difficult cases, coordination is essential if students are to receive beneficial, comprehensive services.

Because school counselors usually serve individual schools, they are a logical choice to lead student services teams. They apply consulting skills to coordinate the services of these professional groups, resolve differences of opinion, and ensure that students' needs are being met by the school and community. Making sure that services are provided in a timely fashion and smoothing differences among professionals whose areas of expertise often overlap is indeed a challenge. For this reason, mediation, negotiation, and facilitation are among the consulting skills required by school counselors in these leadership roles.

Other School Services

In addition to establishing consulting relationships to disseminate information, give instruction, and facilitate conferences, school counselors assist schools in planning schoolwide activities for the benefit of students, parents, and teachers. The following sections illustrate ways that school counselors assume a leadership role in advocating on behalf of all students. Such advocacy seeks to improve the curriculum, provide appropriate services for students, ensure a safe and inclusive school environment, and create services to meet the needs of all students. These activities help schools focus on the development of all students and foster awareness of the factors that influence students' welfare. The ability to maintain a wide-angle focus on students' development is the hallmark of an effective school counseling program and, correspondingly, a successful school.

Many factors contribute to successful schools. As Purkey and Schmidt (1996) noted, everything counts; every program planned, every policy drafted, every process implemented makes some difference, positive or negative, to someone in the school. To ensure that school programs, policies, and processes contribute in positive ways to the development of people, counselors help plan appropriate services and activities. This begins with the guidance curriculum.

Guidance Curriculum. Guidance is the responsibility of everyone in the school and is best implemented when integrated as an essential part of the curriculum. Guidance does not occur at a single moment or as a solitary event when a teacher says, "Students, put your books away; it is time for guidance!" Rather, it is infused with all subjects and in all daily instruction. For this infusion to happen successfully, teachers and counselors plan appropriate activities for classroom instruction.

In elementary and middle schools where teachers join in teams by grade levels or subject areas to plan instructional programs, counselors consult with these groups to share guidance objectives and offer suggestions of activities to use in classroom instruction. In high schools, counselors meet with departments to achieve a similar purpose. This process of planning together allows teachers to use counselors as resources while maintaining their leadership role in the instructional program. These consultations also allow counselors and teachers to share information about particular students who are struggling and in need of additional services beyond classroom guidance.

Individual Student Planning.   Adequate responsive services for students do not occur by accident. They require conscious and careful planning. Likewise, students do not achieve educational career goals without finding a direction and choosing methods to reach their objectives. School counselors help meet individual student needs and assist all students in selecting goals and strategies that will satisfy their aspirations.

As noted, a guidance curriculum provides developmental and preventive activities for all students in the school. This is the primary reason why counselors and teachers integrate guidance into classroom lessons. However, some students struggle with serious concerns that demand attention beyond participation in affective education programs. These students need more intense preventive and remedial services. To select and schedule these types of services for students, counselors consult with teachers and parents so that appropriate plans are made.

In exceptional children's programs, schools develop individual education plans (IEPs) for all identified students. Planning by counselors, teachers, and parents who develop these IEPs is essential in providing appropriate services. The same type of preparation is needed for students who do not qualify for special education services but who nonetheless are failing in school. These students also need special attention and individual plans.

Students who do not have exceptional needs and do not require intensive interventions also consult with counselors to review their educational and career goals. Contacts made by students with their counselors, particularly in middle and high schools, are for the purpose of gathering information and making plans for the future. Sometimes these consultations between counselors and students are brief, single sessions. Other times they may last for several meetings. These sessions are consulting rather than counseling relationships because their emphasis is on sharing information and making plans for the future. In addition, they usually do not reveal any underlying emotional or personal problems that need to be addressed by the student and counselor.

Special Events and Projects.   Many events in elementary, middle, and high schools supplement instructional programs during the year. Counselors become involved in planning some of these events so that they are available to all students and the programs incorporate objectives that parallel broader school goals. Counselors who plan events such as "Substance Abuse Awareness Week," "Good Citizen of the Month Award," and "Special Olympics" illustrate their commitment to the entire school and all student development.

Special events and projects that require planning and consulting on the part of school counselors include teacher-advisor programs, testing services, peer helper programs, and many others included in a comprehensive school counseling program. These programs and services require a high degree of coordination for counselors to be successful in schools. Coordinating is another important service of a comprehensive school counseling program.

Coordinating

By now, it is probably clear that a comprehensive school counseling program consists of a variety of services and activities, some of which counselors provide directly to students, parents, and teachers and others that indirectly affect the welfare of students. Counselors deliver many of these services and have responsibility for coordinating a number of other activities that benefit students and schools. In this section, we examine some essential coordinating activities used by most professional counselors in schools. These activities are not the only ones that counselors use, but they offer a sample of responsibilities assumed and directed by counselors to help schools use appropriate and accurate data, follow through on responsive services, and plan a schoolwide focus for student development.

Data Collection and Sharing

Education begins with the process of determining what students already know so that schools can design appropriate curricula and instruction to enhance and build on existing knowledge. In addition, the design of appropriate curricula and instruction depends on many students' characteristics, including their abilities and learning styles. Throughout students' educational careers, schools gather information to help teachers make accurate decisions about programs and processes related to learning. School counselors are trained in testing and measurement and are available to assist teachers in collecting data to make these important decisions.

One major area of data collection in which schools have become involved in recent years is testing. Most schools, elementary through high school, use standardized tests to assess students' abilities and evaluate students' achievement at the end of the school year. School counselors traditionally have had responsibility for organizing, scheduling, and monitoring the administration of these types of group tests. These responsibilities constitute, in part, the function known as student appraisal, which we examine at the end of this chapter and in more detail in Chapter 9. For now, we consider how the uses of tests, inventories, and other measurement procedures are coordinated in comprehensive school counseling programs.

Test Administration. There are several types of tests and assessments used with students. Tests are generally used to determine students' aptitude and achievement in school. Schools administer aptitude tests at different times during the year depending on how they plan to use the results. For example, if test data will help teachers place children into appropriate instructional programs for the coming school year, the school will administer tests during the spring semester so that scores will be available at the start of the next school year. Typically, schools administer achievement tests toward the end of the year, so that teachers can evaluate the progress of students and share these results with students and parents.

U.S. public schools under the federal dictate of the No Child Left Behind Act (U.S. Department of Education, 2002) have stressed testing results as a measure of a school's performance. This emphasis on "high stakes" testing has placed significant pressure on teachers and administrators to increase student achievement. While this is an admirable goal, NCLB has had its share of critics and its impact on classroom instruction and student achievement nationwide is yet to be determined. For counselors in schools, the challenge has been to help students and parents deal with the realities of testing while supporting their teaching colleagues and administrators in meeting the demands of government and society.

Counselors also administer individual tests and other assessment instruments if the need for information exists. For example, a student new to a school may need to take an achievement test if recent data are not received from the transferring school. Such assessment helps teachers place the student in an appropriate course of study so that valuable instructional time is not wasted.

School counselors often have responsibility for ensuring the proper administration of tests in accordance with standardized instructions. With individual tests, it is the counselor's responsibility to choose appropriate instruments for which he or she is adequately trained and to administer these assessments according to proper procedures. With group testing programs, counselors often assist their schools in coordinating materials, training teachers and test monitors, and scheduling administration of the examinations. In large schools that test students frequently, such coordination is a tremendous responsibility, and sometimes it interferes with other functions of the counseling program. When this happens, counselors rely on teachers' assistance, clerical aides, and parent volunteers to help coordinate materials, monitor test administrations, and schedule makeup examinations. In schools where coordination of the testing program is a major administrative and clerical task, teachers, administrators, and counselors might form a testing committee to assign different responsibilities for various tasks. Or, the school might employ a testing coordinator for the primary purpose of providing administrative services for the testing program. By using alternative methods, coordination of testing is accomplished without interfering with other important services of the program.

Test results are useful only if obtained under the proper circumstances. Therefore, test materials must be secured before and after test administration, students should be properly prepared and ready for the test that is selected, teachers must be familiar with instructions for administering the test, and a proper environment should be created to give students an opportunity to achieve optimal results. When these conditions are satisfied and valid tests are used, schools can be comfortable with the reliability of students' results.

Test Results.   After tests have been administered and scored, the data need to be used for the purposes intended. Appropriate distribution and utilization of test data require adequate coordination. Again, counselors who are trained in testing and measurement have the background to help students, parents, and teachers understand test data and, consequently, to use these results in making educational and career decisions. In addition, counselors assist administrators in understanding the schoolwide results and accurately reporting these outcomes to the school system and local media.

Tests can be useful in diagnosing and assessing student progress, or they can become diabolical tools of the misinformed. School counselors who coordinate the use of test results have an obligation to help schools convey an accurate picture of their instructional program's strengths and weaknesses. At the same time, they must protect individuals from interpretations that lump all students into a single category based on norm-referenced data. For example, when test summaries indicate that the average student's score is below the mean, public reports should also show the range of scores, including the percentage of students above and below the mean. By reporting results in this manner, schools present a clear picture of how the total student population performed on the test. Reporting mean scores alone shows only a single dimension.

The most important role counselors have in coordinating test reports is the use of these data with students, parents, and teachers. Students in elementary, middle, and high schools can gain understanding of themselves by learning about their performance on tests and interest inventories. Of course, the explanations they receive must be developmentally appropriate for them to comprehend, and counselors at all school levels should convey these explanations accurately. Parents also need to know how their children perform on educational tests. With accurate knowledge, they can help children learn about areas of strength and weakness, and they can better guide children in educational and career choices.

Teachers are equally important in the processes of using and interpreting standardized tests and inventories. Tests and other measurement techniques play a vital role in helping teachers plan effective instruction and choose appropriate materials for students. The recent school reform movement in the United States has placed additional emphasis on student assessment and the relationship between teaching effectiveness and student performance. School counselors have the knowledge and training to assist teachers in selecting appropriate evaluative processes and instruments and in using the data collected to improve instruction and student learning.

Chapter 9 presents specific examples of how school counselors help teachers select tests and use results to improve instructional programs. The major point to be made here is that counselors are knowledgeable of testing and measurement techniques, and they use this training not only to administer tests and inventories but also to coordinate the appropriate use of data from these assessment instruments. Such coordination includes planning ways to disseminate accurate information and following up to ensure that the information is used appropriately. As examples, school counselors discuss test results with individual teachers in conferences about specific students and entire classes. They also present in-service workshops to help teachers use test data to identify instructional strengths and weaknesses and in planning adjustments to the curriculum.

Data collected about students usually are filed in cumulative folders. These folders are stored in a central file room in the school to which appropriate personnel have access. Decisions about the use of students' records relate to another area of program coordination for which counselors often have responsibility.

Students' Records.   In most school systems, students' records begin when children enter school for the first time and follow each child through his or her school career. Decisions about what information should be placed in students' cumulative folders are guided by local policies, state regulations, and federal laws. A major guide for schools is the Family Educational Rights and Privacy Act passed by Congress in 1974. This bill, commonly called the Buckley Amendment or FERPA, gives parents of minor students the right to review all school records about their children. After this law was passed, school counselors were encouraged to examine all students' records and avoid misinterpretations by including only information that could be clearly understood by laypersons. Further, recommendations were made to remove material from students' records that potentially violated a student's right to privacy (Getson & Schweid, 1976).

Since passage of this act, schools have become more careful and sensitive about the types of information placed in students' folders. They have also implemented procedures for use when students, parents, school personnel, and officials outside the school request and use information about students. These procedures include policies about who has legal access to students' folders, waivers regarding letters of recommendations written on behalf of students, and permissions required of officials outside the school to access students' records.

Because of their involvement with testing and confidential information, school counselors historically have had a role in coordinating and managing students' records. FERPA focused attention on the need to have clear guidelines for and careful coordination of record-keeping procedures. As a result, while all school counselors may not have primary responsibility for managing and recording data in students' folders, they help the school staff, especially secretaries and clerical assistants, to know about appropriate procedures and legal guidelines. Counselors also advise administrators and teachers about the proper use of students' records. In this way, school counselors act as gatekeepers, coordinating the data that go in and out of students' files and thereby ensuring the rights and privacy of students and parents. To assist counselors in this task, it is preferable that schools assign secretarial staff to the counseling program. Having responsible staff to handle school records ensures their proper use.

Information gathered by schools is also helpful to other agencies that provide services to students and families. Sometimes school counselors and teachers share information about students with community agencies or physicians, psychologists, and counselors in private practice. This process of sharing information brings us to another area of coordination: referrals and follow-up of students who benefit from additional services beyond the school counseling program.

Referrals and Follow-Up

Occasionally, a social, psychological, financial, or other factor hinders a student's progress in school and the school cannot address these obstacles adequately without assistance from others. In such cases, counselors and teachers search for appropriate services in the community to assist students and their families. School counselors are the logical choice among school staff members to coordinate these referrals and follow up in cases of students and families who are being served by outside agencies. Counselors are familiar with the breadth of community services, they design assessment techniques to gather initial data for referrals, and, as members of a helping profession, they establish effective communication with service providers outside the school.

By having counselors coordinate referrals and follow-up activities, schools avoid duplication of effort. This kind of coordination results in more efficient referral processes and subsequently more cooperative relationships with agency personnel in the community. For example, mental-health counselors, social workers, clinical psychologists, pediatricians, and other professionals appreciate communication with one referral source rather than with a large number of teachers from the same school. Counselors who coordinate referrals for their schools can establish consistent procedures that conform to the needs and requirements of particular agencies. At the same time, feedback from these resources can be channeled through the school counselor, who in turn gives accurate reports to teachers and other appropriate personnel.

In coordinating referrals, school counselors typically deal with two primary resources—community agencies and private practitioners. The following sections offer brief descriptions of common referrals made to public agencies, private institutions, and practitioners.

Community Agencies.   In most communities in the United States, several public and private agencies offer services to children, adolescents, and families. School counselors, as coordinators of referrals, attempt to gather current information about these resources so that students, parents, and teachers can make the best decisions about services outside the school. Usually, the number and level of services in a community are related to the size of the population, the tax base to support these services, and the demand of the citizenry to have these services. In poor rural communities, the desire and need for these services are sadly outweighed by a lack of financial resources. In these cases, school counselors may be the only human service available (Sutton & Southworth, 1990).

Typically, schools look for community health services, social services, mental-health and substance-abuse services, residential treatment centers for severe emotional or behavioral problems, recreational programs, and centers that offer educational opportunities to students and parents. In most instances, health programs, social services, and mental-health clinics are provided through county and state departments established and financed with public funds. Because of their public affiliation, these agencies have interagency relationships that, when coordinated properly, facilitate the location and delivery of services to people in the community. School counselors frequently refer students and families to these agencies for evaluation purposes and for more intense counseling and treatment than schools are able to provide.

Recreational programs such as boys and girls clubs, scouts, and camps are also sought by schools to provide additional creative and social outlets for students. School counselors coordinate referrals to these types of organizations by having current literature and applications available to students and parents. Students benefit from involvement in a wide range of recreational and civic activities, and school counselors are one source of information concerning these opportunities.

Churches, synagogues, mosques, colleges, universities, and similar institutions offer other resources for referrals. Students and parents sometimes seek additional educational opportunities to support and enrich the learning process. School counselors invite these institutions to send materials for distribution to students and parents. Usually, this kind of information is offered to students and parents without endorsement from the school. Nevertheless, counselors and other school personnel who distribute this information to students and parents for consideration should be familiar with the programs and services being offered. This is especially true when counselors give information about private organizations and professionals in the community.

Private Practitioners.   In addition to public agencies and programs, most communities have private practitioners and institutions that offer educational, psychological, recreational, and other services for children and families. Counselors in schools coordinate referrals to private resources in the same way that they work with public agencies. Examples of these resources include private residential treatment centers and hospitals; psychiatrists, counselors, clinical social workers, and psychologists in private practice; and educational centers that assist students who have learning problems, want to improve test-taking skills, or desire enrichment activities.

The role of the counselor in coordinating referrals and following up with public and private agencies and practitioners in the community assists the school and the family in locating resources and providing services to enhance student learning and development. Comprehensive school counseling programs offer a wide range of services to meet this goal. By coordinating referrals for additional services beyond their school program, counselors increase the probability that all students will reach their educational goals. At the same time, counselors within the school strive to include all students and encourage development for everyone.

Schoolwide Events

Coordinating the activities of a school counseling program includes planning, organizing, implementing, and evaluating schoolwide events that focus on developmental issues. These activities are either part of ongoing programs in the school or they are special events planned to address particular developmental needs of students. School counselors take an active role in coordinating these events with teachers and other school personnel who share responsibilities for planning and implementing schoolwide activities. The advisory committee of a school counseling program is often the group that initiates plans for these special events.

Countless examples of schoolwide events and programs are found in today's schools. In some instances, teachers plan and create these events, such as a field day, and other times they are sponsored by organizations, such as a beautification project planned by the parent-teacher association (PTA). The following ideas are a few schoolwide events and programs for which counselors might assume some responsibility. These events and programs are examples of how counselors coordinate activities that target developmental goals for all students.

Student Recognition Activities.   Schools consist of diverse student populations in which every child and adolescent chooses his or her individual educational, social, and career goals. Schools are active places with many students achieving and moving toward higher levels of performance. With all this activity, it is sometimes possible to forget particular students who may not excel and therefore do not receive recognition for their accomplishments. Because school counselors and teachers are sensitive to the needs of all students, they create an atmosphere where everyone can succeed and be recognized for their achievements.

Activities that recognize students include a variety of schoolwide events from award ceremonies to bulletin boards giving students multiple opportunities to let their peers know who they are and how they have been successful. Counselors assist with these recognition processes by helping teachers design events and activities for a broad range of objectives related to students' development. In this way, a wide spectrum of students in academic, athletic, drama, art, music, and other ventures receive appropriate recognition for their accomplishments and contributions to the school and community. Through these activities, individual pupils are invited to be an integral part of the school and the student body. By coordinating these kinds of events and programs, counselors and teachers encourage students to participate in the school and create a healthy environment for optimal learning.

Career Awareness Programs.   Career development is an essential goal of education and begins formally when students enter school for the first time. Excellent instruction includes a philosophy about how learning connects with career development and vocational choices throughout the lifespan. In elementary through senior high school, counselors assist with this goal through the counseling and consulting services they provide to students and parents and by coordinating schoolwide events.

Students achieve career awareness as a result of learning activities that are cooperatively planned by teachers and counselors. Classroom guidance lessons, integrated with daily instruction to highlight special types of careers, are one example. As an illustration, imagine that a middle school wants its science classes to focus on health occupations and how the study of science relates to these career choices. To assist with this effort, counselors in this middle school help teachers plan and implement this guidance approach by locating appropriate resources, scheduling health professionals as guest lecturers, and presenting lessons with teachers in the science classes.

In secondary schools, counselors coordinate job fairs, college days, and similar events to help students survey the range of occupational opportunities available and review the educational requirements of various tracks. The time required to plan these types of events is usually substantial, so counselors seek assistance from student organizations, teacher committees, parent volunteers, and the advisory committee of the school counseling program. The success of these types of programs has a positive effect on student development as well as on school-community relationships. Therefore, planning and coordination are essential. Businesses, colleges, and universities that participate in well-planned, schoolwide events form positive perceptions about both the school and the counseling program, and they carry these perceptions into the community. This evaluation process is invaluable in helping the school create an accurate image and enabling the school counseling program to gain broad support.

Teacher-Advisor Programs.   In most schools, the student-counselor ratio is quite high, particularly in elementary and middle schools where counselors frequently serve as many as 1,000 students or more. To assist with advising of students, counselors train teachers in basic communication skills and assign them students as advisees (Gallassi & Gulledge, 1997; Myrick & Myrick, 1990). In teacher-advisor programs, teachers are assigned students whom they advise about educational planning and assist with school progress. In some programs, teachers advise students as these pupils matriculate through all the grades. For example, a high school teacher might be assigned the same group to advise each year as students move through the ninth, tenth, eleventh, and twelfth grades. By designing programs in this way, teachers develop stronger relationships with the students assigned to them.

In teacher-advisor programs, teachers schedule time to confer with individual advisees and to meet with their entire group of advisees on a regular basis. Individual conferences allow students and teachers the opportunity to review academic progress and discuss concerns that may impede growth and development. When teachers believe students need additional help, they refer students to the school counselor. This is also true when teachers present guidance activities to groups of advisees and determine that particular students need more direct counseling services.

Coordinating teacher-advisor programs requires a process for assigning students, designing a schedule for teachers and students to meet, and training teachers in skills to facilitate relationships with their advisees. In addition, school counselors offer resources and topics to help teachers choose guidance activities for their advisee groups. In this way, teacher-advisor programs become avenues by which developmental guidance is integrated with instructional goals and objectives.

Training is a key ingredient of successful advising programs. Teachers who possess adequate communication and facilitation skills and understand the essential characteristics of effective helpers have the potential to provide excellent assistance to students. They also form an important referral network with school counselors to ensure that all students receive appropriate services in the school and from community agencies.

Peer Helper Programs.   Another service that school counselors organize and coordinate to reach a wide audience of students is called a Peer Helper Program (Campbell, 2000; Myrick, 2003). In this program, students are selected and trained to perform various helping functions, such as assisting teachers with classroom guidance activities, tutoring students who need assistance, showing new students around the school, and listening to peers who have concerns. By offering these activities through peer helpers, counselors expand their programs, bringing services directly to students and thereby reaching a wider audience. In addition, peer helpers, like teacher-advisors, form a communications network to help counselors receive referrals of students who have serious concerns or have difficulty overcoming barriers to learning.

Coordinating peer helper programs takes time. It is necessary to train participating students in communication skills and referral procedures. It also requires a clear description and understanding of the role each peer helper will play in the program. Some counselors schedule regular sessions with the peer helpers for supervision and skill building. In high schools, counselors sometimes integrate peer helper selection and training into the curriculum through a psychology or other human services course. In these instances, school counselors team-teach peer helper courses with classroom teachers, and students receive high school credit for their training and participation in these programs. In other high schools, peer helpers present college preparatory seminars or work with dropout prevention programs.

The preceding examples illustrate activities that help counselors and teachers reach a higher percentage of students. Through special events, such as "career night" and other student awareness programs, information can be distributed widely. By the same token, student advising by teachers and peer helper programs allows school counseling services to extend beyond the counseling center, using teachers and students as additional resources to assist a greater number of students in the school.

To determine which students need what services, counselors evaluate the needs, characteristics, and factors affecting students' development. Assessment of these elements includes evaluation processes that encompass the fourth responsive service of comprehensive school counseling programs—appraising.

Appraising

Since the beginning of the school counseling profession, counselors have used appraisal instruments and assessment processes to measure students' needs, interests, intellectual functions, and academic performance. Today's school counselors continue to coordinate the assessment of students' characteristics and school progress in a variety of ways. In addition, counselors and other student services professionals are concerned with the influence of environmental factors on students' development. Chapter 9 explores specific methods and instruments used in student appraisal. By way of introduction, the following sections briefly describe student assessment and environmental evaluation processes used by counselors in schools.

Student Evaluation

School counselors use many assessment processes to help students, parents, and teachers gather accurate data and make sound decisions about educational programs, instructional placements, career directions, and a host of other issues. These evaluations include the use of standardized tests, interest inventories, behavior rating scales, and nonstandardized procedures such as observations and interviews. Tests are among the most common instruments used by school counselors.

Tests. Evaluation through standardized testing is and will continue to be an important service of school counseling programs. In part, this is due to the mobility of U.S. society and the transfer of students from school to school during their educational careers. Sometimes new students arrive at schools with little information and few records about their educational progress. At these times, counselors can help teachers determine appropriate instructional placement by administering individual achievement and aptitude tests. A current measurement of students' abilities and academic achievement assists teachers in placing students at the proper instructional levels and in designing beneficial learning experiences. Without this assessment, teachers can only estimate students' levels and might misplace them in an instructional program. One caveat is necessary here: The selection of appropriate assessment instruments to avoid cultural biases and other factors leading to inaccurate results is imperative.

Expanded services for students who have special educational needs, aided by Public Law 94-142 (see Chapter 2), have increased the demand for individual assessment of students to identify strengths and weaknesses in learning styles and intellectual functions. Sometimes, school counselors begin this assessment process by assisting special education teachers with screening procedures. These procedures include the use of behavior rating scales, short-form ability tests, and achievement batteries. Results of these screening procedures help teachers decide if a complete educational and psychological profile is required to determine appropriate services and placement. If so, the school initiates a referral to the school psychologist or another evaluator.

Inventories. School counselors use a variety of questionnaires and inventories to assist students with their educational and career decisions. In addition, some inventories are designed to help students learn about personal and social characteristics that enhance or inhibit their relationships with others. Interest inventories have the potential for many applications, including helping students learn about interests they did not know they had and contrasting their expressed interests with their assessed abilities.

Selection of inventories depends on the purpose of the assessment and the training of the counselor for using and interpreting these instruments. Because some of these inventories are founded on particular psychological theories, a counselor's theoretical training is an additional factor to consider when selecting these types of inventories.

Assessment of students does not always require standardized tests or inventories. School counselors and teachers often gather valuable information through observations, interviews, and other nonstandardized procedures. These procedures are an important part of the overall assessment process.

Observations and Interviews.   School counselors frequently receive referrals from teachers and parents about particular behaviors exhibited by students at home or in school. The first step the counselor takes after receiving a referral is to gather data to decide who needs what. To determine what services best address the identified concern, counselors use direct observations and interviews to gather relevant data. For example, when a teacher refers a student because of inattentive classroom behaviors, a first step the counselor takes is to observe the student during class while instruction is taking place. Occasionally, counselors will recommend behavioral rating scales for teachers or parents to complete. These rating scales might be developed by the counselor or selected from published sources. In either instance, the findings from these rating scales supplement the observations made by counselors, teachers, and parents. By using these processes, counselors are better able to recommend appropriate services, which could include direct counseling with the student, classroom management techniques for the teacher, or home strategies for parents to encourage appropriate behavior at school.

In addition to rating scales and observations, counselors interview teachers, parents, and students as part of the evaluation process. Structured interviews ask specific questions and focus on particular information. Through these interviews, counselors are able to compare the perceptions of teachers, parents, and students regarding problems. These perceptual differences must be sorted out and explicated if progress is to be made. Students' records provide an added source of information about past events and academic progress that assist in evaluation and decision-making processes. These records also contain information collected in group assessment procedures that enable counselors and teachers to learn more about individual students and how they compare with other students in the school.

Group Assessment.   Schools use group standardized tests to measure the academic ability and progress of students. The two major types of group tests used in measuring student achievement are criterion-referenced and norm-referenced instruments. Criterion-referenced tests measure students' performance in relation to identified criteria or dimensions, such as spelling proficiency. By contrast, norm-referenced exams generate scores that compare students and rank them against one another by using scores derived from sample reference groups. These reference groups are called "normed populations." In schools, the norms are usually established by grade levels or age levels. In other words, students assessed by norm-referenced tests are compared with other students in the same grade level or age range. These types of standardized tests are described in detail in Chapter 9.

Both criterion-referenced and norm-referenced instruments have value in helping counselors and teachers make decisions on behalf of students. At times, decisions need to be made based on performance of a particular skill, and other times schools need to know how students compare with others in their age or grade level. Knowing what kind of information is needed guides the counselor in deciding which type of assessment to use. Some school counselors and teachers also apply sociometric techniques in assessing students' roles and relationships in groups (Gibson & Mitchell, 1999). Basically, these techniques are used to evaluate the acceptance of students in the social structure of their peer groups, such as in classrooms. Additional information about sociometric techniques is presented in Chapter 9.

Environmental Evaluation

A third area of appraising centers on environmental factors that influence students' development and learning. These factors include the school atmosphere, classroom environment, peer groups, and home environment. Gathering data to help students, parents, and teachers make appropriate plans and decisions is incomplete without an evaluation of the environments and social groups that affect student development. An examination of school climate is a logical place to begin this area of assessment.

Assessment of School Climate.   As noted in an earlier chapter, schools might avoid many problems if they adequately assess places, policies, programs, and processes and use this information to create beneficial conditions for optimal learning (Purkey & Schmidt, 1996). In determining which services to provide for students, parents, and teachers, counselors save precious time if they first look at the physical environment of the school, the policies that govern the school, procedures and processes for administering school regulations, and programs established for student learning and development. Part of a counselor's role in the appraisal process is to help the school assess itself.

By creating appraisal processes to help teachers and administrators assess school environments, counselors gather data with which to plan efficient and effective services. Form 5.2 is a sample questionnaire used with middle-graders to help evaluate school climate. Results of surveys such as this one give teachers a way of assessing students' perceptions about the school and its programs. Altering negative aspects of a school and its programs is the first step in creating healthy environments and encouraging students to learn.

Assessment of Families.   The best school environment may not help students who struggle because of deprivation, neglect, or abuse at home. By assessing home environments and family functioning, counselors determine the level of support a child or adolescent is receiving from his or her family structure and use this information to seek appropriate community services.

The processes used to assess home environments and family functioning include interviews, observations, and students' records. For example, home visits enable counselors and teachers to examine the physical and social surroundings in which students live. Golden's "Quick Assessment of Family Functioning" (1988) uses a structured interview approach to assess five criteria: parental resources, chronicity of the problem, family communication, parental authority, and rapport with professional helpers. Assessment of these criteria permits counselors to distinguish between functional and dysfunctional families and, thereby, make appropriate decisions about school services and referrals to outside agencies.

Peer Group Assessment.   A final aspect of environmental evaluation that contributes to the overall appraisal of students is the assessment of social peer groups. Many of the methods already discussed are useful for assessing peer relationships. In particular, structured interviews and observations are viable assessment techniques.

FORM 5.2   *School Climate Assessment*

Students: Please circle your responses to the following statements and return this form to the counselor's mailbox in the school office. Your answers will help us in evaluating our school. Thank you.

1. Is the school building neat and clean?	YES	NO	SOMETIMES
2. Is the cafeteria food good?	YES	NO	SOMETIMES
3. Do you enjoy being in your classroom?	YES	NO	SOMETIMES
4. Are the restrooms clean and supplied with soap, paper towels, and tissues?	YES	NO	SOMETIMES
5. Is the playground safe and well-equipped?	YES	NO	SOMETIMES
6. Does the air smell fresh inside and outside?	YES	NO	SOMETIMES
7. Are windows and doors in good working order?	YES	NO	SOMETIMES
8. Are people friendly in your school?	YES	NO	SOMETIMES
9. Do your teachers listen to you?	YES	NO	SOMETIMES
10. Are the school rules fair to everyone?	YES	NO	SOMETIMES
11. Do the teachers have enough supplies for all students in your class?	YES	NO	SOMETIMES
12. Is the equipment working in your school?	YES	NO	SOMETIMES
13. Do volunteers help in your school?	YES	NO	SOMETIMES
14. Is the counselor a good person to ask for help?	YES	NO	SOMETIMES
15. Are you learning in your classroom?	YES	NO	SOMETIMES
16. Are boys and girls treated the same?	YES	NO	SOMETIMES
17. Is the media center in your school a good place to find things?	YES	NO	SOMETIMES
18. Do students usually follow the rules in school?	YES	NO	SOMETIMES

Having students take stock of their friendships and peer associations adds to their overall self-awareness and contributes to their total profile. When students assess the behaviors, goals, and attitudes of their peers, they also examine and question their own traits, objectives, and beliefs. Part of the helping process is to confront the discrepancy that appears between how a person is and how the person wants to be. Students who want to be successful in their school performance and social relationships can benefit by examining their peers who are most important to them and by determining the contradictions between the way they want to be and the way their peer groups are. A first step in making changes in one's life is to give up traditions and associations that keep a person locked into, or engaged in, nonproductive and destructive behavior patterns.

Appraisal procedures create a diagnostic process by which counselors choose appropriate services for students, parents, and teachers. In this way, appraisal procedures interact with the other services of a comprehensive school counseling program. By using appropriate and accurate assessment instruments and procedures, counselors can determine which responsive services are most likely to generate successful outcomes.

In this chapter, we examined the four responsive services of a school counseling program: counseling, consulting, coordinating, and appraising. These four services form distinct categories that together identify a broad role for professional counselors in schools. The next chapter uses the structure about comprehensive programs presented earlier in Chapter 4 to show how school counselors design their individual programs around these comprehensive services.

Additional Readings

Hitchner, K., & Tifft-Hitchner, A. (1996). *Counseling Today's Secondary Students: Practical Strategies, Techniques and Materials for the School Counselor* (Englewood Cliffs, NJ: Prentice Hall).
A practical resource to help middle and high school counselors collaborate with teachers, administrators, parents, and the community in providing services to students.

Myrick, R. D., & Myrick, L. S. (1990). *The Teacher-Advisor Program: An Innovative Approach to School Guidance* (Ann Arbor, MI: ERIC/CAPS).
This monograph, published as one of a series on guidance and counseling programs, is an excellent resource for planning and implementing teacher-advisor programs. It consists of articles by contributing authors who have established successful teacher-advisor programs in their schools.

Thompson, C. L., Rudolph, L. B., & Henderson, D. (2004). *Counseling Children* (6th ed.) (Belmont, CA: Brooks/Cole-Thompson Learning).
An excellent guide for counseling children, the book offers a wealth of ideas and practices beyond direct counseling for school counselors. Specific problems and issues are presented and counseling approaches or other interventions are suggested.

Vernon, A. (Ed.) (2004). *Counseling Children and Adolescents* (3rd ed.) (Denver, CO: Love).
This book presents a developmental perspective on the range of counseling and therapeutic strategies available to school counselors. Chapter topics also include designing a developmental curriculum, working with parents, and working with families, for example.

Websites

Federal Student Aid Online
www.fafsa.ed.gov
National Child Protection Clearinghouse
www.aifs.gov.arc/nch
National Parent Information Network (NPIN)
www.feps.net/fcs/defaul.asp?prcitem=160
National Peer Helper Association
www.peerprograms.org

National School Safety Center
www.schoolsafety.us
Peer Resources
www.islandnet.com/~rcarr/helping.html
Teacher-Advisor Programs
www.linktolearning.com/tap.htm

Exercises

1. By yourself, brainstorm about factors that influence how much time school counselors choose to spend in a particular service area. List these factors and share them in class. In the class discussion, come to consensus about the three most influential factors. Which, if any, of these factors can be controlled by the counselor? Discuss what your findings mean to the role of a school counselor.

2. A curriculum supervisor in the school system reports to your principal that counselors should not see students in individual counseling for more than four sessions because to do so would be considered "therapy" and counselors are not therapists. Discuss in a small group how you would respond to this situation. Highlight the main points of your discussion with the class.

3. As a school counselor you might spend considerable time coordinating services for students. This could mean spending time on the telephone with agencies, meeting with parents, completing appropriate referral forms, and other functions that go unnoticed by your fellow teachers. Such "invisible" functioning risks criticism from teachers who might say, "I don't ever see the counselor and don't know what the counselor does." What are some active measures you could take as a counselor to keep your teaching colleagues informed about what you do regarding referrals?

4. Create a brochure or flier about a counseling program that illustrates or describes the responsive services provided. What factors are most important to consider as you design this brochure?

6

Program Development

Chapters 3, 4, and 5 described the role of school counselors, presented the components of comprehensive counseling programs, and summarized the responsive services that comprise comprehensive programs in school settings. Together, these chapters provide a philosophical foundation for the practice of professional counseling in contemporary schools. With this theoretical base, we now explore how school counselors actually set up a program of services.

This chapter offers some of the practical aspects of putting together a comprehensive program of counseling, consulting, and coordinating services in a school. These aspects are, of necessity, presented in a general nature, and are applicable across all levels—elementary through high school—of school counseling programs. They are not intended as a detailed description of how to design and develop a comprehensive program, but are an overview of procedures and processes school counselors use to create their programs of services. Readers who wish more specific and detailed suggestions for developing comprehensive counseling programs should consult references cited throughout this chapter and suggested readings at the end of the chapter.

In this chapter, we use the four phases of designing a comprehensive program presented in Chapter 3 as major headings—planning, organizing, implementing, and evaluating. Some of the practical considerations presented under each of these phases include assessing the current program, seeking input and support for change, assessing the needs of students as well as parents and teachers, determining resources, assigning responsibilities, marketing the program, scheduling services, balancing time, providing services, using technology, and evaluating outcomes. The last of these, dealing with program evaluation, is introduced for practical consideration here but is presented more thoroughly in Chapter 11.

Before considering the practical aspects of developing a comprehensive school counseling program, we must pause to recognize that many state and local initiatives in schools across the country influence the actual role of counselors. The educational reform movement begun in the 1980s continues to have an impact on state programs and local perspectives about what counselors should be doing in our schools. Indeed, in some communities school administrators and committees consisting of people other than professional counselors control the counselor's job description. For this reason, students who learn about comprehensive school counseling programs through this text and other notable works will need to apply these ideas within the context of the states and local school systems where they choose to work as counselors. With that caveat in mind, we now consider the phases of a comprehensive counseling program.

Planning

One of the first steps in planning a comprehensive counseling program is to determine what has existed in prior years. This is particularly important for a new counselor coming into a school situation where there has been a program of services. As noted in Chapter 3, Gysbers and Henderson (2000) encouraged counselors to establish an organized plan for moving an existing program forward. In many instances, however, new counselors find that although a counselor was at the school in past years, for all practical purposes there was no comprehensive program of services. In either case, Gysbers and Henderson's encouragement should be heeded—an organized plan for change is essential.

Assessing the Current Program

A first step in formulating this plan is to determine the breadth of services in past years. This means gathering data about what services were provided, how program decisions were made, what processes were used to evaluate services, and how people perceived the counseling program. As part of this assessment, Schmidt (2004) suggested that new counselors formulate questions for principals and teachers of the schools they are considering for employment. From the responses counselors receive to their questions, they could determine what changes to initiate in the overall program. Some sample questions to ask principals and teachers are as follows:

1. Is there an annual plan, with written goals and objectives, for the school counseling program?
2. Is there an advisory committee for the counseling program, and if so, how are the members selected?
3. What data are most important in generating goals and objectives for the program?
4. What service of the counselor was most helpful to students in past years? Most helpful to parents? Most helpful to teachers?
5. What are major needs of students that the counseling program must address?
6. Are classroom teachers actively involved in integrating developmental guidance into the curriculum and their daily instruction?
7. What has been the level of parental involvement in the school and the counseling program?
8. How adequate are the facilities of the counseling center in the school? What are the barriers to improving the facilities?
9. What service of the counseling program, if any, should be increased in the coming year? What service, if any, should be decreased?

In addition to asking the principal and teachers about their perceptions, counselors might use surveys and interviews with parents and students to provide useful information for examining the counseling program. The key element in this process is to gather as many perceptions as possible, so that decisions about changing aspects of the program are made with a broad vision. After the counselor is satisfied that crucial elements of the program have been identified for possible change, a next step is to involve people in the decision-making process.

Seeking Input and Support for Change

By definition, a comprehensive school counseling program is planned as part of an inclusive process. This means that the program does not belong to any single professional, nor is it the sole responsibility of the school counselor. By including as many people as possible in program planning, counselors are likely to have widespread support for their services.

The first person to include is the building principal. Understanding how the principal perceives counseling services in the school and learning that the principal may be willing to adopt new perceptions about program areas is important. Only through an honest exchange of views and ideas are counselors and principals able to establish working relationships through which they can make appropriate programmatic decisions. Once the counselor and principal agree on the key elements of a comprehensive program of services, the next step is to solicit input from teachers, parents, and students. One medium that can facilitate this exchange of information is an advisory committee.

An advisory committee of a school counseling program is a vehicle counselors use to obtain input from teachers, administrators, parents, and students about appropriate services and activities (Studer, 2005; VanZandt & Hayslip, 1994). An advisory committee might be appointed by the principal or selected by the counselor. In some schools, the advisory committee could be combined with other teacher committees, such as a child study committee or a student assistance team. Whatever its organization, the advisory committee assists the school counselor in designing needs assessment instruments, selecting annual goals and objectives, planning major school events to focus on student development, and determining program evaluation activities.

Counselors use a number of processes and systems for gathering information for program development. The advisory committee is supplemented by suggestions from school volunteers; ongoing evaluations by administrators and counseling supervisors; informal conversations with students; feedback from the school nurse, social worker, and psychologist; and ideas learned through involvement with professional associations. These avenues for receiving suggestions enable school counselors to focus on the major services expected for students, parents, and teachers.

Another reason school counselors seek suggestions from students, parents, and teachers is to supplement the findings of the needs assessment process. Typically, surveys of students, parents, and teachers discover some critical concerns and needs of students in the school. Although these critical concerns are imperative to address and often result in crisis-oriented goals, such goals do not begin to satisfy the developmental needs of a majority of the students. Preventive and developmental goals broaden the vision of a school counseling program. In this way, counselors do more than repair wounds, mend fences, and solve mysteries. Instead, they do all these things and, at the same time, create healthy school climates, enhance human relationships, and develop systems for students to strengthen their self-awareness, motivation, and responsibility.

For counselors to identify appropriate services for their programs, they must first have an understanding of the most important critical and developmental needs of students, parents, and teachers. One of the first functions of an advisory committee is to assist the counselor in designing needs assessment instruments and developing assessment procedures.

Assessing Students', Parents', and Teachers' Needs

In determining what goals and objectives to include in a comprehensive school counseling program, counselors first investigate the needs of the populations to be served. As noted earlier, these populations consist of students, parents, and teachers, whose needs will vary from school to school and from community to community. This variability depends on the size of the school, the socioeconomic status of the community and its cultural diversity, the concentration of learning problems found in the school, the educational backgrounds of parents, the community's attitudes toward the school and education, and the leadership of the school and district. Because each of these factors influences schools in unique and different ways, the needs of students, parents, and teachers have a similarly unique influence on the design and implementation of a school counseling program. For example, students and families who come from impoverished backgrounds express quite different needs from students and families of affluence. These differences are reflected in the school as a whole and in the development of a comprehensive counseling program. This is true in elementary, middle, and senior high schools.

As an illustration, elementary counselors in schools with students who require substantial attention to meet their basic needs for food and shelter often find themselves playing the dual role of crisis counselor and social worker. In these situations, the scope and breadth of the counseling program may not span the full spectrum of preventive, developmental, and remedial services advocated in this text. By nature of its school population, this counseling program has more of a remedial focus. Of course, a visionary counselor finds ways to include prevention and development in the program, and teachers in the classroom are agents who carry out this plan, even in schools where communities are affected by serious social and economic adversity. The rationale for such a comprehensive approach is founded in the belief that to remedy existing concerns without helping students learn about themselves and make sound educational choices is merely a Band-Aid solution to a larger social problem.

One way that counselors collect needs assessment data is through surveys with students, parents, and teachers. In large schools, counselors might take a random sample of students in each grade level to cut down on time and paper costs and to streamline the analysis of data. They may do the same with samples of parents. Usually, counselors seek needs assessments from all teachers in the school. Forms 6.1, 6.2, and 6.3 illustrate sample needs assessments to use with students, parents, and teachers.

As noted earlier, needs assessments can be done by using methods of data collection other than surveys. For example, counselors might interview students, parents, and teachers, or they might simply observe the school and community and draw conclusions from these observations. Counselors may also review students' records and other existing data banks, such as absentee rates and other methods of assessment. In comprehensive school counseling programs, counselors use a variety of methods and alter these approaches year

FORM 6.1   *Middle School Student Needs Assessment*

Instructions: Please read the following statements and circle Yes, No, or Sometimes, showing how each one applies to you.

1. I usually do well in school.	YES	NO	SOMETIMES
2. My teachers think I can do better school work.	YES	NO	SOMETIMES
3. I like coming to school.	YES	NO	SOMETIMES
4. I do not have any close friends.	YES	NO	SOMETIMES
5. I want to learn how to study better.	YES	NO	SOMETIMES
6. I am happy about my family life.	YES	NO	SOMETIMES
7. My parents (or guardians) listen to me when I have a problem.	YES	NO	SOMETIMES
8. I would like to talk to someone about a problem I have.	YES	NO	SOMETIMES
9. Most people like me the way I am.	YES	NO	SOMETIMES
10. I am lonely much of the time.	YES	NO	SOMETIMES
11. I want to learn more about jobs and careers.	YES	NO	SOMETIMES
12. I would like to join a group of other students to help them with problems.	YES	NO	SOMETIMES

FORM 6.2   *Elementary School Parent Needs Assessment*

Instructions: Please help us plan this year's school counseling program by completing the following questions. Circle your responses and return this form with your child who will give it to the teacher. Thank you for your assistance.

1. My child likes going to school most of the time.	YES	NO	UNSURE
2. My child has many friends at school.	YES	NO	UNSURE
3. The school is a warm and caring place to be.	YES	NO	UNSURE
4. My child needs special attention for learning.	YES	NO	UNSURE
5. My child is responsible at home and usually does what he/she is told.	YES	NO	UNSURE
6. I would like my child to be in a group with other children to learn about getting along together.	YES	NO	UNSURE
7. I am worried about my child's progress in school and would like to talk with someone about it.	YES	NO	UNSURE
8. I would like to join other parents in a group to talk about children and parenting skills.	YES	NO	UNSURE
9. My child has physical problems that the school should know about.	YES	NO	UNSURE
10. I want my child to see the school counselor.	YES	NO	UNSURE
11. I have some concerns to share with the school counselor.	YES	NO	UNSURE
12. I am available to volunteer at school if needed.	YES	NO	UNSURE

FORM 6.3   *High School Teacher Needs Assessment*

Instructions: Please help us plan the School Counseling Program this year by completing this form. Circle your responses and return the form to the school counselor's mailbox in the office. Thank you for your assistance.

1. I want my students to have access to group counseling this year.	YES	NO	UNSURE
2. I want students to receive more career information.	YES	NO	UNSURE
3. Students need lo learn better study skills.	YES	NO	UNSURE
4. Many of my students have concerns about substance and alcohol abuse.	YES	NO	UNSURE
5. We need to do more about pregnancy prevention this year.	YES	NO	UNSURE
6. I want to integrate guidance activities into my lessons this year.	YES	NO	UNSURE
7. I want to join a teacher support group this year.	YES	NO	UNSURE
8. I have students who seem quite depressed.	YES	NO	UNSURE
9. Some students need help handling problems without resorting to violence.	YES	NO	UNSURE
10. I have difficulty getting support from parents.	YES	NO	UNSURE
11. I need better communication skills with students.	YES	NO	UNSURE
12. I need help with class management skills.	YES	NO	UNSURE

after year to ensure an accurate assessment of their schools' needs. In some instances, counselors might use the results of their annual program evaluation as an assessment procedure.

Once the needs' assessment is complete, the school counselor determines available resources to suggest appropriate services for meeting selected goals. Determining available resources is another aspect of planning comprehensive counseling programs.

Determining Resources

Comprehensive school counseling programs cannot operate in isolation. For this reason, school counselors learn about the various resources and support services available in their schools, districts, and communities. When speaking of resources for a school counseling program, we usually refer to people as the primary resource. A comprehensive program also benefits from the materials, equipment, and space available to the counselor, but without adequate human support all these other elements may make little difference.

Successful school counselors are adept at learning about the talents of their teaching colleagues and are creative in soliciting support from other personnel. They recruit capable volunteers for the school, generate support from businesses and industries that donate money and materials to the program, use student helpers to network with their peers, and cooperate with other student services' team members, such as school nurses, social workers, and psychologists. In addition, successful counselors learn about the services and resources of the communities and states in which their schools reside. By knowing about health services, psychiatric treatment centers, family counseling clinics, recreational programs, and other resources, counselors create professional alliances that ultimately benefit students and families of the school. Without this knowledge, counselors run the risk of working in a vacuum and can become frustrated and overwhelmed by the level of need expressed by their students, parents, and teachers.

Comprehensive programs also consist of adequate materials, equipment, and space to do the job. Counselors measure the adequacy and appropriateness of materials according to the developmental needs of students in the school. Games, educational kits, films, recordings, catalogs, books, and a variety of other items are used by elementary, middle, and senior high counselors, depending on the scope of their programs. Equipment such as computers, modems, recorders, and telephones enable counselors and their support staff to provide efficient and effective services. Adequate space for private counseling, individually and in groups, is desirable. In Chapter 4, you saw the importance of location, design, materials, and equipment to a school counseling center.

To create programs that maintain a realistic vision, counselors assess school needs, interpret these data accurately, and determine what resources are available to provide the most effective and efficient services. Usually, counselors assess students', parents', and teachers' needs in the beginning of the school year and then develop year-long goals and objectives around these established needs. In most instances, counselors identify a few annual goals that remain consistent from year to year regardless of how the student population changes over time. These goals become an ongoing part of the program. For example, in most secondary schools, counselors are concerned with helping seniors make plans for postgraduation. Such plans might include employment, marriage, childrearing, military service, technical school, trade school, or college. Though populations might change over the years, and subsequently students' needs after high school may vary, the process of assisting them with plans for the future continues as an important service in every school counseling program. Other goals for the counseling program may vary from year to year. This is why needs assessment processes are important and can help schools set goals for the counseling program, which moves us to the next phase of comprehensive program development—organizing.

Organizing

Successful counseling programs tend to have several things in common, but most important among the key elements is that the services of counselors are organized as an integral and essential part of the broader school mission (Gysbers & Henderson, 2000). Therefore, in organizing their programs, counselors attempt to set goals that address the identified needs of students, parents, and teachers by integrating activities into the curriculum, providing adequate plans to meet the needs of individuals, selecting appropriate responsive services, such as counseling and consulting, and fostering support from the school system that provides sufficient resources and supervision for the program.

Setting Goals

In setting goals, the counselor summarizes data from surveys, interviews, observations, and other assessment processes and presents results to the advisory committee. At that

FIGURE 6.1   *Sample Planning Sheet for Aligning Needs Assessment with Program Goals*

Middle School Counseling Program

Students' Needs Based on the Seventh-Grade Survey	*Recommended Program Goals*
1. Want more information about abilities and interests (42%)	**1.** Plan small groups for all seventh-grade students to explore their educational and career interests and compare these interests with their performance in school.
2. Concerned about friendships (68%)	**2.** Develop friendship units and integrate with social studies lessons in the fall semester.
3. How to deal with feelings about family separation and divorce (37%)	**3.** Offer small group counseling to students whose families are experiencing change.
4. Need to develop better study skills (35%)	**4.** Develop a study skills unit for teachers to use in language arts block.
5. Have strong feelings of loneliness and am very sad (8%)	**5.** Identify and observe students who are isolates or appear depressed and offer individual counseling or referral services. School may also need to examine issues of cultural diversity.

presentation, the counselor interprets the results, solicits reactions from committee members, and together they determine major goals and objectives for the annual program. Figure 6.1 illustrates a sample planning sheet used by a middle school counselor to identify students' needs and recommend program goals to classroom teachers.

In Figure 6.1, some of the statements show a high percentage of responses indicating that many students expressed these concerns, thereby justifying them as program goals. As one example, item 2, "Concerned about friendships," shows 68 percent of the students shared this concern. At the same time, other items with much lower percentages are also identified as needs, and program goals are recommended. An example is item 5, "Have strong feelings of loneliness and am very sad," to which only 8 percent of the students responded affirmatively. Although this percentage is low in comparison to other items, the serious nature of this question justifies its focus as a student need. If 8 percent of the student population feels sad, lonely, and depressed, this should be a critical concern for teachers and counselors to address.

Some goals are set as a result of local and state mandates and standards that aim at providing equal services to all students. In some states, departments of education set specific learning goals and objectives as part of a guidance curriculum. School counselors and teachers cooperatively decide how and when these goals and objectives will be met in each school's instructional program. All these goals, those set as a result of students' needs assessments and those mandated by the state, become part of a school plan to meet the developmental needs of students. Related to this school plan is the counselor's annual plan of goals, objectives, and services to be provided during the year. Two categories of goals useful in establishing comprehensive services are learning-related goals and service-related goals.

Learning-Related Goals.   School counselors review the data gathered from needs assessments with students, parents, and teachers, and relate these findings to their observations and to the observations of administrators and members of the advisory committee. In some cases, the selected goals relate directly to an identified need. For example, if a high school survey finds that students need to associate their educational success with future career satisfaction, a goal might be *to increase student awareness of the significant correlation between educational achievement and career development.* Such a goal would be a learning-related one for all students and could be addressed directly through the school's curriculum and career guidance activities.

An elementary example of a learning-related goal might be that students need information about personal safety. As a result, the counselor and teachers design activities and compile resources to teach young children the importance of being cautious with strangers, what to do if they feel threatened, and to report to their parents and teachers situations in which they feel unsafe.

Service-Related Goals.   Sometimes goals indirectly address the expressed needs of students, parents, and teachers. In the previous examples of increasing students' career awareness and learning what to do in threatening situations, a counselor might choose broad program goals. For example, to address career awareness the goal might be *to increase the number of career guidance sessions with eighth-grade students.* By choosing this type of service-related goal, the counselor addresses the relationship between educational achievement and career success by assessing how often this information is taught. Service-related goals, such as this one, illustrate ways that counselors assess particular standards by describing comprehensive services.

As you can see from the above categories, goals can take different forms and be addressed through a variety of services and activities. Selecting appropriate services and activities is important, and equally important is how these services are assigned to various professionals and volunteers in the school.

Assigning Responsibilities

As noted earlier, many people, professionals and volunteers alike, have a stake in seeing that an efficient and effective program of services is established in the school. Consequently, a number of people can assume assignments to help meet program goals. A well-organized school counseling program not only identifies important goals but also assigns who is responsible for providing services and activities to address the intended objectives. An advisory committee can provide leadership in assigning responsibilities for activities and services to reach the program's goals. The committee can also be influential in helping to convince the principal and teachers of the importance of having wide involvement and participation in the school counseling program.

Activities that are incorporated into the curriculum, such as developmental guidance, are the primary responsibility of classroom teachers. Sometimes, counselors share this responsibility by co-leading certain guidance lessons with teachers, or they might assume total responsibility for presenting a particular topic or subject matter that addresses an important aspect of student development. How choices are made about who is assigned particular guidance activities varies from school to school, and each advisory committee can help establish the criteria for making these decisions. Such criteria might be determined by asking the following questions:

1. Is the activity appropriate for all students in the school or at a particular grade level?
2. Can the intended goal of the activity be related to other goals or objectives in the curriculum, and is it reasonable to think that its integration into the curriculum will be effective?
3. Do teachers have the necessary knowledge and background to present the activity during classroom instruction?
4. Does the counselor possess special knowledge or skill that is required to lead this activity?
5. Are there existing programs through which this activity can be presented, such as an advisor-advisee program, a peer helper program, or school volunteers?
6. What is the most efficient and appropriate way to deliver this service?

As the advisory committee discusses goals and objectives it begins helping the counselor and teachers plan strategies and activities for the year. For example, assume that a middle school survey has found that eighth-grade students express anxiety about moving to the ninth grade at the senior high school. The goals, objectives, and strategies planned by the advisory committee of this middle school might look like this:

Goal. Students will be successful in high school.

Objectives. Students will:

1. Learn about senior high school courses, credit requirements, schedules, and ninth-grade regulations.
2. Know their way around the senior high school and become familiar with different services that are available to them.

Strategies	Assignment	Timeline
1. Each eighth-grade student will be given an orientation brochure to be discussed in advisor-advisee sessions.	Teacher-advisors	By January 1st
2. Each eighth-grader will write an essay about his or her expectations of high school.	Language arts teachers	By April 1st
3. Each eighth-grader will have a group session with a counselor to discuss special concerns regarding high school.	Counselors	By April 30th
4. Eighth-graders will visit the high school for a half-day program to meet with ninth-grade teachers and counselors and to tour the school's facilities.	Principals and counselors	By May 1st

This plan to help students address anxieties about moving to high school includes services and activities provided by a number of people: (1) teachers who are advisors are actively involved; (2) language arts teachers incorporate learning strategies into their classroom instruction; (3) counselors use small group sessions to consult and counsel with students; and (4) the principal and counselors coordinate an orientation trip to the high school. This example illustrates how counselors and advisory committees analyze needs assessments and summarize their findings into plans for a counseling program. It also shows that the school counseling program involves the services of many professionals in the school and, therefore, consists of more than individual counseling or classroom guidance provided solely by the school counselor. Rather, school counseling includes myriad services and activities planned to meet specific goals and objectives and delivered by designated personnel in the school.

When counselors, teachers, and other team members have organized components of a comprehensive program, the program is announced or advertised to prospective clients and consumers. In a sense, the counselor and advisory committee market the counseling program.

Marketing the Program

Counselors adopt a variety of methods to inform people about who they are and what they do in schools. From speaking to the parent-teachers association (PTA) at the beginning of each year to sitting on community boards that govern services for families and children, school counselors choose many avenues to publicize their programs. These marketing strategies have a twofold purpose. One is to educate people about services available to students, parents, and teachers through a comprehensive school counseling program. A second and equally important goal is for counselors to promote the school counseling profession by being visible in the schools and communities.

Samples of marketing and promotional strategies used by school counselors include

• *Brochures* that briefly define the role of the counselor in the school and describe major services provided to students, parents, and teachers. These brochures are handed out at PTO meetings, placed in orientation packets for new students, and made available in the counseling center. Successful brochures are written clearly in understandable language, are brief in content, and are visibly attractive to the eye.

• *Counselor's column* in the school newspaper or local town newspaper. A regular article in some type of print media, written by the school counselor, educates parents and students about the role of the counselor, provides valuable information about services in the school and community, and promotes other school programs.

• *Websites* about the counseling program and upcoming events and activities use the technology of our electronic age. In addition, using the Internet to communicate with students and parents may facilitate relationships and enhance information searches. Of course, privacy and confidentiality continue to be of primary importance as counselors and their clients use electronic media to communicate.

• *Speaking engagements* at school meetings, civic groups, businesses, educational associations, and other organizations. These opportunities give visibility to both counselors and their school programs and allow counselors to highlight important issues about student development and learning for community members.

• *Class presentations* to students about the counselor's role and services available. This is a fundamental method of marketing services to students. School counselors must be visible in their schools, and these presentations, early in the school year, can help students identify who the counselors are in their schools and learn how to obtain their assistance.

This list provides a brief sample of ways school counselors can market their programs and promote themselves as professionals in the community. As noted, technology is useful in marketing the program and, in addition, it is beneficial in implementing other aspects of the program. Advances in technology for data management, assessment, communication, and information sharing continue to play an increasingly important role in how counselors disseminate information and methods they use in delivering other responsive services.

Using Technology

Technological advances continue to enhance and challenge all aspects of our lives. New tools developed through innovative technology have implications for school counselors at all levels of practice (Casey, 1995; Elias & Hoover, 1997; Gerler, 1995; Hohenshil, 2000; Rust, 1995; Sabella & Booker, 2003; Van Horn & Myrick, 2001). Gerler (1995) observed that the school counseling profession needs to address the challenge of entering the information age with the same enthusiasm used to train new high school counselors following passage of the National Defense Education Act (NDEA) of 1958 and to address the profession's expansion into elementary school counseling during the 1960s and 1970s.

An initial step to address this issue was a special publication by the American School Counselor Association titled *Microcomputers and the School Counselor* (Johnson, 1983). In the early 1980s, the micro- or personal computer was rapidly entering the schoolhouse. Many in the school, including counselors, expressed great hope that this new technology was going to help manage student data, plan programs, and schedule classes, thus freeing time for teachers and counselors to deliver more direct services to students. This anticipated freedom, however, has not been realized. In actuality, the introduction of computers to schools may have decreased the time some counselors spend with students because they have been placed in charge of data management for student records, scheduling, and other functions. It takes time to enter and manage the tremendous volume of data that schools collect and use, and when counselors have primary responsibility for this function, it takes them away from a comprehensive counseling program. In some schools, data management specialists have been hired to handle the input and oversight of this information and that has helped, but in schools where such personnel have not been employed, administrators and counselors struggle to find better ways to manage computerized records, schedules, and other data.

Much of the school counseling literature in the 1980s focused on the selection of computer hardware and appropriate software programs to address developmental needs of students. The most frequently mentioned types of software were career guidance programs. In recent articles, the profession has focused on expanded ways of using computers, the Internet, virtual reality, assessment programs, and other technological advances to design and deliver counseling and informational services in schools. In this section, we explore a few emerging applications by school counselors.

Information Managing and Data Processing.   As noted, schools handle and process a large amount of data. School counselors often share responsibility for monitoring student records, tracking student schedules, and following up on students' grades to provide academic counseling. In addition, counselors might keep data related to student and parent contacts, program management, counseling case notes, and other information to help them be more efficient and effective in providing services. With all these tasks, the computer shows great potential, and at the same time it challenges our ability to keep privileged communications and other private matters confidential (Sabella, 1996).

In a study of elementary, middle, and high school counselors, Owen (1999) found that nearly 98 percent reported the availability of a computer for their use. Of those, middle school and senior high counselors used computers significantly more than elementary counselors. Findings related to how these counselors used computers indicated more time spent on word processing, record-keeping, and scheduling related tasks than on counseling and guidance related functions. In this regard, Owen (1999) concluded that limited resources and lack of computer knowledge and skill contributed to counselors not taking advantage of the technological advances that have been made. He suggested that further research is needed to determine what training is necessary for school counselors to become more adept and sophisticated in using new technology in providing counseling services and guidance information.

Assessment.   Historically, a major function performed by counselors has been in the area of testing and assessment. We will explore this function in detail later in this book, but here we want to briefly address the use of new technology in this area. Assessment is an important part of the overall services that school counselors provide because it is the starting point for helping students, parents, and teachers make appropriate educational, career, and personal decisions. Without adequate and accurate assessment, counselors may not have sufficient information to help people make appropriate and responsible choices.

Although Owen (1999) found that school counselors in his study tended to focus more on word processing and information management, advances in computer hardware and software programs should enable more counselors to find appropriate uses in assessing students' needs, interests, and abilities. New technology and software programs are emerging every day, enabling counselors to administer and score individual tests more efficiently, allowing students to explore educational and career opportunities, and providing opportunities to learn and solve problems through interactive guidance programs.

Interactive Guidance and Counseling.   Beyond the use of computer technology to assist with assessment, school counselors now have available the hardware and software to supplement traditional counseling and guidance strategies and techniques. For example, virtual reality programs are currently being used in the entertainment industry, for recreational purposes, and in the business world. Although there is little indication of virtual reality programs being used in schools, it seems reasonable to expect this medium to be applied by school counselors in the future. It has potential for helping students with peer relationship issues, problem solving, career exploration and decision-making, and educational planning among other topics.

Computer-assisted learning to help students with problem-solving skills has been studied by Elias and Hoover (1997). They examined the effects of computer-facilitated counseling with at-risk third-grade students over a six-month period and found positive results. Although this study did not specifically study the efficacy of computer-assisted learning, it demonstrated one example of how computers could be used to deliver counseling services.

The Internet.   Perhaps no other aspect of the information age has had such a profound and universal impact on people's lives than the Internet. Indeed, the World Wide Web has altered how we communicate, how families and institutions function, where we get information, how we spend leisure time, and how we spend our money. For better or for worse, these changes are taking place around the globe.

An emerging use of the Internet for professional counselors has been online counseling. As new technology alters routines, customs, traditions, and other aspects of people's lives, it is certain to influence the way that professional counselors offer services to clients, including students, parents, and teachers in schools. As with other innovations, online counseling offers an array of benefits, but also raises caveats for professional counselors and their clients (Haas, 2000; Sussman, 2000). One advantage of using electronic mail and Internet chat rooms to assist students is the convenience and access that the technology provides. For example, students can send messages to their counselors during off-hours, thereby not missing instructional time in classes. Their counselors could respond to these inquiries either immediately or the following day, depending on their schedule and the nature of a student's concern. Another advantage is that students, parents, and teachers could seek a counselor's assistance from the total privacy of their home without ever entering the counseling center. The new technology for online counseling also allows counselors to keep a full record of sessions, which eliminates the need to take notes for appropriate follow-up and supervision requirements.

Some of the risks and disadvantages involved with online counseling include concerns about confidentiality. Because the technology is so new, procedures of ensuring confidentiality and preventing other people from reading exchanges between counselors and clients are still being developed and tested. Another concern about using electronic means to counsel students is the lack of affect and nonverbal cues accorded by face-to-face counseling. Diligent use of their responding and questioning skills by counselors who use cybercounseling will be complemented by more frequent follow-up to ensure accurate understanding of clients' perceptions (Bloom & Walz, 2000).

Regulation of the use of electronic methods for counseling is another issue for school counselors to consider. The state of California has already passed legislation governing the practice of psychotherapy and restricting the administration of mental-health services to clinical psychologists and medical doctors licensed in the state (Sussman, 2000). Other states are sure to follow. School counselors will want to monitor legislation in their states to see if laws and regulations governing online counseling might affect their services. In addition, counselors want to be aware of ethical standards established by professional counseling organizations such as the American Counseling Association, which included a section on Technology Assisted Services in its latest ethical code (2005).

The Internet provides seemingly unlimited information through thousands of websites created by individuals, institutions, businesses, associations, and other organizations. Much of the information that students, parents, teachers, and counselors find through the Internet will be beneficial, but some of it might be inaccurate and misleading (Bloom &

FIGURE 6.2   *Illustration of School Counselor Home Page*

Walz, 2000). School counselors can assist students and others by becoming familiar with popular websites and monitoring the accuracy and appropriateness of the information found. They can also search for sites that might be unfamiliar to students, yet provide useful educational, career, and personal/social information. Schools across the country have websites and counselors are included with home pages where students locate information, send messages to their counselors, and find links to other useful sites. Figure 6.2 illustrates a fictional school counselor's web page.

Coming decades will most likely bring more innovations in technology that will have an increasing impact on how counselors serve students, parents, and teachers both in and out of the schoolhouse. This will influence how school counselors offer direct services, such as counseling and consulting, as well as services that disseminate information and provide learning experiences for students. These changes will also increase the need to have counselors who meet professional standards and hold appropriate credentials to practice in school counseling programs.

One outcome of all the discussed organizational processes is that counselors are able to assign themselves appropriate services within the school. As noted earlier, appropriate services and activities to assign school counselors include individual and group counseling, student appraisal, parent education programs and consultation, and small group guidance for selected students. As these assignments are made, counselors begin to establish a schedule of services for their programs. Depending on school and program goals, a counselor's schedule might span a week, month, a grading period, a semester, or the full year. Designing a schedule for the counseling program is the initial step of implementing services.

Implementing

To provide a comprehensive program, school counselors gain control of their time and subsequently schedule services to satisfy the goals and objectives of the program as well as the critical needs of students, parents, and teachers. Having a schedule helps counselors plan and allot time for selected services and, at the same time, illustrates for everyone the comprehensive nature of the school counseling program.

Scheduling Services and Setting Priorities

As specialists who focus on broad areas of student development, school counselors have a unique role that distinguishes them from their teaching colleagues. One illustration of this difference is how counselors and teachers structure their time and establish their schedules. Classroom teachers have schedules set by administrators or by committees of teachers who design curricula, schedule courses, and assign students to classes. A teacher's schedule is therefore consistent from day to day. This may vary from elementary schools where teachers are responsible for the same students all day long to high schools where teachers maintain identical or similar schedules every day. In elementary and middle schools, for example, teachers have flexibility and control over their schedules because frequently they decide when particular subjects or certain activities take place. At the senior high level, however, schedules tend to be more rigid. Teachers are responsible for instructing specific subjects, but the schedule is usually set by the administration.

In contrast to teachers' schedules, school counselors usually have more control over their daily routine. The degree of control may vary from school to school, depending on administrative policy, but most counselors are able to design programs and establish schedules that reflect desired services and activities. The schedule of a comprehensive school counseling program illustrates its attention to a wide range of preventive, developmental, and remedial issues.

School counselors seek suggestions from teachers and administrators in establishing their schedules so that their services complement rather than interfere with the instruction of students. By collaborating with teachers, counselors are better able to determine the best times to schedule individual counseling, group sessions, classroom presentations, parent education programs, and other activities of their programs. Many counselors post their schedules, weekly or monthly as the case may be, to announce services and to let people see how they are spending their time.

A counselor's schedule is also influenced by the goals and objectives selected after a needs assessment is complete. A challenge for each counselor and advisory committee is to take these identified goals and objectives and begin setting priorities. The process selected for setting priorities influences the schedule of services. Myrick (2003) proposed several different ways for counselors to systematically approach their schedules. The first way, which we have already presented, is to set priorities according to the needs identified and determine which can be addressed through classroom interventions and which need the special services of a counselor. A second method is to set priorities based on current crises being experienced by individual students, the school, or the community. Again, decisions can be made about what group or individual services address the crisis situation most effectively and efficiently.

Another way of setting priorities is by emphasizing the different types of services the counselor is able to offer in the school. This method suggests a ranking of services. Assuming all types of interventions are equally effective, Myrick (2003) concluded that group work deserves a higher priority because the number of counselors to meet the needs of individual students is inadequate.

A fourth method of setting priorities is by time management. Simply stated, the counselor examines the total amount of time in a day and determines how much time is needed to deliver each of the planned interventions—a certain amount of time for individual counseling, group work, classroom activities, and so forth.

None of the preceding methods by themselves are sufficient to set priorities for a counseling program and establish a reasonable schedule for the counselor. Each, however, makes a contribution to this process. What is equally important, as mentioned earlier, is for counselors to seek input from others, attempt to coordinate their schedules with the instructional program, and let people be aware of their schedules.

By seeking suggestions from others, establishing schedules that fit the instructional program, and posting their schedules for others to see, school counselors accomplish several important goals. First, they demonstrate that the most important function of the school is to educate children and adolescents, and programs such as school counseling should enhance this process. When school counseling services and activities detract from student-teacher relationships or impede student learning, they contradict the purpose of a comprehensive counseling program. Second, collaboration and cooperation with teachers place counselors in the visible role of letting people know what services are offered and when they are being implemented. Such visibility eliminates doubt and confusion about the role of a school counselor. Last, by seeking suggestions and establishing visible schedules, school counselors demonstrate that the services they offer are essential to the development of all students and are an integral part of the school. The underlying challenge that counselors face in establishing a workable schedule is how to balance their time among the demands being made.

Balancing Time

Nearly every resource that has been written to help school counselors establish comprehensive programs stresses the importance of time management (Baker & Gerler, 2004; Myrick, 2003; Schmidt, 2004; Stone & Dahir, 2006). There is no mathematical formula or magic process that can help counselors balance their time across the varied services in their programs, but the different methods of setting priorities, presented in the previous section, provide a good starting point. Other factors to consider are the critical needs of students and their families served by the school as well as school programs and community agencies available as referral sources. Counselors in schools with many children who have severe learning difficulties or that serve a high percentage of families in economic distress plan services that appear quite different from counselors in other schools.

In addition to examining the priorities set by their advisory committees, counselors can identify the proportion of students who have critical needs. Typically, 10 to 20 percent of a student population is in need of some type of direct intervention. This is consistent with mental-health estimates for the population at large. If that percentage is accurate, a counselor in a school of 500 students can expect a group of fifty to one hundred students who need direct service for one reason or another. These students become the "focus group" of the counseling program and should be given a high priority for individual and small group counseling services.

Once these "focus students" are identified and the counselor determines whether individual or group services are most appropriate, developmental needs of the remaining students should be addressed. These needs are best identified through the formal and informal assessments done with teachers and students. As these needs are prioritized by the advisory committee and counselor, decisions about how best to meet these needs can be made. Activities that focus on developmental concerns include guidance lessons integrated into the curriculum by classroom teachers, special presentations by the counselor in the classroom, and schoolwide events and initiatives.

Figure 6.3 illustrates a sample schedule of a middle school counselor. This fictional counselor is the only counselor in a middle school of 400 students. The percentage of exceptional students with learning problems is about 15 percent, which is relatively high for this school system. Over 40 percent of the students qualify for the free lunch program, and one of the school's goals is to increase parental involvement.

The sample schedule shows an attempt to balance services for approximately fifty "focus students," while also providing educational programs and consultation for parents. About seven hours for individual counseling are scheduled during the week. The counselor sees students in half-hour sessions; therefore, this allows time for fourteen students to be counseled individually each week. An additional seven hours are scheduled for group

FIGURE 6.3 *Sample Schedule for a Middle School Counseling Program*

Keystone Middle School Counselor's Weekly Schedule for September

Time	Monday	Tuesday	Wednesday	Thursday	Friday
7:45	Parent consultation	Parent consultation	Peer helper supervision	Planning and coordinating	Parent program
8:45	Individual counseling	Class presentation	Class presentation	Group counseling	Individual counseling
9:45	Class presentation	Group counseling	Group counseling	Observation	Individual counseling
10:45	Individual counseling	Testing/ assessment	Observation	Class presentation	Parent program
11:45	Peer helper supervision	Teacher consultation	Class presentation	Group counseling	Group counseling
1:00	Individual counseling	Individual counseling	Group counseling	Testing/ assessment	Principal consultation
2:00	Class presentation	Group counseling	Individual counseling	Teacher consultation	Planning and coordinating
3:00	Parent consultation	Teacher consultation	Referrals and follow-up	Referrals and follow-up	Planning and coordinating

counseling. Assuming that each group has five to six members, thirty-five to forty students may participate in group counseling sessions. Thus, individual and group counseling services combined could provide services for the fifty "focus students."

Parent consultation and parent programs are allotted five hours per week to address the school's goal to increase parent involvement. Teacher consultation is given three hours per week, and classroom presentations are scheduled for six hours. Because the schedule is intended for September, many of these class presentations are probably used to orient sixth-grade students to the school and the school counseling program. Additional presentations would focus on topics that seventh- and eighth-grade teachers identified in the needs assessment.

The schedule also shows that the counselor supervises a peer helper program and allows two hours per week for training and supervision. Testing and observation of students use four hours per week, program planning and coordinating have three hours scheduled, and two hours per week are designated for referrals and follow-up.

The preceding example briefly shows how counselors might process the needs of a school to establish a reasonable schedule of services and program leadership. One important aspect about a school counselor's schedule is that it must be flexible. Counselors are often asked to handle "crisis" situations, and at those times, they may not be able to adhere to a posted schedule. Another important aspect is that, while counselors are responsible for setting their schedules, they seek input from the advisory committee, administrators, and teachers so that their schedules can best meet the needs of the school population. By having an acceptable schedule, counselors are better able to manage their time, provide leadership for a comprehensive program, and develop a range of responsive services.

Counseling

As noted earlier, counseling services include individual and small group relationships in which counselors help students, parents, or teachers focus on specific concerns, plan to address these issues, and act on these plans. Counseling in schools covers a wide range of issues and concerns, from peer relationships to suicidal thoughts. As such, counseling can address academic areas, personal adjustment, career decisions, and a host of other topics. Generally, school counselors offer short-term counseling relationships when dealing with serious and critical concerns. If progress is not realized in these brief relationships, counselors refer students to other professionals such as mental-health counselors, counseling psychologists, or psychiatrists in the community. In some cases, students with normal developmental concerns establish relationships with school counselors and continue these helping relationships throughout their school years. In these long-term relationships, the counselor addresses different topics and issues and observes significant growth and development.

The sample schedule in Figure 6.2 shows that group counseling can help schools reach a larger number of students than through individual counseling. In schools, group counseling is an essential service, yet it is often difficult to incorporate into the program because of scheduling problems, lack of suitable space, and misunderstanding about what it is. Teachers in U.S. schools are under increased pressure to show evidence of student achievement, so it is understandable why many are so protective of their instructional time. Consequently, they are reluctant to excuse students from class to participate in activities and programs they view as "noninstructional," such as group counseling.

Establishing Groups.   When organizing and scheduling group counseling sessions and group guidance activities, school counselors develop a plan that informs the administration, educates the faculty, introduces groups to students, develops an acceptable schedule, and involves parents when appropriate to do so. The first step in this process is to determine what needs of students are best met through group processes and which type of group is most appropriate—group counseling or group guidance. Next, counselors must convince the school administration and their teaching colleagues of the value of these group services.

Informing the Administration.   Because group guidance and counseling services require special consideration to remove students from normal class schedules and instruction, counselors should inform their principals about the nature and value of these activities. To do so effectively, counselors must be knowledgeable about group procedures, clear about their goals, and up-to-date about current research on group procedures in schools. School principals want effective services for students, but instructional time and teacher satisfaction are two sacred elements that cannot be disturbed by new approaches started on a whim. To convince principals, counselors in schools must readily demonstrate that group guidance and group counseling complement classroom instruction by helping students examine behaviors, attitudes, and perceptions that inhibit learning and restrict their development.

Once school counselors persuade administrators that group sessions are worth implementing in counseling programs, the next step is to sell the idea to teachers. Teachers are important allies of counselors. Without teachers' support and confidence, services such as group counseling are not likely to succeed or even be approved.

Persuading the Faculty.   Successful school counselors convince teachers of the importance of new services by demonstrating positive results in the services they already provide. Competent, reliable school counselors are respected by their colleagues and have a decided edge over counselors who are uncertain and inconsistent with their practices. Beyond their overall capabilities, effective counselors illustrate to teachers the relationship between student self-development and school achievement. Research on students' self-concepts and beliefs about themselves as learners demonstrates a connection with school achievement (Purkey, 2000; Purkey & Novak, 1996). Group procedures, particularly group counseling, facilitate the process of self-exploration, self-learning, and self-acceptance because:

1. As with all people, students are social beings, and by belonging to a group they interact with one another, reflect and evaluate perceptions of who they are, and practice new behaviors in a safe, nonthreatening environment.
2. Group members help each other, often more effectively than a counselor can individually with a student. In groups, students relate to what other members are saying, they compare similarities and differences in the concerns shared among group members, and they pool their ideas to offer a range of suggestions and alternatives to assist each other.
3. Groups offer a sense of belonging and camaraderie to students who feel isolated, rejected, and alone. Through group counseling and small group guidance, students bond with other members, form friendships and alliances, and recognize the value of caring, helpful relationships.

4. Groups allow participation without demanding that students be active. Some students are not very verbal or are not as outgoing as other students. In groups, these students still benefit from the helping process by listening and watching other members. In time, with the appropriate encouragement and support, they may become more active, but even if not, they can learn about themselves and others by observing the proceedings of the group.

5. Groups are an efficient use of counselors' time. By establishing helping relationships with more than one student at a time, counselors are able to reach a broader population, offering more services to a greater number of students.

In summary, persuading teachers of the value and importance of group processes in a school counseling program is grounded in the assumption that students who work together learn essential skills and strengthen their self-perceptions. For example, Rose (1987) described skills training groups with elementary students that demonstrated positive results in helping students develop social competence. Similarly, Marianne and Gerald Corey (2002) reported favorable comments from teachers, parents, and counselors after students participated in group sessions. Children improved their self-understanding, altered aggressive behaviors, and demonstrated increased willingness to belong and get along with others. Gladding (2003) cited several studies of group work with children that indicate benefits in improved self-concepts, coping skills with family stresses, school adjustment, and academic achievement. These results translate into responsible student behavior and academic progress, two strong selling points with teachers.

Introducing Groups and Selecting Students.   School counselors introduce their groups to students in a variety of ways. In elementary and middle schools, counselors present classroom guidance activities with teachers and use these opportunities to introduce other topics suitable for small group sessions. Through this introductory process, counselors assess students' interest in participating in these groups. At the same time, counselors observe students during classroom guidance lessons and identify those who will benefit from either individual or group counseling.

Teachers, parents, and students are the referral sources who bring group ideas and suggestions to counselors. One senior high counselor reported that he approached a female student who was overweight and seemed withdrawn and isolated in the school. The student discussed her feelings and perceptions about her weight and relationships she had with her peers. During this exchange, the counselor asked the young lady if she thought other students might have similar concerns and would want to share them in a group. The next day the student returned with seven classmates who wanted to establish a support group to work on their self-concepts.

When counselors select students to participate in small groups, they take precautions to assure compatibility of group members. This is not to say there can be no differences among participants, but a wide divergence does not lend itself to cohesiveness that is important to the group process (Toseland & Rivas, 2001). Although group cohesion is difficult to define and evaluate, common descriptions include "the mutual attraction among members of a group and the resulting desire to remain in the group" (Johnson & Johnson, 2000, p. 110).

In selecting students for small groups, school counselors consider age differences, language development, types of concerns, degree of concerns, and social class. A wide disparity within any one or more of these factors may inhibit sharing, supporting, and relating among group members. For example, an elementary counselor who places 5-year-olds in the same group with 10-year-olds may find the age spread is too great and the students have little in common to share adequately in group sessions. Likewise, students who are in groups because of acting out behaviors may not relate well with students who are shy, withdrawn, and overly anxious about school. Sometimes, however, divergence is helpful in groups. For example, by including students of different cultures to share their feelings and observations, counselors create an excellent forum for learning sensitivity and acceptance among students.

Selection processes are essential in creating successful groups (Corey & Corey, 2002; Gazda, Ginter, & Horne, 2001; Ivey, Pedersen, & Ivey, 2001). Gladding (2003) suggested an individual or small group interview with potential members. In these interviews, the counselor introduces the group idea to students, explains the purpose of the group, listens to students' reactions, and assesses whether a student would make a good group member. At the same time, the counselor hears what the student's expectations of the group might be if he or she were to join. Corey and Corey (2002) imagined this screening process as an opportunity for the counselor to assess students and ascertain what they expect from the group. It is also an opportunity for students to become familiar with the counselor and the group counseling program. In this interviewing process, the counselor explains the group rules and seeks commitment from students to abide by the rules and work on concerns if they join the group.

By using a clear selection process, school counselors retain control over group membership. This is critical to their success as leaders of small group guidance and counseling. At times, school administrators and teachers recommend students for counseling, either individual sessions or group counseling, and they insist that the students receive counseling services. When counselors relinquish their professional role and responsibility to assess students' needs and determine the suitability of particular interventions, they diminish their control of, and thereby jeopardize their overall effectiveness in, the school counseling program. Counselors want to accept referrals from others, assess situations properly, and make informed, responsible decisions about what services to provide for whom. Sometimes students who are referred for counseling may benefit more from other services such as a medical examination and consultation, assistance from social services, or participation in a youth program. Other times, it may be that teachers or parents may benefit from instructional or informational services that indirectly help students. On the occasions when counselors decide that group services will be beneficial to students, their next step is to schedule the sessions.

Scheduling Groups.   In designing group schedules, counselors determine the frequency of meetings, the length of each session, the place where they hold sessions, and the number of sessions if they plan a closed group. Suggestions from teachers are essential in helping counselors design reasonable and efficient group schedules. The counselor's advisory committee, consisting of teachers, administrators, parents, and students (at the middle and high school level) can assist with the task of designing an appropriate schedule that satisfies the faculty, is reasonable to the counselor, and meets the expectations of the groups.

Scheduling large group guidance is not difficult if teachers and counselors integrate these lessons into daily instruction. As emphasized throughout this book, the most effective large group guidance occurs in the classroom as a result of a collaborative relationship between the teacher and counselor. When integrated as part of the ongoing curriculum, classroom guidance poses few logistical hurdles. By having teachers and counselors co-lead classroom guidance, the schedule allows for flexibility. For example, if a crisis occurs and the counselor is needed elsewhere in the school, the teacher is able to continue the guidance lesson without interruption.

Small group guidance and small group counseling are more difficult to schedule, particularly if a counselor leads many groups involving a large number of students. In elementary and middle schools where individual teachers or teams of teachers instruct the same students during the day, scheduling should be coordinated between the counselors and teachers. To prevent students from missing the same subject matter every time their group meets, one solution is to stagger the times of the group meetings. For example, the first group session might begin on Monday at 10:00 a.m. The second session would meet the next week on Tuesday at 2:00 p.m., and so forth. This method of changing the day and time is also reasonable to use with groups at all levels—elementary, middle, and high school. By scheduling group sessions in this manner, counselors avoid taking students from the same teacher and out of the same course for the entire duration of the group. Instead, students miss only one or two classes from a given subject area.

Involving Parents.   Because group counseling and group guidance complement the instructional program of the school, counselors want to inform and involve parents in selecting children to participate in these services. In most instances, parental permission is not required for student participation in these programs, unless there is a local, state, or other policy that stipulates the need for parental approval. In general, professional counselors follow the guidelines and procedures of the agency or institution where they are working (Gladding, 2003). School counselors are wise to inform parents of group opportunities through their presentations at school functions such as parent-teacher association (PTA) meetings and by publishing and distributing brochures about their school counseling program.

When screening and selecting students for groups, counselors inform parents about their children's participation. This is not necessarily a request for permission but rather a courtesy extended to parents to include them in the helping process. One counselor uses the following announcement to parents:

> Your child has asked to be in a group led by the school counselor. The group will meet once a week for eight weeks and will focus on school achievement, student relationships, and other aspects of school life and concerns of students. I encourage you to talk with your son or daughter about his or her participation and contribution in the group. Please call me if you have questions about the group or your child's participation.

In some instances, students may want to join groups without their parents' knowledge. Whenever possible, counselors should honor and protect this request. For example, students who have been physically or sexually abused have the right to receive support and treatment without fear of retribution at home or elsewhere. By informing administrators, persuading faculty, involving parents, and implementing the other steps mentioned above, counselors will be successful in establishing group procedures as part of their programs.

Their ultimate success depends on each counselor's leadership abilities, knowledge of counseling theories and approaches, and communication skills.

One approach counselors can use in persuading their teaching colleagues, principals, and parents of the benefits of group work is to run groups that will have positive effects on student study habits, attitudes toward school, and similar topics that may enhance student achievement. As counselors demonstrate positive outcomes in such groups and relate those outcomes to student performance in class, more teachers, administrators, and parents will see the value of group processes. We will examine individual and group counseling, as well as other group processes, in greater detail in Chapter 7.

Consulting

School counselors assist parents and teachers with many aspects of child development and behavior. In most instances, counselors take the role of a consultant, bringing to the relationship a level of knowledge about human growth and development, needs of children and adolescents, and approaches for assisting students with behavioral changes. Many of the communication skills used in counseling relationships are similar to those found in consulting processes. The difference between counseling and consulting relationships may lie more in their design and structure than in actual process differences.

Parent education programs and teacher in-service activities are forms of group consultation. School counselors who design comprehensive programs offer these types of services as an indirect method of assisting students. For example, parents who learn behavior management skills or how to structure homework time are better able to support and guide their children in beneficial ways. Likewise, teachers who hear about different learning styles are better prepared to create appropriate instructional activities for students in their classes.

Counselors also use consulting services when working with professionals outside the school. They frequently consult with health officials, social service workers, and professionals in other agencies to seek the most appropriate services for students and families. In forming these consulting relationships, school counselors share their expertise, including student information when it is appropriate to do so, and they learn about the programs and services of the agency from which assistance is sought. Gathering information from agencies, making initial referral contacts, and ensuring that the referrals are followed through are processes that relate to another primary service of a school counseling program—coordinating.

Coordinating

Because a comprehensive school counseling program consists of several components and activities, it must be coordinated efficiently. Research has shown that school counselors spend a significant portion of their time coordinating events and activities (Kameen, Robinson, & Rotter, 1985). Later research indicated the demand for collaboration and coordination is increasing (Hobbs & Collison, 1995). Functions and skills that relate to program coordination include scheduling services, providing clear communication, setting timelines, delegating responsibilities, following up services and commitments, and time management. Given this expansive list of functions and skills, it seems that almost every service provided by a school counselor, every activity performed, in some way relates to program coordination. In addition, special education services and increased systemwide testing programs that have resulted from school reform initiatives require significant coordination effort that often becomes the responsibility of school counselors.

As seen above, coordinating consists of many skills and processes, which gives it a general, perhaps indefinable connotation. Although coordination may have a broad, apparently all-encompassing meaning, it is nevertheless essential to successful programs. If a comprehensive school counseling program includes a variety of related services, all these services must be organized to be in harmony with the school's educational program. As an example, the counselor who provides effective individual counseling but fails to follow up referrals from teachers and parents finds that services are requested less frequently. In contrast, a counselor who accepts referrals, makes prompt contact with students, and provides appropriate responses to parents and teachers is appreciated and valued.

Appraising

To offer effective services, school counselors begin by gathering the necessary information to make appropriate and accurate decisions. When students are referred to counselors, a process of assessing the situation, appraising the student, and choosing appropriate responsive services is required. In comprehensive programs, counselors know that all students do not need and do not necessarily benefit from individual or group counseling. Other responses, such as small group guidance, parent education, and teacher in-service programs may be more appropriate in addressing some concerns brought forth by students, parents, and teachers.

Gathering and using data from various sources, analyzing information, drawing accurate conclusions, and making recommendations to address the concerns of students and others are important aspects of effective counseling programs in schools. When counselors fail to appraise situations fully and resort to using the same mode of operation regardless of the case at hand, they limit their power as leaders and collaborators and restrict the services of comprehensive programs. Counselors who perform adequate appraisals, make accurate diagnoses, and select appropriate services win the respect of their colleagues and the people who seek their assistance. This is a hallmark of all professional counselors regardless of the setting in which they work. Student appraisal is discussed in detail in Chapter 9.

All these functions are important to the overall implementation of a comprehensive school counseling program. As noted, a key to the counselor's success is found in the design of a reasonable and flexible schedule that accomplishes three important purposes:

1. Takes active control of time management for the counseling program
2. Informs school personnel about the important functions and services provided by the school counselor
3. Solicits the participation of administrators and teachers in planning how the responsive services are scheduled during the school day

Suggestions from teachers and administrators in the design and schedule of a school counselor program also contribute to the annual evaluation of the services offered. In comprehensive school counseling programs, evaluation is a final element that defines the program, establishes its credibility, and demonstrates the vital role that counselors play in the school.

Evaluating

Accurate needs assessment, as seen earlier, is important to establish desirable school counseling services. Adequate evaluation is essential in determining the value of the services that counselors render. Chapter 11 of this text describes evaluation procedures in detail, so the following section serves as an introduction and highlights a few important elements of evaluation, particularly its practical considerations when developing a program.

A successful school counseling program is one that gets results. By this I mean that students who receive counseling and related services are able to improve school performance, increase social skills, make sound educational and career decisions, and realize other identified goals. At the same time, all students in the school benefit from the counselor's presence by information received or through instruction about important developmental tasks and issues. Teachers and parents benefit from consulting services as demonstrated by their increased knowledge of child and adolescent behavior and higher level communication skills for improving listening and teaching processes.

Evaluation in school counseling is an ongoing process of collecting data from students, parents, and teachers to assess services and activities. It is also an annual process of gathering reactions and opinions regarding the counseling program as a whole. Counselors who design ongoing and annual evaluation processes demonstrate their effectiveness, alter services that are not achieving desired results, and continuously assess the direction of their programs. In addition to using surveys of students, parents, and teachers, school counselors use procedures, such as those endorsed by the American School Counselor Association (Dahir et al., 1998), and work with their principal or other school system evaluators to design appropriate and accurate annual performance appraisal systems (Schmidt, 1990).

Competent school counselors select appropriate and effective services to meet the needs of students, parents, and teachers. This is what we mean by counselor accountability—the ability to show what services are being offered and the difference these services make in the lives of people. Counselor accountability has long been an important professional issue (Baker & Gerler, 2004; Myrick, 2003; Schmidt, 2000; Stone & Dahir, 2004). Without demonstrating positive results, counselors are unable to validate their essential role in the school. Simply "being there" is not sufficient to warrant the cost of developing and staffing a school counseling program. Today's counselors must show that the program services they lead and deliver help the school reach its educational mission.

From a practical standpoint, an important consideration in designing evaluation processes is to keep it simple. School counselors do not have to develop elaborate systems of evaluation that take time away from the services they are attempting to deliver. That would be counterproductive. For this reason, counselors may find the advisory committee helpful in designing reasonable and efficient methods of evaluating services.

As indicated earlier, adequate evaluation enables the counselor and school to return to the assessed needs of students, parents, and teachers and the overall goals of the school counseling program. In this cyclical process renewed planning, organizing, and implementing services continues. Each time this cycle is completed evaluation helps the counselor recommend changes for future services. In a comprehensive school counseling program, all the procedures associated with this cycle of planning, organizing, implementing, and evaluating are coordinated by the counselor in cooperation with the school principal, the advisory committee, and the supervisor of counseling services.

All the components of a comprehensive program contribute to the development and implementation of successful services. The responsive services of a comprehensive program are described in detail in the next four chapters beginning with Chapter 7.

Additional Readings

Bloom, J. W., & Walz, Garry R. (Eds.) (2000). *Cybercounseling and Cyberlearning: Strategies and Resources for the Millennium* (Alexandria, VA: American Counseling Association).

This is a timely text in which various authors provide a variety of perspectives about counseling and learning over the Internet and the use of other electronic technology. Forty-eight authors discuss the challenges of this emerging field and its implications for professional counseling.

Hitchner, K. W., and Tifft-Hitchner, A. (1996). *Counseling Today's Secondary Students* (Englewood Cliffs, NJ: Prentice Hall).

This book is a practical guide for secondary counselors to design a comprehensive program of services for a broad range of students. It provides a structure for developing an identity as a school counselor and offers usable ideas and strategies to address a range of issues with students, parents, and teachers.

Schmidt, J. J. (2004). A *Survival Guide for the Elementary/Middle School Counselor* (2nd ed.) (San Francisco: Jossey-Bass).

This book is a guide for elementary and middle school counselors to establishing comprehensive programs, developing effective services, and evaluating their performance. It encourages counselors to look beyond their immediate survival and design programs in which they can flourish as professional helpers.

Websites

Comprehensive Counseling and Guidance Program
http://counselingoutfitters.com/vistas/vistas06/vistas06.41.pdf
Strengthening K–12 School Counseling Programs
www.therapeuticsources.com/82-58text.html

UCLA School Mental Health Project (information on program accountability)
www.smhp.psych.ucla.edu/specres.htm
Note: Numerous state sites exist under "comprehensive school counseling programs."

Exercises

1. Design a brochure for an elementary, middle, or high school counseling program. Present the brochure to your class and ask them to critique it for clarity, brevity, and attractiveness.

2. Role play with another student and pretend that you are being interviewed on a radio program about being a counselor in a school.

3. Assess your time management behaviors. Make a list of the positive aspects of your time management, and then list the barriers to becoming a better time manager. How will you overcome these barriers when you are a school counselor?

4. Visit a school counselor for a day, and observe how that counselor organizes the program, implements services, and manages time.

5. Create a website that describes the mission and goals of your school counseling program. What services would be listed and what links would you include on this website?

6. In small groups develop persuasive arguments that you could present to a school principal who thought a school counselor's time was best spent in coordinating special education services, the school's testing program, and other administrative functions.

7

Individual Counseling and Group Processes

The counseling profession takes its name from the function that defines and describes a primary role of its members. As noted in Chapter 1, counseling emerged as a major function of the profession because of the work of Carl Rogers and other theorists in the 1950s and 1960s. Throughout the development of the profession, counseling has continued as the mainspring for all other practices and services. This is true in all professional settings in which counselors work, whether they are in mental-health centers, family clinics, prisons, hospitals, or schools. The basis for most services provided by professional counselors is a knowledge of counseling theories and the effective use of helping skills.

Effective and efficient helping skills encompass a wide range of behaviors, techniques, and practices that are compatible with the counselor's theoretical and philosophical perspectives. Successful counselors are adept at choosing and developing strategies that bring their theoretical beliefs to life for them and their clients. The hallmark of an effective counselor is the ability to take a particular theoretical stance, mold it to fit one's unique perspectives and beliefs, and acquire the communication and facilitation skills necessary to use these views and assumptions in helping oneself and others achieve optimal development. Today's counselors also adapt their skills and perspectives to facilitate relationships with diverse clients, many of whom might not be helped by models based on European and Western views (Schmidt, 2006). School counselors must be particularly sensitive to this issue as they serve students and families with varied cultural backgrounds.

In this chapter, we examine individual counseling and group procedures as two essential and complementary services in a comprehensive program. In addition, some counseling approaches are briefly presented with particular attention to brief counseling models suitable for counseling in school settings. Before exploring the processes and models associated with the practice of counseling individuals and groups, we address some fundamental questions: What is counseling? For whom is it intended? What is its purpose?

What Is Counseling?

The counseling profession has discussed, presented, debated, and labored over this question since its beginning. The term *counseling* has been defined extensively in the professional literature, but this effort has not always resulted in consistent definitions. In part, this inconsistency is because of the varied settings in which counselors practice and the abundant theories on which these definitions have been based. In answering the question, "What is counseling?" it is helpful to review some historical sources. One approach in answering this question has been to establish a clear meaning of counseling by distinguishing it from psychotherapy. This was common in earlier writings (Shertzer & Stone, 1966; Stefflre & Grant, 1972), and today the tradition continues in much of the counseling literature. For example, Gladding (2004) noted that psychotherapy focuses on

- Past events more that present experiences
- Personal insight more than behavioral change
- Detachment of the counselor
- An expert role for the counselor

Years earlier, Blocher (1966) listed five parallel conditions that define counseling and the relationship between counselors and counselees. These conditions include the following:

1. Clients are not "mentally ill," but rather capable of setting goals, making decisions, and being responsible for their behaviors.
2. Counseling is concerned with the present and the future.
3. Counselors are essentially partners and teachers, and clients are collaborators as they move toward mutually defined goals.
4. Counselors do not impose values on their clients, nor do they attempt to hide their own values, feelings, and moral beliefs.
5. The goal of counseling is to change behavior, not simply to gain personal insight.

While noting that the profession "has not made a clear distinction between counseling and psychotherapy," Nystul (1993) nevertheless persisted that there are "subtle differences between these two processes" (p. 7). He distinguished the two across four factors: types of clients, goals of the relationship, treatment approaches, and professional settings. In his view, clients who seek counseling have problems related to life choices, whereas the problems of clients who are in psychotherapy are more complex. Similarly, the goals of counseling are short-term while those of psychotherapy involve long-term commitment. According to Nystul (1993), treatments used in counseling are preventive, whereas psychotherapy is again more complex and deals with unconscious processes. He noted that counseling is practiced in a variety of settings, but psychotherapy is usually found in private practice, hospitals, and mental-health clinics.

In a humorous vein, Eysenck (1961) described psychotherapy as "an unidentified technique applied to unspecified problems with unpredictable outcomes. For this technique we recommend rigorous training" (p. 698). For others, this debate is more serious because many authorities have delineated the differences between counseling and psychotherapy.

Generally, these efforts have examined the goals of each process, the types of clients served, the training of counselors and therapists, and the work settings in which the helping relationship occurs. For example, Nugent (2000) noted that psychotherapy and counseling differ in terms of the severity of problems that clients present. Counseling approaches tend to be short-term with emphasis on developmental issues and concerns. In contrast, psychotherapy focuses on more debilitating psychological and emotional problems, which require more intense and often longer treatment.

Despite these attempts to clarify differences between counseling and psychotherapy, many authors believe the distinction is unnecessary. Shilling (1984) wrote that attempts "to distinguish counseling from psychotherapy have been less than totally successful. Some think that no distinction is necessary; others think it is essential" (p. 1). Likewise, George and Cristiani (1995) noted, "Some practitioners . . . use the two terms synonymously" while others "feel that such a distinction must be made" (p. 3).

George and Cristiani (1995) advocated a position that is closest to the view I hold and present here. They wrote that "both counseling and psychotherapy utilize a common base of knowledge and a common set of techniques. Both involve a therapeutic process but they differ in terms of severity of the client's situation, in terms of the client's level of problem and/or functioning" (pp. 5–6). For the purpose of this text, there is no need to make further distinctions or to point out additional similarities between counseling and psychotherapy. Overall, the processes of both are similar, with many overlapping elements and skills. In this book, we are more concerned about what counseling *is* than about what it is *not*.

Contemporary definitions of counseling illustrate the profession's focus on a wide range of human needs, including preventive, developmental, and remedial relationships. In 1984, Pietrofesa, Hoffman, and Splete presented counseling as a process facilitated by trained professionals for persons "seeking help in gaining greater self-understanding and improved decision-making and behavior-change skills for problem resolution and/or developmental growth" (p. 6). Nugent (2000) echoed this perspective by stating, "Regardless of where they work, counselors help individuals, families, and groups resolve conflicts, solve problems, or make decisions in a social, cultural context" (p. 2). By constructing a broader purpose for their helping relationships, counselors offer services for an array of people who are basically healthy, functioning individuals. Among this group, some people have psychological and social concerns, and others seek information and support for developmental decisions they are making for the future. Gladding (2004) summarized these elements by defining counseling as a brief relationship founded on a theoretical model or models to help relatively healthy people make life decisions.

Schools are specific settings in which the counseling process is practiced. As with other professional settings, the primary mission of schools colors the practice of counseling with its focus on the educational goals of students, parents, and teachers. As such, counseling in schools is a process of helping students, parents, or teachers learn about themselves; understand how their personal characteristics, human potential, and behaviors influence their relationships with others; and make choices to solve current problems while planning strategies for optimal development. By using a broad definition, school counselors assess which students, parents, and teachers will benefit from counseling relationships and determine whether they are the best professionals to provide this service to these groups.

Who Needs Counseling?

In elementary, middle, and senior high schools, counselors provide services for a multitude of reasons. They offer a wide range of related and interrelated services to help people resolve problems and make decisions. Unfortunately, because counseling has retained a mystical aura in much the same way that psychology and psychiatry have, some people believe that counseling is the answer to all problems. In short, counseling should "fix people" who are not behaving the way others want them to. For example, sometimes teachers bring students to school counselors with a combined plea and command that a "student is not doing work in class and needs counseling." Although such students may benefit from helping relationships with counselors, it may be equally beneficial in these situations for teachers to learn about the student's academic needs, learning styles, or other characteristics that impede progress in school. In such cases, a consulting relationship with the teacher might be as helpful as counseling with the student. These are the types of leadership decisions counselors make in comprehensive programs.

When receiving referrals from students, parents, and teachers, school counselors first ask themselves, "Who needs what?" In deciding whether or not counseling is an appropriate service in a given situation, counselors investigate a number of criteria and ask several questions. The information they collect and the answers they generate from this investigation enable them to make appropriate decisions. Some of the questions counselors ask in reviewing criteria are the following:

1. *Does the counselee see the situation in ways similar to those who made the referral?* There is little reason to counsel someone about a problem identified by others when the individual does not see or admit that any problem exists. At the very least, the individual who is referred must know that a conflict exists with the person who made the referral.

2. *Does the counselee perceive a need for assistance and accept counseling as a method of addressing this concern?* Not all individuals enter counseling relationships with a strong desire to change. Gladding (2004) observed that a majority of clients are reluctant or unmotivated to change. In such instances, success is possible when counselors and counselees establish genuine working relationships. As counseling research has repeatedly documented, genuineness on the part of counselors is fundamental in developing effective helping relationships (George & Cristiani, 1995). In instances of reluctance and discouragement on the part of counselees, counselors use persuasion and confrontation to encourage counselees to take initiative and pursue helping relationships (Corey, 2001; Ivey & Ivey, 2003).

3. *How much control does a prospective counselee have in bringing about necessary change?* One criterion that enables counselees to be successful is their ability to gain control of the situation in question. Students in schools rarely have total control over situations in their lives. This is particularly true with younger children in the primary and intermediate grades. Family relations, parental substance abuse, socioeconomic status, and a host of mitigating factors are beyond the control of individual students. Furthermore, cultural heritage, traditions, and world views are also influential in developing self-views (Schmidt, 2006).

In deciding whether counseling is appropriate, counselors identify the behavior or situation that needs to change and determine the degree to which the counselee will be able to effect that change. If students have the capability to control situations, make necessary adjustments, and choose new behaviors to cope in the future, counseling may be appropriate. At the very least, individual counseling might offer support for students who are trapped in circumstances beyond their control and might suggest coping skills to survive what appears to be an unbearable situation. In today's schools, students bring an array of critical concerns about domestic violence; physical, sexual, and emotional abuse; substance abuse; and other issues that require immediate attention. Individual counseling can help students acquire coping skills to survive these oppressive situations. By surviving initially, students gain time to make long-term plans, develop new skills, and strengthen positive self-perceptions.

4. *Is the counselee committed to making changes, learning new behaviors, or seeking alternatives to the present situation?* Counseling that begins and continues without eliciting commitment is a one-sided and often frustrating process for both the counselor and the counselee. Commitment may not exist at the start of the counseling process, but if the counselor establishes a genuine relationship in which the counselee's views are accepted, it eventually emerges. Without some level of commitment, there is no counseling relationship.

The preceding questions and answers help counselors assess their clients' readiness for counseling and willingness to enter beneficial helping relationships. The questions and answers above focus on problem-solving and crisis-oriented counseling. As noted before, school counseling serves other purposes as well, including developmental goals and objectives. In developmental counseling relationships, the need is established by a referring agent (such as a parent or teacher) or a client (student) who has the desire to explore opportunities, assess potential, and energize interactions with other people. By helping students cultivate opportunities for development and growth, school counselors move from problem-oriented perspectives to broader views of their helping relationships. The answer to the question "Who needs counseling?" depends on the goals and objectives of these helping relationships. Effective counseling is achieved by establishing appropriate and clear goals.

Goals of Counseling

What are the goals of counseling? On the surface, this appears to be a simple enough question, but it is not easy to answer. Determining the goals of counseling relationships depends on whose goals we are talking about—the counselor's or the counselee's. Sometimes the goals of counselors and their clients differ. For example, a high school student may seek ways of "getting my parents off my back about college," whereas the counselor's goal is to assist the student in self-assessment, career planning, and educational decision-making. In many instances, people who ask counselors for assistance are searching for answers and ways to solve problems without taking any risks. They wish to avoid the issue of changing their own behaviors or of making important decisions and instead want others to change or make decisions for them. George and Cristiani (1995, p. 6) presented five major goals that are emphasized in most counseling theories and models. An adaptation of these goals includes objectives to

1. Facilitate changes in one's behavior.
2. Improve social and personal relationships.

3. Increase social effectiveness and one's ability to cope.
4. Learn decision-making processes.
5. Enhance human potential and enrich self-development.

Imbedded in most, if not all, of these objectives is the importance of heightening one's cultural awareness and acceptance of cultural diversity. In schools today, counselors and other professionals cannot ignore the importance of helping students become more aware of their own cultural influences and become sensitive to the cultural differences that surround them. This awareness and sensitivity add richness to one's life and contribute to social harmony and progress.

Setting goals in counseling relationships is particularly important in school settings where finding solutions and alleviating difficulties in a timely manner are essential. The primary purpose of school counseling is to enhance educational planning, expand opportunities for learning, and strengthen students' achievement. Given this primary purpose, successful counselors consider the following guidelines when selecting goals for individual counseling:

1. Relate goals to some aspect of learning. When counseling students in schools, the ultimate objective is to enhance learning and development. Therefore, the goals of counseling should connect in some way to this outcome. Whether the main concern is social, such as in peer relationships; personal, such as with the loss of a loved one; or psychological, such as with fears and anxieties, the counseling relationship needs to address these issues in the context of their impact on the student's educational development.

2. Generalize the achievement of educational goals to other relationships. Because time is precious in schools, it is helpful for students to take the knowledge achieved in counseling and apply it toward other relationships and situations in school and at home.

3. Share learning experiences and skill development with others. The assistance that individual students receive in counseling can be magnified and expanded if they share experiences with others. Group counseling, classroom guidance, and peer helper programs are a few vehicles that school counselors and students use to accomplish this goal.

4. Involve parents whenever possible. Students of all ages, children through adolescents, benefit from the support and nurturing of caring parents. In counseling relationships, school counselors are wise to win the cooperation of students and persuade them of the importance of parental involvement. In some counseling relationships, such as in child abuse cases, parental involvement may not be feasible, but in the majority of school counseling relationships, as noted in Chapter 3, this goal is not only possible, it is desirable.

Knowing what counseling is, determining who needs what kind of counseling service, and establishing appropriate goals for counseling relationships enable school counselors to create beneficial relationships. Counseling is a process. It has a beginning, it is characterized by a series of sequential steps or stages, and it ends when identified goals are achieved. Just as there is an abundance of counseling theories, there is also a wide selection of helping models from which to choose (Stone & Dahir, 2006). Having effective models on which to base their counseling relationships permits counselors to structure and direct effective helping processes. In schools with young students, structure and direction are appropriate, even in counseling relationships.

Individual Counseling in Schools

Models of counseling range from three to a multitude of stages. The following sections illustrate a four-stage approach to the counseling process. Specific stages, such as those that follow, offer a blueprint for counselors to build effective relationships. By mentally processing different stages of their helping relationships, school counselors stay on course and consistently encourage students and other clients to move closer to their identified goals.

Establishing a Relationship

Counseling is a process of disclosing personal hopes, desires, concerns, fears, and failures in an attempt to change behaviors, alter external factors, and set future goals. This kind of intimate sharing and communicating is only possible in relationships founded on acceptance, understanding, and positive regard. Counselors demonstrate empathic understanding when they make every effort to perceive the world (or situation) the way clients do and accurately communicate this perceptual comprehension back to them.

Respect is another essential condition of the first phase of counseling relationships. Sometimes referred to as "unconditional positive regard," respect includes the ingredients of equality, equity, and shared responsibility. In counseling, nothing is more important than the people in the process; therefore, it recognizes the rich complexity and unique value of each human being. In schools, this condition of respecting the person's value is vital to the successful outcome of helping relationships with students.

School counselors have an obligation to demonstrate actively and visibly a regard for students, showing that students have value, can be responsible, and are deserving of respectful treatment. This respect is not easily achieved. Counselors who practice honorably, with care, and at the highest level of professional performance are able to win the respect of students, parents, and teachers. On the other hand, those who neglect their obligations, divulge confidences, behave in nonaccepting ways, use ridicule, and defame the education and counseling professions demonstrate disrespect toward themselves and others and invariably are avoided by students, parents, and teachers.

Genuineness relates to respect in that counselors who are accepting of others are in a better position to disclose their true feelings and reactions to the concerns expressed by their clients. At the same time, genuine counselors demonstrate consistent behaviors without discrepancies between what they say and do. Genuineness, sometimes called *congruence,* is a characteristic that allows counselors to be who they are without playing a role or hiding behind a façade. This congruence emerges from respectful relationships to let clients, especially students, know how they appear and come across to others.

One caveat is appropriate here; genuinely facilitative responses are not blunt, frank reactions and reflections to "let students know what life is *really* all about." Quite the contrary, a genuine counselor balances empathy and respect with honest opinions and feelings in quest of a mutually beneficial relationship. Through the process of sharing feelings and perceptions, school counselors and students establish beneficial interactions in the helping process and move from this introductory phase to a deeper and more meaningful exploration of concerns.

Exploring Concerns

Counseling is more than simply forming a relationship. It is the process of using the helping relationship to focus on concerns, either developmental or problem-oriented, and make decisions to remedy a situation, acquire new skills, or enhance one's self-awareness. Relationships that fail to move to this next stage cannot be viewed as counseling. They may be friendships, conversations, or other types of interaction, but they are not professional helping.

Sometimes, school counselors seem unable to move their counseling relationships beyond the phase of building rapport and toward a deeper exploration of issues and concerns. In part, this may be due to their lack of understanding of specific counseling theories and practices. All counseling approaches use similar skills and behaviors in the initial phase to establish a viable working relationship. Beyond this first stage, however, the language, assumptions, and beliefs of various counseling theories and models begin to distinguish themselves from one another. School counselors who have a clear understanding and command of specific approaches are more able to assist students in further exploration and to take action that addresses their concerns.

The exploration phase is characterized by constructs, language, techniques, and strategies created and endorsed by particular approaches selected by counselors. For example, Adlerian counselors focus on birth order, family constellation, goals of behavior, and feelings of inferiority, and they use lifestyle assessment techniques to help clients understand their private logic and its relationship to success in life (Sweeney, 1998). In contrast, behavioral counselors identify specific problem behaviors, collect baseline data, examine stimuli and antecedents of behaviors, and develop behavioral techniques, such as skills training, relaxation training, and systematic desensitization, to correct or change behaviors during the next phase of the counseling process (Corey, 2001).

School counselors who know their theoretical foundations and have command of basic skills and techniques that are compatible with their assumptions about human development are in a position to be a beneficial presence in the lives of others. In particular, they guide students through adequate exploration of pertinent issues and toward selection of alternatives for resolving conflicts, gaining greater awareness, and making life-enriching decisions. This moves the relationship into the next stage, sometimes called the *action phase* of counseling.

Taking Action

A relationship that fails to include definitive action to address a client's concerns is not counseling. Earlier, you learned the importance of goal-setting in the initial phase of the counseling process. The action phase of counseling relationships enables clients and counselors to realize the goals they have chosen. Similar to the exploration phase of counseling, the action phase is influenced by the theoretical beliefs and helping models embraced by practicing counselors. Psychodynamic approaches, for example, usually feature development of insight, reorientation of attitudes and beliefs, redefining goals, and choosing alternative behaviors. In contrast, behavioral strategies tend to include social modeling techniques, behavioral contracts, skills training, self-monitoring, decision-making models, and similar approaches.

In the action stage, the counselor and client agree on a particular plan and strategy, monitor the implementation of that plan, and evaluate the outcome of the strategy used. When evaluation indicates that the problem has been resolved, the counselor and client have the opportunity to examine other issues or other areas for developmental growth. If their decision is to continue in a helping relationship, they return to the exploration phase once again. When the client identifies no other concerns or issues to address, the counseling relationship can end.

Ending the Relationship

All relationships come to an end, either naturally or circumstantially. Counseling relationships are no different. They too complete a final stage, which is called *closure* or *termination*. In this stage, the counselor and counselee arrive at a point where the purpose and goals of their relationship have been successfully achieved, and now it is time to move on to other goals and other relationships.

Gladding (2004) emphasized that this phase of counseling is the least understood and most neglected of all the stages. Perhaps this is because in many successful helping relationships, both the counselor and counselee find it difficult to sever the ties that bind them. In some ways, the idea of ending a helping relationship is contradictory. By definition, a helping relationship is continuous. On the other hand, a counseling relationship that sets no time frame for closure may continue indefinitely without adequate attention to the exploration of concerns, commitment to change, and decisions about appropriate plans of action. This is a poor use of counselors' time and passive deceit of counselees who believe they are being helped.

In school counseling, the process of ending or concluding a helping relationship deserves extra care and consideration. Because students remain in school with the counselor, the closing of specific helping relationships takes on a different meaning than when counselors end relationships with clients in agency settings. Students who see counselors for individual sessions also interact with them in other ways during the school day. They may talk with counselors about career information, participate in classroom guidance, or be supervised by a counselor in after-school extracurricular activities. Because these interactions are ongoing, closure of an individual counseling relationship is planned and carried out gradually.

In some cases, the decision to end counseling with a student may be made jointly with the child, parents, and teachers involved in the process. Ending counseling relationships with students is also facilitated by preparing them gradually for termination during the latter phases of counseling. By reinforcing the progress students have made, emphasizing the skills they have attained, encouraging them to express their feelings about ending the counseling relationship, and helping them learn about other avenues for continued support, school counselors bring appropriate closure to successful helping relationships.

Because school counselors provide a range of services and work with large populations, they usually do not have time to continue long-term counseling relationships. Although no exact number of sessions can (or should) be assigned to counseling relationships in schools, contemporary approaches have encouraged models for brief counseling.

School counselors should be adequately trained to perform interventions with emphasis on establishing helping relationships and brief counseling.

Brief Counseling

As presented in this text, counseling is both an educational and therapeutic process. School counselors attempt to help students identify concerns that may detract from their development and learning. At the same time, school counselors help students address areas that they could enrich to improve their lives. Brief counseling endeavors to address a developmental issue or to remedy an existing concern over a relatively short period of time, perhaps in a few sessions. In general, brief counseling is appropriate for helping students enhance their immediate situations by resolving pressing difficulties or making educational and career decisions.

Brief counseling is advocated in the literature (Bruce, 1995; Davis & Osborn, 2000; Lopez, 1985; O'Hanlon & Weiner-Davis, 1989) and applies to both psychodynamic and cognitive-behavioral approaches (Nugent, 2000). It is particularly valuable in schools where time constraints are crucial to counselors (Bonnington, 1993; Bruce & Hooper, 1997; Harrison, 2000). By way of summary, brief counseling usually centers on specific concerns or behaviors of students and tends to be an action-oriented approach. In most cases, brief counseling follows a sequence of steps or questions that the counselor follows or the student addresses. As examples, three separate, yet similar, models follow.

Lopez (1985) presented a four-step model of brief counseling that is adapted here for school counseling:

1. *Ask the student to describe in concrete terms what he or she would like to change.* In this step the counselor explores with the student concerns, worries, or behaviors that are hindering development. The counselor assesses the situation and attempts to narrow down the student's most critical concerns.

2. *Examine what the student has done already.* Most students know when they have a concern or when they face an obstacle, and they make attempts to resolve these problems. In this step, the counselor helps the student look at all the attempts that have been made thus far to see if any have further use and, if so, how they might be changed to be successful.

3. *Clearly identify a goal.* Counseling in schools must be purposeful to be successful; therefore, school counselors and students need to establish measurable goals to know when the helping relationship has been effective.

4. *Develop and implement strategies.* To ensure success, counselors and students must create reasonable strategies aimed at reaching their identified goals.

Using this four-step model, Bruce and Hooper (1997) studied fifty-four students in grades 2 through 7 in four midwestern schools. They found that "specific action within the capabilities and control of the student yield rapid results and maintenance" (p. 182).

Myrick (2003) created a similar sequential structure for brief counseling, but his consists of four questions. He calls this approach the Systematic Problem-Solving Model. With it, counselors ask students to process these questions: (1) What is the problem or situation? (2) What have you tried? (3) What else could you do? and (4) What is your next step? As with other approaches to helping, Myrick's model requires a high level of facilitative responses during the initial questions. This strengthens the relationship and allows the action questions to be processed more quickly (Harrison, 2000).

Solution-focused counseling is another approach to brief therapy that has potential in school counseling (Bonnington, 1993; de Shazer, 1985; Harrison, 2000). Basic to this approach is the hypothesis that students' problems are maintained by their belief that the difficulty is constantly occurring. According to Harrison (2000), these students often "see themselves as flawed or having something wrong with them as people" (p. 92). The goal for counselors in working with these students is to focus on "what is right" rather than "what is wrong" with them. One intervention to address this goal is the "miracle question" developed by de Shazer (1991). Essentially this question asks the student, "What will happen if you wake up tomorrow morning and you no longer have this problem? What will be different and how will you know the problem is solved?" Key to the question is the focus on "what *will*" as opposed to "what *would*" happen. The word *will* more emphatically states that without this problem there *is* a difference.

Bonnington (1993) noted three tasks that summarize solution-focused counseling. In schools, counselors can adapt these three tasks by (1) evoking descriptions of differences from students, (2) helping students to magnify these differences, and (3) assisting students in continuing to make changes (p. 127).

By having an uncomplicated structure for brief counseling school counselors take a pragmatic course and encourage short-term relationships with students. This serves several purposes. First, it demonstrates to students that they are not "sick," "disturbed," or "abnormal." Rather, they are healthy individuals who can resolve their concerns. Second, forms of brief counseling are an efficient use of counselors' time. With such approaches, counselors are more accountable to their students and the schools that employ them. Finally, short-term approaches to counseling encourage independence and foster self-responsibility and self-reliance, all of which are admirable goals for students in school.

As with all other approaches to counseling, models of brief counseling are always practiced with the best interests of students in mind. Efficiency in counseling is marvelous, but not when it compromises the integrity of the student or the counseling process. As noted earlier, brief counseling requires the same level of facilitation as other models of counseling. For this reason, forms of manipulation and the use of unreasonable control as a pretense for helping are a gross misuse of the counselor's position and, if not blatantly unethical, are at least questionable practices.

Another application of brief counseling models is crisis intervention. Schools reflect the trends and concerns found in society, and as a result, crises that occur in families and communities are often brought into the schoolhouse. For this reason, school counselors need to be prepared to counsel students who have critical concerns.

Crisis Counseling

In addition to counseling students who have developmental concerns or relationship problems, school counselors enter crisis-oriented relationships with students. In doing so they establish initial helping processes that precede referrals to other professionals and agencies in the community. Crises require immediate intervention that begins with assessment to determine the degree of risk and the level of crisis that students face. Assessment includes interviews with students, parents, teachers, and others, observations of students' behaviors, review of medical records, use of questionnaires, and whatever other methods are appropriate for the situation.

Crisis counseling, by nature, tends to be directive and action-oriented. When students are in crises, counselors do not have the luxury of time to allow students to pause for self-reflection or in-depth exploration of their perceptions and concerns. "Typically, students in crises want direction, and it is only after they are stabilized and secure that they are able to assume some decision-making responsibility. This responsibility comes gradually, after an initial plan of action has been established and the student has experienced preliminary success" (Schmidt, 2004, p. 149).

A final aspect of crisis counseling, as with all other forms of helping relationships, is the follow-up and evaluation of outcomes. When students have made changes, adjusted behaviors, chosen directions, or made other significant decisions that parallel the goals and objectives of the counseling relationship, school counselors assess the results. Even though students may make progress in the helping relationship, school counselors sometimes decide that they have gone far enough within the scope of their competencies and program guidelines. In these instances, they refer students to other services in the school system or community.

As with brief counseling, crisis counseling is usually a systematic, structured, step-by-step procedure. During a crisis intervention, the primary focus is on the safety and welfare of the client. In schools, crises may occur in countless ways, from the sudden death of a student or teacher to multiple acts of violence perpetrated by an intruder. Therefore, to tap the expertise of many staff members, administrators, counselors and teachers often use a team approach. By developing a strategic team approach, the school assigns every professional specific responsibilities to handle the crisis effectively. This means that the school counselor is in the forefront as a team member and offers first-line assistance to students and teachers who are in crises. After assessing the situation, determining what immediate services are necessary, and securing the client(s) who is (are) most vulnerable or at risk, the counselor meets with other team members to plan further actions. In this way, a team approach capitalizes on the expertise and skills of several professionals, with the school counselor assessing individuals' needs as well as the overall school atmosphere. As a team member, the school counselor offers initial counseling services and other types of support for students and teachers.

Counseling Approaches

School counselors receive training in many different theories and approaches to helping. Though there appear to be countless theories and models from which to choose, a few approaches have gained prominence in school counseling. In practice, most school counselors, similar to counselors and psychologists in clinical settings, embrace an *eclectic* philosophy (Corey, 2001). Eclectic counseling is the integration of a number of related theories, approaches, and techniques into a personalized and systematic process. Over the years, eclectic practice has been both encouraged and condemned in the counseling literature (Rychlak, 1985). When counselors select approaches systematically, with purpose and understanding, their integrative styles allow them to expand options for their clients. On the other hand, when this selection process is haphazard and without any rationale, the counseling process may appear unfocused and without clear direction.

As noted earlier, there are numerous counseling theories and approaches from which counselors must make logical choices. Simultaneously, school counselors face the challenge of helping students, parents, and teachers evaluate their situations, explore concerns, examine alternatives, and make decisions within a reasonable period of time. These two conditions make it palatable for school counselors to adopt an integrative posture, choosing from a range of approaches found to be successful in school settings. In doing so, they search for common elements among compatible theories and approaches and recognize the important differences that exist when merging various philosophies and practices. Counselors who borrow from different perspectives to establish an eclectic practice are successful when they choose intentionally with adequate knowledge of the approaches selected, are aware of related research findings, and have a clear understanding of their therapeutic purposes and goals.

Group Processes

School counselors search for interventions that enable all students to develop their fullest potential. Although individual counseling relationships are effective in helping certain students, one-to-one processes are not always the most efficient use of a counselor's time and resources. More important, individual relationships do not capitalize on the human resources available to counselors through the expertise of students, parents, and teachers. In contrast, group methods allow counselors to reach out to more people and effectively use the helping potential of others.

Chapter 5 introduced two main types of group processes used by school counselors: group counseling and group consultation. Group counseling is a confidential helping relationship in which the counselor encourages members to focus on developmental, preventive, or remedial issues with which they are concerned. Group consultation encompasses a range of activities that utilize instructional, informational, and problem-solving processes. Examples of group consultation include teacher in-service activities, classroom guidance lessons, and parent education programs. In determining what types of groups to establish in comprehensive programs, school counselors want to have a clear rationale with which to persuade administrators, teachers, and parents.

A Rationale for Group Processes

In the history of education, many philosophers and scholars have encouraged schools to take a proactive role in instilling values and developing students' character. Kohn (1991) proposed that this process of character education should include caring about others: "If we had to pick a logical setting in which to guide children toward caring about, empathizing with, and helping other people, it would be a place where they would regularly come into contact with their peers and where some sort of learning is already taking place" (p. 499). Schools offer this ideal setting, and school counseling programs, in the context of group guidance and group counseling, provide the structure to help students learn empathic behaviors, problem-solving skills, and a host of cooperative, pro-social attributes.

Today's schools are under fire from all directions and all segments of society to overhaul their services, improve instruction, and increase learning. School counselors should be part of this movement and, in fact, should be leaders for change. An essential role for school counselors is as an agent for change (Erford, 2003; Stone & Dahir, 2006). This role is implied in all the major functions, particularly group work, addressed in this text. By advocating more group processes in the instructional and counseling programs of the school, counselors lend their expertise to the process of restructuring education and enhancing student development and learning.

In the next section, we focus on two types of group processes used specifically with students: group counseling and group guidance. This section presents the purposes of these two types of groups, their advantages and limitations, and how counselors offer them in schools. We begin by defining and differentiating group counseling and group guidance.

Group Counseling and Group Guidance

Group counseling and group guidance are two processes used by school counselors to handle a wide range of students' concerns and interests. Many students in schools have concerns that are similar in nature. Sometimes these are normal, developmental issues such as making friends, becoming comfortable with physical changes, making educational decisions, and learning problem-solving skills. Other times, students confront major problems, often of crisis magnitude, that must be dealt with expeditiously. Group procedures offer efficient and effective formats for assisting students with many different issues, from educational planning to grieving over the loss of a loved one. Groups also allow diverse activities with dissimilar audiences who have various goals and objectives. Part of the school counselor's role is to select appropriate group processes to meet these expanded needs.

Many texts and articles have described group processes in detail (e.g., Corey & Corey, 2002; Gazda et al., 2001; Gladding, 2003; Jacobs, Masson, & Harvill, 2002), and school counseling literature has encouraged the use of group guidance and counseling since the late 1950s, beginning with Driver's now classic book, *Counseling and Learning through Small Group Discussion* (1958). Today, the American School Counselor Association identifies group counseling and guidance as responsive services of elementary, middle, and secondary school counselors.

By using group counseling, school counselors encourage interaction among students, thereby facilitating their willingness and ability to help each other. Under the leadership of a trained counselor, students share concerns, self-disclose in a safe environment, listen to the ideas and opinions of other group members, and give one another support and suggestions about the concerns they have raised.

Purpose and Nature of Groups

An essential difference between group counseling and group guidance is that counseling creates a confidential and personal relationship, and group guidance is more instructional and informational in nature. Gladding (2003) described the purpose of group guidance as the prevention of personal or societal difficulties through information sharing and skill development. In general, group guidance, originally developed for school settings as psychoeducational groups, focuses on development through learning. Myrick (2003) has encouraged counselors to differentiate large group guidance from small group counseling by observing the purposes of various types of groups and the ways in which they function.

The purpose of group counseling is for members to explore issues affecting their development and to form intimate relationships in which they accept and support one another in the process of resolving and coping with their concerns. As noted above, group guidance is more instructional in nature and differs from counseling in the depth of personal interactions and the level of sharing among group members. Though many of the leadership skills used in group counseling and group guidance are similar, group guidance activities tend to be more didactic than group counseling sessions. Typically, guidance groups focus on specific learning objectives or information needed by students for their development. In summary, the differences between group counseling and group guidance are found in the purposes of the groups, the level of personal interactions among group members, the leadership behaviors of the counselor, and the size of the groups.

Size of Groups.   Determining the size of groups depends on the purpose of the group, the ages of the group members, the number of sessions scheduled, and the nature and severity of problems mentioned by prospective group members. With young elementary children, Gazda and colleagues (2001) recommended limiting group counseling to no more than five students. With adolescents and adults, groups may be slightly larger, but as the size of the group expands, cohesiveness among the members diminishes (Jacobs, Masson, & Harvill, 2002). Regarding group size in general, Corey and Corey (2002) list four determining factors that include the age range of group members, the leader's group work experience, the type of group formed, and the issues/concerns of the group. They surmise that an effective group "should be big enough to give ample opportunity for interaction and small enough for everyone to be involved and to feel a sense of 'group' " (Corey & Corey, 2002, p. 107).

Myrick (2003) defined large group guidance as processes that include more than ten students. He observed that if the size of a counseling group is larger than ten, the process becomes less clear and could change the group's purpose. When this happens, the group process becomes different from counseling; it becomes more instructional and informational and personally less intense for the group members.

Group Processes and Comprehensive Programs.   Both group guidance and group counseling are essential functions in comprehensive school counseling programs. Yet, literature indicates that some school counselors neglect group process because of resistance from teachers, difficulty of scheduling, and lack of confidence in their group leadership skills. Too often, counselors resist the use of group processes due to feelings of inadequacy regarding their leadership skills and abilities. In a 1987 national survey of elementary, middle, and senior high school counselors, Bowman summarized counselors' views regarding group work:

1. Counselors at all levels agreed that small group guidance and counseling are important functions to include in their programs.
2. Counselors used groups to focus on a variety of topics depending on the developmental age and needs of students.
3. Counselors agreed that their school counseling programs would be more effective if they increased the number of groups they scheduled, but at the same time they noted

the difficulty of restructuring the time available to do this and the challenge of obtaining teacher support.

4. Senior high counselors indicated that scheduling and leading groups in their schools is more difficult and less practical than at the elementary and middle grades.

5. Opinions were mixed among the counselors regarding their training to run small group guidance and counseling effectively as part of their programs. A total of 22 percent of the counselors indicated they needed additional training to implement effective groups.

Here in the twenty-first century, time, level of school practice, counselor preparation, and confidence in one's group leadership abilities continue to be influential factors in a counselor's use of group processes in schools.

The important role of group process in comprehensive school counseling programs continues to be sustained in the literature, in counselor training programs, and among practicing counselors. Counselors who examine this issue and choose to establish group counseling and group guidance services in their school programs begin by selecting the types of group structures most conducive to their setting.

Group Structures.   In small-group guidance and group counseling, there are essentially two types of structures—open and closed. Open groups allow students to enter and leave the group as needed, and the schedule of group sessions is for an indefinite period of time. By contrast, a closed group begins with identified members who continue with the group until it ends. In closed groups, a specific number of members are selected through a screening process. These participants attend all sessions and remain in the group until the last session. One problem with closed groups occurs when too many members stop attending and the support network discontinues. In contrast, open groups replace members who leave with new members who rejuvenate the group by bringing fresh perspectives and ideas. Although this open structure may afford new stimulation, adding new members to a group runs the risk of adversely affecting the cohesiveness established earlier in the group.

Closed groups, by definition, are structured and tightly scheduled, which may be more appealing to teachers and administrators who want to adhere to more precise schedules and routines. Open groups may be confusing and difficult for students who have to remember which group they are in and when their groups meet. Furthermore, students in closed groups have the advantage of knowing when their group sessions will end. In practice, this helps students focus on their concerns, bring up issues more readily, and attempt new behaviors to address their problems. By knowing when groups will end, students and counselors set a time line of sorts that they use to influence and facilitate desired changes. In contrast, open groups may unintentionally encourage members to procrastinate and put off disclosing their concerns or making the necessary decisions to effect change.

One aspect related to group structure and success is member participation. In particular, each member's voluntary participation in a group, as opposed to involuntary assignment, can make a significant difference in how a group functions. In schools, students are sometimes asked to participate in groups to address their behaviors, academic progress, alcohol and drug use, or other problematic aspects of their development. In these cases, students may be assigned to groups as a condition of their continued progress and attendance in school. Such students may be reluctant participants at best. School counselors who use group procedures follow ethical guidelines regarding voluntary participation and enlist the cooperation of all group members (Gladding, 2004).

Even though some students are assigned by counselors to particular groups involuntarily, it is essential that their actual participation—sharing, self-disclosing, and supporting others—remains voluntary. Though counselors may initiate groups as a result of referrals from parents, teachers, and administrators, the students *must voluntarily participate.* Students in groups may choose *not* to actively contribute in the group sessions to which they are assigned without their consent. Effective counselors, who are highly skilled in group relationships, call on all their leadership abilities to encourage these students and invite them to participate for their benefit and the good of other group members.

By determining the types of groups to include in their programs and carefully choosing the processes for establishing particular groups, school counselors identify their professional role in developing and leading groups. Because teachers and parents sometimes oppose services that remove students from classes, counselors want to have a clear process for establishing groups by informing people about the program, carefully selecting and including students, scheduling sessions, and obtaining permissions when required. Earlier in Chapter 6, ideas for establishing groups within a comprehensive program were presented.

Leading Groups

Small-group counseling requires the same knowledge of theory and approaches that individual counseling demands. The process of group counseling is similar to individual counseling in that the group members start by forming relationships, continue by exploring concerns and issues of importance to them, examine alternatives and strategies, and create individual action plans. When all issues have been adequately addressed and action plans implemented, the group reaches closure. Active listening, appropriate questioning, adequate structuring, and other communication and leadership skills are required in group work with students.

Small group guidance involves communication skills similar to those used in counseling and presentation skills used in classroom guidance. Because small group guidance takes the form of instructing or informing, counselors tend to use more didactic skills and approaches in these sessions with students. Sometimes group guidance consists of a single session to focus on a particular learning objective. In these instances, the counselor's effective use of time, preparation of materials, group management skills, and acceptance of comments from students to evaluate the lesson ensure that the session's goal is reached with most, if not all, the students.

In both group counseling and small group guidance it is important that counselors retain their leadership role. To achieve this, counselors set ground rules with each group member during the screening interview, and they reiterate these rules at the start of the group and during subsequent sessions as needed. Sample ground rules used with students in group counseling and small group guidance are as follows:

1. Set your goals early in the group and stick to your commitment to address these learning objectives and behavioral goals.
2. Present your concerns clearly to the group and discuss them honestly.
3. Listen to the opinions and concerns of other group members and respect their points of view.

4. Keep information discussed in the group confidential; you may discuss what you say with your parents, but you must not discuss what other members reveal in the group sessions.

5. Be on time for the group and remain for the entire session.

6. Accept and respect the counselor's role to lead the group.

7. Agree that group decisions will be made by consensus.

Ground rules set the foundation for cooperative relationships in the group process. Combined with effective counseling skills, ground rules and other structural aspects of establishing groups increase the likelihood that group counseling and small group guidance sessions will be successful. To ensure the appropriate use of group services, counselors understand all the advantages as well as the limitations of these helping relationships.

Advantages of Group Counseling

1. Group counseling offers a social setting in which students can share concerns, practice new behaviors, and support one another in a safe, nonthreatening environment. In groups, students have the opportunity to exchange ideas, test assumptions about themselves and others, and compare and contrast their views with others. Individual counseling does not offer the opportunity for such broad experiences and exchanges.

2. By sharing their concerns in groups, students learn about and identify with common issues and perceptions held by others. This process of identifying with others increases cohesiveness and enhances understanding about students' concerns.

3. Group counseling encourages listening and facilitates learning. For group members to reach an acceptable level of understanding, empathy, and helpfulness with their peers in the group, they must develop effective listening skills. Any services that help students improve their listening skills should be beneficial to the learning process.

4. Controlled peer pressure can be used in groups to encourage and confront students about their behaviors, goals, and attitudes that inhibit their development and progress in school. Under the direction of a competent group counselor, students gently persuade and cajole their peers to accept the group's consensus about changes they need to make and to choose appropriate plans of action.

5. Group counseling is action oriented. The purpose of placing students in groups for counseling is to help them select goals, identify changes they want to make in their lives, formulate plans of action, and implement steps to realize their objectives. These decision-making processes and skills are valuable to students in all areas of learning and development.

6. Group counseling can be less intense and threatening than individual counseling. In one-to-one relationships, students are sometimes overwhelmed by the presence of the counselor and feel inhibited about sharing personal concerns without support from others.

7. Group counseling is economically more efficient than individual counseling because more students can receive services in the same time span. While this is an advantage, it is not so important that individual counseling should be relegated to a lower priority in school counseling programs. Both individual counseling and group counseling

are important services and school counselors should consider each on the basis of students' needs, objectives of the helping relationships, and preference of the students who seek services.

Limitations of Group Counseling

1. Effective group work takes a high degree of leadership skill. Group counseling is more complex than individual counseling because the factors to consider and the dynamics of the process are multiplied. Some school counselors may be overwhelmed by the students' needs and the facilitative skills required to be successful group leaders

2. Group counseling requires a high energy level from the counselor to keep track of the group direction, address members equally, and establish effective relationships. Fatigue can occur when counselors attempt to lead too many groups in a given period of time. Keeping track of the dynamics in the group and relating to each group member effectively can be emotionally draining as well as physically exhausting.

3. Scheduling groups, as noted earlier, can be difficult. It is much easier for school counselors to call in one student at a time than it is to schedule groups of students out of classes. Counselors who work closely with their teaching colleagues in designing group schedules are likely to be successful with their group counseling services.

4. Group counseling may not be suitable or effective with some students. Students who have severe behavioral disorders or other dysfunctions may not be suitable for group processes. Disruptive behaviors, limited cognitive abilities, and severe emotional disabilities, for example, may limit the likelihood of success in groups.

Advantages of Group Guidance

1. In group guidance, counselors and teachers can impart information or instruction to larger numbers of students. Group guidance reaches more students than individual consultations and opens avenues for discussion and sharing that may not occur with individual students.

2. Group guidance does not require any special training in counseling theories and techniques because it uses instructional processes. Effective teachers who have strong facilitative skills can be quite successful in leading group guidance.

3. Guidance is best implemented as an interdisciplinary approach. Group guidance can be integrated with other subjects in the school curriculum, such as language arts, social studies, mathematics, physical education, and others.

4. Group guidance has the potential to enhance the total environment of the classroom or school by emphasizing positive aspects of human development and relationships. Information learned and behavioral skills achieved through classroom guidance can be generalized by students to address personal, educational, and career goals in their lives.

Limitations of Group Guidance

1. Because guidance groups are more educational and informational than they are therapeutic or personally enhancing, they may not result in significant changes in students who have critical conflicts or serious difficulties in their lives and in school. However, group guidance activities often help to identify such students, so teachers can refer them to the counselor for more intense intervention.

2. Depending on the size of the group, guidance activities do not allow as much inter-action among group members as do group counseling sessions. Therefore, personal support, caring, and the development of trust are not as in-depth as they are in group counseling.

3. Group guidance does not necessarily offer individual assistance toward specific personal, educational, or career goals for all group members. When group guidance is designed to present a series of topics, it is possible that attention to individual needs of students may be overlooked in an attempt to reach the instructional objectives of the guidance lessons. In contrast, group counseling focuses directly on the individual needs and expectations of each group member.

4. Because group guidance uses instructional processes and techniques, and the size of groups is sometimes twenty-five or more students, counselors need to be more structured and directive in these activities. This leadership style may seem contradictory to counselors who prefer helping relationships with more freedom of expression for students.

When determining whether to use individual counseling, group counseling, or group guidance approaches in school programs, counselors consider all the advantages and limitations of each approach, the primary goals and objectives of counseling services, their individual and group skills, and the acceptance of the school and community for these services. In addition, counselors become familiar with the research about the effectiveness of the counseling models they choose and the different types of group services they offer.

Research on Counseling

Much of the research on counseling has focused on the "core conditions" first proposed by Rogers (1951). Although he developed the person-centered approach, and subsequently these conditions have been closely associated with this perspective, research of other counseling models has indicated that these qualities are universally important to all helping relationships. The now classic research efforts of Rogers, Carkhuff, Truax, Berenson, and many others have extensively examined the contribution of genuineness, empathy, positive regard, and concreteness to the establishment of beneficial relationships and the attainment of successful outcomes in counseling (Carkhuff & Berenson, 1967; Rogers et al., 1967; Truax & Carkhuff, 1967). In addition, investigations by these and other researchers have expanded this list of essential conditions to include further dimensions of effective counseling.

Currently, the research does not support any particular approach to counseling as being more effective than others. In a summary of research examining the effectiveness of counseling approaches and techniques, Sexton and Whiston (1991) confirmed past findings and reported that successful counseling relationships include "mutually interactive" processes in which counselors are empathic, involved, warm, and credible in the eyes of their clients. In addition, most benefits occur in the "first 6 months of weekly sessions" (p. 343). These authors also noted that the "most crucial aspect of counseling . . . seems to be the skillfulness of the counselor implementing the intervention" (pp. 343–344). On this basis, effective counseling is best measured by the degree to which counselors help their clients focus on identified problems, set goals to master these situations, and gain independence in learning to solve life's difficulties (Sexton, 1999).

Beyond knowing what the research says about fundamental characteristics of effective counselors and about basic skills essential to positive outcomes, school counselors must stay current in their knowledge of prevailing practices. In a 1992 review of research of comprehensive school counseling programs, Borders and Drury noted that the purpose of counseling interventions is "to promote students' personal and social growth and to foster their educational and career development" (p. 491). They cited numerous studies from the 1970s and 1980s that indicated students who received counseling services showed improvement in attitudes, behaviors, and academic performance.

Sink (2005) summarized several studies that support the use of brief counseling and its application in school settings. Combined, these studies provide quantitative data and qualitative findings indicating success of brief counseling methods across an array of issues including academic, career, personal, and social issues and across culturally diverse populations.

Effective school counselors keep abreast of research findings about counseling and other services they provide. This means reading professional literature and reports about approaches that demonstrate success with students in school. It also means learning how to assess the value and effectiveness of counseling approaches selected in one's own school program.

Examples of research studies can be found in numerous scholarly journals, including *Professional School Counseling,* the national journal of the American School Counselor Association. School counselors should be aware of research studies that examine different approaches to use with students, and they should adapt available research to select viable strategies and interventions to use in individual counseling.

Because school counselors have responsibility for a wide spectrum of student needs, and they provide such an array of different services for students, parents, and teachers, they usually find that more than one view and approach to counseling is required to satisfy all their program goals and objectives. They also know that individual helping relationships have limitations and absorb a considerable amount of time. For this reason, research on group processes is equally important to a comprehensive school counseling program.

Research on Groups

In 1989, Gazda noted that research studies of group processes have increased in the counseling literature in recent years. He analyzed 641 research studies published between 1938 and 1987 according to the following variables: type of controls, treatment period, type of group, assessment instruments, statistics used, type of study, experimental designs, size of samples, and the nature of outcomes. On the basis of his analysis, Gazda (1989) concluded that the research on group counseling has generally made considerable progress in identifying variables related to group effectiveness. Although research methodology has improved in recent years, Gazda noted that some areas of group counseling need additional study, and some existing problems with research methods need to be corrected. Gladding (2004) noted that early group research was deficient for several reasons, including the lack of sophisticated designs and statistical analysis. However, Gladding (2004) echoed Gazda's (1989) optimism for new methods of research used by group investigators.

Whiston and Sexton (1998) reported on several studies that examined large group and classroom guidance sessions. According to Sink (2005), research on large groups, while not extensive, illustrates a level of effectiveness across a wide range of topics that include self-esteem, career development, study skills, cultural knowledge, and other issues.

The remainder of this chapter presents research studies of group counseling and group guidance. The studies presented here form a sample of research to give a broad view of the types of groups used by school counselors and illustrations of results reported in the counseling literature. We begin with group guidance research.

Group Guidance Research

Although the school counseling literature has advocated the use of small and large group guidance for several years, research on the effectiveness of guidance activities has been limited when compared to the number of studies on individual and group counseling. In some instances, reports of research studies do not clearly indicate whether the groups were guidance-oriented or group counseling sessions. The following are studies of groups that appear to be instructional or informational in nature and therefore are classified here as group guidance.

Stickel (1990) reported on a multimodal group project with kindergarten students to improve social skills, develop problem-solving skills, increase cooperation in small groups, and enhance their expression of feelings. Four groups of five children each made up the study, and each group met for seven sessions, twenty minutes every other day. The sessions consisted of three segments including a leader-directed activity, a student-involvement activity, and a sharing time among group members. Each session focused on one of the modalities described in the BASIC ID paradigm of the multimodal model. Although the researchers did not report statistical findings in the results of this study, the kindergarten teacher "noted increased cooperation and interaction among certain children following the groups and thought it allowed the counselor to get to know the children better as individuals and give them some needed individual attention" (p. 286).

A 1986 study in Florida demonstrated that classroom guidance units can generate positive results in altering student attitudes and behaviors (Myrick, Merhill, & Swanson, 1986). Fourth-grade students in sixty-seven elementary schools were randomly assigned to either treatment or control groups. A pretreatment assessment by teachers rated each student's attitude. Counselors presented a six-lesson guidance unit to the treatment groups. Sessions focused on (1) understanding feelings and behaviors, (2) learning about perceptions and attitudes, (3) helping someone new to the school, (4) making positive changes, (5) experiencing the "I am lovable and capable" activity, and (6) looking for personal strengths. Results from thirty-seven schools were complete enough to use in the analysis. Data were collected using teacher and student inventories of their perspectives on a number of behaviors and attitudes. The results indicated that students who participated in classroom guidance "were significantly different from those in the control group in terms of finishing class assignments on time . . . and saying kind things to others" (p. 247).

In this study, teachers' perceptions of the control groups and treatment groups also demonstrated significant differences. Teachers viewed treatment groups more positively than control groups on a number of factors, including: (1) getting along with others, (2) working hard on assignments, (3) following directions, (4) liking their teachers, (5) being liked by their teachers, and (6) believing they were important and special persons. These positive results were noted across student populations, from those in preassessment who were identified with poor attitudes to students who were rated highly on the attitude scale. All students seemed to benefit from the classroom guidance sessions. The Florida study was replicated in Indiana with 731 fourth-graders and similar results were found.

A study using affective education to improve reading performance of second-grade students indicated positive results in a twelve-week program (Hadley, 1988). Three treatment groups and four control groups of second-graders were included. A program consisting of self-esteem activities to diminish negative attitudes, improve patience, and enable students to handle anxieties was presented to the three treatment classes. Results indicated a significant impact on academic growth as measured by reading scores on the Stanford Achievement Test for students who participated in the classroom guidance program.

Gerler and Anderson (1986) investigated the effects of classroom guidance on students' attitude toward school, achievement in language arts and mathematics, and classroom behavior. In this study, 896 fourth- and fifth-grade students from eighteen different schools were presented a classroom guidance unit entitled "Succeeding in School." The unit consisted of classroom guidance lessons presented by the eighteen counselors in the participating schools. Results of the study indicated that the program had a positive effect on students' classroom behaviors. In comparison with control groups, the treatment groups improved behaviors while the control groups remained the same or became worse. Attitudes about school and academic achievement were additional variables indicating favorable results for the treatment groups.

Lee (1993) used the "Succeeding in School" lessons (Gerler & Anderson, 1986) in a follow-up study. She found that fifth- and sixth-grade students significantly increased their math achievement over a control group of students. Increases in language and conduct scores were also noted.

A group guidance stress-control program demonstrated some positive effects with elementary students from an inner-city school (Henderson, Kelby, & Engebretson, 1992). A total of sixty-five students were randomly assigned to either the experimental or control group. Nine 50-minute sessions were conducted for the treatment group by two graduate assistants who were trained in classroom guidance. The sessions included topics on stress, relaxation, exercise awareness, time management, assertiveness, handling anger, expressing other emotions, friendship, and creative problem solving. Significant differences between the treatment and control group were found in two aspects of self-concept related to stress in school—behavior with peers and school-related tasks. The treatment group also reported significantly more appropriate coping strategies after the program than the control group.

Research of a study skills program with 118 fourth-grade students demonstrated significant increases in average test scores on the California Test of Basic Skills (Carns & Carns, 1991). Over a single year of participating in the study skills program, students' mean scores increased an average of three years, one month in grade equivalency scores.

More recently, Schlossberg, Morris, and Lieberman (2001) investigated the impact of classroom guidance units with ninth-grade students. Their study of ninety-three students in a large urban high school used six 45-minute developmental guidance lessons that were facilitated by counselors and teachers together in the classroom. Results of the study indicated significant differences in student ratings on scales measuring behavior, attitude, and information favoring the students who participated in the developmental guidance lessons. Also, teacher ratings on these same students showed significant differences in the areas of attitude and information learned.

These and other research studies demonstrate that classroom guidance, also referred to as affective education, developmental guidance, and psychological education, can have positive effects on students' attitudes and behaviors. Although changes in attitudes and behaviors have occurred in many studies of guidance groups, significant change in self-concept as a result of classroom guidance has not been consistently found. This is not surprising since self-concept theory postulates that self-perceptions create a certain stability in the human personality (Schmidt, 2006). As such, we can expect change in the self-concept to occur gradually after intense treatment over a period of time. Classroom guidance does not allow for this type of intense, long-term intervention. Group counseling, however, is more conducive to establishing this type of helping relationship.

Group Counseling Research

Research on group counseling covers a broad area of treatment topics, student behaviors, and models of counseling. Borders and Drury (1992) reported that "a number of empirical studies have verified the positive effects of group counseling interventions" (p. 491). In studies cited by the authors, students showed significant improvement in school attendance, school behaviors, achievement, attitudes, and self-esteem among other characteristics. The following are a few examples of studies from the 1980s into the twenty-first century using group counseling with student populations.

In 1985, Myrick and Dixon identified twenty-four students in two middle schools who demonstrated poor attitudes about school. Six students in each school were randomly assigned to group counseling and the other six were placed in a comparison group to receive counseling later. Group counseling consisted of six sessions that focused on topics related to feelings about school, how feelings relate to behaviors, consequences of behaviors, giving and receiving feedback, taking the first step toward improvement, and being positive. Data collected on the two groups indicated that teachers rated the students in group counseling significantly higher in improved classroom behavior. This was true for both boys and girls in the groups. Students who participated in the groups reported positive feelings about themselves and a greater understanding of others.

Omizo, Hershberger, and Omizo (1988) examined the use of group counseling with elementary-grade students who were identified as aggressive and hostile by their teachers. Students in the study were assigned to either experimental or control groups. Those in the experimental groups participated in group counseling using cognitive-behavioral techniques, modeling, role-playing, and positive reinforcement. Results indicated that students in group counseling tended to decrease their aggressive and hostile behaviors to a greater degree than students assigned to control groups.

Divorce has been a popular topic for group counseling with students. Tedder, Scherman, and Wantz (1987) used group counseling with fourth- and fifth-graders whose parents had divorced and who were referred by teachers or parents because divorce adjustment was a concern. Two groups of students participated in eleven sessions of group counseling and guidance. Parents and teachers completed two instruments, the *Walker Problem Behavior Identification Checklist* (Walker, 1962) and the *Child Behavior Rating Scale* (Cassel, 1970), in pretest and posttest assessments for all the children. Results showed that teachers' ratings of students' behaviors did not change, but parents noted that children were less distractible and exhibited fewer behavior problems at home.

Omizo and Omizo (1987) also investigated the use of group counseling with children of divorce. A sample of sixty elementary students from divorced families were randomly assigned to an experimental or a control group in a study that examined differences in student aspiration, anxiety, academic interest and satisfaction, leadership initiative, identification and alienation, and locus of control. The experimental group met for ten sessions in which the counselor specifically addressed divorce using bibliotherapy, role-play, and discussion. Findings indicated significant differences between students in the group counseling and those assigned to the control group in aspiration, anxiety, identification versus alienation, and locus of control. Group counseling was found to be "beneficial for enhancing some areas of self-concept and an internal locus on control among elementary school children experiencing divorce" in this study (p. 51).

De Luca, Hazen, and Cutler (1993) reported on the effectiveness of group counseling with elementary school girls who had experienced sexual abuse. Seven girls participated in a ten-week counseling program in which 90-minute sessions focused on "feelings about the offender, responsibility, guilt, fears, assertiveness, social skills, problem solving, sex education, and prevention" (p. 104). Results of this preliminary study suggest that group counseling can have a positive effect on anxiety and self-concept. The authors encouraged counselors to evaluate the possibility of using group approaches with students who have experienced sexual abuse.

In a group study of children of alcoholics, Riddle, Bergin, and Douzenis (1997) found that students showed benefits of participating in group counseling. Self-concept scores improved, social skills increased, and anxiety scores decreased over the fourteen-week period that the group met. The forty students who participated in the program also learned about alcoholism and ways to cope in families suffering with this disease.

Many research studies of group counseling and group guidance offer similar results to those listed above. School counselors who want to persuade their principals and teachers of the efficacy of group work should become familiar with research findings to make a strong case. In addition, counselors want to develop a rationale for using group processes to help students learn from one another, instruct them in social skills, and enable them to become caring, cooperative members of society.

Through their leadership in group counseling and group guidance, school counselors contribute to the broad effort and mission of educating the whole student. Group guidance, especially when integrated into the curriculum by teachers and counselors, uses the classroom as a social setting to explore issues and values essential to students' character development. This is not a new concept. Good teachers have applied these ideas in their relationships with students since schools began. Therefore, group guidance and group counseling are vehicles with which counselors can assist teachers in continuing beneficial traditions in education.

Additional Readings _____

Corey, M. S., & Corey, G. (2002). *Groups: Process and Practices* (6th ed.) (Pacific Grove, CA: Brooks/ Cole).

A practical and readable guide, this book gives a thorough overview of various group processes for children, adolescents, and adults.

Davis, T. E., & Osborn, C. J. (2000). *The Solution-Focused School Counselor: Shaping Professional Practice* (Philadelphia, PA: Accelerated Development).

An excellent resource for school counselors who want to take a fresh approach in helping students, teachers, and administrators try strategies that work.

Johnson, D. W., & Johnson, F. P. (2000). *Joining Together: Group Theory and Group Skills* (7th ed.) (Boston: Allyn and Bacon).

The seventh edition of this readable text helps counselors move from theory to practice by using experiential exercises and numerous examples throughout each chapter.

Kottler, J. A. (2001). *Learning Group Leadership: An Experiential Approach* (Boston: Allyn and Bacon).

This practical guide is an introduction to the basic skills and knowledge needed to be successful as a group leader. Personal applications, reflections, and class activities offer numerous experiential opportunities to learn and practice group processes.

Websites _____

Association for Specialists in Group Work
www.asgw.org
Cooperative Learning
www.clcrc.com/pagescl.html

Effective Group Counseling
www.ericdigests.org/1994/group.htm
Guidance and Counseling
www.edu.gov.mb.ca/k12/specedu/guidance/ group_work.html

Exercises _____

1. Visit a school for a few hours during the day. Your goal during this visit is to observe the one-to-one interactions between students and teachers, students and students, and students and counselors. Note differences and similarities among these three pairs of interactions. Present your findings in class and discuss their implications.

2. In a small group, talk about the many one-to-one interactions a school counselor has with students, parents, and teachers during a typical day. List as many of these as your group can in a minute. Once your list is made, determine which of these interactions would be considered "counseling relationships." What factors did you use to identify those interactions that are counseling?

3. List five beliefs you now hold about human development, based on the following: (1) Why do people choose the behaviors they do (What causes behavior?) (2) What conditions affect a person's success in life? and (3) How can people change? After you have written your list of beliefs, share them with a classmate and decide which theory of counseling is most aligned with your assumptions.

4. Several research studies have found that group guidance can have positive effects on student variables. Review studies of group guidance effectiveness within the past ten years, and note how many of them compared counselor-led groups with teacher-led groups. Summarize your findings for a class discussion.

5. In a small group, think of topics that might *not* be appropriate for group counseling in a school setting. If there are such topics, how would you suggest school counselors address them if not through group processes?

6. A new school counselor has confided her apprehension about doing large group guidance with middle-grade students. She was a mental-health counselor before coming to the school setting and has never worked with large groups of students. What recommendations would you give that would decrease her anxiety and build confidence in her ability to lead groups?

8

Collaboration and Consultation

Although school counselors have primary responsibility for developing comprehensive programs, they cannot fully meet this challenge without assistance and support from other professionals in the school system and the community. For this reason, school counselors systematically initiate collegial relationships with a variety of educational, medical, and other professionals who provide auxiliary services to school populations. These alliances of counselors and other helping professionals are essential for delivering the broad spectrum of services expected in a comprehensive school counseling program. They ensure the availability of appropriate responsive services for students, parents, and teachers who seek the assistance of school counselors.

Forming successful alliances requires a clear understanding of the services needed and knowledge of the types of services offered in the community. At the same time, professionals who work in community agencies, health departments, family centers, and other organizations need to know about the role and training of school counselors. By achieving a mutual understanding of their professional roles and functions, school counselors and community practitioners establish beneficial relationships with students, teachers, and families, as well as collaborative relationships with each other.

These collaborative relationships are not limited to professionals in the school and community. Rather, they include, and perhaps begin with, the cooperative associations that school counselors create with parents. Parental involvement is a vital ingredient of successful school counseling programs at all levels. Because this is so, counselors in schools make every effort to establish lines of communication with the home, invite parents to plan educational goals for their children, advertise services of the school counseling program, and, when appropriate, include parents in learning about the critical concerns of their children and adolescents.

Collaboration is an important aspect of all consulting relationships formed by school counselors. In this chapter, you will learn about many individuals, professionals, and agencies with whom school counselors create and maintain working relationships on behalf of students, parents, and teachers. Some authorities distinguish between the terms *consultation* and *collaboration,* whereas others present varying models of collaborative consultation in the literature (Brown et al., 2006). For example, Fishbaugh (1997) offered three models of collaboration, including a consulting model, a coaching model, and a teaming model. Each model, according to Fishbaugh, has a particular focus and purpose. The consulting model tends to take a traditional approach of offering expert advice. In contrast, she defined coaching as creating equality in a relationship that follows a cycle of supervision (Brown et al., 2006). The teaming approach advocates an interactive process within which participants address identified problems and create possible solutions. The teaming approach is one advocated in recent transformation literature (Stone & Dahir, 2006). Offering another perspective, Dettmer, Dyck, and Thurston (1999) proposed a *collaborative school consultant* approach that calls upon the counselor's facilitative communication skills, cooperative relationships among school personnel, and coordination of the services that are needed.

Numerous views of collaboration and consultation have been presented (e.g., Brown, Pryzwansky, & Shulte, 2006; Caplan & Caplan, 1999; Mostert, 1998; Parsons & Kahn, 2005). Consequently, school counselors want to be familiar with the professional literature regarding collaboration and consultation so that they can communicate their understanding of the terms to other student services team members, teachers, and parents. In this text, we take the view that collaboration is one form of consulting. It is particularly useful in schools because of its emphasis on building partnerships with parents, teachers, student services professionals, and other personnel in the school system and community. Because authorities have varying views on the use of these terms, what seems important is that school counselors attain their own understanding and use the terms consistently to define and describe their program of services. Readers are encouraged to refer to the sources cited in this chapter to expand their knowledge of collaboration and consultation and arrive at an understanding of what these terms mean for them.

This chapter presents an overview of the consulting skills and processes that enable counselors to establish and facilitate collaborative relationships with different participants. Counselors who develop effective consulting skills are in an excellent position to create superior programs of expanded services for their schools. They learn about the various agencies and services offered in their communities, develop effective communication networks, and use this knowledge and skill to establish strong alliances that benefit students and their families.

The next two sections examine many groups and professionals with whom school counselors consult and collaborate to establish effective services for students. For clarity, these groups are classified into two categories: school services and community agencies.

School Services

Today's schools and school systems consist of a multitude of professionals and volunteers who provide countless services to students, parents, and teachers. In comprehensive programs, school counselors interact, directly and indirectly, with all these groups. This is not an easy accomplishment. The demands on their time often prevent counselors from seeking supportive services beyond their own counseling program.

Because their primary role is to provide direct services to students in the school, counselors occasionally create a narrow focus for their programs by overemphasizing their own counseling and consulting services with students. As a result, they neglect to collaborate and consult with agencies and individuals who could supplement these services. In some cases, the tendency to overlook school or community programs misses a vital service that counselors could use to assist students more directly and effectively than they are able to do by themselves. The first step in ensuring that this does not happen is to learn about all school-based services and the professionals who perform these functions. At the same time, counselors learn about parents and other guardians of students in the school. As mentioned before, collaboration with parents and guardians has significant impact on direct counseling services with students.

Parents and Guardians

Although families in the United States have various configurations, in most instances one or two adults in a given family play significant leadership and guardian roles. In traditional two-parent families, these adults would be a mother and father. In others, a single parent, stepparent, grandparent, aunt or uncle, foster parent, or friend of a parent assumes a leadership role. In all these cases, whether the child is relating with a parent or other guardian, school counselors have responsibility for establishing collaborative working relationships.

Chapter 3 noted that parental involvement may be strong in the elementary years and then taper off as students move through the secondary school level. As such, we might expect that collaborative relationships are more apparent in the primary and intermediate grades than in secondary schools. Although this may be true, parental involvement continues to be an important factor during the early adolescent years, and in contemporary U.S. society, it seems to retain importance well into early adulthood. This extended role for parents is due in part to the higher percentage of people attending college and pursuing advanced degrees in professional and graduate schools.

Economically, parental involvement appears to be an essential ingredient that enables young people to continue their formal education well into their twenties and beyond. At the same time, employment trends and the cost of living have necessitated continued parental support in providing housing for children who are beginning careers and in offering financial assistance for young couples who are just starting out.

This trend toward longer parental involvement in children's developmental and decision-making processes has an effect on the overall involvement that parents expect to have in their children's education. The result is that schools, teachers, and counselors must form cooperative working relationships with parents and guardians in designing educational programs for students, selecting helping processes and strategies, and making plans for future educational and career directions. The first step in this process is for counselors to learn about the families served by their schools and determine the needs of parents by assessing the role they expect to play in the schooling of their children.

Through needs assessment procedures, counselors determine which services to offer parents, the types of programs to which parents will respond, and the services for which parents will volunteer in the school. A comprehensive school counseling program touches all these areas because counselors (1) counsel and consult with parents and guardians, (2) design informational and instructional programs for parents, and (3) invite parents to assist with functions such as student tutoring, test monitoring, career guidance, and educational information (Perry, 2000).

The relationships that counselors establish with parents and guardians are often important ancillary functions to individual and small group counseling with students. This may be particularly true for elementary counselors, because they serve students who have little control over the environments and situations influencing their lives. Parents of young students and middle-graders have a tremendous impact on the choices their children make regarding school performance, career direction, friendships, and other developmental elements. By consulting with parents, school counselors design support networks and channels of communication to complement the goals and objectives of counseling with students. Parents and guardians who want children to benefit from these helping relationships welcome the opportunity to meet with school counselors, gain understanding about their children's needs, and develop strategies to nurture positive parent-child relationships at home.

When collaborating with parents and guardians, school counselors create many avenues through which they provide direct services or offer indirect assistance. For example, counselors frequently contact parents about students' progress in school and consult about ways to support their educational development at home. Relationships such as these illustrate a cooperative effort that says, "We are together in this effort to help children learn and develop their fullest potential." Such a stance is more facilitative than one that views parents as the opposition, a "them against us" mentality. Counselors who believe facilitative relationships are essential for improving home-school communications work to establish mutual respect between parents and teachers.

Another direct service that counselors provide for parents is educational programs. Parenting is a challenging role for which few of us are prepared in any formal sense. The parenting skills most of us have learned, we adapted from the parenting styles of our parents and guardians when we were children. Unfortunately, these behaviors are not always conducive to healthy, affirmative relationships. To assist in the parenting process, school counselors facilitate parent meetings, establish support groups, and lead parent education programs. Sometimes these events are informal get-togethers where parents exchange ideas about what works with children in their families. For example, one elementary counselor I know holds periodic "coffee and doughnut" gatherings for parents on their way to work in the morning. Such exchanges are beneficial as ways of brainstorming limitless strategies to assist parents in communicating effectively with their children and adolescents. By facilitating these exchanges and designing educational activities for parents, counselors demonstrate the school's willingness to cooperate and work with parents in creating optimal learning opportunities for all students.

In Chapter 3, we discussed how some educational programs for parents are packaged and marketed commercially. Typically, these programs have a trainer's manual for the counselor to follow and a participant's handbook for parents. Parent education programs can be organized in a single session or in a series of meetings to present specific information about child behavior, leadership strategies, and other issues of interest to parents. Some programs continue for several sessions and cover a wide range of issues and topics about child development and parenting skills.

School counselors arrange their work schedules to accommodate parent education programs. Often, parent groups meet at night to fit work schedules, but occasionally, counselors lead parent groups during the daytime, when students are in school. When counselors schedule groups during the day, they seek suggestions from their principals and advisory committees to examine the ramifications of using school time to assist parents. If positive parenting skills equate to increased learning and participation of students, counselors are able to convince principals and teachers of the importance of these daytime activities.

Support groups for parents usually center on a particular concern or issue, such as being a single parent, and counselors lead these groups in discussion of common concerns and exploration of actions to handle everyday problems. Parents' support groups endorse each member as an "expert" on his or her child. The assumption is that no one knows the child better than the parent. This expertise is "pooled" in group discussions, and counselors use this collective knowledge to assist individual parents who need help or alternative ideas to handle current situations or problems. Groups such as these allow parents to see that they are not alone in their struggles and, at the same time, enable them to gain support from the collective wisdom of the group. During this process the counselor is the facilitator of discussion, the keeper of time, and the coordinator of the group activity.

Few students develop at optimal levels without support and encouragement from their parents and guardians. Through services such as these, counselors let parents know about available resources to help students. One way of informing parents is through direct contact. By consulting directly with parents, counselors provide current information, instruction, and essential problem-solving services.

Counselors who address the informational and educational needs of parents ensure that schools and parents move in the same direction and have similar goals for students. To verify this parallel movement, counselors also consult and collaborate with teachers in their schools.

Teachers

No school counseling program is successful without the support of teachers. Teachers are a vital link in the integration of affective education into the curriculum. They are the first-line helpers in the school counseling program, and they are referral sources for students in need of additional assistance. For these reasons, counselors at all levels of educational practice wisely cultivate collaborative relationships with all the teachers in their schools.

One of the first signs of collaboration between counselors and teachers is the input counselors request about the nature, scope, and focus of comprehensive school counseling programs. Counselors who send these requests are well received and respected because they demonstrate mutual regard for teachers and the teaching profession. This partnership is not merely a mutual admiration society but shows a genuine respect for what it takes to be an excellent teacher, balanced by an acceptance of the unique role that counselors play in school programs.

Counselors collaborate with teachers in many other ways, some of which are similar to the individual and group processes for parents described earlier. For example, teachers and counselors consult with each other to identify the needs of individual students, gather data to assess these needs, make decisions about practical strategies to assist students, and evaluate outcomes of these strategies. Counselors also consult and collaborate with teachers in group sessions, such as team meetings in middle schools and departmental meetings in senior high schools. Counselors who are sought out by individual teachers and invited to team meetings are respected for their collaborative skills and empathic understanding of the teacher's role. By the same token, these counselors seek out teachers for their guidance and suggestions and thereby demonstrate respect for teachers' knowledge of curricula and command of instructional methods.

Teachers' support groups are another medium by which school counselors collaborate with their colleagues. As with parents' support groups, teachers' groups rely on the expertise of group members to explore concerns, identify pertinent issues, suggest alternatives, and plan reasonable action. The emergence and application of this kind of "teachers' expertise" is made possible through the facilitative skills of the counselor as a group leader. By relying on the observations and suggestions of other teachers in the support group, counselors lead these groups in discussions while avoiding the role of expert. This is another way that counselors learn to appreciate the difficult role of teachers in elementary, middle, and high schools. At the same time, teachers in a support group have an opportunity to watch the communication and facilitation skills of their counseling colleagues.

Collaboration between counselors and teachers also occurs when they cooperate to plan and present in-service activities for staff development. Sometimes counselors give these presentations as a result of suggestions from teachers. Other times, counselors recruit teachers who are skilled in particular areas of instruction or child development. Experienced teachers who are skilled facilitators are often the best people to present faculty in-service in schools. Instructional and informational programs for school faculties are successful when teachers and counselors cooperate by setting staff development goals, planning appropriate activities, and following through on these action plans.

Teachers of Exceptional Children.   Other teachers who are especially important collaborators with school counselors are those who teach exceptional children. These professionals are highly trained to identify and provide instruction for children and adolescents who require special education services.

Coinciding with the development of special education programs in the 1970s, as you learned in Chapter 2, was the emergence of a professional specialty for teachers of exceptional students (sometimes called special education teachers). These teachers are trained in pedagogical theories and methods of curriculum and instruction, and they have specialized knowledge and skills to address the needs of students identified with specific challenges. Educable handicapped, learning disabled, emotionally disabled, academically gifted, physically impaired, and multihandicapped children and adolescents are among students who are served by special education teachers.

Because school counselors provide services for all students in schools, they especially want to collaborate with special education teachers in assessing students' needs, locating school and community resources, planning counseling services, and examining school policies that have positive or negative effects on the educational progress of challenged children and adolescents. Special education teachers assist counselors in all these functions and, in addition, collaborate to keep counselors up-to-date about current regulations and research findings regarding various areas of exceptionality. At the same time, counselors offer these teachers support and understanding as they create and deliver appropriate instruction for the school's most challenging, and most challenged, students.

School counselors and teachers of exceptional students also cooperate by helping parents and guardians of these children adjust to the challenges of nurturing, guiding, and caring for them. Parents of these children face obstacles unknown to most mothers and fathers. This is particularly true of students who have a debilitating mental, emotional, or physical handicap. The guilt sometimes associated with having borne a child with any type of disability, combined with the challenges of daily care, supervision, and parenting, often seems insurmountable. Counselors and teachers who offer parents support and guidance can help immeasurably.

Counselors who form close alliances with teachers of challenged students are better able to create effective helping relationships with these students and their parents. They are informed about the exceptionalities, disabilities, and handicaps with which the family and child are dealing and, therefore, are in better position to design and implement successful interventions and services. Counseling these students and consulting with their parents have special features that require particular knowledge and skills. By collaborating with teachers of exceptional students, counselors in schools are able to acquire this knowledge and skill.

School counselors have a responsibility to include special education students in their comprehensive program of services. Too often, counselors neglect this population because of unreasonable counselor-student ratios, unnecessary administrative obligations, and the mistaken perception that the special education teacher provides sufficient individual attention for these students. By collaborating with teachers, counselors can provide guidance lessons in special education classes, place students in appropriate small group counseling and guidance activities, and see particular students for individual counseling. To plan appropriate counseling and guidance services for these students, it is essential that school counselors be actively involved in developing each student's Individual Education Plan (IEP) as noted in Chapter 2.

Principals

Schools are managed by principals trained in educational administration, curriculum, law, and other aspects of school governance. These administrators are ultimately responsible for everything that goes on in school buildings and in educational programs. Therefore, every service and activity scheduled and provided by school counselors is directly or indirectly supervised by a school principal. This awesome responsibility makes it essential for principals and counselors to collaborate about the design of the counseling program, selection of major goals and objectives, identification of appropriate functions, evaluation of services, and countless other details related to comprehensive school counseling programs. This collaboration between principals and counselors is an ongoing process that enables counselors to include their principals in program planning processes and, at the same time, to inform school administrators of issues affecting students' educational development.

Many of the activities planned by counselors have a schoolwide focus to meet the needs of a broad spectrum of students, parents, and teachers. In determining goals and strategies for these schoolwide events, counselors collaborate with school principals to check on the feasibility and appropriateness of particular activities. Principals have knowledge of local policies, financial limitations, and other restrictions that guide the selection and implementation of activities planned for the school. By establishing working relationships with their principals, school counselors are better informed about the parameters within which their programs of services need to function. Similarly, effective communication with administrators allows counselors the opportunity to convey their assessment of students' needs and the overall school climate and how these two elements interact in the school.

When sharing information with principals, counselors are careful to follow ethical standards and legal guidelines regarding confidential matters and privileged communications. Counselors frequently receive confidential information in their relationships with students, and this information must remain private unless there is imminent danger to students or others. Ethically, school counselors cannot reveal confidential information to principals or other people without the consent of their clients. However, because counselors are privy to information that reflects on the overall condition and climate of the school, they have an obligation to inform principals about these conditions. For example, if a senior high counselor has learned from students that a number of girls are pregnant, the counselor needs to inform the school administrator of this situation. Of course, the counselor cannot reveal the identities of the young women, but he or she can tell the principal that the condition exists. By having this information, the school administrator is in position to plan educational services these students will need and to consult with the school nurse about appropriate health services to provide. In addition, the principal might confer with the counselors and teachers about preventive services the school should develop for the future.

By collaborating with their principals, counselors take charge of school counseling programs. They inform the administration about their annual plans; they focus on essential services for students, parents, and teachers; and they keep lines of communication open to receive advice from their school administrators. In addition, counselors become the coordinators for all student services, including those provided by school nurses, psychologists, and social workers.

Nurses, Psychologists, and Social Workers

Some schools and school systems have student services beyond the elements of a comprehensive counseling program. These additional components include nursing and health, psychological, and social services, and they are provided by highly trained professionals in each respective area.

These student services overlap to some degree in that they each focus on the physical, emotional, and social health and welfare of students and families. Because their functions overlap, student services professionals realize it is imperative to collaborate with each other and coordinate their activities. In schools where counselors work full-time, it is logical for them to coordinate student services. This is especially true when the nurse, psychologist, and social worker are at the school part-time. As a full-time employee, the school counselor coordinates referrals, follows cases, schedules team meetings, and performs other functions to make certain students receive appropriate services.

One form of collaboration is a team approach where student services staff members meet on a regular basis. Through these regular meetings, the counselor, nurse, psychologist, and social worker share information, update cases, assign responsibilities, and avoid duplication of services. They also focus on specific cases to ensure that students are receiving appropriate services from the school and that referrals to community resources are adequately pursued and monitored.

Effective collaboration among these student services professionals begins with a mutual understanding and respect for their unique roles in schools and regard for their individual areas of expertise. In situations where this respect and regard are not achieved, student services are not well coordinated, and as a result, students' needs are inadequately addressed. In today's schools, students, parents, and teachers face sufficient challenges to require the services of all these professionals. Adequate coordination and timely collaboration provide appropriate and effective service for all concerned.

Collaboration within the school and school system helps counselors stay abreast of students' needs and select appropriate services to meet these demands. Sometimes, schools seek assistance from agencies and resources within the local community and from county and state organizations. By collaborating with available agencies, counselors give their schools an edge in initiating referral procedures and receiving timely services for students and families. This is most important in rural areas, where schools and communities do not always have the resources and funds to meet the demands of students and families. As a result, counselors in these schools use their creative and leadership abilities to help people join forces to reach program goals. The next section presents a few of the agencies typically used by schools to locate social, health, psychological, and family services for their students.

Community Agencies

Schools comprise a major agency in a community, but alone, they cannot offer all the human services necessary to help a town, city, or county educate its citizens, provide healthcare, and offer basic services to improve the human condition. The primary mission of schools, and simultaneously the primary mission of school counseling programs, is to ensure the educational development of all students. In their attempt to reach this goal, school personnel offer an array of related services such as counseling, psychological evaluation, healthcare consultation, and social services. They offer these services to assist the school in its primary mission of education. The assumption is that as personal needs, health concerns, and learning difficulties of students are identified and addressed, students' educational progress is assured and their opportunity for success in life is enhanced.

When services offered by schools are insufficient to remedy the concerns of students and families, counselors and teachers turn to community resources. Not all communities have ample services, so school counselors locate those that exist and establish collaborative professional relationships to benefit students, parents, and teachers. Successful collaboration rests, in part, on the school's ability to convey its role and mission to these community resources, while also learning about the agencies' roles. The primary mission of public agencies and private practitioners in the community is to assist in one or more of the human service areas. For example, most communities have access to a health department that offers a wide range of medical services and health education programs.

Health Departments

School counselors and other student services professionals collaborate with health departments in a variety of ways. Elementary and middle school counselors rely on community health services to assist families with medical checkups and offer recommendations to the school about health and medically related issues affecting the educational development of students. In some communities, health consultants work closely with the school to develop appropriate guidance activities on the physical growth, sexuality, and healthcare needs of students. Similar services are available to senior high schools and, in addition, health services exist for pregnancy, sexually transmitted diseases, substance abuse, and other critical problems.

A strong cooperative relationship between the school and healthcare professionals is vital to student welfare. When schools and healthcare professionals form active partnerships, adequate services are accessible and accurate information becomes available to students and their families. When health concerns appear to be other than physical, schools turn to community mental-health services.

Mental-Health Centers

At times, the emotional and personal concerns mentioned by students to counselors, nurses, psychologists, and social workers require in-depth, intensive interventions. Although student services professionals may be competent to offer these interventions, time, schedules, and other factors associated with comprehensive school-based programs make it appropriate to refer these students and their families to mental-health centers.

Mental-health counselors, social workers, and psychologists spend a majority of their time in one-to-one and small-group therapy helping clients remedy social, emotional, and behavioral problems that interfere with development and learning. Collaboration between school counselors and mental-health practitioners is essential because, while students are receiving treatment at the centers, they usually remain in school and continue their contacts with school counselors regarding classroom work, academic progress, and school behavior. By collaborating, mental-health counselors and school counselors are careful not to confuse students in their respective helping relationships. In most instances, the agency counselor has primary responsibility for focusing on immediate social, emotional, or behavioral concerns. The school counselor supports this intervention by encouraging the student at school, locating and establishing support systems, and implementing strategies suggested by the mental-health professional and agreed on by the school, classroom teachers, and parents.

Social Services

Among the challenges faced by U.S. families in today's society is the real prospect of economic disadvantage, unemployment, and financial ruin. The gap between the lower and upper classes of our society continues to widen. Frequently, students and their families are confronted by job loss, homelessness, lack of heating fuel, need for food, or other critical concerns. Counselors and teachers are usually the first to learn about severe economic losses and limitations of families, and therefore, they are frequently in touch with departments of social services in their communities.

In addition to these severe economic needs, children and adolescents in many families are increasingly at physical and emotional risk due to neglect and abuse. In part, economic stress contributes to this social illness, but alcohol and substance abuse are often found to be significant factors. Federal and state laws require school personnel to report instances of suspected child abuse to the appropriate authorities, and in most communities this is the protective services of the department of social services (DSS) or a similar agency.

Because the issue of child abuse and neglect is so sensitive and potentially explosive, counselors collaborate with DSS to ascertain the proper reporting procedures, the responsibilities of each agency, and the role of the school in handling these cases. Without this type of communication and cooperation, reporting procedures may be misunderstood, responsibilities blurred, and the safety of children unattended. It is essential for school counselors to be aware of federal and state laws regarding child abuse reporting, know their school system's policies and procedures, and follow reporting guidelines of the local child protective services.

Family Services

When children and adolescents struggle in their educational development, contributing factors often emanate from familial disturbance and dysfunction. Conversely, students' educational problems sometimes contribute to family stress and hardship. Often, it is impossible to separate students' concerns from their interactions with family members. For this reason, school counselors establish collaborative relationships with clinics and professionals who specialize in family counseling services.

Frequently, mental-health centers and departments of social services employ counselors, psychologists, and social workers who specialize in family interventions. Other community resources include family counseling services sponsored by United Way agencies, churches, universities, and other nonprofit organizations. Knowing which agencies and institutions offer these kinds of services enables school counselors to pursue appropriate avenues for referral.

By collaborating with family services in the community, school counselors recognize the influence of family dynamics in child and adolescent development. Harnessing this influence and using it to establish positive goals and strategies are imperative, and cooperative relationships between schools and family practitioners are avenues through which to accomplish these objectives.

Counselors can use opportunities to form collaborative relationships between the school and family practitioners. For example, family counselors can educate school personnel about family needs and stresses and thereby encourage involvement and inclusion of parents and children in schools in nonthreatening ways. These community professionals can sensitize the school to family breakups that have destroyed what were once loving relationships, but which now fuel resentment and bitterness among family members. Consultations between school counselors and family counselors allow the school, especially teachers, to become informed about stress and difficulty affecting children's daily lives.

In some instances, school counselors work with entire families (Hinkle, 1993; Nicoll, 1992; Sink, 2005). Models of family counseling for implementation in school counseling programs have been encouraged in the counseling literature. For example, Williams, Robinson, and Smaby (1988) proposed a "group skills model that incorporates techniques associated with problem solving and interpersonal communications" (p. 170). They designed a model for intervening in childhood and adolescent problems that stem from dysfunctional family relationships. Amatea and Fabrick (1981) recommended the family systems approach as an alternative to traditional counseling with students. Adlerian counseling, another approach to family service, is also encouraged in school counseling practice and counselor training (Nicoll, 1992). Sink (2005) deduced that "school counselors are in a strategic position to support and counsel families because they have an understanding of the school system, a background in child and adolescent development, and knowledge of family dynamics and counseling interventions" (p. 127).

Invariably, those who advocate family counseling and other family-oriented services by school counselors suggest that the integration of these approaches requires an adjustment in school counselors' schedules to allow evening and weekend hours when necessary (Palmo et al., 1984). In addition, family interventions should cover a wide range of services, including family counseling, parent education activities, and parent support groups in a comprehensive program of services.

Colbert (1996) advocated for a model of collaboration and coordination efforts that encouraged counselors to establish partnerships with families. He maintained that such efforts were consistent with school reform initiatives and redefine the role of school counselors in comprehensive programs. Similarly, Keys and Bemak (1997) suggested, "the school counselor's 'school only' focus is too narrow to provide the multidimensional services needed to effect long-term change . . . help for an individual must occur within a larger network of school-community interventions targeted at families and students" (p. 259).

Comprehensive counseling programs, in contrast to traditional services, plan activities for parents and attempt to focus on entire families when situations suggest a link between a student's development and family functioning. In most comprehensive school counseling programs, however, family counseling and parent education services are limited. For this reason, school counselors who provide family services continue to rely on community agencies and private practitioners as primary referral sources. In some communities, where public services are insufficient to meet the tremendous needs of student populations, school counselors rely on psychologists, psychiatrists, counselors, and other therapists in private practice to assist students and their families.

Private Practitioners

Physicians, counselors, clinical social workers, and psychologists in private practice offer an array of services to children, adolescents, and families to assist with educational, psychological, and social development. By identifying private practitioners in their communities, school counselors expand the list of resources available to students, parents, and teachers. The longer the list, the more options and alternatives are available.

When school counselors suggest community resources to assist students and parents with identified concerns, it is best to have a list from which people can choose. In this way, counselors rely on their clients to make the final selection and thereby demonstrate respect for their ability to make responsible decisions. Parents and students consider costs, personal preferences, and other factors when selecting agencies and professionals for additional services. It is best for the referring counselor to provide as much information as possible, offer a list of two or more options, and let the individual make the decision about where to seek further assistance.

In all these collaborative relationships with parents, teachers, administrators, specialists, community agencies, and private practitioners, school counselors call on their training in communication and consulting skills to establish successful associations. In many respects, these consulting skills are similar to the competencies that counselors use in individual and group counseling relationships (Gladding, 2004; Schmidt & Osborne, 1981). While this is so, the consultative roles assumed by school counselors when working with parents and other professionals have a distinct purpose and make a unique contribution to the development and implementation of comprehensive school counseling programs.

Counselors as Consultants

Consultation is not new to the school counseling profession. According to Aubrey (1978), its place in school counseling was first advanced in a 1966 joint report of the American School Counselor Association (ASCA) and the Association for Counselor Education and

Supervision (ACES). In the late 1960s, Faust gave particular emphasis to the consulting role of school counselors in his book *The Counselor/Consultant in the Elementary School* (1968b). Similarly, Fullmer and Bernard (1972) referred to the school counselor-consultant as an "emergent role" in the profession (p. 1). Since that time, many articles and books have examined various ways that school counselors use consulting skills and processes with students, parents, teachers, and other professionals. As school counselors help students, parents, and teachers face increasingly complex problems, the expectation is that consultation will continue to be a major function (Parsons & Kahn, 2005).

School counselors spend considerable time in consulting relationships. In particular, counselors consult with teachers about students' progress, motivation, and classroom behaviors. As seen earlier in this chapter, they also serve as referral agents for parents and teachers in locating information and resources with which to help students, and instruct students, parents, and teachers in issues, topics, and skills to assist all groups in realizing their educational and career goals. Many perspectives and approaches to consultation exist for counselors to consider, depending on the purpose of their helping relationships. For a comprehensive overview of consulting models and processes, consult the references cited in this section.

In Chapter 5, we introduced different ways that counselors consult with students, parents, and teachers to distribute information, give instructions, assist with problem-solving services, encourage curriculum changes, and plan schoolwide events. The skills and processes associated with these different consulting roles are similar to other helping relationships established by school counselors. Yet, structurally there are differences. In this section, we examine some of the aspects that distinguish consulting relationships from direct counseling services.

Consulting Processes

In his now classic mental-health model, Caplan (1970) defined consultation as "a process of interactions between two professional persons—the consultant, who is a specialist, and the consultee, who invokes a consultant's help in regard to a current work problem" (p. 19). Likewise, Bergan (1977) described consulting relationships as problem-solving processes.

School counselors use consultation in a broader context that includes educational, informational, and problem-solving relationships. As Parsons and Kahn (2005) noted, this perspective views consultation as an umbrella for many services of a comprehensive program rather than as a solitary technique. As an example, in some instances counselors assume consulting roles to help their schools prevent problems. In other cases, counselors consult with teachers, parents, and others to plan activities that focus on developmental needs of students. These consultations form a triadic relationship consisting of the counselor-consultant, a consultee, and a situation with another person (the client) or other type of external concern.

One way to visualize consulting relationships is as a triangular relationship that consists of a consultant, a consultee, and a situation. In such consultations, the counselor-consultant assists the consultee in finding and implementing solutions to the problem situation. Sometimes group conferences may include more than one consultee, but the triangular structure is still applicable.

Another perspective on consultation is of situations that demand a preventive response. In consultations with a preventive focus, identified problems or situations receive attention through instruction or by sharing information. For example, if middle school teachers want to hone their communication skills to enhance advisor-advisee relationships, the counselor may serve as an instructional consultant. In this scenario, the teachers are the consultees, and the situation would be teacher-student communications. Figure 8.1 illustrates the triangular nature of most consultations used by school counselors. The arrows in the diagram indicate communications, fact-finding processes, and responses among the three elements in the consulting relationship.

The triangular view of consultation differs from direct counseling relationships because the ultimate goal is to address or remedy a situation or other aspect external to the relationship between the consultant and consultee. In this sense, the consultant works with the consultee who in turn makes adjustments or intervenes with the identified situation. In contrast, a counseling relationship assists another individual in making direct changes in his or her life. Hansen and colleagues (1990) noted that, unlike counseling relationships, "consultation is not primarily used for private motives of the individual consultee" (p. 5).

In an early article, Kurpius and Robinson (1978) outlined different modes of consultation that include various purposes. Later, Kurpius and Fuqua (1993a) delineated four generic modes of consultation. These modes offer different roles that counselors can adopt when performing consulting functions. The first role is one of an *expert*. In this mode, counselors provide answers to problems by offering expert information to students, parents, and teachers. In some instances, the "expert" consultant uses direct skills in "fixing" a broken situation. Similar to the "expert mode" is the *prescriptive role* that counselors assume when they gather information, diagnose situations, and recommend solutions. A third consulting role used by counselors is that of a *collaborator* when, as we saw earlier, the counselor works in partnership with consultees to define areas of concern and design strategies to affect change. *Mediation* is a fourth mode of consultation described by Kurpius and Fuqua (1993a). Sometimes, when counselors assist consultees who are at odds with each other or with an external situation, the consultation takes on the appearance of negotiation or mediation. In these instances, it is the counselor-consultant who becomes

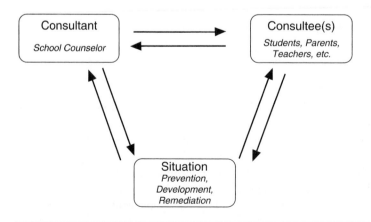

FIGURE 8.1   *Triangular Structure for Consulting in School Counseling Programs*

the *mediator* and *negotiator.* The counselor attempts to find common ground between conflicting views and sometimes negotiates compromises. To these four modes, I add *instructor* as a fifth consulting role for school counselors. This is usually the role school counselors take in parent education programs, teacher in-service, and classroom guidance with students.

The consulting role that counselors assume as *collaborator,* which we addressed earlier, establishes an equal relationship among participants to facilitate change (Kurpius & Fuqua, 1993a; Kurpius & Robinson, 1978). The collaborative mode is generally accepted as a viable role for school counselors when consulting with students, parents, and teachers (Brown et al., 2006). The collaborative mode is also effective in consulting with school administrators, social workers, and other professionals who seek ways to enhance the educational opportunities and developmental progress of students.

In schools, instructional and informational consultation is clearly different from counseling relationships. However, problem-solving consultations resemble counseling processes because the feelings of the consultee are considered in the exploration and selection of viable alternatives and strategies. The use of consulting processes in school counseling programs to convey information, offer instruction, or resolve difficult situations requires the application of different processes. As a result, the roles and processes chosen by school counselors are determined in large part by the goals of the consultation itself.

Informational and instructional consultations require processes such as preparation, presentation, feedback, and evaluation. Problem-solving consultations, on the other hand, have a slightly different focus, and therefore require different skills and processes. In problem-solving consultations, counselors gather information, identify the main problem, help consultees explore alternatives and strategies, facilitate decision-making, win agreement, follow up this agreement, and evaluate outcomes. We now consider these different consulting roles and the processes associated with each of them.

Informational and Instructional Consultation. The processes and skills used to convey information and present instruction are similar. Counselors plan programs with teachers, lead parent education groups, and facilitate classroom guidance and other instructional activities using similar behaviors. In many respects, the skills and processes used by school counselors in these types of activities resemble instructional approaches used by classroom teachers. Instructional approaches can be classified into four categories including information processing, social interaction, individualized education, and behavior modification (Good & Brophy, 1994). School counselors use all four of these approaches in various instructional and informational activities with students, parents, and teachers.

Information processing is one type of instruction used by school counselors to disseminate educational and career materials to students and parents. Presenting course information, discussing financial aid opportunities, and reviewing community resources are a few examples of informational presentations planned and implemented by school counselors.

Social interaction approaches are used in teacher in-service, parent education, and group work with students. In these relationships, participants are encouraged to interact with each other to learn about the topics addressed in the program. By using social interaction procedures, school counselors rely on the combined expertise of group members to find solutions, offer ideas, and explore alternatives. In this way, counselors avoid becoming sole experts and instead become facilitators of the learning process.

Individualized consultations provide information and instruction in brief contacts with students, parents, and teachers. The counselor-consultant in these instances acts as a sounding board and enables individuals to choose a direction, find appropriate materials, learn a necessary skill, and reach an identified goal. An example of this type of consultation is when a high school student seeks a counselor's assistance in deciding to which college to make an application. The counselor shows the student how to review resources, administers interest inventories about college selection, and gives other assistance to enable the student to narrow down choices.

Behavior modification strategies are helpful in both individual and group consultations. Behavioral approaches with individual students can be helpful in teaching a skill or learning to cope with particular situations and can be used to instruct parents and teachers in management skills for home and school. Sometimes, behavioral instruction is a strategy used in problem-solving consultations as well.

Each of the above approaches relies on particular processes and skills on the part of the counselor-consultant. Generally, these processes and skills include behaviors related to preparation, presentation, feedback, and evaluation.

Preparation.   Successful instruction and information sharing require adequate preparation of materials and time. Counselors who present classroom guidance activities, teacher in-service, and parent education programs are successful when they choose instructional goals carefully, plan appropriate learning activities, and schedule their presentations within a reasonable time frame. For example, when counselors present classroom guidance, they plan developmentally appropriate activities for all students in the group. The content of their lessons and the activities they choose for instruction include vocabulary and concepts that elementary, middle, or high school students understand. At the same time, counselors allow adequate time for the lesson in accordance with the age and development of students. Elementary, middle, and high school students tolerate various types of presentations for different lengths of time. Knowing these differences and planning programs accordingly increases the likelihood that students will attend to the presentation and achieve the intended learning objectives.

When counselors choose developmentally appropriate objectives, use materials and media to which participants will be responsive, and schedule beginning and ending times that facilitate optimal learning, their presentations to students, parents, and teachers are more likely to be successful. Adequate preparation begins this process and is followed by effective presentation skills.

Presentation.   In many respects, successful guidance, in-service, and other presentations by school counselors depend on skills similar to those used by effective teachers. Research on effective teacher characteristics has not produced conclusive findings, but consensus among educators highlights teaching skills and behaviors that distinguish effective instruction (Ryan & Cooper, 1988), including:

1. Design lessons and state goals to let students know what is expected and what they will learn.
2. Monitor students' progress with regular feedback and task-oriented assignments.
3. Use well-paced instruction to maximize the content covered in the lesson.

4. Ask high-level questions that require students to analyze, synthesize, or evaluate information.
5. Communicate high expectations for all students.
6. Manage classrooms with appropriate skill, positive reinforcement, and attention to student achievement.

This list is by no means all-inclusive. Other teacher behaviors relate to student learning and instructional effectiveness. The next list focuses on those behaviors that are particularly useful in presenting effective lessons such as classroom guidance.

1. Start the lesson promptly and use time efficiently.
2. State the purpose of the presentation clearly.
3. Give clear instructions and directions.
4. Encourage participation of all students.
5. Demonstrate adequate group management skills.
6. Facilitate the session with listening, questioning, reflecting, clarifying, and summarizing skills.
7. Respect the individuality of students.
8. Affirm and reinforce students' willingness to contribute.
9. Provide effective feedback to students.
10. Use evaluative measures to assess the outcome of the lesson.

These behaviors may also be associated with presentations to parents and teachers for instructional or informational purposes.

Regardless of the type of presentation, counselors use effective behaviors and evaluate the outcome of their services. In sum, successful presenters are deeply involved in their activities, encourage exchanges between themselves and their audiences, facilitate appropriate interaction among group members, use management techniques that maintain order without inhibiting participation, and pace presentations to keep a high degree of interest without moving so quickly that some members of the group get lost.

Feedback. For instructional and informational consultations, counselors set goals to distribute information or teach knowledge and skills to selected audiences. To create learning environments in which people accept information and attain skills, counselor-consultants seek ongoing feedback from participants. In this way, their presentations become more than didactic discourses. Instead, they encourage a free exchange of ideas and opinions about the subject matter being presented. Classroom guidance often teaches character education, citizenship qualities, and other traits revered in society. Although it is appropriate and proper to include these objectives in a guidance curriculum, teachers and counselors remain open to views that express different and sometimes conflicting opinions about important issues. A healthy exchange among students, parents, and other participants in these types of presentations fosters acceptance and instills democratic principles embraced by society and its schools.

Evaluation. Counselors measure the effectiveness of their presentations by asking two questions: (1) Has the information or content of the activity been acquired by the participants? and (2) Have the participants indicated their satisfaction with the presentation?

They answer the first question by observing the skills acquired by participants or by assessing whether participants have obtained the information and knowledge desired. For example, a counselor who presents conflict resolution strategies to middle-graders might evaluate the effect of this activity by having classroom teachers monitor student behavior and measure the acquisition of negotiation and mediation skills. Another evaluative process the counselor might use is to have the students complete a questionnaire to measure their understanding of the information presented as well as their satisfaction with the group program. Form 8.1 illustrates a sample questionnaire a counselor might use with a middle school group on conflict resolution.

By evaluating their presentations, school counselors are able to make adjustments in their programs and accurately meet the needs of students, parents, and teachers. There is little reason for counselors to continue activities that do not result in desired outcomes or are dissatisfying to participants. Because time is limited, counselors must evaluate their activities and services based on how well they meet the needs of intended populations and discard those that have minimum effect on program goals and objectives. In Chapter 11, we examine some of the evaluation processes that school counselors can use to assess programs and services.

Problem-Solving Consultations.   In addition to group presentations that focus on developmental learning and facilitate the dissemination of information, school counselors assist consultees in examining problems, exploring solutions, choosing strategies, and evaluating outcomes. Many problem-solving models have been developed and presented in the consulting literature for school counselors (Brown et al., 2006; Kurpius, 1978; Kurpius & Brown, 1985; Parsons & Kahn, 2005; Schmidt & Medl, 1983; Umansky &

FORM 8.1 *Sample Group Evaluation Form*

Your participation in the Conflict Resolution Group has been appreciated. Please evaluate our group by answering the following questions. Indicate your answers by circling either YES, NO, or UNSURE. Thank you.

1. Did you learn about yourself in this group?	YES	NO	UNSURE
2. Did you learn about other people in this group?	YES	NO	UNSURE
3. Was the group helpful in teaching you about conflict?	YES	NO	UNSURE
4. Did you learn ways to handle conflict?	YES	NO	UNSURE
5. Did the counselor listen to the people in the group?	YES	NO	UNSURE
6. Were you allowed to give your opinion?	YES	NO	UNSURE
7. Did other group members help you?	YES	NO	UNSURE
8. Was being in this group helpful to you?	YES	NO	UNSURE
9. Did the counselor's leadership help?	YES	NO	UNSURE
10. Would you recommend this group to other students?	YES	NO	UNSURE

Holloway, 1984). Generally, consulting models consist of similar phases or stages. The variations found in these proposed stages, or with the language used to describe processes within stages, are usually related to differences in theoretical foundations of the models. For example, behaviorally oriented consultations differ from Adlerian approaches, not because of any fundamental difference in consulting structures, but because of the way each theory views human development and behavior. Behavioral views focus on external factors that influence behavior and development, whereas Adlerian theory emphasizes people's perceptions and interpretative powers in self-creating a unique view of the world and their role in it.

Problem-solving and situational consultations performed by school counselors can be illustrated by a generic four-stage model that can be adapted to different, divergent theoretical perspectives. This model consists of an introduction, exploration, implementation, and evaluation phase.

Introduction.   In this phase, the counselor-consultant meets the consultee, makes introductions, states the purpose of the meeting, and hears the main concern. The essential goal of this phase is for the consultant to help the consultee clearly identify and express the concern. In this stage, the consultant and consultee establish rapport and begin gathering information that will enable them to agree on what is the main issue and the actual problem that needs immediate attention.

An additional reason for gathering information in the introduction phase is to enable the consultant and consultee to have data and other material to assist in the exploration of alternatives and possible solutions. Counselor-consultants use observations, tests, inventories, records, interviews, and other processes to gather pertinent information. This gathering is a nonjudgmental process in which the consultant accepts input from the consultee as it is given. Later, by evaluating and sorting various pieces of information, the consultant formulates opinions about various data to give an accurate direction to the consultation, but in this early stage information is simply collected.

Exploration.   After the relationship is established and a clear understanding of the problem is attained, the roles of the participants must be explored and clarified. This process is essential so that all persons in the relationship know their responsibilities as well as the other obligations assumed by everyone else involved. For example, when a parent consults with a school counselor about a child's behavior at home, both the counselor and parent agree that the counselor's role is not to go to the home and manage the situation, but rather to offer resources, information, and instructional opportunities from which the parent can select strategies to handle the problem successfully.

When roles are clarified, the participants in the consultation are ready to explore the situation and consider strategies to address it. In this phase, the information that was gathered earlier is closely examined, strategies and approaches attempted previously are discussed, and additional possibilities are debated. Sometimes consultants encourage brainstorming techniques to expand the alternatives. Brainstorming is a process of listing all the ideas available, regardless of how outrageous, impractical, or unlikely they might be. Once they generate this list, the consultant and consultee begin to narrow down the alternatives. Whatever process the consultant chooses to explore possibilities, the result of this phase of the relationship is to identify and agree on one or more strategies to implement.

Implementation.   Exploration without action leads nowhere. A successful consulting relationship uses the agreement reached in the exploration phase to design a plan of action, assign responsibilities, and make a commitment regarding these assignments. An action plan lets each participant in the consultation know what will be done, by whom, and when it will be accomplished. Only by designing and implementing an action plan with clear assignments and time lines are counselor-consultants able to perform adequate follow-up and evaluation of their consulting relationships.

Evaluation.   A successful consultation is not complete until follow-up and evaluation are done. In this phase, the school counselor (consultant) makes contact with all participants in the relationship, receives responses from each of them, and ascertains whether assignments were fulfilled according to the plan. If the counselor discovers that consultees did not complete assignments, the consultation returns to the exploration phase for further clarification of roles and examination of selected strategies. If all assignments are completed, then an assessment of change is needed. Closure in the consulting relationship is possible when the identified problem or concern has been adequately addressed and resolved by implementing the action plan.

This four-phase model for problem-solving consultations provides a structure by which school counselors can process information with students, parents, teachers, and other professionals and formulate agreements to carry out specific plans of action. In all these phases, there are specific skills that consultants incorporate to move the consulting process toward a successful conclusion.

Figure 8.2 illustrates a problem-solving model using the four phases of consultation presented above. Consulting skills are listed with each phase, and objectives are stated. Each skill, of course, is useful throughout the consulting relationship and may be found in more than one phase. In 8.2, the skills listed are essential for the phase in which they are indicated, but they are also useful during other stages of the consultation. Because so many skills are recommended for different types of consulting relationships, a few cautions are necessary. First, the counselor-consultant must be knowledgeable and skilled in the use of these facilitative behaviors. Skills used without proficiency are potentially damaging to relationships. Second, the frequency with which a particular skill is used can affect the success of a given session or interaction. For example, a consultant might be very knowledgeable and proficient in the use of paraphrasing, but if he or she uses this skill repeatedly, the consultee will begin to tire of it. Eventually, the relationship will falter and the consultant's assistance will be rejected.

A third caveat in using consulting skills relates to timing. Even the best intentions miss their mark when they are ill-timed. Successful consultants know *what* to do, and, equally important, they know *when* to do it. A well-intentioned question asked at an inappropriate time will not achieve its goal. Successful consultations, like magic shows, require precise timing of proficient skill.

Research on Consulting

Research on consultation is plentiful, but as some authors have noted, methodological problems are prevalent, making it difficult to draw concise and accurate conclusions (Brown et al., 2006; Froehle & Rominger, 1993). For one thing, consultation lacks clear

FIGURE 8.2   *Consulting Phases, Skills, and Objectives*

PHASE	SKILLS	OBJECTIVES
Introduction	Listening and attending Responding to content and feeling Clarifying Summarizing for understanding	Establish rapport Identify concerns and problems Gather information
Exploration	Questioning Structuring Focusing Clarifying roles Interpreting data Instructing/Informing Brainstorming	Narrow concerns List options Seek agreement on possibilities Move toward action
Implementation	Mediating/Negotiating Confronting Prioritizing Planning	Choose strategies Assign responsibilities Set goals and time lines
Evaluation	Observing Documenting Assessing Summarizing	Evaluate results Follow up on agreements Reach closure

description and definition due to the variety of structures and models proposed in the literature and used by counselors in schools. Also, research studies have not compared the effectiveness of processes used by different professional helpers in various programs of services. Much of the literature and research in school consultation, for example, appears in both school counseling and school psychology sources. Yet, these two professional areas have not been compared to determine if differences exist in the effective practice of consultation with parents, teachers, and other professionals. Future research might examine how counselors and psychologists use these approaches to determine whether professional focus and training make a difference in consulting relationships.

In school counseling, research has focused on a few theoretical approaches, namely Adlerian (Frazier & Matthes, 1975; Jackson & Brown, 1986; Williams, Omizo, & Abrams, 1984) and behavioral programs (Giannotti & Doyle, 1982; Henderson, 1987; Weathers & Liberman, 1975), in examining the effective use of consultation. Some research has reported the effects of special training and consultation programs, such as support groups for abusive parents (Post-Krammer, 1988).

Although a number of studies that examine the efficacy and effectiveness of parent consultation programs have been published, research on counselor-teacher consultation is limited. In one study, Cunningham and Hare (1989) reported success in instructing teachers in child bereavement processes. By training teachers in death education and child bereavement, counselors were able to increase teachers' effectiveness in helping children through the grieving process (Hare & Cunningham, 1988; Molnar-Stickels, 1985).

Generally, limited research indicates positive results with many types of consulting services and programs used by school counselors. However, more and better designed studies are needed. By way of example, a few studies are summarized here. Henderson (1987) reported positive results in improving children's alternative thinking skills by combining affective education programs with parental involvement. Students received classroom guidance instruction and parents participated in a seminar titled "Helping Our Children with Reading." Although the study failed to show significant results on all variables, students whose parents participated in the seminar performed significantly better on alternative thinking measures than students whose parents were not involved. Alternative thinking was defined as children's ability to generate alternative solutions to different types of interpersonal problems.

Giannotti and Doyle (1982) used Parent Effectiveness Training (PET) with parents of children with learning disabilities to investigate parental attitudes, children's perceptions of parental behavior, children's self-concepts, and children's behavior in school. Using a pretest-posttest control group design, the study found significant differences on all four variables. Parents who participated in PET reported more confidence in their parenting skills, a greater awareness of the effect their behavior had on their children, better understanding of their own needs, and more willingness to trust their children than did parents who were not in PET. In addition, children of parents in the PET group scored higher on self-concept measures than those whose parents were in the control group. Teachers' ratings of student behavior also indicated significant differences in some areas. Students whose parents were in PET were seen as less anxious about school achievement, having more self-reliance, and seeking more positive relationships with their teachers.

Two studies of *Systematic Training for Effective Parenting* (STEP), a program based on Adlerian principles, demonstrated some support for this type of consultation. A 1984 study measured changes in parents' attitudes after participating in a STEP program (Williams et al., 1984). The study also investigated changes in locus of control measures for the children of participating parents. All of the children in the study were identified as learning disabled. Parents were assigned to either the experimental group (STEP) or a control group. The STEP program was presented to the experimental group for nine consecutive weeks in two-hour sessions. Results indicated that the experimental group showed significant differences from the control group of parents. As measured by the Parent Attitude Survey (PAS) in a pretest and posttest design, STEP parents were more accepting and trusting after participation in the program, and they perceived their own behavior as more of a contributing factor in their children's behavior.

Another study of STEP placed twenty-five parents in an experimental group and twenty in a "waiting list" control group and used an eight-session format of one-and-a-half hours per session (Jackson & Brown, 1986). The study investigated changes in children's self-concept, perceptions of parent behaviors, and parents' attitudes. Unlike the first study reported above, this investigation found only one significant difference in parent attitudes. Parents in the STEP program scored higher on the trust scale than parents in the control group. No other significant results were found on either parents' or children's variables. The authors concluded that these results failed to support findings of previous research, but they noted that the modest support found for the STEP program "should be encouraging to counselors who hope to influence positively the attitudes of parents toward their children" (Jackson & Brown, 1986, p. 103).

Classroom guidance is another type of consultation used by counselors to provide information or instruction, and research studies pertaining to this service were reviewed in Chapter 7. In their review, Borders and Drury (1992) explained that the movement toward more comprehensive programs in school counseling has advocated the integration of guidance with the curriculum. This "infusion" of guidance into daily instruction can be accomplished only if school counselors take the lead in encouraging teachers to adopt this philosophy, help teachers plan the integration, and provide resources for teachers who want to include guidance objectives in their daily instruction. To take such a leadership role, counselors should be conversant in what the research says about the effectiveness of guidance activities in the classroom.

Although more research needs to be done in studying the effectiveness of consulting approaches, consultation remains an emerging and important practice in school counseling. Through individual and group consultation, counselors extend their services to a broad audience and collaborate with other professionals to design and implement appropriate and effective services for students, parents, and teachers. An important aspect of these collaborative relationships is gathering accurate, reliable information to make suitable decisions about programs and services. This process of gathering information brings us to the next essential service of comprehensive school counseling programs, student appraisal, which is explored in Chapter 9.

Additional Readings

Brown, D., Pryszwansky, W. B., & Schulte, A. C. (2006). *Psychological Consultation and Collaboration: Introduction to Theory and Practice* (6th ed.) (Boston: Allyn and Bacon).
This text is a thorough yet understandable treatment on consultation. It provides historical and theoretical perspectives on consulting and presents information on important processes and skills to use with parents and teachers.

Caplan, G. (1970). *The Theory and Practice of Mental Health Consultation* (New York: Basic Books).
This classic book is used as the foundation for much of what is called consultation today. This is especially true for consulting models as applied in the helping professions such as counseling and psychology.

Kurpius, D. J., & Fuqua, D. R. (Eds.) (1993b). Special Issue: Consultation: A Paradigm for Helping, I, *Journal of Counseling & Development, 71,* 593–708.

Kurpius, D. J., & Fuqua, D. R. (Eds.) (1993c). Special Issue: Consultation: A Paradigm for Helping, II, *Journal of Counseling & Development, 72,* 113–198.
These two volumes by Kurpius and Fuqua repeat the focus on consultation and update models of practice.

Parsons, R. D., & Jahn, W. J. (2005). *The School Counselor as Consultant: An Integrated Model for School-Based Consultation* (Belmont, CA: Brooks/Cole—Thomson Learning).
A contemporary guide to various uses of consulting in schools, this text presents a new integrated model of consultation. As such, consulting is not simply a service but rather an overarching structure under which all school counseling services exist.

Websites

Components of a Crisis Prevention Program
www.renew.net/prevstat.htm
National Association of School Nurses
www.nasn.org

National Association of School Psychologists
www.nasponline.org
School Social Work Association of America
www.sswaa.org

Exercises

1. Investigate available services in your community. Use the local telephone book, the Internet, and other resources to compile a list of services that could be used as referral sources for students in schools. Divide these services into categories such as "family services," "substance abuse services," and others to determine the range of services available.

2. Form a group of four with other students in your class. Design a role-play situation where one student is the counselor-consultant, a second is a parent, and a third is the teacher. Make up a situation in which the parent expresses a concern about the child's progress in school. During the role-play, the fourth member of your group is an observer who will give feedback about the various roles and skills observed.

3. Contact school counselors in the community and ask what, if any, parent education programs are used in the school. Establish a list of the most prevalent programs used by elementary, middle, and high school counselors. Some programs used by counselors may be original designs, and you may want to ask the counselor for a copy to share with your class.

4. Interview a school nurse, psychologist, or social worker. Ask them about their understanding of a school counselor's role and preparation. Ask what they know about a comprehensive school counseling program. Share your findings in class.

9

Student Appraisal

Early in its development, the school counseling profession established a strong focus on student assessment, particularly with the use of standardized tests. Since its inception, the profession has argued for and against the use of assessment instruments and processes in counseling relationships. Today, the controversy continues, and with the increased emphasis on school accountability and public demand for higher student achievement, there appears to be no end in sight to this debate. States across the country are using test results as benchmarks for student progress, instructional accountability, and evaluation of individual school performance. Unfortunately, neither these purposes nor the "high stakes" testing climate they create truly meets the instructional and educational needs of students. In contrast, school counselors have historically applied assessment techniques to help students gather data about themselves to make appropriate educational plans and decisions.

Counselors in schools often coordinate schoolwide testing programs, administer educational assessments to individual students, and interpret test data to parents, teachers, and professionals who provide services to students. Student appraisal functions—those procedures used to collect and interpret data about students' abilities, achievements, interests, attitudes, and behaviors—remain an essential part of the school counselor's role.

Student appraisal was briefly introduced earlier as one service of a comprehensive school counseling program. Now, we examine this function in greater detail. The chapter concludes with a brief consideration of the *Diagnostic and Statistical Manual of Mental Disorders,* commonly known as the *DSM-IV-TR* (American Psychiatric Association, 2000), and a rationale for why an understanding of this manual is useful to school counselors.

This is not a comprehensive treatment of the subject of measurement and appraisal in schools but, instead, a brief description of how student appraisal fits into comprehensive school counseling programs. For more in-depth information about this function and related processes, consider the sources cited throughout the chapter and listed in the references.

Before reviewing common appraisal instruments and assessment processes used by school counselors, an explanation of the terms used to describe and define measurement in counseling is appropriate. Several terms describe the scope of assessment and appraisal procedures in counseling (Drummond, 2004). Through an understanding of these terms, school counselors are able to take an appropriate role in student appraisal.

Appraisal is synonymous with *evaluation* and encompasses processes for measuring a range of student attributes, abilities, and interests and for making professional judgments based on the results of these measurements. Student appraisal (sometimes referred to as *evaluation*) involves collecting data from a variety of sources, forming opinions and making comparisons with those data, and drawing conclusions with which to guide students and others in educational and career decisions.

Assessment comprises the instruments and procedures to gather data for student appraisal. Educational tests, psychological evaluations, interest inventories, interviews, and observations are samples of assessment procedures used by school counselors, psychologists, teachers, and other school personnel.

Individual analysis is a description of a student's behaviors with emphasis on strengths and weaknesses. It is a process that includes the observation and interpretation of behavior and therefore is a special form of student appraisal.

Interpretation refers to processes that explain and give meaning to various data, observations, and information that counselors gather in student appraisal. In particular, counselors interpret behaviors to give them meaning and purpose within the context in which they are observed. School counselors interpret test results and school policies to help students, parents, and teachers understand problematic behaviors.

Measurement is a process to determine the degree and boundaries of specific traits and characteristics being assessed. Measurement assigns a numerical value or an evaluative description to the trait or characteristic in question. As such, it is the aspect of appraisal that tells us "how much?" or "how often?" By themselves, measurement data are of limited use. Only when applied statistically or comparatively do they acquire any meaning.

Diagnosis is an aspect of appraisal that refers to specific identification, grouping, and categorization of measurement results to make the *best guesses* or *best judgments* about student behavior and performance. Diagnosis has not always been a comfortable, acceptable term for school counselors. Perhaps this is due to its "medical" and "analytic" implications. Nevertheless, diagnosis is one aspect of appraisal and is an important element of the decision-making process used by school counselors to select appropriate services for students and other clientele.

Standardized Testing

In the controversy surrounding student appraisal, no single issue has raised more concern, fueled more heated debates, and caused more public uproar than the use of standardized tests. This controversy has focused on the plight of education in the United States and what some see as the failure of our students to compete successfully with students from other developed countries. An outcome of this concern has been an increased demand by politicians, parents, school board members, and other decision makers for more testing and evaluation of student achievement. In states and school systems across the country, money and energy have been spent developing, purchasing, administering, and analyzing test results. Thus far, despite all the time, effort, money, and best of intentions beneficial outcomes across the nation are uncertain at best. In other words, a link between emphasis on increased standardized testing and higher student achievement has not been identified.

Research findings in the school counseling profession related to the use of tests to improve student achievement and development are also lacking. Seemingly, the use of tests, in and of themselves, has had little impact on student development. What Goldman concluded in 1982 continues to have significance today:

> [T]ests seem to have made little difference in the decision-making, problem-solving, and planning activities of pupils and clients. There is very little evidence from research that tests as used by counselors have made much difference in the lives of the people they serve. (p. 70)

One major criticism of using tests in schools and other settings is their limitation with culturally diverse populations and the possibility of test bias. Lee (1995) posited that "culturally responsive school counselor[s] should have the ability to consider the dynamics of culture/ethnicity when interpreting data from standardized tests and other assessment tools. [They] should be able to recognize possible cultural bias in assessment instruments and consider this when making educational decisions about students from culturally diverse backgrounds" (p. 194). Several concerns related to the testing and assessment of minority students continue to be relevant to the selection and use of assessment instruments in today's schools. These concerns offer guidelines for counselors and other school personnel to use in assessment:

1. Assessment is unfairly discriminatory when students are not tested in their native or dominant language. The purpose of tests is to discriminate, but when unfair biases and inappropriate items are used, the validity of tests and reliability of results are questionable.

2. Tests are unfairly discriminatory when developed with white, middle-class sample populations and administered to culturally diverse populations. The student populations to which tests are administered should reflect the normative populations on which tests are developed.

3. When school counselors are poorly trained in assessment and the characteristics of culturally diverse students, they contribute to test bias and discriminatory practices.

4. When certain groups are overrepresented in special education programs (such as programs for the educable mentally retarded) and underrepresented in others (such as gifted and talented), there is evidence of test bias or improper assessment practices.

5. The practice of permitting students to remain in ineffective educational programs for years of schooling without demonstrating reasonable progress is indicative of cultural bias and unreliable assessment procedures.

6. Parental involvement is essential to appropriate assessment practices. When parents are excluded from decision-making processes or are uninformed about tests, testing procedures, and their children's results, full and accurate use of data is questionable.

7. Decisions made on limited test data place students at risk of being deprived access to educational and career opportunities. Proper appraisal consists of a wide range of information and data.

8. Tests and testing results used to reinforce prejudices and stereotypes are a violation of legal rights and clear examples of unethical practice. Schools must use tests to enhance opportunities for learning and create possibilities for student development rather than to discourage, demean, and deny their potential for growth.

9. When tests intentionally or unintentionally limit a student's choices for educational and career development, they contribute to existing prejudices and contradict the mission of our schools.

10. When schools use tests in isolation without consideration of other types of information and data, they violate basic principles of assessment and equity. School counselors who wish to create equitable procedures for all students attempt to include a wider spectrum of people in the decision-making process to ensure proper selection and use of assessment instruments. (Adapted from Oakland, 1982)

Another aspect of the debate on testing involves the misuse and misunderstanding of test results. Enthusiasm for finding a method of assessing academic progress has, unfortunately, been dampened by hasty decisions, improper procedures, unreliable scores, and inaccurately interpreted results. None of these conditions adds to the acceptance of assessment processes or measurement instruments in schools. As professionals prepared in appropriate use of tests and other standardized assessment instruments, school counselors have responsibility for proactively assisting their schools and school systems in the selection, administration, and utilization of tests and test results. The first step is to understand the meaning of standardization and to know the different types of standardized tests.

Standardization

A test is a standardized measure when administered and scored according to uniform procedures. When tests use the same procedures during every administration with every individual or group of students, it is possible to compare performance over time or to compare an individual's scores with the scores of other students. Test standardization, therefore, requires uniform testing conditions every time a particular test is administered.

Responsibility for adequate standardization rests with both the developer and user. The developer formulates specific test directions as part of the standardization procedure, and the user must adhere to these directions without deviation. Standardization includes the oral instructions given, materials used, time constraints, demonstrations, methods of handling students' questions, and other details related to test administration. In addition, other subtle factors may alter test administration to such a degree that it violates standardization. For example, if a counselor reads the directions at a pace much quicker than called for by the standardized procedures, such an administration may render the test scores unreliable and invalid.

Another aspect of standardization that allows for the comparison of scores across test administrations, or among students who take a particular test, is the use of *norms*. Standardized tests are developed and administered to a large representative sample of subjects, known as the *standardized sample,* for whom the tests are designed. Norms are the average scores of specified groups within the representative sample. For example, if on a spelling test, the average 10-year-old correctly answers fifteen out of thirty items, then the *10-year-old norm* would be a raw score of 15 correct. When reporting scores, standardized tests use either *age norms* or *grade norms*. The preceding example is of an age norm.

Standardized test scores are derived from normal curve distribution theory, which says that on a given trait, individual scores cluster near the center of the range of scores and gradually taper off as the extreme low and high scores are approached. The central score of this curve is called the *mean, median,* or *mode* depending on the type of statistical average used. These three different types of averages are called *measures of central tendency.* The statistical term used to describe the degree to which students vary from the average score is the *measure of variability,* and two types of variability are the *range* and *standard deviation.* Figure 9.1 illustrates a normal curve with the percentage distribution of cases across the range of scores.

In addition to age and grade norms, test scores of students are commonly reported by percentile ranks or standard scores. *Percentile ranks* indicate the percentage of students who fall below a particular raw score and show the relative position of students within the representative sample. For example, a percentile score of 45 means that 45 percent of the students in the sample obtained a lower raw score. Although percentiles are relatively easy to understand, they are often misinterpreted and misunderstood. All testing manuals that explain percentile scores warn that percentiles *do not* represent percentages of questions correct. Therefore, the percentile rank of 45, given above, *does not* mean that the student answered 45 percent of the items correctly. Percentile rank alone does not indicate how many items were on the test or how many correct responses were achieved. This is important for school counselors to remember when interpreting percentile scores to students, parents, and others who may not be test-sophisticated and may mistakenly interpret a percentile rank as the number of answers correct.

Another type of score, a *standard score,* indicates students' performance by the distance above or below the average score for the group. Standard scores express students' performance in terms of standard deviation units from the mean score. The *mean* is the average score for the sample population, and the *standard deviation* is the measure of variability or spread of the scores across the group. As seen in the normal curve distribution illustrated in Figure 9.1, standard deviation of plus or minus 1 presents scores in either direction of the mean and includes approximately 68 percent of the sample population. Accordingly, we would expect 68 percent of the students' scores to fall within this range of −1 to +1 standard deviations.

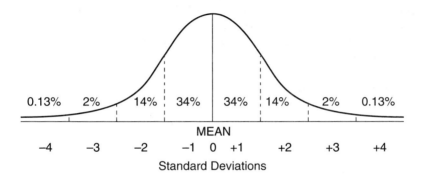

FIGURE 9.1 *Normal Curve Distribution with Percentage of Cases across a Range of Scores*

Unlike percentile bands, standard scores have the advantage of consisting of relatively equal units. Therefore, equal bands of standard scores indicate approximately the same performance difference along the distribution. For example, the difference between the scores of 400 and 500 on a test is roughly the same as the difference between the scores of 600 and 700. Percentile bands do not have this characteristic. The difference in students' performance from the 35th to 45th percentile rank cannot be equated to the difference between the 75th to 85th band. Another advantage of standard scores over percentile ranks is that they can be averaged mathematically.

Examples of tests used by school counselors and reported in standard scores are intelligence tests and college admissions exams. Intelligence tests that use deviation intelligence quotients set a score of 100 as the median (i.e., *median* IQ = 100), and a standard deviation of 15. As such, the range of plus or minus 1 standard deviation from the norm is 85 to 115. College admissions exams, such as the Scholastic Aptitude Test (SAT) developed by the College Entrance Examination Board, also use standard scores. For example, SAT scores range from 200 to 800 (not including the essay and writing subtests). Suppose the College Board reports a mean score of 500 on the SAT and a standard deviation of 100. Using the normal curve distribution, therefore, we may assume that 68 percent of the students who took this administration of the SAT scored between 400 and 600.

Stanine scores are a widely used type pf standard score (Drummond, 2004). A stanine system uses a 9-point scale, where 9 is high and 1 is low, and the mean is 5. Stanines 1 and 9 cover the tails of the normal curve distribution. Each of the remaining stanines, 2 through 8, includes a span of raw scores with a width equal to one half of the standard deviation.

Stanines are popular scores, particularly for reporting local norms, because they are easy to translate and explain to students and parents, and scores on different tests can be compared (such as between mathematics and language arts). In addition, stanines are easily recorded due to their single-digit form, and they are computed in the same way as percentiles, yet have the arithmetic advantages of standard scores (Gronlund & Linn, 1990).

The preceding description of standardization and different types of test scores does not do this topic justice. Readers who desire more in-depth explanation and information should consult the references cited in this section. At this point we examine two types of standardized tests used in schools: norm-referenced and criterion-referenced.

Norm-Referenced Tests.   Tests that compare an individual student's performance to the performance of a group are norm-referenced tests. Scores on these tests, such as percentile ranks and stanines, illustrate a student's relative standing in the normative sample. For example, a stanine of 6 in a language arts subtest indicates the student scored within the first standard deviation above the mean for the group. Likewise, a percentile rank of 34 in mathematics indicates the student scored better than 34 percent of the students in the representative sample (same age or grade level, for example). These tests report scores based on local, state, or national norms, therefore the term *norm-referenced* tests.

Norm-referenced tests are helpful in comparing students' performance and achievement with other students in their age or grade level, but they have limits when evaluating student knowledge or mastery of subject matter. As an example, if ten students were evaluated using a norm-referenced mathematics test, the results would show each student's relative position in comparison to the normative sample on which the test was developed. Yet, these scores alone would not help teachers learn the mathematical strengths and weaknesses of each student. All ten students could be quite able in math, but their scores would simply rank them against a sample population. One would be ranked highest and one lowest despite their comparable knowledge of mathematics. To evaluate these students' mathematical knowledge, teachers use a second type of assessment called a criterion-referenced test.

Criterion-Referenced Tests. These tests are designed to assess student performance in terms of specific standards or learning objectives. Returning to the example of the ten math students, a criterion-referenced test enables students, teachers, and parents to identify which math skills each student has mastered and which areas of knowledge and skill need additional attention. Typically, criterion-referenced test results are reported as the percentage of correct items in a particular knowledge or skill area. In the case above, for example, a student might score 35 percent correct in arithmetic computation for addition and 80 percent correct for subtraction. If the criterion for mastery is 75 percent correct, then this student has mastered subtraction skills but has not mastered addition.

Norm-referenced and criterion-referenced tests have purpose and benefit in student appraisal. Criterion-referenced tests enable counselors and teachers to describe the performance of students in relation to some set of learning goals and objectives. This information is helpful in designing and restructuring instructional programs to meet the needs of all students. This is of particular benefit in curriculum development. By contrast, norm-referenced results allow schools to make comparisons within the school and among schools in a district, state, or region. These comparisons help schools look at student placement, grade assignments, broad instructional issues, and demographic concerns in schools and school systems. Both types of tests have value. The important issue for counselors, principals, and teachers is knowing why they should select a particular test and whether or not it is a reliable and valid measure of the trait being assessed.

Selection of Tests

Because school counselors are professionals that are knowledgeable on tests and measurement, they often help their schools with the selection of instruments to use in testing programs. In addition, counselors select assessment instruments, including tests, to use in individual student appraisal. To give adequate assistance to their schools, and to select appropriate instruments for individual appraisal, counselors need to be knowledgeable and prepared to give guidance in making the best selections.

Counselors use a variety of sources to learn about new tests and keep abreast of research on testing. One essential source of information is the *Mental Measurements Yearbook* published by the Buros Institute for Mental Measurements. Each yearbook contains descriptions of various tests, test reviews written by testing specialists, selections of test reviews published in other sources, bibliographies for specific tests, and reviews of books on tests and measurement. The Buros Institute also publishes *Tests in Print,* a guide for locating information and descriptions about specific tests that are currently published. *Tests in Print* is cross-referenced with past editions of the *Mental Measurement Yearbook* to enable counselors to locate tests and research past reviews. The Institute, located at the University of Nebraska in Lincoln, maintains an electronic database and search engine that counselors may use to purchase reviews of available tests and inventories.

Other sources for test information include the ERIC Clearinghouse on Assessment and Evaluation at the University of Maryland (http://ericae.net); the *Standards for Educational and Psychological Testing* (www.apa.org/science/standards.html), published by the American Psychological Association; the *Responsibilities of Users of Standardized Tests* (http://aac.ncat.edu/Resources/documents/RUST2003%20v11%20Final.pdf), prepared by the Association for Assessment in Counseling (AAC); and a number of professional journals. One journal, *Measurement and Evaluation in Counseling and Development,* is published by the Association for Assessment in Counseling, a division of the American Counseling Association. Another source of information is test publishers' catalogues, which contain brief descriptions of tests, costs, and other facts useful in the selection process. After counselors have obtained sufficient resources about available tests, they are ready to start the selection process. They begin by identifying the purpose that underlies the need for gathering test information.

Identifying the Purpose of a Test.   Why is a test needed? This is the first question that schools, counselors, administrators, and teachers must answer in selecting appropriate assessment instruments. When tests are selected without a clear purpose, reports might be misused or underused, and time and the cost of administration are wasted. In making an appropriate selection or giving recommendations for particular tests, counselors identify the goals and objectives of the testing process. What is the school, teacher, student, or parent trying to find out? How will the results be used? Based on the research of existing tests, which ones appear to offer what we need?

If schools want to assess the reading level of students in third grade, do they want to know reading levels as defined by learning objectives or as a comparison of students in the third grade? The answer to this question will narrow the decision between criterion-referenced and norm-referenced tests. In addition, a focus on students' reading levels enables counselors and teachers to eliminate full-battery achievement tests and limit their selection to reading tests. In sum, knowing the intended use of the test and the type of score reports desired helps schools to initiate the screening and selection process.

Considering Administrative Conditions.   After identifying the purpose of testing, counselors consider administrative factors that influence the selection of particular tests. Several questions are deliberated. For example, will the test be administered individually or to groups of students? Do budgetary restrictions preclude the selection of particular tests? How much time will be required to administer the test? What preparation for teachers and students will create an appropriate testing environment? Are other conditions or materials required that will affect the selection of particular tests?

There is little purpose in selecting an appropriate test only to have it administered in a haphazard manner. Therefore, all factors for administering the test correctly are carefully weighed before making a decision. As learned earlier, standardization requires strict adherence to published testing procedures and directions. Any deviation from these violates standardization and jeopardizes the testing results.

Acquiring Specimen Sets.   When schools narrow their decision to a few possible choices, they usually order specimen sets of the tests from publishers. These sets can be purchased at nominal cost and include a copy of the manual, a sample test booklet, and information about scoring and score reports. Examination of these materials helps to narrow the choices further. In particular, counselors and teachers want to examine the test manual to ascertain the uses for which the test is designed, the training and qualifications of test administrators, the knowledge and qualifications needed for interpreting results, evidence of validity and reliability, directions for administering and scoring the test, and information about the normative sample. A thorough examination of the test manual and review of specific test items in the booklet provide valuable information to make an appropriate selection. At this stage, it is essential to pay particular attention to the validity and reliability data presented by the publisher and to reviewers' critiques if such reviews are available.

Validity and Reliability

Test *validity* pertains to the degree to which an assessment instrument actually measures what it says it does. For example, does a math achievement test measure math knowledge and skill, or does it measure a student's ability to *read* and respond to mathematical questions? Another example of validity is whether IQ tests actually measure the elusive construct called "intelligence," or do they simply measure knowledge and skill based on experience, background, and education? Anastasi (1988) summarized three major types of test validity as content, criterion-related, and construct:

> *Content validity* indicates that the items on a test are a fair representation of the domain of knowledge or tasks the test purports to measure. Content validity is commonly applied in evaluating achievement tests that assess students' performance in particular subject areas.

> *Criterion-related validity* involves the effectiveness of a test in predicting a student's performance in certain situations. Specifically, the student's performance on a test is compared to some *criterion* that is an independent measure of what the test is intended to predict. Such a criterion may be reflected in either concurrent or future situations. For example, a typing test may give results that are compared with the current average speed and performance of secretaries already hired by the firm. By contrast, the Scholastic Aptitude Test (SAT) is presented by the College Entrance Examination Board as a predictor of future success in college, based on research of college performance of past examinees.

> *Construct validity* is concerned with abstract, psychological characteristics that a test claims to assess. In schools, counselors and teachers frequently use self-concept questionnaires and other scales to assess students' perceptions of themselves. An assumption of these instruments is that a construct, in this case the self-concept, is measurable. In many instances, instruments that rely on construct validity are evaluated by comparing them to other reputable instruments that claim to measure the same construct. Comparable results indicate that the instruments may measure the same quality or characteristic.

> *Reliability* is another important factor to consider in selecting standardized tests. This factor refers to the consistency of test results and outcomes from other assessment processes. If a teacher administers a reading achievement test to a student on two successive

occasions within a short period of time, we would expect the results to be similar. In this way, reliability refers to the results obtained with particular instruments rather than to the instruments themselves.

There are many different types of reliability and each uses statistical procedures to quantify the relationship between different sets of test results. When quantified, this relationship is assigned a statistic called a *correlation coefficient,* which counselors and teachers use to examine the reliability of tests. When applied specifically to reliability, this statistic is called a *reliability coefficient.* The reliability coefficient is expressed as a single digit ranging from –1 to +1, where both extremes of the range indicate a perfect correlation and 0 indicates no correlation at all. Therefore a coefficient of +0.95 indicates that two sets of data (such as two separate administrations of the same test) are strongly related in the same (positive) direction. This would be a desirable finding if we were examining the reliability of reading achievement tests.

A correlation coefficient of –0.95, on the other hand, also illustrates a strong relationship between two sets of data, but in the opposite (negative) direction. This finding is desirable when we examine two measurements whose results contradict each other. For example, if we develop an anxiety scale where a low score indicates minimal anxiety, and we want to compare it with a mechanical skills test, we would hope to find that lower anxiety scores correlate with higher mechanical performance. Conversely, if we found the same instruments to be negatively correlated, we would expect higher anxiety scores to relate to lower mechanical performance.

The most important aspect of reliability is its relationship to validity. A test that does not offer reliable results cannot be valid, and a test that is valid yields, by definition, reliable results. At the same time, reliability is not a *sufficient* condition for test validity. It is possible to have a highly reliable instrument that produces very consistent scores without measuring what it intends to measure. For example, an intelligence test that produces consistent scores but is more an assessment of educational and cultural experiences than it is of cognitive functioning cannot be accepted as a valid measure of innate intelligence.

Determining Test Usefulness

Another aspect to consider in test selection is the usefulness of the instruments being considered. Once the school has determined the purpose of a test and assessed its empirical soundness, the staff needs to evaluate how useful this instrument will be in the overall educational program. The same is true for counselors who examine individual tests and inventories to use in their school counseling programs. When establishing criteria to evaluate test usefulness, counselors and teachers consider the following questions:

1. Will the time they devote to planning, administering, and interpreting the tests be well spent? In schools where time is at a premium, it is a challenge to cover all the curriculum and provide all the special services such as counseling. Consequently, will time be available for this particular assessment?

2. Will the test produce usable results to develop an appropriate curriculum or to alter instruction to meet individual students' needs? Will it enable people to make important educational and career decisions? Tests given to satisfy local or state policy without generating usable results are a waste of time, resources, and money.

3. Are the test results reported clearly so that all persons who read them will understand them? Test results should be clear to students, parents, teachers, counselors, and others who will use the information to create beneficial learning programs and services in the school. Testing procedures that simply receive and file results in cumulative folders because no one understands them should not be tolerated. Either the test should be eliminated or users should receive adequate training to better understand and use the results appropriately.

Using Standardized Tests

Counselors and teachers who select appropriate tests and use the results for the benefit of individual student development and improved instruction for all students want to ensure the proper use of standardized tests. In schools where counselors are responsible for coordinating testing services, the task of delineating testing procedures rests on their shoulders. In this section, we examine some of the steps counselors consider when coordinating the use of standardized tests in schools. These steps take up where the selection process ends. They begin with test security.

Test Security

All standardized tests should be kept in a secure location. Test information that is disclosed to students intentionally, or learned by students incidentally, jeopardizes the reliability and validity of the results. For this reason, counselors who are charged with test coordination have access to a secure storage facility and caution teachers about using information or items from the test in their instruction.

When schools use certain tests frequently, particularly group achievement tests, there is the risk that some of the items will become familiar to teachers who administer the test. Consequently, they may unintentionally incorporate this test information into classroom lessons. To protect against this potential violation of test security, schools should review tests periodically and select new tests or new forms as the need arises.

Administration

Any deviation from required testing procedures threatens the standardization of norm-referenced and criterion-referenced tests. Therefore, testing coordinators should take pains to help teachers who are administering these tests learn proper procedures and adhere to specific published directions. This is also true for counselors who administer individual tests to students for screening purposes in special education or placement in classroom instruction. Competent counselors follow test directions explicitly, even during individual assessment sessions. Drummond (2004) noted that proper testing procedures are described in three documents with which school counselors should be familiar: *Code of Fair Testing Practices in Education* (American Psychological Association, 1988), *Standards for Educational and Psychological Testing* (American Educational Research Association, 1985), and *Responsibilities of Users of Standardized Tests* (American Counseling Association, 1989). A third edition of this last document was revised in 2003 by the Association for Assessment in Counseling (AAC), a division of ACA.

In addition to following correct procedures and specific directions, test administrators want to create testing environments conducive to producing reliable and valid results. Locating a quiet room for individual testing and stopping all interruptions and extraneous noises (like school bells) during group testing contribute to proper testing environments. Having all the necessary materials at hand, providing accurate timepieces, checking the lighting, and making arrangements for emergencies (such as a student who becomes ill during testing) are other aspects to consider. The goal of adequate test coordination is to create a setting in which students achieve optimal results so that accurate decisions and appropriate educational plans are made.

Interpretation

When schools receive test scores, counselors, teachers, and administrators use the results in a variety of ways. Accurate analysis and interpretation of these results are essential for the testing program to achieve its intended goals. School counselors are involved in the interpretation of test data with students, parents, and teachers, and they attempt to use test results with each of these groups to provide adequate instruction, proper placement, and assistance in educational and career decisions.

Students can learn about their test performance to identify strengths and weaknesses and use this information in making decisions about study habits, time management, tutoring, or other processes to help them learn. Some tests, such as aptitude tests, can disclose previously unknown abilities to students. Consequently, these data can help students look at career directions in which to apply these aptitudes towards lifelong goals. Other students might benefit from learning that their abilities compare favorably with their peers', and this knowledge may instill self-confidence to reach for higher goals. At the same time, test data enable students to accept realistic expectations from themselves and from the helping relationships they form with their school counselors. Of course, this is only the first step of a continuous assessment process that is essential to achieve successful helping relationships.

Interpretation of test results with parents is another responsibility of school counselors (Baker & Gerler, 2004; Lyman, 1998). When students complete group achievement or aptitude tests, the score reports usually include a summary for the parents. Counselors assist the school and parents by explaining and interpreting these reports in group meetings or individual sessions. In group meetings, counselors distribute test reports and explain in general terms the meaning of scores and how parents can interpret their children's results. In most instances where test companies include a parent or home report, the results are given in both numerical form and narrative explanation. Figure 9.2 shows an example of a parent report for a fictional School Achievement Test. In this example, the student's scores are reported in both national percentile ranks and confidence bands. A percentile band illustrates the range of scores in which the expected "true score" lies. Counselors usually reserve specific explanations of individual students' scores for private sessions with parents and the students.

In addition to group test results, scores on individual aptitude tests, achievement batteries, career interest inventories, and other appraisal instruments are typically interpreted to parents and guardians by counselors in individual conferences. Sometimes counselors plan these conferences with other school specialists, such as a teacher of exceptional children or a school psychologist. This is particularly true in situations that address exceptionalities and involve placement in special education programs. Helping teachers

FIGURE 9.2 *Parent Report for Fictional School Achievement Test*

Parent Report

School Achievement Test

Student: Melissa Smith   *Grade*: Three   *School:* Hope Elementary

On March 2, 2007, your child took the School Achievement Test for third-grade students. The results of your child's performance are printed on the chart below. The Total Battery Score shows that your child performed at the 75th percentile. This means that your child scored better than 75 percent of the third-graders who took this test when it was standardized. On the chart beside the Total Battery Score is a group of Xs to illustrate a percentile band. This band indicates that your child's score would fall within this range if she took the test several times.

Following the Total Battery Score are percentile scores for the different parts of the School Achievement Test. Your child's scores on these sections are: Reading, 94; Language Arts, 87; Mathematics, 55; Science, 67; and Social Studies, 70. As with the Total Battery Score, these scores are also reported as percentile ranks.

These scores show only how your child compares with other students in the third grade across the nation. To determine whether a score is good or not good, other information is needed. Teachers and counselors at the school can share additional information to help you better understand and evaluate your child's performance.

Tests	National Percentile	National Percentile Bands														
		1	2	5	10	20	30	40	50	60	70	80	90	95	98	99
Total Battery	75										XXXX					
Reading	94												XXXX			
Language Arts	87											XXXX				
Mathematics	55								XXXX							
Science	67									XXXX						
Social Studies	70									XXXX						

understand test results and encouraging them to use the reports to improve instruction is another essential aspect of test interpretation. Counselors who coordinate testing programs in schools are responsible for assisting school administrators and teachers in using test reports properly. This responsibility means more than interpreting results to parents and preparing reports for the superintendent and local school board. It includes examining students' performance within the context of the school curriculum and the instructional program. In this way, test results not only contribute to student appraisal, they also affect program planning and evaluation. The process of using test results to examine the instructional program is best fitted to criterion-referenced tests or to norm-referenced tests where publishers include item analyses categorized by learning objectives. There has been a trend by test publishers to develop combined types of standardized tests that provide norm-referenced data as well as criterion-referenced information (Gronlund & Linn, 1990). With criterion-referenced information, counselors are able to assist administrators and teachers in examining specific strengths and weaknesses of students across learning objectives. Figure 9.3 illustrates a school summary report for third-grade reading on the fictional School Achievement Test. The summary report is complemented by a sample worksheet

School Summary Report

School Achievement Test

School: Hope Elementary

Grade: Third

Reading	% below Standard	% at Standard	% above Standard
Total Score	35	45	20
Word Analysis	30	50	20
Consonants	45	35	20
Vowels	25	55	20
Vocabulary	45	35	20
Reading Comprehension	25	45	30

FIGURE 9.3   *Partial School Summary of Fictional School Achievement Test, Third-Grade Reading Results*

(Figure 9.4) developed by the school counselor to assist teachers in reviewing test results for their classes and for planning instructional changes. Specifically, teachers want to identify learning objectives on which their students performed below the average student in the school and determine what instructional methods need redirection or new emphasis. Appropriate use of test results and adequate interpretation to students, parents, and teachers are essential responsibilities of the testing program coordinator. Without proper use of these results, the school's testing program is meaningless. This is true for group testing of all students as well as for individual assessment for educational and career decision-making. Schools use a variety of standardized tests, and if counselors are responsible for

Classroom Testing Results

Teacher Worksheet

Learning Objective	School % at or above Standard	Class % at or above Standard	% Difference	Priority Rank
Total Reading	65	57	− 8	N/A
Word Analysis	70	63	− 7	N/A
Consonants	55	45	− 10	1
Vowels	75	69	− 6	3
Vocabulary	55	58	+ 3	4
Reading Comprehension	75	66	− 9	2

FIGURE 9.4   *Teacher Worksheet for Reviewing and Analyzing Reading Test Results on the Fictional School Achievement Test Scores*

Note: Figure 9.4 is an example of a teacher worksheet. In practice, a standardized achievement test reports results for many more learning objectives than are shown here. This sample is for illustration only.

coordinating the testing program, they must be thoroughly familiar with different types of tests that contribute to student appraisal.

Types of Assessment Instruments

Tests and other assessment instruments available to counselors and teachers cover a wide range of devices that are developed as norm-referenced or criterion-referenced tests and are administered to either groups or individuals (Drummond, 2004). In addition, tests and other assessment instruments differ in characteristics and structure. For example, some are timed precisely, such as group achievement and aptitude tests, whereas others allow students a generous amount of time to respond. Some tests require responses to objective multiple-choice or matching items, while others call for subjective answers and, subsequently, subjective scoring. Counselors consider all these factors as they help schools select assessment instruments and as they choose tests and inventories to use in student appraisal. The following sections offer brief descriptions of the major types of tests and inventories used by schools and school counselors.

Achievement Tests

Perhaps the most common standardized tests used in schools are achievement tests and batteries. These tests are similar to teacher-made classroom tests in that they attempt to measure what students know about particular subject areas such as reading, mathematics, science, and social studies. Achievement testing most commonly occurs in the elementary through the middle grades. Assessment of student progress and achievement of basic skills is critical in the early years of schooling. Gibson & Mitchell (1999) indicated that the purpose of achievement testing is to measure

1. The amount of student learning
2. The rate of student learning
3. Comparisons with other students or one's achievement in other subject areas
4. The level of student learning in subareas
5. Students' strengths and weaknesses in particular areas of learning
6. Predictions of future learning (p. 246)

Achievement batteries, surveys of a range of subject areas and learning objectives, are perhaps the most popular form of testing in schools. They are efficient, cost-effective assessments that provide a broad overview of student performance. One of the disadvantages of these batteries is that, because they cover such a wide range of areas, they are limited in what they assess for any given subject. For this reason, counselors and teachers sometimes use standardized tests that are specific to certain subject areas. As an example, some of the most common tests used at all levels of education are reading tests. These are used to assess the effectiveness of reading instruction, identify students who need special attention in reading, predict students' success in other subject areas, and screen for possible learning problems (Gronlund & Linn, 1990).

Counselors also use individual achievement tests in the student appraisal process. These types of tests are either survey batteries or separate subject tests administered to one student at a time with questions usually answered orally or pointed to by the student. Individual achievement testing has increased as a result of special education services to students with handicaps and the need to screen all students being considered for placement in these programs. School counselors also use individual achievement tests to gather data about students new to the school and for whom few records are available to help teachers with appropriate classroom placement and instruction. On occasion, counselors might use individual achievement tests to verify a student's performance on previously administered group batteries.

Aptitude Tests

A second common test administered to students in schools is the aptitude test. *Aptitude* is defined as a characteristic that reflects a student's ability to achieve in a given area or to acquire knowledge or skills necessary for performing in that area. Thus, aptitude assumes that an individual is endowed with an ability that under the right conditions can be developed to its maximum potential. Traditionally, tests designed to measure a person's learning ability were called *intelligence tests*. While some tests of mental ability remain in use today, controversy surrounding intelligence testing and the meaning of *intelligence* has contributed to the decline of these terms in favor of *ability* and *aptitude* tests.

Aptitude tests are sometimes in the form of multiple batteries of aptitudes, such as the Differential Aptitude Test (DAT), the General Aptitude Test Battery (GATB) used by the U.S. Employment Service, and the Armed Services Vocational Aptitude Battery (ASVAB). Tests such as these provide scores for a range of aptitudes such as verbal reasoning, mechanical ability, clerical speed and accuracy, language ability, numerical ability, and others. Some group aptitude tests used in schools provide two or more scores on subareas as well as a total aptitude score. The Cognitive Abilities Test, which yields scores for verbal, nonverbal, and quantitative test batteries, is one example. Another is the Scholastic Aptitude Test (SAT), which gives verbal and nonverbal scores, and these are totaled or used separately by colleges and universities in admissions processes. Sometimes, school counselors use individual ability tests to obtain a quick estimate of verbal and nonverbal functioning. Two examples are the Peabody Picture Vocabulary Test-Revised (PPVT-R) and the Slosson Full-Range Intelligence Test (S-FRIT). Some group ability tests, such as the Henmon-Nelson Tests of Mental Ability, can also be administered individually to students.

Interest Inventories

Because student appraisal consists of more than testing, school counselors incorporate other types of standardized instruments into their assessment processes. Among these are interest inventories such as career questionnaires. By assessing students' interests and comparing these results with achievement and aptitude, counselors are in a better position to provide adequate assistance in educational and career counseling. With data from interest inventories, counselors and students can verify career and educational choices, identify previously unknown or unrecognized areas of interest, relate interests to educational and career choices, and stimulate exploration of educational and career opportunities.

In some instances, interest inventories are the vehicles that enable counselors and students to establish initial helping relationships. When administered to students in groups, these instruments yield profiles that counselors explain and interpret in groups and with individual students. During these sessions, students use their profiles to raise concerns with counselors, often leading to self-referrals for group or individual counseling.

Examples of interest inventories used in school counseling programs include the Strong-Campbell Interest Inventory (SCII), the Self-Directed Search (SDS), the Ohio Vocational Interest Survey (OVIS), The Career Key (www.careerkey.org), and many others. The SCII is based on Holland's theory of career development (Holland, 1985) and is scored and interpreted according to the similarity found between the student's expressed interests and the interests of people in particular occupations. Holland developed the Self-Directed Search (SDS) based on his theory of six personality and environmental themes related to career choice. The SDS is self-administered and self-scored and can be self-interpreted by the student. After scoring, the student derives a code from across the subtests of the SDS, compares the code with a list of more than 450 occupations, and matches the code from SDS with jobs having the same code. When matches are identified between the student's code and job codes, the student continues to follow instructions for further career planning.

Another inventory, developed for use with high school students, is the Ohio Vocational Interest Survey (OVIS). Based on the career model used by the *Dictionary of Occupational Titles,* the OVIS reports its results on twenty-four different scales generated from responses to a student questionnaire, a local information survey, and an interest inventory (Gibson & Mitchell, 1999).

The Kuder General Interest Survey and the Kuder Occupational Interest Survey are two additional instruments used by counselors. There are several forms of these inventories, which are either computer-scored or self-scored, offering a student profile on ten areas of occupational interest: mechanical, scientific, persuasiveness, literary, artistic, musical, social service, clerical, computational, and outdoor activities.

Personality Inventories and Tests

A number of instruments are available to assess students' characteristics and traits that may be termed "aspects of personalities." Of course, the concept and construct of *personality* are vaguely defined and rarely agreed on factors in the assessment field. Furthermore, if there is such a trait as personality, can it be measured? Researchers and developers of personality assessment instruments respond to this question affirmatively, as do many practicing counselors and therapists.

Two types of personality assessment include personality inventories and projective techniques. Personality inventories usually consist of a series of questions to which the student responds *yes, no, not sure,* or a similar range of choices. These inventories compare the student's score on one or more personality variables with scores of a sample population. Types of variables measured by these instruments include self-concept, social adjustment, problem-solving styles, sexual adjustment, and other traits.

Though personality assessment is intriguing to both lay people and professionals, many hazards exist, particularly with self-reporting processes. First, students and others who take these instruments may deliberately fake their responses to put themselves in a "better light." Some inventories contain items that attempt to control for this likelihood, but it is impossible to eliminate all false answers. As a result, self-reporting procedures inherently include the possibility of producing an inaccurate picture of the client and an invalid assessment of the personality variables being investigated. Second, some authorities question whether all clients have the personal insight to respond adequately to these instruments. With individuals who have personal problems or poor social functioning skills, this lack of insight may further distort their self-image and responses to survey questionnaires. Finally, the nature of personality inventories and the questions involved allow for multiple interpretations by respondents. Questions that include modifiers such as "mostly" and "frequently" invite a range of interpretations, which affect instrument consistency and reliability.

Two examples of personality inventories used by school counselors are the *Mooney Problem Checklist* and the *Myers-Briggs Type Indicator* (MBTI). The *Mooney Problem Checklist* presents a list of problems to which students respond by underlining ones that are of *some* concern to them, circling items that are of *most* concern, and writing a summary in their own words. The MBTI is based on Carl Jung's theory of personality types and includes forms that can be used with high school students. Though not designed as a vocational assessment, the MBTI is widely used in career development counseling and planning.

A second type of personality assessment, the projective technique, is rarely, if ever, used by school counselors. Projective techniques and instruments are less structured than inventories and more subjective in their scoring. Examples of projective techniques include the *Thematic Apperception Test,* the *Draw-a-Person Test,* and the *Children's Apperception Test* (Drummond, 2004). These assessment instruments require special training and supervision.

All of the preceding tests and instruments contribute significantly to student appraisal in schools. They are, however, only part of a comprehensive appraisal process. To develop adequate appraisals of students, school counselors and teachers incorporate a variety of other assessment procedures, which we will now review.

Other Assessment Techniques

Student appraisal consists of more than individual and group testing to measure achievement, aptitude, or some aspects of personality. School counselors use a variety of assessment procedures to gather data with which to make effective decisions in counseling students and to help teachers plan and implement appropriate instruction.

Adequate student appraisal occurs at the beginning of, during, and after the counseling relationship. Assessment is an ongoing process that is multidimensional in nature and helps to establish direction in the decision-making process. Through these varied assessment activities, school counselors gather data and information to establish goals, plan strategies, and evaluate the effectiveness of their helping relationships.

Ongoing student appraisal involves different activities including observations, interviews, child study conferences, self-reports, and sociometric methods. Sometimes these activities are formal and include structured sessions and instruments such as rating scales. At other times, they occur informally and naturally as events happen. Two assessment activities that fit easily into school structure and student appraisal are observations and interviews.

Observations

Observation "is the best means we have for evaluating some aspects of learning and development" of students (Gronlund & Linn, 1990, p. 375). At the same time, it "can be one of the most abused techniques in human assessment" (Gibson & Mitchell, 1999, p. 267). Because observations fit so naturally into the school setting and can be enhanced by the reports of parents, it is understandable why they are readily used and recommended as an assessment technique. At the same time, however, caution is needed. Observational techniques are limited due to the perceptual biases and resulting inaccuracies of the observers. Human perception is a mysterious and powerful phenomenon, but it is imperfect as an assessment procedure. Simply ask any police officer who has investigated a traffic accident in which more than one "eyewitness" has reported the event, and you will see how limited human observation can be in gathering accurate, consistent information.

With student appraisal, observations occur in many settings, under different conditions, and for countless purposes. Teachers, parents, and counselors are constantly observing students' actions, interactions, and reactions, both individually and in groups. Parents observe children at home and in other settings and summarize these perceptions in conferences with teachers and counselors. Teachers observe students in classrooms and other locations in the school, making mental and written notes or using rating scales to report on behavior and performance. Counselors also observe students in various settings within the school and as part of their counseling relationships. All of these activities add to a comprehensive assessment of students' needs and performance and enable counselors to recommend appropriate services and strategies to facilitate and enhance student development.

Observations of students in schools can be formal or informal and occur in different settings at varied times and with distinctive structures. Sometimes observations occur naturally in classrooms, on playgrounds, and in other areas of school life. When teachers and counselors observe students doing class work or relating to peers, they may use observation instruments, such as rating scales or anecdotal notes. On other occasions, counselors might structure group activities in the counseling center to observe particular students and record their interactions and reactions. During such observations, counselors may impose specific conditions on the activity to see how students handle peer relationships, conflict resolution, rejection, or other situations. Other methods of observation include surveys to gather data on specific behaviors. For example, parents might complete a survey of their observations about how children interact and get along with siblings and friends at home and in the neighborhood.

School counselors rely on parents', teachers', and their own observations to add to the student appraisal process and formulate decisions about services. In using observational techniques, counselors become familiar with different methods, locate recording processes and instruments, and learn about the advantages and limitations of the procedures used. Some of the methods and instruments used by school counselors include anecdotal records, checklists, rating scales, direct measurement of products, frequency counting, and interval recording and time sampling.

Anecdotal Records.   Observations that enable teachers, parents, and counselors to record descriptions of particular student behaviors during a given situation are methods of anecdotal reporting. Since schools began, teachers have recorded notes about students'

Observation Notes

Student: Melissa Smith

Date: April 4, 2006

Melissa was observed assisting a student who was standing alone on the playground. The teacher observed her approach another child without hints or encouragement, and she asked the student if he wanted to play on the swings. This is the second time this week that Melissa has approached another student in a positive manner.

FIGURE 9.5   *Anecdotal Record of Observation Completed by Teacher*

behaviors and academic progress. Often, these observations were haphazardly done and the resulting records consisted more of biased perceptions and conclusions than of factual data. Today, largely as a result of the Family Educational Rights and Privacy Act of 1974, students' records contain less of this type of biased information. Proper anecdotal procedures, however, remain useful as observational techniques.

We find two primary methods of anecdotal observations in schools and school counseling programs. One method asks teachers to record significant events and observations as they happen or as soon after as is reasonably possible. These observations gather data on the overall functioning of students, or they track the occurrence of specifically identified behaviors. In training teachers to gather anecdotal information, counselors encourage objective reporting, free from interpretations and conclusions. The idea behind anecdotal records of this kind is to gather as many observations as possible to give a full picture of the trait or behavior of concern. After the reports are used in making decisions about instruction or special services, they are destroyed. Their usefulness is limited, and their long-term application is questionable. Figure 9.5 illustrates a sample anecdotal record completed by a teacher.

A second method of anecdotal recording used by counselors observes particular students for given periods of time in class or other situations during school. This process is especially useful to counselors who have received referrals from teachers about students' behaviors in classes. School counselors observe students as part of their diagnostic procedures to determine what services would be most beneficial. In developing observation procedures and techniques, counselors may find the following steps useful:

1. Inform teachers at the beginning of each school year about the policy for accepting referrals and incorporating classroom observations. To gather the most accurate data to make the best decisions about services, the counselor should observe students where and when teachers believe it will be most informative and helpful.

2. Arrive on time when observing students in classrooms. Sit at a desk in an inconspicuous corner of the room and leave without fanfare after you have recorded sufficient observations. Generally, 40 to 50 minutes of class time should allow ample observation.

3. Design an observation form to record the student's behavior or use a note pad with time intervals written in the margin. As with other anecdotal reports, counselors should record only what they see during these observations and avoid all interpretations and judgments at this time.

4. Schedule a follow-up meeting with the teacher to share the observations and receive the teacher's reactions to what occurred in class. In this conference, the counselor finds out if the observed class, particularly the behaviors of the identified student, was typical. Often, when observers enter a classroom, students behave differently than normal. The teacher will verify whether or not the class session was typical during the observation.

5. Observe more than once when possible, or have another professional observe at the same time. Comparison of observations helps avoid bias and can lead to more accurate conclusions.

Rating Scales. When gathering observational data, counselors frequently find that a structured form, such as a rating scale, helps the observer—teacher, parent, or counselor—remain focused on the behaviors, characteristics, or traits being evaluated. Generally, rating scales consist of lists of characteristics or behaviors to observe and an evaluative scale on which to indicate the degree to which they occur. Rating scales designed to gather data on students' attributes and behaviors typically have a numerical or descriptive format. With a numerical scale, each number indicates a degree to which the behavior is observed. For example, on a five-point scale, the numbers might be assigned values accordingly: 1 = strongly disagree; 2 = disagree; 3 = somewhat agree; 4 = agree; 5 = strongly agree. Each item on a rating instrument that uses descriptive formats is followed by a separate scale of descriptive terms on a line that is checked by the observer. Figure 9.6 shows a sample descriptive scale.

Some commercially produced rating scales are used in schools. However, counselors and teachers often find that designing their own scales allows them to tailor instruments to specific situations, and they can easily revise them as needed. In designing rating scales, counselors should

1. Determine a clear purpose for the instruments.
2. Choose characteristics and behaviors that are directly observable.

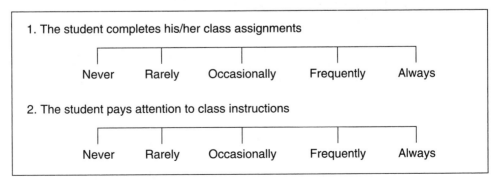

FIGURE 9.6 *Example of Descriptive Scale for a Behavioral Rating Form*

3. Write items that clearly and directly relate to the attributes being observed.
4. Determine descriptors for the scale (usually a minimum of three and a maximum of five points).

When designing a new scale, it may be helpful to have a trial run using "practice observers" to check the clarity of items and directions. In addition, counselors should (1) determine who will rate the attributes, (2) train raters in the use of the instrument, (3) instruct raters to ignore items they feel unqualified to judge, and (4) use as many raters as reasonably possible. Gathering data from many different raters increases the reliability of the process. For example, when rating a student's responsible behaviors, the counselor may desire ratings from parents and all the teachers who have this student in class.

Checklists.   Observers' checklists are similar to rating scales. One difference is the type of judgment required from the observer. As seen above, rating scales ask evaluators to indicate a degree or frequency with which a behavior or attribute exists. By comparison, checklists ask the observer only to mark *yes* or *no* to indicate whether he or she observed a trait. Although easier to develop and use, these instruments provide a basic, rudimentary assessment and should always be combined with other appraisal procedures.

Counselors use rating scales and checklists to assess other types of student performance and information beyond observable behaviors. These methods include direct assessment of products, such as students' homework, frequency counting, and interval recording procedures.

Direct Measurement of Products.   Students produce many items and products that are useful in the appraisal process. In addition, school records include data that can be screened and incorporated into a comprehensive assessment of student development and needs. Examples of students' products, which teachers and counselors can evaluate by using a rating scale, a checklist, or simple narrative form, include homework papers, art work, class projects, and journals. In many schools, these data and material comprise student portfolios, which are used in the overall assessment of student performance and progress. Counselors and teachers can also evaluate school records such as attendance reports, health cards, test records, and grade reports.

Frequency Counting.   Sometimes parents and teachers can add to the assessment of particular problematic behaviors by keeping a record of the frequency with which these behaviors occur. Usually there is a specific time frame within which the identified behavior is monitored (such as between 9 and 10 a.m., during a class period, or during recess on the playground). Methods of counting the behavior could include pencil and paper tally sheets and electronic or mechanical counters. Frequency counting is particularly useful with behaviors that are clearly defined. That is, they are identified by distinct beginnings and endings.

Interval Recording and Time Sampling.   When behaviors and attributes are not clearly defined and observable, interval recording and time sampling are appropriate techniques for assessment. There are several different types of interval and time-sampling procedures. With most, the evaluator determines the length of the observation period and divides it into equal segments or intervals. An observer then records when the identified behavior occurs

Student: <u>Melissa Smith</u>   Date: <u>September 17, 2002</u>

Location: <u>Mr. Juarez's Classroom</u>   Observer: <u>Karen Fox, Counselor</u>

Behavior Counted: <u>Off-task behavior</u>

Time Frame: <u>9:00 A.M.–10:00 A.M.</u>

Time	On-Task	Off-Task
9:00–9:20	X (20 minutes)	
9:20–9:30		X (10 minutes)
9:30–9:45	X (15 minutes)	
9:45–9:50		X (5 minutes)
9:50–9:55	X (5 minutes)	
9:55–10:00		X (5 minutes)
	Total Off-Task Behavior	20 minutes
	30% of time Off-Task	

FIGURE 9.7   *An Observation Record Using a Time-Sampling Method*

during the time period, counts the number of intervals when the behavior was observed, and computes the percentage of time the behavior occurred. Figure 9.7 illustrates an observation record using a time-sampling method.

In using interval and time-sampling procedures, counselors should be aware of different time-sampling observations. Some observations require that an identified behavior occur for an entire time interval. This is *whole-interval time sampling,* which observers use when it is imperative to know that the behavior is uninterrupted. Other observations use a partial-interval time-sampling technique in which only a single occurrence of the behavior in a given time period is required. A third process, momentary time sampling, observes behaviors that occur at the moment a particular time interval ends.

Interviews

Another method that school counselors use to gather data and information is interviewing. In a comprehensive assessment of student developmental needs, interviews with students, parents, and teachers are essential. In addition, counselors interview teachers who have had students in former grades, social workers who have assisted students and families, physicians who have examined and treated students, and other professionals who might add to the profiles being developed.

Sociometric Methods

Sociometric methods help teachers and counselors evaluate student relationships and identify students who are most often chosen by their peers and those who are social isolates. Although sociometric methods are easy to develop and administer, counselors and teachers should use them cautiously. Gibson and Mitchell (1999) suggested that counselors consider the following conditions when using sociometric methods:

1. The length of time the group of students has been together influences the results. The longer a class or group of students has interacted, the more meaningful is the outcome of a sociogram.

2. The age of students affects the reliability of students' responses. The older the students, the more reliable and valid are their responses.

3. Groups that are too small or too large may provide less useful information. There may be too few or too many selections with no distinct patterns emerging.

4. A meaningful group activity provides a logical and natural opportunity for students to select partners and give honest responses. In designing a sociometric method of assessment, counselors and teachers choose an activity familiar to students.

5. The group chosen for the sociogram should be appropriate for the particular appraisal process. If, for example, the assessment is investigating a particular student's comfort in social studies, then that class is where the teacher or counselor should use a sociogram.

Figure 9.8 is a sample sociogram for a fifth-grade class. In the activity, the students were asked to select one to five of their classmates with whom they would or would not want to work in a group. The students in the center circle of the diagram are those most often selected by their peers. Students in the outer circle are those chosen least often. They are the class loners and isolates. Six students in the class were rejected by classmates and one student (19) was rejected by two students. By using the same questions over a period of time during the school year and watching for changes in the sociograms that are generated from these students' selections, counselors and teachers are able to assess the effects of strategies and services they implement to help individuals and groups of students with peer relationships and social skills.

Child Study Conferences

An additional method used by counselors, particularly in the elementary and middle grades, is a child study conference, sometimes called staffing or team building. At these meetings, counselors, teachers, psychologists, social workers, nurses, and other professionals pool their knowledge and assessment results to make decisions about services to offer students and families. Some schools hold these meetings regularly and, depending on the cases being presented, invite community practitioners to participate. These practitioners might include mental-health counselors, physicians, protective services, case workers, and others. The shared information discussed at these meetings enables counselors, administrators, and teachers to plan effective school services and refer to appropriate community services.

Counselors and other evaluators typically perform all the preceding student appraisal procedures *with* or *to* students. In some cases, such as with checklists and rating forms, students may respond directly, giving their opinions and observations about themselves. For example, checklists and self-rating scales can be developed to have students assess their attitudes about school, feelings of self-worth, or beliefs about their potential as learners. In addition, counselors use informal methods of having students self-report about themselves and their

These five categories were designed as guidelines to help clinicians organize information, symptoms, physical problems, and other issues presented by mental-health clients. Today, the *DSM-IV* continues to present these five axes as the most popular diagnostic system of mental disorders in the United States (Morrison, 1995). In 2000, the American Psychiatric Association published a text revision of the *DSM-IV*, which became the *DSM-IV-TR*. The goals of the text revision included the need to: (1) correct factual errors identified in the *DSM-IV*, (2) ensure that all information was up to date, (3) improve the educational value of *DSM-IV*, and (4) update classification codes. There were no substantive changes made in criteria sets and no new disorders, subtypes, or appendix categories were proposed in this revision.

Because school counselors are often in the first line of professional helpers who work with children and adolescents, it may be useful for them to have a working understanding of the *DSM* system, particularly as they coordinate referrals to community mental-health counselors, clinical psychologists, and psychiatrists. Knowing the lexicon that these professionals use in making diagnoses can help school counselors communicate their referrals more clearly, thereby coordinating cases more efficiently for students and their families (Geroski, Rodgers, & Breen, 1997).

Counselors who choose to become familiar with the *DSM* system will need special preparation and will also want to understand the limitations and concerns surrounding this manual. Certainly, a major concern is the potential for misuse. As House (1999) cautioned, "Labels (informal and formal) can be hurled as weapons, and the emotional pain that can result is just as palpable as physical pain" (p. 197). Among the criticisms and concerns voiced about the *DSM* is the classification of behavior problems for children and adolescents. School counselors who use the manual when consulting with community agencies and clinical practitioners should note this concern. Future editions of the *DSM-IV-TR* might adequately address this and other issues, which gives additional reason for users to stay abreast of these revisions.

All the techniques and activities described in this chapter add to comprehensive student appraisal. In school counseling programs, counselors carefully plan procedures that contribute to the development of a clear, usable student profile. An important caveat for school counselors is that no single assessment instrument, process, or result should be used when making program decisions or planning intervention strategies. Proper assessment of student development and appraisal of the individual needs of students always include several measurements to design instructional programs adequately or choose appropriate counseling services.

Additional Readings _____

House, A. E. (1999). *DSM-IV Diagnosis in the Schools* (New York: Guilford).
A usable guide and practical resource for counselors and other student services professionals.

Lyman, H. B. (1998). *Test Scores and What They Mean* (6th ed.) (Boston: Allyn and Bacon).
An easy reading guide to using test results. An excellent resource for counselors who interpret test results to parents and teachers.

Morrison, J. (1995). *DSM-IV Made Easy: The Clinician's Guide to Diagnosis* (New York: Guilford).
Another readable guide to help counselors learn the language of mental health diagnosis.

Websites _____

American College Testing
www.act.org
Buros Institute of Mental Measurement
www.unl.edu/buros
The College Board
www.collegeboard.org

Educational Testing Services
www.ets.org
Note: In addition to this list, several websites are
mentioned in the chapter.

Exercises _____

1. In a small group, participants disclose an experience
   from a test-taking situation. As your group discusses
   these events, consider what factors or conditions
   would have made the experience different for you.
   Ask a group member to record these comments to
   share with the class.

2. Review the sociogram in this chapter and identify
   students you think would benefit from counseling
   services. What type of counseling do you think
   would be helpful to these students? How would you
   approach these students to offer services?

3. With another student, visit a classroom in an elementary, middle, or high school and observe for an
   hour. Record your observations on a notepad, using
   the margin to record time intervals. After your observation, compare notes with the other student and
   check the consistency of your observations.

4. Design an assessment instrument to evaluate physical surroundings. Use the instrument to assess the
   building in which you hold class, and discuss your
   findings. How will this type of assessment fit with
   your role as a school counselor?

5. In a small group, discuss the topic of "high stakes"
   testing in schools. Make a list of positive features of
   this phenomenon, and share for an open discussion
   with the class.

10

Educational and Career Development

A premise of this text is that a comprehensive school counseling program targets two major goals: to assist students with educational planning and related academic success, and to encourage students to explore a wide range of options and make appropriate decisions to satisfy their career development. Chapter 4 introduced these two goals and indicated that they were complemented by two additional goals of assisting students with their personal and social development. In practice, all four of these objectives are important and interrelated in the broad scope of student development.

Students have the opportunity to select from a wide range of career options when they attain basic skills and acquire sufficient knowledge of language, mathematics, science, social studies, and other academic areas. Likewise, students increase their potential to achieve academically when their personal lives are free of barriers and their social lives reflect appropriate, responsible, and accepting behaviors. As seen in the preceding chapters, counselors offer direct and indirect services to help schools plan appropriate instruction, assist parents in removing obstacles to development and learning, and counsel students about a full range of issues. In this way, school counselors assist students with their educational, personal, and social development to achieve academic success and choose appropriate career direction. This is the primary purpose of professional counselors who practice in school settings.

Primary Purpose of School Counseling

All of the responsive services described in this text come together in a comprehensive program of counseling, consulting, coordinating, and appraising activities that encourages all students to develop their fullest potential, achieve educational success, and select appropriate career goals. Gysbers and Henderson (2000) described this as the "life career development" perspective (p. 49). This perspective includes four areas of student growth and development first presented by Gysbers and Moore in 1981: (1) self-knowledge and interpersonal skills; (2) life roles, settings, and events; (3) life career planning; and (4) basic studies and occupational preparation. Although our ever-changing world will continue to in-fluence career choice and development, these four areas still provide a schema by which we can examine career activities in a comprehensive school counseling program.

Self-knowledge and interpersonal skills are achieved through counseling and related services that increase students' self-awareness and acceptance of others. With individual and small group counseling, in group guidance activities, and through schoolwide events, counselors and teachers introduce students to concepts and processes that encourage self-exploration and heighten students' awareness of their personal traits and characteristics. At the same time, counselors design programs and activities to help students learn appropriate communication skills and problem-solving strategies. The level of self-awareness achieved by students is vital in helping them make appropriate educational choices and plan careers. Everything that takes place in a school setting has as its ultimate goal the lifelong enhance-ment of education and the satisfaction of individual career interests. Counselors contribute significantly to this goal through comprehensive programs of essential services.

Life roles, settings, and events emphasize the interconnection among various life roles, the settings in which students live, learn, and work, and the situations and events that will impact their development over a lifetime. One continuous challenge for schools has been to connect the learning objectives of daily instruction to the broader goals faced by students in their overall development. By creating activities and responsive services to help students make this connection, counselors and teachers breathe life into the curriculum and give meaning to the educational process. Students who are able to accept a relationship between school and their future life goals successfully progress through their develop-mental years and continue the educational process through a lifetime. They understand the interrelationship of school life and aspirations for future career success, and view their school years as a relatively short-term challenge when compared to their lifelong ambitions.

Life career planning is another essential aspect of the overall educational process. A goal of school counselors is to help students master decision-making skills with which to explore a wide range of career interests, match those interests with their own characteris-tics and abilities, and make decisions accordingly. Again, the array of services and activities initiated by counselors in comprehensive programs assists with this broad focus. For example, individual contacts in counseling and consulting relationships enable students to explore their personal traits and characteristics, receive appropriate up-to-date information, and begin exploring future goals. Form 10.1 is a sample educational and ca-reer planning form that students and counselors could use in secondary schools. In con-ferences with school counselors, students would use this form to examine their goals and assess progress in light of their academic and extracurricular achievements. These conferences might take place during individual contacts with their counselors or in group sessions with other students.

In group experiences, such as small group counseling and classroom guidance, students also have the opportunity to gather information, increase their self-awareness, and learn decision-making skills. Through group processes, students are more able to test the appropriateness of future goals by checking their perceptions with those of their peers. Group work of this kind, as we saw earlier, allows students to test reality in safe environments with minimal risk of failure. Life career planning activities, in groups or individually, help students make responsible choices, gather necessary information to make decisions, develop adequate interaction skills, and plan their futures.

FORM 10.1   *Sample Planning Form*

Alexander High School

Student Planning Form

Student: _____   Date: _____

My Career Interests:

1. _____
2. _____

My Long-Term Educational Goal: _____

Course Work Needed to
Realize My Goal:

	Courses Taken	*Year Completed*	*Final Grade*
Communication Skills	_____	_____	_____
Technical Reading	_____	_____	_____
Literature	_____	_____	_____
Foreign Language	_____	_____	_____
Mathematics	_____	_____	_____
Statistics and Logic	_____	_____	_____
Sciences	_____	_____	_____
Social Studies	_____	_____	_____
Art/Music/Drama	_____	_____	_____
Vocational Courses	_____	_____	_____
Other Courses	_____	_____	_____

Extracurricular Experience: _____

My Planning Conferences with Counselor(s) (or Teacher/Advisors):

Date	*Decisions/Plans*	*Counselor or Teacher*
_____	_____	_____
_____	_____	_____
_____	_____	_____

Post-Secondary Tasks I Need to Accomplish (college applications, scholarship applications, entrance exams, job interviews, résumé writing, etc.):

Task	*Date Completed*
_____	_____
_____	_____

Basic studies and occupational preparation encompass the fourth domain of life career development, which consists of all the learning objectives found in a school's curriculum. The challenge for teachers and counselors in this arena is to design and implement a meaningful curriculum by which students can make the connection between their educational development and career satisfaction. Students must have access to knowledge and skills that enable them to keep abreast of ever-changing career developments. Outdated, outmoded skills and knowledge are of little value to students entering the world of work now and in future years. School counselors have a role in helping teachers, administrators, and curriculum supervisors stay ahead of career trends and the technological advances that are influencing these trends. The skills and knowledge base that schools teach today must be useful not only to current student development but also to students' futures as contributing, productive members of society. This is true at all levels of education and, for this reason, school curricula are living documents and processes that evolve and develop to meet the needs of all students.

The role of school counselors is clear in helping teachers and other educators create instructional programs with a focus on these four domains. The primary purpose for employing counselors in schools is to provide program leadership and delivery of services and activities that help all students to achieve academically, reach higher levels of functioning in basic skills, assess their strengths and weaknesses, and gather appropriate information about career development. Sometimes, before counselors provide these types of services and activities, they need to assist students with personal and social development. This is understandable because optimal learning and career development are less likely to occur if personal and social barriers remain in place. Therefore, personal adjustment counseling frequently is a bridge over which students travel in realizing their educational and career goals.

Although career planning and development are widely acclaimed as essential areas of focus for school counseling programs, educational planning has received less attention. Perhaps this is because schools are inherently involved in the education of students, so planning is assumed to happen simultaneously. In practice, however, most educational planning is done by the adults who have responsibility for teaching, guiding, and supervising students. Parents, teachers, counselors, and others share information, assess students' abilities, set instructional goals, and place students in educational programs. Although most of these planning procedures are appropriate, students are frequently left out of the process. As emphasized in this text, educational planning is a key ingredient in school success and career development. For this reason, we assign special importance to the school counselor's role in educational planning with all students.

Educational Planning for All Students

Throughout a lifetime, people make many decisions that affect their development and learning. In some instances, they make these decisions as part of a well-designed plan, and other times these decisions are haphazard and accidental. People who have respect for learning and educational development make intentional plans regarding their educational and career goals, thereby demonstrating a high level of self-caring. They demonstrate this caring during years of schooling and throughout their adult lives.

In schools, teachers and counselors observe a wide range of commitment to education by students and parents. Some students enter school in the primary years with a keen thirst for knowledge and an enthusiastic curiosity for learning. They have benefited from healthy home environments in which parents communicate frequently with their children, read to children during preschool years, and generally encourage a wide range of educational pursuits. Sadly, not all children experience these types of relationships in their formative years. They come to school undirected and misguided in their educational goals, and they are unfamiliar with what other children have learned about the relationship between knowledge and successful living.

Schools are challenged by students at both ends of this spectrum and in between. Students who are enthusiastic, curious, and excited about learning continue to be invited to the celebration of their own development by an appropriate curriculum and instruction. When bright and talented students are allowed the freedom to explore, learn at an accelerated pace, and choose educational plans that stretch their potential, they excel in schools and in life. At the same time, students who arrive at school from less advantaged environments require special attention in designing plans and activities to incorporate educational aspirations into their life's goals. All these students, from the most advantaged and enthusiastic to the most underprivileged and disinterested, benefit from individual and group services to encourage educational planning, learn decision-making skills, and set goals for lifelong learning and achievement.

With academically talented students, schools sometimes overlook the need for appropriate educational planning because these scholars come prepared to learn. This stance may be an erroneous one. The error a school makes with these types of students is to assume that they do not need special attention because they are bright and that they will achieve regardless of the plans made to provide appropriate curriculum and instruction. On the contrary, when schools remain rigid in their curricular and instructional processes, these students become bored, unchallenged, and disruptive. Such behaviors negate the positive attributes they bring to school and contribute to antagonistic relationships between home and school.

At the other end of the continuum, schools sometimes spend so much effort designing and offering remedial instruction to students from disadvantaged homes that they neglect to inspire, encourage, and plan for future possibilities. While basic education is important, it, alone, without optimistic processes to examine and explore future goals, fails to lift less fortunate students out of their status toward successful career development. The challenge presented by Shertzer and Stone (1966) more than a half century ago remains true today. Appropriate planning and placement services must be provided for "disadvantaged youth to remove some of the obstacles to their economic and social betterment. . . . Education will have to be made realistic for them in new and more effective ways. Unless such youth are helped by planning and placement, many will continue to remain alienated from education and society. By engaging in planning, such youth learn to manage their problems, mobilize their resources, and gain the capacity to continue on their own" (Shertzer & Stone, 1966, pp. 327–328).

School counselors have an obligation to assist schools in developing and implementing activities that offer a meaningful educational focus for all students. The essential goal for all services of a comprehensive school counseling program is to help schools create appropriate learning activities, design individual educational plans, and incorporate adequate career exploration for all students throughout their school years. In essence, the role of the school counselor, whether in elementary, middle, or high schools, is to advocate for appropriate educational planning and programming for all students, regardless of their backgrounds and preparedness for school.

Student Advocacy

A major responsibility of all school counselors is to assist school administrators and teachers in designing and implementing policies, programs, and processes that equitably support the educational and career development of *all* students. This has always been a fundamental purpose for employing counselors in schools (Studer, 2005). Accordingly, counselors have been viewed as student advocates. This is not to say that other school professionals do not advocate for the well-being of the pupils. Quite the contrary, student advocacy is essential in all aspects of school life by all personnel employed to serve students. Foremost among this group are classroom teachers, who are charged with the educational, social, and personal welfare of their students.

Unlike teachers, who are responsible for grading students' progress, school counselors are not typically involved in evaluative relationships with students and, therefore, may be viewed as more *student-oriented* than *school-* or *curriculum-oriented.* In this sense, counselors in schools have special responsibility for student advocacy and work closely with teachers and administrators to ensure the welfare and protect the rights of students.

School counselors contribute to this endeavor by monitoring the placement of students in instructional programs and special services; consulting with parents, teachers, and administrators about the educational progress of individual students; and helping schools avoid stereotypical and prejudicial procedures that discriminate against individuals and groups of students. The consulting role often taken by school counselors is particularly suited for student advocacy (Kurpius & Brown, 1988; Parsons & Kahn, 2005). Through contacts with parents, teachers, and other professionals who serve students, counselors attempt to ensure that every child and adolescent is given adequate and appropriate attention in his or her educational planning, instructional activities, and other services to reach optimal learning and development. Sometimes, because teachers face many challenges and have many responsibilities beyond providing essential instruction, they need assistance from counselors to be sure students are not forgotten by the system.

There is no single service or activity by which counselors demonstrate their advocacy role. Every aspect of a comprehensive school counseling program has as its goal an improved learning environment and academic success on the part of the student. Counselors advocate by consulting on a regular basis with teachers about their instructional programs and the placement of students in classes. They also participate in special education placement processes, and, in particular, they advocate for challenged students through their contacts with parents. For example, policies and procedures should be explained to parents in understandable language so they can make informed decisions about their children's placement in these programs. Counselors have the skills to assist with this process and, as noted earlier in this text, can help parents in the preparation of the Individualized Education Plan (IEP) for these students.

Counselors also advocate for students when they assist school administrators in reviewing and revising policies. Some regulations or procedures may simply be outdated and, as a result, unintentionally discriminate against particular students. For example, an elementary school changed its tradition of having a "fathers' luncheon" once a year because so many students without fathers were unable to participate. Instead the school sponsored a "visitors' luncheon" program, which enabled all students to invite an adult to share lunch with them at school. By slightly changing the focus of the event, more students were included, rather than excluded, from a worthwhile activity. There are limitless opportunities for counselors to examine school programs, such as athletics, extracurricular activities, and special services, with administrators and teachers to ensure that the rights and privileges of students are not abridged. Counselors use their observational skills to assess particular aspects of school life and offer suggestions to administrators and teachers on how to affect student development more positively.

Counselors, teachers, and other school personnel also advocate for students in the community by encouraging town governments, city officials, and business leaders to sponsor programs that benefit children and adolescents. Recreational opportunities, creative outlets, and educational experiences all contribute to the efforts begun by the school. By advocating for these types of programs, schools join their communities in a cooperative venture to improve the educational and social lives of children and adolescents. In this way, educational planning and development become community goals and responsibilities rather than the sole obligation of the school.

One way that school counselors use their positions to advocate for students and make connections with community professionals is through committees that focus on individual students' needs. Sometimes called child study committees or student assistance teams, these groups include counselors, teachers, nurses, psychologists, and social workers from the school as well as health, social services, law enforcement, and other community professionals. The overriding purpose of these committees is to make certain that all avenues for helping a child or family are explored, while at the same time protecting the student from negligence by the educational system. Through the combined efforts of many concerned professionals, schools are more likely to examine situations, generate appropriate ideas for solving educational concerns, and focus on the needs of students being served.

In addition to their consulting roles, school counselors advocate for students through their counseling services and guidance activities. In individual and group counseling, as well as through classroom guidance, counselors help students learn about themselves, acquire behavioral skills—such as study skills and relaxation techniques—to improve their educational performance, and understand their rights in school and society. Through all these responsive services, counselors help students achieve a sense of value and self-worth and develop assertive behaviors to seek appropriate educational programs and beneficial career directions. Implicit in this process is the aim of counselors to instill in students the notion that educational planning and career development do not end when they graduate from high school or college. Rather, these are lifelong processes that depend on a foundation established during years of schooling. As such, the goal for all students is one of lifelong learning.

Lifelong Learning

Formal education in the United States and other countries emerged as a need to educate the citizenry to govern themselves, become self-sufficient, and contribute to the overall productivity of the nation. Through various historical and economic eras of past decades, the need for improved educational systems has been documented. As we continue is this twenty-first century, the focus on improving education for all people in all communities continues to be a dominant political and social theme highlighted and debated in a variety of settings from living rooms to national conventions across the land.

In all this debate and with all of the restructuring, reforming, transforming, and redesigning of education, one element seems to be consistently overlooked. Education is not an isolated, individual process, aimed at accomplishing finite goals. Instead, it is a continuous endeavor beginning at birth and ending with death. It is a lifelong pursuit with limitless goals and divergent purposes. As we look at educational structures and policies in the United States, it becomes clear that this idea of learning for a lifetime has escaped the consciousness of educational planners, leaders, and decision makers.

Learning is an integral part of living. Education is not simply a means to an end; it is a fuel that ignites inspiration, desire, compassion, and a host of other human dimensions and emotions that enable us to live our lives fully. The pervasive attitude that only so much learning is needed by any individual or group is as misguided as the notion that people no longer need food and drink once they are full. No matter how many changes we implement, no matter how much money we allocate to improve our schools, we will continue to struggle in this endeavor unless we rethink the purpose of learning and its role in human development.

School counselors play a key role in this effort through the services of their comprehensive programs. The first step is to encourage schools to focus on the broad picture of school climate, parental involvement, mastery of learning, and other conditions noted in the effective schools' research. Purkey and Schmidt (1996) identified these elements as people, places, policies, programs, and processes. When schools pay attention to the elements that contribute to healthy educational environments and foster the desire for lifelong learning, they enhance student development and increase the likelihood of academic and personal success. A wide-angle perspective is needed to achieve this goal, and school counselors facilitate this process through all of their responsive services. In particular, counselors foster lifelong learning by encouraging schools to

1. Infuse affective education into daily instruction. As noted in earlier chapters, "guidance" does not occur in isolation but rather as an integral part of the curriculum. Teachers who incorporate life skills into their daily instruction bring their subject areas to life and demonstrate how all learning contributes to successful living.

2. Examine grading, promotion, and other policies that establish the structure by which students move through the educational process. Do school policies contribute to or detract from the notion of lifelong learning? By achieving academic milestones, such as grade promotion or diplomas, are students reaching out for knowledge or simply going through the motions of academic achievement? Education should be more than "learn it, bank it, and forget it," but to view it otherwise, students have to be included in decisions regarding their participation and movement through school.

3. Invite parental participation. Research demonstrates the vital role parents and the home play in student development. Findings consistently show that parental involvement with schools and their children's learning makes a difference in the quality of education and student success (Stone & Dahir, 2006). School counselors assist in this effort by establishing parent volunteer programs, designing and leading parent education groups, consulting with parents about student development and progress, and training teachers on

consulting skills and processes to facilitate relationships with parents. Many of the essential services described in this book contribute to this effort.

4. Recognize the value of learning by demonstrating how adults continue to develop throughout their lives. School counselors plan appropriate in-service programs for staff members throughout the school year, seek scholarships to enable teachers and others to return to school, and celebrate learning by announcing staff participation in a variety of educational pursuits. For example, a list of professional and personal development activities being attended by staff members could be posted in the school for students and others to see. These activities include a host of adventures from graduate school studies to piano lessons. No learning experience is insignificant; all activities should be valued.

5. Focus on career development and its relationship to lifelong learning for *all* students. Educational planning and lifelong learning are interconnected with career and vocational choices that people make, beginning with their school careers and continuing throughout their lives. In all the responsive services designed and implemented by school counselors, career planning and decision-making skills are critical elements.

Career Planning and Decision-Making

Throughout its development, the school counseling profession has been closely associated with vocational guidance and career development. The industrialism of the late 1800s altered working conditions and vocational needs of society rapidly and immensely (Zunker, 2002). As noted in Chapter 1, these changes influenced the early vocational guidance movement initiated by Jesse B. Davis, Frank Parsons, and others. In the decades since, the focus of vocational guidance on the selection of an occupation has broadened considerably to include all aspects of career development. In addition, the interaction among educational planning, personal development, career choices, and successful living has become clearer. These relationships are affected by a number of technological, industrial, social, and political changes that are rapidly sweeping the globe (Herr, Cramer, & Niles, 2004).

In 1999, Gibson and Mitchell highlighted several aspects of the changing nature of the world of work that continue to have meaning for counselors in a variety of professional settings, particularly school counseling. These aspects include the diversity of vocational opportunities, the dangers of gender and cultural stereotyping, the relationship between education and career development, and the future of occupational opportunities. A comprehensive school counseling program in cooperation with the school's curriculum and instructional programs should address each of these aspects.

Career development is a lifelong process of opportunities and probabilities. The future holds a multitude of vocational possibilities for most people. Gone are the times when people would select a career early in youth and follow that choice for a lifetime. Students who enter schools in this twenty-first century and beyond will be bombarded with ever-changing and rapidly advancing discoveries that alter the workplace and the range of services required of the work force. Already it is common for people to change careers several times, sometimes within the scope of a broad vocational area, but also more drastically from one occupational pursuit to a dissimilar one.

School counselors need to assist students with these future decisions by presenting a wide range of career possibilities and encouraging long-term educational planning. It is difficult to forecast exactly where technological advances will lead us; educational preparation is essential to increase vocational flexibility and career options (Isaacson & Brown, 2000).

Gender and cultural stereotyping in career selection must be eliminated. Although much more progress is needed, women and men in the United States are becoming equal participants and partners in career development. Some bastions of resistance toward equality remain and women continue to be paid unequal pay for the same work, but current trends indicate that the process is reversible. In recent decades women have moved into careers formerly believed to be for "men only" such as construction work, truck driving, airplane piloting, politics, engineering, and countless others. At the same time, men are entering career tracks once considered exclusively for women. Nursing and secretarial work are two examples.

As the world continues to shrink in light of expanded communications systems, cultural integration is inevitable. Stereotypical thinking with regard to diverse groups and divergent cultures will continue to be an impediment to career development. Counselors and teachers have major responsibility in helping people from diverse cultures remove these barriers from their own thought processes and belief systems, as well as educating majority groups about prejudicial, stereotypical views and behaviors that are destructive to the welfare of society as a whole.

Schools make a major contribution to the continued integration of the sexes and cultural groups within society. Textbooks and multimedia avenues chosen to illustrate career choices must depict a variety of nontraditional occupational opportunities for women and men, as well as the career integration of people from all cultures. School counselors support this process by consulting with administrators and teachers about the texts and materials selected for the curriculum and by planning career awareness, exploration, and decision-making activities that allow students to experience the full scope of career possibilities.

Higher education will not necessarily equate to greater career satisfaction. Although college education may be necessary for many future careers, some technical occupations may require educational studies somewhere between a secondary school and a college education. If this is true, it is essential that students plan educational careers to match their vocational interests without closing the door on future possibilities. Technical training at all levels of education may be appropriate for a large percentage of students, but, as noted earlier, this decision should be tied to lifelong educational pursuits that encompass not only career goals but also personal objectives for successful living. Although a four-year college education might not be necessary for many workers in the twenty-first century, this does not mean that college graduates will find their education unfulfilling. On the contrary, it may mean their lives consist of balanced goals, satisfied through a wide range of occupational, vocational, and leisure activities. The object in educating people must encompass goals for personal satisfaction as well as career objectives.

The present no longer predicts the future. It has always been a dangerous posture for counselors and other helping professionals to predict what the future holds for individuals. Today and in the future, this may not only be dangerous, it may also be impossible. As Gibson and Mitchell (1999) cautioned, "changing technology affecting the workplace, plus drastic changes in the international marketplace, and changes in the makeup of our workforce have made it increasingly difficult, if not almost impossible, in recent years to adequately predict the future by examining only the present and the past" (p. 315). One aspect of the future we can be sure of is that, in light of all the technological, scientific, and medical advances being made today, it will be different from the present, and this includes occupational needs and opportunities.

Because career forecasting is so difficult, counselors assist students best by offering communication and decision-making skills to set career goals based on today's knowledge with an eye toward the future. This means acquiring the ability to know oneself, having access to information about career possibilities, and developing interaction skills to connect with people in positive ways and increase opportunities for career choices. This reliance on others as well as oneself is a final aspect of career development.

Career development is an interactive process. In the past, individuals could set their course and create their own fate. Today, because of the complex interaction of so many variables and forces in the world, the likelihood of this happening is remote. Striking out on one's own today, without support from others, is in the purest sense of the term "risky business." For this reason, successful students learn how to seek support, gain access to accurate information, and build a foundation for career development. In this process, they learn human relationship skills and coping mechanisms for overcoming barriers to success. In most instances, the failure of people to reach personal and professional goals is less a result of their formal education and training than their inability to form healthy, caring relationships with others. It is through these types of relationships that people learn to cope with life's difficulties and nurture the resolve to overcome career obstacles. The preceding aspects of career development, adapted here from Gibson and Mitchell's (1999) symptoms of "the changing nature of the world of work" (p. 314), are addressed in comprehensive school counseling programs and by appropriate school curricula. Through appropriate curricula and comprehensive counseling services, students learn about themselves, career opportunities, and educational requirements that fit their life's goals. School counselors in elementary, middle, and high schools contribute to this learning process by designing services that focus on specific needs of students. In addition, they base these services on particular theories of career development. Most texts on career counseling and development highlight and differentiate between various theories of career development (Herr, Cramer, & Niles, 2004; Zunker, 2002). Readers who are unfamiliar with the broad field of career counseling and development should locate these and other sources to learn about the different theories associated with career awareness and decision-making. For our purposes, this section focuses on how school counselors incorporate counseling and guidance activities into comprehensive programs to enhance student awareness, invite career exploration, and encourage appropriate decision-making at all levels of education.

School counselors are charged with a wide range of responsibilities, including career counseling and developmental activities for all students. Consequently, counselors in collaboration with their teaching colleagues set priorities, develop learning objectives, plan activities, and deliver services to address the areas of student awareness, career exploration, and decision-making skills.

Student Awareness

Typically, the school counseling literature has used aspects of career development, such as awareness, exploration, and decision-making to structure career activities and design a career focus for programs at the elementary, middle school, and high school levels. This structure and focus generally emphasize career awareness activities and services in the elementary grades, exploration of occupational choices in middle school and junior high programs, and job placement and career decision-making during the high school years. As Zunker (2002) and others have noted, however, these areas of career focus are not limited to any single level of education or development. True, elementary children may need assistance with self-awareness and career awareness, but the need for increased familiarity with and understanding of one's personal interests and goals within the context of career opportunities is a continuous process that affects learning objectives and activities at all levels of schooling. It is through exploratory experiences that children in elementary schools become aware of themselves, others, and the world around them, including the world of work. Therefore, exploratory activities in the curriculum and school counseling program are appropriate at all levels. Likewise, decision-making skills are continuously acquired and perfected throughout life, and therefore their acquisition should not be limited to one developmental stage of learning.

One difference regarding various approaches to career development is in how counselors and teachers at different educational levels assist students in increasing their awareness of themselves and their career interests. In elementary schools, for example, self-awareness and career awareness goals and objectives are incorporated into the curriculum rather than isolated as separate entities focused on by one specialist, such as a school counselor. This incorporation of guidance objectives is important at all levels—elementary, middle, and senior high school. School counselors use these types of objectives to assist classroom teachers in developing curriculum goals and designing instructional strategies to address career awareness for students. Knowledge of school curriculum and student development is essential for counselors to provide adequate guidance for teachers in this endeavor.

In middle schools and high schools, the incorporation of career guidance into the curriculum continues and is complemented by individual counseling and small group work with students facilitated by the school counselor. As learned in earlier chapters, counselors use individual and small group counseling sessions to enable students—in private, confidential relationships—to discover their inner selves and acquire a deeper, more personal level of understanding. Through this process of self-discovery, students become more able to benefit from classroom and small group guidance that addresses various aspects of career awareness and development.

To facilitate students' self-awareness, school counselors use assessment processes as part of their helping relationships. As discussed in Chapter 9 on student appraisal, these assessment procedures include aptitude testing, career interest inventories, and a host of other measures that assist students in learning about their academic strengths, personal characteristics, and traits related to career interests and decision-making. Several computerized career assessment programs are available for school counselors to use to help students acquire pertinent information and guide students toward appropriate decision-making. Computer-assisted career information systems provide students with a structure to search for specific occupations and offer background information, such as educational requirements, for the occupations selected in a search. With some of these systems, assessment data such as test scores are introduced as a starting point for the computer search of appropriate occupations.

In past years, the development of computer-assisted career information systems was buoyed by the availability of grants from the Department of Labor and the National

Occupational Information Coordinating Committee (NOICC). These funds gave impetus to the development of career information systems in a number of states. Federal funding for NOICC ended in 2006, but many states continue to offer career information systems as well as local and regional information (search for SOICCs on the Internet). The Internet includes countless other career information websites. As with most areas of computer technology and software development, the availability of career information systems is ever-changing. As a result, counselors need to stay informed through their professional associations, journals, and other media.

Other types of computer-assessment programs, career guidance systems, tend to have a broader focus than simply the dissemination of information. These systems take students beyond the search of occupational possibilities and into areas including self-assessment processes, instructional modules, planning activities, and decision-making steps. One widely used computer guidance program is the *System of Interactive Guidance and Information* (SIGI-Plus) from Valpar International Corporation. The SIGI-Plus program consists of nine modules to assist students and their counselors: (1) introduction to the process, (2) self-assessment, (3) search of possible occupational choices, (4) information about possible occupations, (5) skills, (6) preparation, (7) coping skills necessary to do what is required, (8) decision making, and (9) developing an action plan (http://www.valparint .com/s1.htm).

Another popular computer assessment system is *DISCOVER,* published by the American College Testing Service (ACT). *DISCOVER* is an interactive, computer-assisted system designed to provide (1) self-assessment, (2) opportunity to explore the world of work, (3) strategies to identify occupations of interest, (4) detailed information about hundreds of occupations, and (5) educational requirements to assist in career planning.

In this technological age, computer-assisted systems are ever more prevalent as a method of informing students about career choices. Baker and Gerler (2004) noted that this increasing popularity of computer technology in school counseling programs has raised several important issues. Among them is the question of the effectiveness of computer-assisted programs. Preliminary research on the effectiveness of some systems is promising, but additional research is needed in this area. It seems clear that computer technology will be an integral part of student learning in the future. Therefore, school counselors need to be aware of the available systems, plan how they will incorporate systems into the counseling program, be informed about their cost effectiveness, and keep up with research regarding the use of computer-assisted systems with students.

Another avenue that school counselors and teachers use to enhance student awareness, particularly about career opportunities, is special events during the school year. These events might include "career fairs" in middle and high schools; field trips to businesses, industries, colleges, and other locations; guest speakers for classroom guidance presentations; and many other activities. In elementary schools, for example, a simple program is to invite parents into classes to talk about how they spend their days at work. Two primary school counselors I know organized "Truck Day" at their school to introduce children to firefighting, medical assistance, trash removal, and a host of other occupations.

School counselors help their teaching colleagues focus on student awareness through a variety of instructional activities, computer-assisted programs, counseling services, and special events during the year. These services and activities help students learn about themselves, their interests and abilities, and the career choices available to them or those that may be available in the future. Related to this process of developing self-awareness and an understanding of career opportunities is the necessity for students to explore the world of work and the countless possibilities that exist for each of them.

Exploration

Career exploration begins at the elementary school level as an expansion of guidance activities in the classroom and as special events such as field trips to local points of interest. Appropriate career exploration is reflected in the careful selection of books, films, and other media that schools select for their curricula. Media that are void of sexual and cultural stereotyping and encourage all students to seek a wide range of career possibilities are imperative to student development and learning. As young students become aware of themselves and the opportunities that surround them, they are more ready to explore available career options during their adolescent years.

At the middle-grade and high school levels, career exploration becomes more clearly defined and focused for students. Now, their interests, abilities, strengths, and weaknesses begin to take form and gain clarity. During these years, schools can design activities for students to examine careers that fit their personal and professional interests and abilities. In middle schools, it is common for the curriculum to include career classes to assist with this exploration process. At the high school level, career exploration most likely occurs as a result of special events or individual and small group counseling. Ideally, high school curricula, as in elementary and middle schools, should include classroom career guidance so teachers incorporate career aspects of their subject areas into daily instruction. In this way, while studying poetry in English classes, for example, students might discuss the career of a poet or other types of writers. At the same time, the teacher and students could explore the impact of future technology on these literary professions. How will voice-activated printing or voice-activated videotaping change the artistic and creative worlds of poetry and literature? Likewise, in chemistry and other science classes, future career opportunities might be discussed and offered for consideration. By incorporating career exploration in their lessons, secondary school teachers bring subject areas to life with real meaning and purpose for their students.

In individual and small group counseling, as well as in classroom presentations, school counselors use computer-assisted programs to encourage career exploration. They also use other media and resources to facilitate this learning process. The *Dictionary of Occupation Titles* (DOT), formerly published by the U.S. Department of Labor, is now available online through the *Occupational Information Network* (O*NET) and other sources (http://online.onetcenter.org). The *Occupation Outlook Handbook,* also published by the U.S. Department of Labor, is now online at www.bls.gov/oco. All these examples illustrate the power of the Internet and how technology will influence the way students access information in the future.

Research has not yet identified one single method of career exploration that is significantly better than others are. The rapidly changing world of work and technological advances anticipated in the future make the likelihood that any single method or approach will emerge as a dominant theme unrealistic. For this reason, school counselors at all levels must ensure that the curriculum, their direct services, and special programs allow a variety of opportunities through which students can learn about present and future trends and directions in a broad spectrum of occupations. Only through adequate assessment and a wide range of exploratory activities are students able to make clear plans and appropriate decisions about their future careers.

Decision-Making

Children and adolescents at all levels of education must be guided in their educational planning, because it is through this developmental process that students increase their likelihood of making appropriate decisions and, consequently, successful career choices. Zunker (2002) explained that decision-making is a learned skill that should be a component of every student's educational program. Career counseling and decision-making skills go hand-in-hand. Many decision-making theories and models have been presented, and these are important for counselors to understand in choosing or designing their approaches. Simple steps can be designed to instruct students in decision-making skills, but the complexity of the decision-making process is revealed when individuals begin to use the steps learned and add their own values and unique characteristics to the choices made (Zunker, 2002).

In assisting students with decision-making skills and processes, school counselors often find that group sessions facilitate learning and skill development. This may be particularly true for career decision-making, in which students in groups share information, reflect on each member's individual assessment, give helpful feedback, and support individual group members in their decisions. As noted in Chapter 7, when personal attributes and other private information are part of the sharing process, group counseling is an appropriate setting because it offers a safe, nonthreatening, confidential relationship. On the other hand, when students need to acquire career information or learn new skills, instructional activities, such as group guidance sessions, are legitimate helping processes. For example, when a counselor is going to teach a decision-making model to students, group guidance is an appropriate process to use. To guarantee appropriate procedures and media for teaching decision-making skills, counselors want to be aware of current research and literature on the most promising approaches (Herr, Cramer, & Niles, 2004; Zunker, 2002).

The approaches chosen by school counselors and teachers to facilitate decision-making and planning for career development ideally offer a wide range of options to students and at the same time encourage future flexibility in the planning process. Because future career trends cannot be predicted with absolute certainty, all students are best assisted by information and skills that identify many career options and paths for reaching identified goals and attaining satisfying life experiences. Methods and approaches that limit options and restrict career choices are detrimental to student development and raise questions about ethical practice on the part of the school counselor. In sum, the methods and models of teaching decision-making skills should open doors for students, not close them. Responsive services and essential purposes of comprehensive school counseling programs require a range of counseling and consulting approaches, technical skills, philosophical beliefs, leadership abilities, and professional characteristics that counselors bring to their helping relationships. The following case studies offer brief illustrations of how these approaches, skills, and beliefs merge in an expanded view of a school counselor's role.

Case Illustrations of Comprehensive Programs of Responsive Services

Case Study of Johnny

Johnny was a third-grader in an elementary school that served a wide socioeconomic student population. He started at the school two years previously in first grade and during that time had gained a reputation as a "behavior problem." Johnny's behavior problems according to anecdotal records by his first- and second-grade teachers included being out of his seat, excessive talking, not completing his assignments, picking fights with other students, and simply being a "pest."

At the start of third grade, Johnny met a new counselor at his school. The counselor had heard about Johnny from his former teachers and the school principal, and the third-grade teacher made a referral to the counselor early in the year based on previous year's academic performance. The counselor met with Johnny individually to get acquainted and for him to learn about the counselor's role in the school.

The counselor learned from Johnny that he lived with his maternal grandmother and came from a neighborhood across town. Children from that neighborhood were bused to the school on a forty-five-minute ride. Johnny's father was in prison for burglary and his mother lived in another city. He saw his mother occasionally when she came home to visit. He did not remember his father and only knew him from pictures he had seen. At the end of this first session, the counselor told Johnny about the availability of counseling services in the school and indicated that, if he wanted, they could talk about other things in the future.

Following this initial session, the counselor arranged with Johnny's teacher to observe him in the classroom. During that observation, the counselor noted that Johnny was quite active in the room, although he seemed attentive to what the teacher was doing and what was taking place in the lesson. He seemed most distracted when the teacher was using the writing easel, charts, or PowerPoint presentation in front of the class. The counselor also noticed that Johnny seemed to have a good sense of humor, which unfortunately got him in trouble when he made jokes about things some of the students or the teacher said in class.

After the observation, the counselor and teacher met to discuss the case and review Johnny's records. One finding was that Johnny had been recommended for an eye exam in second grade, but there was no indication of follow-up on that recommendation. The counselor also noticed that there were no standardized assessment data to indicate a level of aptitude. The counselor asked his teacher what she thought about Johnny's abilities, and she responded, "He is much brighter than people think." The counselor shared the observation about his sense of humor, and the teacher concurred, "He is very quick with his wit, and that sometimes gets him in trouble with students and teachers." Together they agreed to initiate a referral for educational assessment and screening.

The counselor also contacted the grandmother and asked about any eye examinations Johnny had in the past year. Evidently, no one had followed up on that earlier recommendation, so the counselor asked the grandmother if she would do that. The grandmother agreed but was concerned about the cost. The counselor offered to contact the school social worker and nurse to see what financial aid or other support might be available. An eye exam was eventually scheduled and found that Johnny's eyesight needed correction. Eyeglasses were prescribed.

The educational assessment, administered by the school counselor and psychologist on two separate occasions, found that Johnny was indeed quite intelligent and might qualify for gifted and talented services of the special education program. The grandmother was contacted about these results and a conference was held with her and the teachers to develop an Individual Education Plan (IEP).

The counselor began seeing Johnny individually to discuss all this new information and how he was feeling about the changes in his life—starting third grade, having new eyeglasses, and being placed in the gifted and talented program. Johnny seemed quite pleased with being in the gifted and talented program, although he was intimidated by some of the other students in the resource class. He liked his new glasses and did not mind wearing them. He proudly exclaimed, "I can read what the teacher writes on the board."

Eventually, the counselor asked Johnny about forming a group of students from his gifted and talented class, and he welcomed the idea. They chose a few students (with the special education teacher's recommendation and approval) and invited them to join a group. The purpose of the group was to help Johnny learn more about himself and gain support for his relationships with other students in the program. During one group session, Johnny expressed interest in working with animals. Consequently, the counselor and teacher planned a field trip to the animal husbandry division of the nearby agricultural program at the university.

As the year progressed, Johnny became more successful in school and he got in less trouble with teachers. He remained an active boy with a quick wit but had a clearer direction and was more satisfied with himself and with school. Third grade proved to be a successful year.

Case Studies of Latisha, Rhonda, and Rebecca

Early in the school year, three girls were referred to the middle school counselor by teachers because of behavior problems ranging from being withdrawn and unproductive to being aggressive and disruptive in class. The counselor met individually with each of the students to establish a relationship and determine each girl's perception of the situation. Latisha was a quiet seventh-grader with few friends and an unremarkable school career. In reviewing her records, the counselor learned Latisha had progressed through elementary school without significant incident and teachers consistently cited her shy, quiet disposition. Her academic achievement, however, did not reflect the high aptitude scores from her third- and sixth-grade assessments. Latisha lived with her mother and older sister. Through initial individual sessions, the counselor learned that Latisha's mother and father divorced when she was three years old, and since then the mother had relationships with two live-in boyfriends.

Rhonda and Rebecca were eighth-grade students, but Rhonda was retained in fifth grade. Rhonda's records illustrated a student with above average ability but less than stellar grades, particularly from fourth grade on. In addition, she had been suspended at various times in seventh and eighth grades for fighting or being disrespectful to teachers. Rebecca's academic profile was similar, but she had no record of suspensions. Rhonda lived with her mother, stepfather, and an older stepbrother. Rebecca lived with her mother, father, and two younger brothers.

During initial counseling sessions with each student, the counselor learned that they all had experienced sexual abuse during their childhood years, and in Rhonda's case the abuse was continuing. The counselor was the first person Rhonda ever told about the abuse by her older stepbrother, which began during her fourth grade. According to state and federal law and professional ethics for counselors, the counselor informed Rhonda that this information could not be kept confidential, but that she would stand by Rhonda and offer as much protection and comfort as possible. With Rhonda's consent, the counselor called the mother and scheduled a conference with her and Rhonda. The counselor also contacted Child Protective Services to report the suspected abuse.

Latisha's abuse was by one of her mother's boyfriends when she was about five years old. The mother learned of the abuse, never reported it, and ended the relationship with the man. Latisha did not have any counseling following the abuse and had never spoken about it until disclosing to the school counselor. The counselor told Latisha that she would have to contact her mother about the abuse because the law required it. The counselor involved the school social worker in a conference with the mother and together they provided her with information about the law and guidance about calling the authorities. Because the boyfriend was not a caretaker for Latisha and the abuse happened several years earlier, the counselor and social worker suggested that information from Child Protective Services would be appropriate. CPS was in position to determine if the case was abuse or sexual assault and whether to involve the police in its investigation now.

Rebecca's abuse was by an uncle who babysat for the family when she was in elementary school. When her mother and father found out, they called the police and the uncle was arrested, charged with sexual abuse, and convicted. He subsequently served time in prison. Rebecca has had no contact with him since then and does not know where he is. She participated in brief therapy with a psychologist, but did not recall much about that relationship. Since entering middle school, Rebecca had not talked with anyone, including her parents, about her experiences.

In each of these cases, the counselor received permission from the girls to meet with their parents. The purpose of these conferences was to encourage the parents to seek additional counseling if the girls wanted it. The counselor also contacted a therapist at a local nonprofit agency, The Hope Center, which specialized in counseling victims of sexual abuse or assault. That contact produced information about the center, services available, and any applicable fees. As a result, each of the parents decided to take their daughter to the center.

The school counselor also asked the girls if they would be willing to meet each other in a small group and share their goals about school, careers, and life expectations. The girls agreed and began meeting regularly with the counselor to help each other with school, career, and friendship issues. The school counselor kept in touch with the therapist at The Hope Center to keep her informed of the group's progress. Eventually, the therapist asked the girls if they wanted to form a group at the center.

One of the many challenges facing these students, as is the case for most victims of abuse, was strengthening their self-worth and gaining confidence in their ability to form healthy, intimate relationships. At the same time, they want to be able to empathize with other victims of abuse and mistreatment. The school counselor contacted a couple that had a farm of rescued animals and asked if the girls could visit the farm. The couple was delighted to have the girls and an informal program, in collaboration with The Hope Center, was eventually established to offer young girls and women who had experienced abuse in their lives an opportunity to take care of animals that had been abused and neglected. For Latisha, Rhonda, and Rebecca, the combination of group counseling in school, group work through The Hope Center, and hands-on activities with animals at the farm proved to be successful interventions to encourage higher school achievement, healthy friendships, and overall brighter disposition about life.

Case Study of Gertrude

Gertrude was an 18-year-old student in her junior year of high school when she and the new counselor first met. She was standing in the middle of the counselor's office, sullen and unkempt, and when the counselor entered, she said, "I'm Gertrude, you're my counselor, and if people don't stop picking on me, someone is going to get it." The counselor had learned about Gertrude from the school principal and the chair of the counseling department, both of whom indicated, "Something has to be done about her this year. We cannot allow the fighting and hostility to continue."

Gertrude's file, examined by the counselor after their first encounter, was extensive. In brief, she was identified as educable mentally retarded, had spent over a year in an adult sheltered workshop prior to coming back to high school, had a history of epileptic seizures for which she was prescribed medication, had repeated two grades in school, and lived with her mother, stepfather, and brother. Her stepfather was employed with the city sanitation department and her mother was unemployed. As an African American female with all these challenges, Gertrude's future seemed bleak.

After reviewing the folder and interviewing Gertrude, the counselor made tentative plans to

1. Establish a relationship with Gertrude in which she would make a commitment to stop fighting and select some attainable goals to achieve during the year.
2. Check with her neurologist about the medication she was taking.
3. Evaluate her academic record, including the year spent in the sheltered workshop.
4. Contact her parents to assess their involvement in this relationship.
5. Collaborate with the principal and teachers to determine an appropriate educational program.
6. Contact the vocational rehabilitation counselor who had been assigned to her case to ensure appropriate career services.

In the initial stages of their relationship, Gertrude and the school counselor met once or twice a week. The counselor used a person-centered approach to establish rapport and develop trust. Early in the relationship, Gertrude stated that she wanted to graduate from high school. Because the requirement for graduation included a state competency test, this would be a tremendous accomplishment for Gertrude. Given her exceptionality, the counselor wondered if it were a realistic goal. Together, they decided to work toward completing all requirements, taking the state exam, and achieving either a diploma or certificate of attendance.

After several sessions, Gertrude brought the counselor a poem she had written about their counseling relationship. The counselor was intrigued with the idea that an educable handicapped person wrote poetry. He put the poem up on his bulletin board, and

Gertrude beamed with delight. The next session she brought a large loose-leaf notebook filled with poems she had written over the years. These lyrics, primitive in form but rich in spirit, were a strong indication that Gertrude had a willingness and a desire to learn and improve her life.

In their individual sessions, the counselor learned that Gertrude was unsure how much medication she was taking. The counselor called the mother, but she added little information. The counselor scheduled a meeting with the neurologist for Gertrude and her mother. No medical evaluation was recorded in over two years and Gertrude had not had a seizure since elementary school. After the evaluation, the physician decided to lower the dosage of medication by half. The counselor agreed to keep the physician informed of any changes noticed at school. Within the first few weeks, everyone noticed a change. Gertrude became less sullen, and, although she was still quick-tempered, she was much more congenial and affable at school.

The counselor and principal reviewed the coursework Gertrude completed at the sheltered workshop to determine if any high school credit could be awarded. After the review, the principal granted six credits for the work completed and promoted Gertrude to a senior class homeroom. This change in status made a world of difference in her attitude, because Gertrude could now dream of finishing high school with reasonable chance of it becoming a reality. Now she wanted a diploma more than anything. To receive a diploma, she would have to pass the state competency test.

The counselor and classroom teachers met with the competency skills teachers to design a plan of action. Because Gertrude had made noteworthy strides in her behavior at the beginning of the year, the teachers were enthusiastic about helping. The competency skills teachers agreed to take her in one of their remedial groups, and the counselor scheduled time to work with all the students in the class on their peer relationships. In this way, the competency skills class was a support group for Gertrude and the other students.

The counselor continued individual sessions with Gertrude and made contact with her parents by phone and in meetings at home and in school. In these sessions, the counselor outlined the goals Gertrude had chosen and reported on the progress she had made during the year. No specific requests were made of the family except to support Gertrude in her efforts to finish school. Unexpectedly, when Gertrude returned to school after Christmas break, she was a different person. She wore fine dresses that her mother bought at a local thrift shop and gave to her as presents. She was clean and attractive, so much so that her appearance drew favorable comments from the same boys with whom she used to fight in school!

An appointment was made with her vocational rehabilitation counselor, who began sessions with Gertrude at school to discuss future plans and options. Teachers in her classes also offered her guidance about what to do after high school. At the end of the year, Gertrude graduated with a state diploma. She had completed all requirements and passed the state competency test in reading and mathematics.

These three case illustrations demonstrate the wide range of services that school counselors deliver in helping students, parents, and teachers address a variety of issues. In the case of Johnny, the counselor collaborated with teachers, grandmother, the psychologist, social worker, and nurse to arrange services. She also used individual and group counseling to assist Johnny with changes in his life and cooperated with the local university to encourage career exploration. Similarly, the counselor of Latisha, Rhonda, and Rebecca used individual and group processes with the students, and consulted and collaborated with parents, the school social worker, Child Protective Services, and the sexual abuse counselor. In addition, the school counselor collaborated with the couple who ran the farm for neglected and abused animals. Likewise, in the case of Gertrude, individual counseling enabled the student and counselor to establish a trustful relationship in which specific goals were identified and commitments were made. Collaborative relationships with teachers, the principal, Gertrude's parents and physician, and others moved this case forward. Group processes were established with teachers and students in the competency skills class, and school policies were used to review the educational record and award credit for work completed in the sheltered workshop. In this way, comprehensive services, orchestrated to focus on specific goals, resulted in a successful outcome.

In this and previous chapters, we surveyed the components of a comprehensive school counseling program and described the responsive services provided by professional counselors. These chapters emphasized that educational planning and career development are the ultimate goals of a comprehensive school counseling program. Because the range of responsive services provided by counselors in a comprehensive program is so extensive, evaluation of the program is a legitimate concern. How do counselors know that the services being provided are the most needed, and how do counselors demonstrate the effectiveness of these services? In the next chapter, we examine the role of evaluation and accountability in school counseling programs.

Additional Readings _____

Herr, E. L., Cramer, S. H., & Niles, S. G. (2004). *Career Guidance and Counseling Through the Lifespan: Systemic Approaches* (6th ed.) (Boston: Allyn and Bacon).

Isaacson, L. E., & Brown, D. (2000). *Career Information, Career Counseling, and Career Development* (7th ed.) (Boston: Allyn and Bacon).

Purkey, W. W. (2000). *What Students Say to Themselves: Internal Dialogue and School Success* (Thousand Oaks, CA: Corwin).
This brief treatise on internal dialogue or "self-talk" offers counselors and teachers insight into the nature of students' inner voice and its impact on educational planning and success.

Zunker, V. G. (2002). *Career Counseling: Applied Concepts of Life Planning* (6th ed.) (Pacific Grove, CA: Brooks/Cole).
These popular texts offer a comprehensive view of career counseling and development for school counselors. They also provide an overview of the important theories that have created this field of counseling and student development.

Websites _____

College and Career Planning
http://apps.collegeboard.com/myroad/navigator.jsp
Learning Styles
www.namss.org.uk/careers.htm
National Career Development Association
www.ncda.org

Occupational Information Network (O*NET)
www.onetcenter.org
Welcome to Mapping Your Future
www.mapping-your-future.org

Exercises _____

1. Think about your decision to study and join the counseling profession. List the factors or experiences that led you to this decision. Discuss with a classmate or a small group these factors; discuss differences and similarities.

2. Interview a worker in any profession or line of work. Through your questions, discover how the individual came to choose his or her career track. Assess the person's satisfaction with the choice and inquire what he or she would change about that career choice, if anything. In class discussions, compare findings of these interviews.

3. In a small group, list career changes that have been brought about by technological advances in the past ten years. After making this list, have your group predict which of these changes will be significantly altered again in the next ten years.

4. Review the case studies in this chapter. In a small group, discuss the way each counselor approached the case. What challenges were faced, risks taken, and decisions made that played a significant role in each situation?

11

Evaluation of School Counseling Programs

In its infancy, the school counseling profession focused on the role of the school counselor and individual helping relationships with students. As the profession moved into the 1950s and 1960s, the literature afforded more attention to the development of counseling theories and models of practice. In addition, group processes in school counseling gained prominence during this period. Beginning in the 1960s and continuing to the present day, the issue of accountability emerged as a requisite to the role and function of school counselors (Aubrey, 1982; Crabbs & Crabbs, 1977; Hohenshil, 1981; Schmidt, 2000; Stone & Dahir, 2004). Specifically, attempts to define and describe the role of counselors in schools have included an urgency to demonstrate effective practices.

In some respects, the same historical events that fueled the expansion of school counseling also contributed to calls for program evaluation and counselor accountability. The national alarms that resulted from *Sputnik I* in 1957, the *A Nation at Risk* report of 1983, and the No Child Left Behind Act of 2001 are examples of the profession reaping the benefits of governmental action and at the same time experiencing pressure to demonstrate *what* they do and *how well* they do it.

Over the years, some authors have noted that counselors as a group are reluctant participants in this movement towards accountability (Baker & Gerler, 2004). A typical response has been that counseling is such a personal relationship and counselors do so many interrelated activities that it is impossible to measure a counselor's effectiveness or evaluate a program of services. Such avoidance of program evaluation and professional accountability continues as an obstacle to public recognition and acceptance of school counselors as essential contributors to effective educational programs. As I noted in an earlier book, "Some counselors believe they are valuable to their schools because they are always 'busy.' To survive as a school counselor, you want to move beyond the notion of 'being busy' toward the realization that the services provided *make a difference* in the lives of students, parents, and teachers" (Schmidt, 2004, p. 8). The future credibility and efficacy of the profession depend on counselors taking the lead and demonstrating their value to the school community and to the educational process.

In 1985, Lombana listed several explanations as to why some counselors are reluctant to demonstrate accountability. Still relevant today, her reasons included (1) the lack of time counselors have to plan and assess their programs; (2) resistance to measuring what counselors do in helping relationships; (3) confusion about the difference between research and accountability; and (4) fear of what the outcomes might be should counselors gather data to assess their effectiveness. Each of these reasons has validity. Time is a critical, precious commodity for everyone. Because school counselors have responsibility for program leadership and delivery of so many services, it is understandable, if not acceptable, that they spend little time measuring their effectiveness. It is indeed difficult, and at best imprecise, to measure the effects of counseling and consulting services. This imprecision, the difficulty of demonstrating cause-and-effect relationships, understandably contributes to anxiety about the results that evaluations might produce. In part, this lack of confidence is an outcome of school counselors not receiving sufficient preparation in research and evaluation methods. These perceptions and feelings are understandable, but they should not deter counselors from acquiring the necessary skills to demonstrate their value and worth to the public who use their services and to the decision-makers who employ them.

In this twenty-first century, there is little new evidence in the school counseling literature to indicate that accountability methods are being widely applied. The educational reform movement in the United States has done little to encourage counselors to embrace comprehensive programs of services or to establish methods of accountability. Quite the contrary, the focus on testing of students as a primary reform initiative frequently distracts counselors from efforts to design, deliver, and evaluate comprehensive programs. This dilemma contributes to questions about the professionalism and identity of school counselors. As Johnson (2000) admonished, "Without accountable performance, promoting the professional identity of school counseling is just 'smoke and mirrors'" (p. 39). However, the transformation movement of the school counseling profession has encouraged accountability processes (Stone & Dahir, 2004), and this encouragement has resulted in an emphasis on program evaluation and other accountability processes in comprehensive models of school counseling programs (American School Counselor Association, 2003; Gysbers & Henderson, 2000).

Comprehensive program evaluation and counselor accountability consist of a variety of activities beginning with the needs assessments described in Chapter 6. In addition, activity evaluations; surveys of students, parents, and teachers; self-rating scales; and performance appraisal processes are all part of a comprehensive process to evaluate a school counseling program and assess the counselor's effectiveness in delivering services.

In this chapter, we examine two aspects of counselor accountability: program evaluation and counselor effectiveness. The purpose of preparing counselors in these evaluation processes is threefold: (1) to help counselors gather data with which to plan their own professional development; (2) to enable counselors to make a case for their value and worth to the decision-makers who plan school programs and services; and (3) to invite counselors to participate in research efforts that lend credibility and validity to accepted practices and the future development of their profession.

Several models and methods of accountability have been presented in the counseling literature (Fairchild, 1986; Gysbers, Lapan, & Blair, 1999; Krumboltz, 1974; Stone & Dahir, 2004). In general, they suggest the following principles and guidelines:

1. The goals of a school counseling program must be defined and agreed on by all who will participate in the evaluation process. Counselors who seek input from students, parents, and teachers, and who are evaluated by supervisors and school principals must clearly describe their program goals, and these goals must be understood and accepted by those involved in the program. Regrettably, school counselors in some systems are evaluated according to standards and practices applied to classroom teachers. These evaluations are likely to be invalid if in fact the counselors are employed to provide comprehensive counseling and consulting services to students, parents, and teachers. Goals that differentiate school counseling from classroom instruction should be reflected in these services.

2. All people who participate in, or are served by, the school counseling program should be involved in the evaluation process. Counselors serve students, parents, and teachers. At the same time, teachers assume an active role in the school counseling program through classroom guidance activities and as advisors to students. Assessment of program goals and evaluation of effective services need to include comments from these groups as well as from the counselor, supervisor, and principal.

3. The instruments and processes used for gathering evaluation data should be valid measures of services and goals of the school counseling program. For example, survey instruments should reflect the goals and objectives of the program. At the same time, the functions and competencies of school counselors should be assessed by valid instruments that relate to counselor preparation and employment expectations.

4. Program evaluation is a continuous process aimed at identifying beneficial services and effective methods of service delivery. In school counseling, strategies for performing ongoing evaluation should be developed and assessed as an integral part of a comprehensive program. As such, evaluation procedures are not implemented simply to appease decision makers or placate the public during crucial times. Rather, they are viewed as vital components in the process of designing, developing, and delivering services to students, parents, and teachers in schools.

5. Strong state and local leadership is imperative (Gysbers et al., 1999). School counselors who do not have support from local directors/coordinators and clear state initiatives that encourage comprehensive programs, responsive services, and reasonable methods of accountability will be challenged to overcome seemingly insurmountable pressures to perform administrative, clerical, and other unrelated functions.

6. The central purpose of counselors' performance appraisal is to assist counselors in helping the school achieve its mission. Evaluation of school counselors, by definition, should enable supervisors and principals to demonstrate that the services provided in a comprehensive counseling program contribute to the school's ability to educate all students.

7. Equally important to helping the school reach its goals is the related purpose of enhancing the counselor's professional development and encouraging skillful improvement. Evaluations that enlighten and educate counselors about their strengths and weaknesses and involve these counselors in making decisions about their professional development far surpass methods that simply identify weaknesses and call for personnel action to remove or reassign counselors.

8. Both program evaluation and counselors' performance appraisal imply that action will be taken as a result of the findings gathered in the assessment process. When school counselors assess their programs of services by asking students, parents, and teachers to comment, they commit to review the results of this study and make changes in the program that, based on their findings, are professionally sound and ethically appropriate. Likewise, when supervisors and principals use reliable and valid methods to evaluate counselors, there is follow-through on the recommendations of these evaluations. To accomplish these goals, school systems offer professional and financial support to counselors to help them further their education, attend workshops, and pursue other avenues to develop and strengthen their knowledge and skills.

9. Evaluations are most helpful and effective when they emphasize positive goals. Program evaluation focuses on the benefits of services provided by school counselors and teachers while identifying unmet goals of the program. Likewise, counselor performance appraisal identifies weaknesses for which counselors may need assistance but also highlights strengths for which counselors should be recognized. As one example of recognition, a counselor could be invited to share particular knowledge and skill with colleagues through in-service activities. By focusing on positive as well as negative aspects, evaluation methods offer a balanced perspective and encourage both program improvement and personnel development.

10. If the purpose of hiring counselors for schools is to help students be successful in their academic achievement, then measures related to student success are appropriate variables to use in accountability procedures (Stone & Dahir, 2004). Schools gather and maintain many pieces of data related to school attendance, academic progress, discipline action, and other factors related to school success. These data are available to counselors in searching for appropriate measures to evaluate comprehensive programs of services.

Types of Program Evaluation

Program evaluation consists of a variety of procedures that focus on different aspects of a comprehensive school counseling program. Baruth and Robinson (1987) offered, "Evaluation of the counseling program is generally of two kinds. These are process evaluation and outcome evaluation" (p. 345). *Process evaluation* indicates whether the services and strategies planned for the program were carried out and answers questions such as: How many people were served? How much time was spent on service delivery? How many sessions were held? *Outcome evaluation,* as the name implies, is an assessment of the outcomes of the services that counselors provide in comprehensive programs. As seen throughout this text, a comprehensive school counseling program consists of a variety of interrelated services. The overall purpose of these services is to assist students in their educational, social, personal, and career development; therefore, outcome evaluation investigates the degree to which specific services assist students in reaching these intended goals. Accordingly, outcome evaluations are performed during the intervention process to assess progress toward the intended goals, as well as at the end of the service to determine whether the goal was reached.

The following sections review four methods of program evaluation. These methods cover the scope of process and outcome procedures available to evaluate school counseling programs. The first of these, goal attainment, focuses on the implementation of strategies and services to meet stated program goals.

Goal Attainment

Inherent in every school counseling service or activity is the belief that it has a meaningful purpose that ultimately contributes to the broader educational mission of the school. This ultimate purpose is found in the goals and objectives chosen for a school counseling program. Usually these goals and objectives, as noted earlier, are chosen as a result of needs assessments performed by the counselor with students, parents, and teachers. Program goals can be evaluated as one of two types: (1) learning-related goals, or (2) service-related goals, which were presented previously in Chapter 6.

Learning-Related Goals. Evaluating this type of goal requires the development of assessment instruments and processes to measure particular learning that is expected of the population being served. For example, for students who participate in career awareness activities, a counselor might create a questionnaire to assess students' knowledge before and after participation in the program. In some instances, the trait being measured might be assessed through commercially produced tests or other types of instruments. Form 11.1 is a sample questionnaire for students who have participated in a career awareness program.

Service-Related Goals. There are three ways to evaluate service-related goals. The first is to simply report the number of occasions on which a service is provided. A second is to

---

FORM 11.1 *Student Career Awareness Questionnaire*

Students: Please respond to the following statements to indicate your feelings and thoughts about the Career Awareness Group in which you have participated. Circle one response for each statement. Thank you.

---

1. This group helped me learn things about myself that I did not know before.	YES	NO	UNSURE
2. This group helped me learn about different careers.	YES	NO	UNSURE
3. I have a better understanding of what education I need for the job I want to have.	YES	NO	UNSURE
4. The counselor listened and understood my concerns.	YES	NO	UNSURE
5. I would recommend this group to other students.	YES	NO	UNSURE

Students: Please write down some of the careers that interest you and the educational goal you would achieve to pursue the careers on your list. (Educational Goals are: High School, Technical School, Two-Year College, Four-Year College, Graduate School, Beyond Graduate School).

Careers of Interest: Educational Goals:

_____   _____

_____   _____

FORM 11.2   *Sample Report of Counselor's Group Work*

Month: April

1. Number of small group counseling sessions held during the month _____
2. Total number of students who participated in group counseling this month _____
3. Number of group guidance sessions led this month (small groups and classroom guidance) _____
4. Total number of students who participated in group guidance_____

Group Counseling Issues and Topics:

_____

_____

_____

Group Guidance Topics:

_____

_____

_____

count the number of people who participate in a given service. The third method is to survey people to obtain their observations about a particular service. This last method is a measure of consumer satisfaction.

Form 11.2 is a sample report about group counseling in an elementary school that uses the combined method of counting sessions and participants. On this form, the counselor reports the number of groups led and the number of students who participated during the month. As noted earlier, such "process evaluations" *quantify* how counselors spend their time and show the amount of services provided and the number of people served. A quantitative analysis is important when counselors want to show how their time is used, the case loads they are serving, and the expenditure of their time across varied services and activities that comprise a comprehensive school counseling program.

Form 11.3 is an example of a survey in which teachers are asked to report their observations about group counseling services. Results from this survey indicate how the counselor is spending time and the level of teacher satisfaction. Both Forms 11.2 and 11.3 address the same counseling service, group counseling, but examine its implementation from different perspectives. The type of evaluation procedures chosen by counselors, therefore, depends on what questions need to be answered.

Measuring the number of participants receiving services or the amount of time devoted to a particular activity ensures that counselors offer a broad spectrum of services to meet the needs of a wide population. If school counselors provide only a few services or meet only the needs of narrowly defined populations, they do not design comprehensive programs to deliver a wide range of responsive services. By quantifying their services, counselors begin to make decisions about how to adjust their programs and where to place emphasis to meet the needs of more students, parents, and teachers. Here is an example of how counselors can use process evaluation to assess and refocus program services:

FORM 11.3   *Teacher's Evaluation of Group Counseling*

Teachers: Please complete the following questionnaire to help us evaluate the counseling groups that have been part of the school counseling program this semester. Indicate your response to each item by circling the appropriate number, 1–5, where 1 means you strongly disagree and 5 means you strongly agree. Thank you.

	Strongly Disagree				Strongly Agree
1. The students who have participated in group counseling have benefited from the service.	1	2	3	4	5
2. I have observed behavior changes in some students who have participated in groups.	1	2	3	4	5
3. The counselor has given me appropriate feedback about students who have participated in groups.	1	2	3	4	5
4. I would like more students to have the opportunity to be in group counseling.	1	2	3	4	5
5. The counselor had a sufficient number of groups available this semester.	1	2	3	4	5
6. The focus of the group counseling sessions seems to be appropriate, based on information received from the counselor.	1	2	3	4	5
7. The feedback from students about their participation in group counseling has been mostly positive.	1	2	3	4	5
8. The group schedule has not interfered with student class work.	1	2	3	4	5
9. Parents have expressed concern about their children participating in these groups.	1	2	3	4	5
10. I need more information about what goes on in these groups.	1	2	3	4	5

A new director of counseling services was concerned about how counselors were spending their time. The counselors and director developed a monthly reporting form and found that while the elementary and middle school counselors used group processes frequently, senior high counselors did virtually no group counseling. In discussing these results with the counselors, the director learned that most of the secondary counselors were uncomfortable with group processes and uncertain of their group leadership skills. As a result, a consultant was hired to lead group workshops for all the counselors. Follow-up surveys the next year showed that some secondary counselors began implementing group counseling in their programs. One experienced counselor who had never led groups before enthusiastically reported success in starting groups at his high school.

Reports that enable counselors and supervisors to examine where time is being spent and how many students, parents, and teachers are being served are important for program evaluation. However, these reports do not adequately address the effectiveness of services—especially as related to outcomes of student progress in school. To do this, counselors must examine identified measures and the effect of responsive services on particular student outcomes.

Student Outcomes

School counseling services help students to obtain information, develop coping skills, adjust behaviors, and achieve other objectives. In all cases, the responsive services that counselors provide to reach these goals should produce some measurable or observable result. In other words, if counseling services complement the learning process, we should be able to assess their impact through student outcomes. Sometimes, outcomes are generalized across populations. For example, a school might focus on one outcome that covers the entire student body. Let us say that the goal is: *To decrease the student absentee rate by 10 percent.* This goal can be measured simply by taking account of the student absentee rate before the service begins and comparing that finding with the student absentee rate after the service is complete.

One problem with this type of outcome evaluation is that it fails to identify how individual students have functioned; it simply looks at whether the broad goal has been achieved. In the example above, we might find that the school absentee rate has improved because students who had relatively good attendance improved their rate even more. On the other hand, students who had high absentee rates might continue to be absent and simply because the overall school rate improved, these students would receive little, if any, notice.

To address the needs of individual students, outcome data for individual cases and small groups should be reviewed. Say, for example, an elementary counselor is seeing a child who is mildly school phobic. The counselor helps the child by using individual play therapy, consults with the teacher about classroom strategies, and confers with the parents about how to handle "getting ready for school" in the mornings. The outcome of all these responsive services is measured by asking parents to report instances of high anxiety at home, receiving feedback from the teacher about the student's frequency of remaining in class without crying, and observing the child's adjustment to the school schedule and classroom environment.

Program evaluation methods to assess student outcomes can take several different forms. For example, evaluation can be based on predetermined or prearranged standards such as: "At least 85 percent of the eighth-grade students will be able to complete the course preregistration card correctly." This type of outcome is generally based on some minimally acceptable level that teachers and counselors believe can be attained.

Another type of outcome procedure compares students in a specific program with ones who have not yet participated. This type of research or evaluation design uses a control group format to demonstrate that the service was a possible causal factor in bringing about a desired change.

For example, at the beginning of the school year, a counselor plans a study skills group of middle-graders who participate for nine weeks. After this period, students show higher grade point averages in comparison to their grade reports for the previous year. A second group of students, called the "waiting group," begins the study skills program after the first nine weeks of school are over and the first report cards are issued. This second group, a matched sample of students, shows no significant difference in grades from last year's report to the first nine weeks' report. After the first nine weeks of school, this matched group is placed in the study skills program, and the experiment is replicated during the second grading period. In this replication, significant changes in grades for the second group of students occur between the two grading periods similar to the findings with the first group of students. Given these results, the counselor can be reasonably certain that the study skills program had a positive effect on helping groups of students improve their grades.

A third outcome procedure asks students about their reactions and involvement in a particular service or asks parents and teachers to observe and record their findings regarding changes in students' behavior and learning. This type of assessment might examine students' attitudes, knowledge, and behavioral changes as measured through surveys, behavioral checklists, rating scales, or case study reports. As noted earlier, the reliability and validity of these assessment instruments are vital to the appropriate development of evaluation procedures and the subsequent interpretation of findings.

A fourth outcome assessment uses a pretest and a posttest comparison. In this procedure, the counselor gathers data to show the student's current standing. The counselor then includes the student in a specific service, such as group counseling. After a period of time, the same instrument or process used in the pretest is repeated and results are compared with the earlier findings. As an example, an elementary counselor who assists a school-phobic child might use a pretest and posttest procedure that involves observing and recording behaviors when the child is referred and then noting the changes after counseling and consulting services are offered. Another example of a pretest and posttest design is a group counseling program with middle-graders who have high absentee rates. Students' absences could be monitored for a few weeks before beginning the group counseling program and then again, when the students have concluded the group sessions. Positive differences between these absentee rates would demonstrate that the group experience encouraged students to attend school on a regular basis.

Another form of goal attainment is to examine specific outcome measures. For example, a comprehensive schools counseling program may target student achievement in a specific area such as mathematics. Several interventions by teachers, counselors, and volunteer tutors are planned throughout the year with the counselor leading the design and implementation. At the end of the year, math scores are compared with scores of the same students from the year before indicating a measure of progress in math achievement.

All these methods of evaluating student outcomes are available to school counselors. Measuring student outcomes is essential, but it is also important to satisfy the clients who seek school counseling services. Counselors realize that the end does not necessarily justify the means, so consumer satisfaction is another method of demonstrating counselor accountability.

Consumer Satisfaction

Collecting data to measure individual student outcomes for all students receiving responsive services may be an impossible task given all the responsibilities of a school counselor in a comprehensive program. Some outcome research is essential to demonstrate the efficacy of counseling services, but if this is all that counselors did, they would have little time to deliver the services they were attempting to evaluate. In evaluating school counseling services, programs can use *empirical* measures or *perceptual* measures. It is the latter, perceptual measures, which fall into the realm of consumer satisfaction.

School counselors use different methods to gather data from students, parents, and teachers in assessing the overall level of satisfaction with program services. Informally, counselors may have follow-up conversations with students and teachers or make phone calls to parents. More formally, counselors design questionnaires for students, parents, and teachers to complete, expressing their views and opinions about school counseling services. Myrick (2003) suggested that it is important and advisable to ask students, parents, and teachers—the consumers of counseling services—what was important from their perspective. For this reason, school counselors use methods to gather information about how these consumers perceive the services of a school counseling program. Figure 11.1 is an example of a high school student survey.

Based on the results shown in Figure 11.1, we can conclude that most students believe the counselor is available, listens to students' concerns, and maintains confidential relationships. The counselor might be concerned that 33 percent of the students did not feel, or were unsure, that the counseling sessions helped them make decisions (question 3). Nevertheless, a strong percentage said they would recommend the counselor to other students who needed services.

One way in which school counselors use consumer feedback to influence decisions about their counseling programs and services is to compile results from all the counselors and summarize these findings for the district administration and school board to review. Comments from students, parents, and teachers are important in demonstrating the value of comprehensive counseling services and in illustrating what role and functions are essential for counselors to fulfill in schools. Sometimes, administrators and board members are unaware of all the services counselors provide. By distributing an annual summary of their program evaluation, counselors take control of who they are and what services they should offer in helping students reach their educational, personal, and career goals.

FIGURE 11.1   *High School Student Survey of Counseling Services*

Summary Report

Instructions: Please indicate your satisfaction with the counseling services you received this year by circling your responses to each statement. Thank you for your assistance.

	YES	NO	UNSURE
1. The counselor was available to see me when I needed assistance this year.	77%	15%	8%
2. The counselor listened to my concerns and seemed to understand me.	70%	20%	10%
3. The counseling sessions helped me focus on my concerns and make decisions.	67%	25%	8%
4. The counselor kept information I shared in counseling confidential.	98%	1%	1%
5. I would recommend the counselor to other students who need services.	85%	5%	10%

An annual evaluation also enables supervisors of counseling services, school principals, and counselors to make decisions about which services to expand and which to deemphasize. Adequate assessment of all counseling programs across the school system places administrators and supervisors in a better position to make decisions about personnel, budget, staff development, and program changes. In contrast, without adequate evaluation, such decisions are made arbitrarily or intuitively with little or no basis in research evidence. Program and personnel decisions made in this manner reflect a serendipitous management style and, likewise, assume that counseling is a fortuitous process without foundation in specific knowledge bases, helping skills, or efficacious models of professional practice. Such a position does disservice to the counseling profession and to the students, parents, and teachers who expect reliable and dependable services.

By gathering data from the consumers of school counseling services, counselors and their supervisors are in a stronger position to make purposeful and meaningful decisions about future directions for the program. This posture of having purpose and direction has been referred to as counselor intentionality (Schmidt, 2002). When related to the process of evaluation, this characteristic refers to an awareness and willingness to receive feedback from others and use that feedback to alter behaviors, develop plans, and change direction to meet the needs of those being served. Though this kind of internal feedback from students, parents, and teachers is valuable to school counselors, sometimes an external review of programs is also beneficial.

Expert Assessment

Perceptions of local supervisors, including school principals, and from students, parents, and teachers offer counselors an opportunity to broaden their assessment of what services are effective and which new services may be needed. However, if only these types of internal perspectives are used, counselors and their supervisors will limit annual evaluations to restricted and repetitious views of *what should be.* In addition, they risk neglecting broader visions that reflect national and international trends and issues in the school counseling profession. To guard against this kind of parochial stance, counselors and supervisors occasionally seek assistance from outside experts in school counseling who offer an external perspective to the evaluation process (Schmidt, 1996; Vacc, Rhyne-Winkler, & Poidevant, 1993).

Expert assessment of school counseling services includes a range of evaluation processes from observing a single counselor in an individual activity to gathering data about all the services of a comprehensive program across an entire school system or state (Gysbers et al., 1999). By using outside experts to gather information, counselors and supervisors increase the objectivity of the evaluation process and thereby ensure results that are more reliable. Because of the expense of hiring outside consultants to perform this type of evaluation, this method is not used often. For this reason, internal evaluations should be used in conjunction with the external reviews for comparison purposes.

In designing an external evaluation of school counseling programs, counselors and supervisors formulate several questions. By asking appropriate questions and giving serious thought to their responses, counselors and supervisors ascertain the potential value of an external review and determine whether the time and cost will produce results to strengthen their program of services. Some questions that counselors and supervisors might entertain are:

1. *What do we want to know?* A proper evaluation begins by asking clear questions about what counselors and counseling supervisors want to learn about the program of services. These questions can be generated in meetings with counselors, administrators, and teachers. Generally, the questions focus on specific areas of concern, such as: Are the essential services being provided by counselors an efficient way of addressing the needs of students in our school? Given the personnel available, are school assignments and ratios of counselors to students appropriate at all levels? Are there more effective and efficient methods of providing services than are currently being done?

2. *Who should be involved in designing the evaluation?* Because school counseling services are an integral part of the educational program, a wide representation of school populations should be included in planning an external review. School counselors should join with supervisors, principals, teachers, other student services specialists, and parents to ensure that a broad area of concerns is considered. In secondary schools, student representatives should also be included.

3. *Who are the outside experts to conduct the evaluation?* Depending on the location of the school system and the availability of external resources and internal funds, an evaluation committee will recommend to the superintendent the evaluators who should be invited on the review team. By using questions formulated during the planning phase, the committee can narrow the field of reviewers needed. Examples of possible external reviewers include counselor educators from local and state colleges and universities, consultants from state departments of education, counselors and counseling supervisors from neighboring school systems, renowned professionals in counseling, and officials in state and national school counselor associations. Credentials of potential reviewers and cost factors are considered in making this recommendation to the superintendent and local school board.

4. *What instruments and processes will be developed as part of this evaluation?* In most instances when an external consultant is hired to perform an evaluation, the design of the study, including the instruments to be used, is part of the contract. The evaluation committee presents the major questions and issues to be reviewed, and the consultant designs the instruments and the processes for gathering data. In some instances, the evaluation committee might ask consultants to design a study and sample instruments as part of the process of selecting an external reviewer.

5. *Who will receive the results of the study and how will they be used?* As with other types of assessment processes, such as testing and observing students, program evaluation requires careful and appropriate use of data. The evaluation committee is responsible for determining how the results will be reported and for whom the report is intended. These decisions are guided by the overall purpose of the external review and the specific questions included in the design of the study. In most cases, the report of an external review is shared with the local school board through the superintendent's office.

Over the years, I have been involved in external reviews of school counseling programs and have consulted with other evaluation teams. In most instances, these reviews were invited by superintendents who wanted an outside evaluation of their school counseling programs. Often these requests were a prelude to the decision of whether to add new counselors to the system. Typically, these external reviews consisted of surveys designed cooperatively with the school system and administered to students, parents, and teachers and onsite visits to schools to interview the principal and counselors. Form 11.4 illustrates a typical student survey used in these reviews. Similar parent and teacher questionnaires are used to gather observations across matching items. In the onsite interviews, a structured interview is usually desired. Form 11.5 shows sample questions that could be used with principals during an onsite visit.

The preceding evaluation processes, from service-related accounting methods to external reviews, aim at helping counselors, supervisors, and school principals assess the direction and benefits of a comprehensive school counseling program. Evaluation methods, such as those suggested in this section, provide an overview of programs and assess the

FORM 11.4 *Student Survey Form for External Review*

School Counseling Program Review
Student Evaluation of a School Counseling Program

Dear Student: This questionnaire is part of a review of the counseling program in your school. We appreciate your help and ask that you answer these questions about the counseling program. Thank you for assisting us with this review.

School: _____ What grade are you in this year? _____

Check One: Male _____   Female _____

Circle your responses for each of the following questions.

1. Do you know who your school counselor is?   YES   NO   UNSURE

2. **a.** Did you meet with your counselor
   individually this year?   YES   NO   UNSURE

   (If "No," skip item 2b. If "Yes," about how many times did you meet with
   the counselor? _____)

   b. If you met with the counselor individually
   this year, was the counselor helpful to you?   YES   NO   UNSURE

3. Would you recommend the counselor to your
   friends if they needed to talk to someone?   YES   NO   UNSURE

4. Did the counselor meet with your parents
   this year?   YES   NO   UNSURE

5. Did the counselor talk with your class or do an
   activity in your class this year?   YES   NO   UNSURE

6. Were you in a small group led by your counselor
   this year?   YES   NO   UNSURE

If you participated in a small group with the counselor this year, please answer questions 7 and 8. If you were *not* in a group with the counselor, *skip these two questions.*

7. Was the group helpful to you?   YES   NO   UNSURE

8. Do you believe the group was helpful to other
   students?   YES   NO   UNSURE

(*continued*)

FORM 11.4   (*Continued*)

School counselors do many things. What do you think should be the *three most important* services the counselor does in your school? Please check [✓] the three (3) most important items.

___help students with personal problems	___help students make decisions about school	___information about summer programs
___help students and teachers get along	___give information about the community	___help with referrals for school and agencies community services
___work with groups of students	___do classroom presentations	___help parents
___help students get along	___help teachers	___help with class schedule
___career (job) information	___college information	___do paper work (forms, etc.)
___help families with problems	___scholarship and financial aid	___supervise or give tests

Is there anything the counselor *does not* do in your school that you would like to see done? If so, what is it? _____

_____

_____

Is there anything the counselor does that you think takes too much time away from more important services? If so, what? _____

_____

_____

value of specific counseling and consulting services. An equally important aspect of the evaluation process is the performance appraisal of school counselors.

School Counselor Evaluation

With increased attention on the performance of our schools, the educational community has placed greater emphasis on evaluation and accountability of professional personnel. For the most part, this emphasis has been on evaluating classroom teachers with little attention paid to other professionals and specialists in the schools. Overall, adequate evaluation of school counselors has been a rare occurrence. When counselor performance appraisal has occurred, little written documentation has justified the evaluation processes used or, worse, the performance of counselors has been rated on instruments and with processes designed for teacher evaluation.

The importance of counselor evaluation was highlighted by Wiggins (1993) in his ten-year follow-up study of counselor effectiveness. Over 230 counselors who participated in the original study ten years earlier completed demographic surveys and gave permission

FORM 11.5   *Structured Interview Form for External Review*

School Counseling Program Review

Structured Interview

Principal: _____

School: _____

1. Overall satisfaction with the school counseling program. What are some strengths and weaknesses of the program?

2. What is the MOST IMPORTANT service the counselor(s) performs in the school? What is the LEAST IMPORTANT activity of the counselor(s)? Is there anything the counselor(s) does that you believe SHOULD NOT be done? If so, who should be doing this?

3. How does the counseling program tie into the school goals? (Is the program an integral part of the school? Is the counselor on the school improvement team? How do the teachers integrate guidance into their classes?)

4. Are *all* students' needs being met by the program? If not, what are the barriers that the counselor(s) has to overcome? (What about exceptional children, at-risk, vocational students, etc.?)

5. How is the counselor supervised? (What about counselor evaluation? Methods of data collection? How are summary ratings reached?)

6. How does the school counselor(s) interface with other student services professionals, e.g., psychologists, social workers, nurses? (Look for team approaches, collaborative efforts, etc.)

7. As the school leader, what is your involvement in the counseling program?

8. How is the program perceived by students, parents, and teachers?

9. Anything else you want to share about the program?

for their supervisors to complete a "Satisfaction with Performance Blank" (SWPB). A total of 193 surveys were usable and results showed that only twelve counselors improved their ratings since the original study. More distressing, thirty-three counselors received lower ratings than they did ten years earlier, and 81 percent of the counselors who were rated low in the first study remained in that category ten years later. This latter finding not only emphasizes the consistency of ratings for low-performing counselors but more tragically stresses that little is done to help these counselors improve.

In the 1990s, there was some indication that evaluation of school counselors received more serious attention. Some states and local school systems developed specific criteria and designed processes particularly suited for school counseling practice (Breckenridge, 1987; Housley, McDaniel, & Underwood, 1990; Schmidt, 1990). Generally, the standards for assessing school counselors included criteria related to program planning and organization, group and individual counseling skills and processes, consulting skills and processes including group guidance presentations, coordination of services, ethical practice, and professional development.

Evaluative objectives used in counselor performance appraisal parallel the process and outcome goals used in program assessment described earlier in this chapter. Specific procedures for gathering data related to these standards and goals, however, have not been systematically developed. Furthermore, when processes have been developed, it remains unclear who are the most suitable observers and evaluators to gather data and make judgments about school counselors' performance. These issues help outline some of the major concerns surrounding the evaluation of school counselors. The first is to determine what needs to be evaluated.

What Will Be Evaluated?

Despite an extensive range of literature and research explaining the role of school counselors, developing models of practice, and creating theories of counseling, uncertainty remains about the counselor's role and purpose in schools. As Ficklen (1987, p. 19) pointed out, "the basic problem for administrators . . . is this: What, exactly, are counselors supposed to be accomplishing?" This question is not only critical for determining the overall role and major services of school counselors, it is also essential in identifying the practices that illustrate effective functioning (Schmidt, 1990).

The first step in developing appropriate evaluation procedures for school counselors is to determine their major functions and identify specific activities that define these functions. In this text, the functions that comprise a comprehensive school counseling program have been identified as planning, organizing, implementing, and evaluating. Aligned with these functions are many activities and responsive services to help all students be successful in school. Broad categories of responsive services include (1) counseling individuals and groups; (2) consulting with students, parents, and teachers, individually and in groups; (3) appraising students' interests, abilities, behaviors, and overall educational progress; and (4) coordinating student services in the school. In addition, counselor evaluation examines the extent to which these practices are ethically and legally performed and the attention the counselor pays to his or her own professional development.

Once we have described the major functions and practices of school counselors, the next step in the evaluation process is to determine the nature of measurement to be used to assess performance. Here, we consider three possible approaches. One, as we saw earlier in program evaluation, is to assess the outcomes of particular practices and activities selected by a counselor to address identified concerns. For example, a counselor who uses group guidance activities with middle-graders to help them develop friendships might be evaluated, in part, by a questionnaire on which students indicate what they have learned in the group and how many new friendships they have attempted as a result of the group. A second way to assess counselor success, as with program evaluation, is to examine performance in relation to an agreed standard. An example of this is when a counselor chooses individual counseling to assist students in decreasing their absentee rates, with the goal that all students who participate will decrease unexcused absences by at least 50 percent. In this approach, the counselor is evaluated not by the outcome itself, but by the level at which the outcome is observed. For example, if a majority of students who received counseling for absenteeism decrease their absences by 50 percent or more, the services would be highly successful. A third way to measure counselor performance is by combining the first two procedures—that is, by stating what outcomes should be observed and at what level of performance these outcomes are expected.

Identifying major functions and responsive services and determining the standards of performance provide the overarching framework for an evaluation process. The next step is to design and create specific methods to gather data with which judgments can be made about whether services have been rendered and the level of performance at which they have been delivered.

How Will Evaluation Be Done?

Because school counselors assume a leadership role and provide a wide range of services and activities, it is difficult to narrow down or limit the methods of evaluating their performance. Unlike teacher evaluation, which depends heavily on classroom observations, school counselor appraisal relies on diverse methods of data collection and documentation. Included in these methods are observations, interviews, simulated activities, self-assessments, product development, video- and audiotapes, schedules, consumer feedback, records of services, and memos of personnel action. The variety of activities expected of a school counselor and the confidential nature of some services in a school counseling program raise questions about methods of gathering data for performance appraisal. For this reason, it is important that counselors and supervisors jointly plan and agree on the methods to be used. Ideally, this planning process takes place at the beginning of the school year, and the supervisor and counselor determine which major functions are going to receive attention and how to collect data to assess their performance.

Observations.   Although some counseling services cannot be observed directly due to their confidential nature, other activities used by school counselors can be evaluated through observation. Large and small group guidance, parent education programs, and teacher in-service presentations are examples of activities that supervisors can observe to assess a counselor's instructional and communication skills. These activities usually have an instructional or informational purpose without the element of confidentiality. Sometimes observations can occur during helping relationships, such as in parent or teacher consultations, but these must be carefully planned and permission of all participants is recommended.

One type of observation used to gather data includes structured, planned observations that usually occur with specific activities and focus on a particular skill or practice agreed on by the supervisor and counselor before the observation. Another type of observation is less structured and more informal. Such incidental observations might include a counselor's interactions with students and staff in the office, conversations in the hallways, participation at faculty meetings, and exchanges with administrators. The focus on these types of observations should be factual data and information that has some bearing on the counselor's performance of one or more of the major functions. When incidental information has little or no relationship to essential practices, cannot be documented by formal observations, and cannot be altered through additional training or other assistance, it should not be part of a school counselor's evaluation.

Audio- and Videotaping.   When an observation would be an intrusion to the helping relationship, other methods of evaluation are recommended. An alternative method of collecting information is through the use of video- or audiotaping. Students of school counseling use video- and audiotaping to demonstrate basic helping skills and these same methods are available to supervisors and counselors in assessing performance on the job. When tapes are used as part of the evaluation process, clients grant permission and understand how these tapes will be used. Elementary school counselors should seek parental permission because of the uncertainty, in a legal sense, of a young child's ability to give permission.

Supervisors who listen to or watch tapes to assess performance and assist counselors with their professional development should be knowledgeable of the skills they attempt to evaluate. Supervisors who are not trained in counseling, such as school principals, are unable to offer much assistance and guidance in helping counselors identify specific goals for further development. Since a major purpose of performance appraisal is to help individuals identify areas for professional growth and development, supervisors who are unable to provide this information offer little assistance. Such an assessment is, at best, incomplete.

Interviews.   Another method of gathering information about a counselor's performance is to interview the counselor about program plans, specific services, and student outcomes. The most effective use of interviews is with a structured format that focuses on specific issues, skills, or other aspects of the school counseling program. General interviews that have no specific focus do not generate clear information with which to assess strengths and weaknesses. In addition, a single interview may not be sufficient. Ideally, a series of structured interviews about the same topic may be the most desirable format.

Self-Assessments and Portfolios.   An evaluation is incomplete if it does not consider the counselor's perspective. One way to include the counselor's perspective is a self-assessment. An honest self-assessment can assist the supervisor and counselor in identifying initial areas of focus for annual performance appraisal. One way for counselors to do self-assessment is to keep a portfolio of data, products, and material about their performance during the year. Figure 11.2 illustrates categories and evidence that school counselors could collect to place in their portfolios. With the technology available today, counselors can compile and manage their portfolios with computer programs that include PowerPoint presentations, video and audio segments, scanned photos, and other material to depict their performance of different services.

Self-assessment processes enable counselors to identify their own strengths and weaknesses and recognize these aspects of their professional practice. By identifying areas for further development, counselors are in a stronger position to seek assistance, both supervisory and financial, and to develop plans of action to improve their performance. In addition, self-assessment procedures allow counselors to gather evidence of appropriate and adequate practice to share with supervisors and evaluators during performance appraisal conferences throughout the evaluation cycle. Form 11.6 shows a brief self-assessment questionnaire for school counselors.

Products.   School counselors create many products and reports for their schools and programs. These items can be assessed as part of the overall performance appraisal process. Specific competencies that might be addressed by examining materials and reports produced by school counselors include writing, program planning, and public relations. Examples of products that counselors and supervisors might review are the annual

FIGURE 11.2   *Sample Evidences for a School Counselor's Portfolio/Counselor Functions and Sample Evidences*

Program Planning
- Needs assessments (e.g., instruments and results)
- Written annual plans (with goals, strategies, assignments, and time line)
- Evidence of work with advisory committee
- Weekly/monthly schedules
- Evaluation instruments and procedures

Counseling
- Case studies (anonymous)
- Sample interventions used with students
- Outcome data (e.g., teacher and parent feedback, survey of students)
- Structured interview summary
- Evidence of follow-up
- Group counseling topics and schedule

Consulting
- Summary of consultations with teachers and parents
- Audience feedback of presentations (e.g., teacher workshops)
- Evidence of using assessment data
- Schedule of group presentations (e.g., classroom guidance and parent education)
- Summary of meetings with student services team members

Coordinating
- Samples of written communication (e.g., program brochure and newsletter)
- Documentation of coordination of student services (e.g., meeting agendas)
- Assisting teachers with guidance integration (e.g., notes from faculty meetings)
- Outcome data from referrals made to agencies (e.g., mental health)

Student Appraisal
- Evidence of using assessment results with students, parents, and teachers
- Written instructions to assist teachers with schoolwide testing
- Summary of individual student assessments (anonymous)
- Meetings with parents and students to explain testing results

Professional Performance and Development
- Involvement in school activities (e.g., faculty sponsor of club or activity)
- Professional workshops and conferences attended
- Presentations at professional conferences
- Publication in professional journals/newsletters
- Membership and activity in professional counseling associations
- Awards and recognition received as a professional counselor

---

plan for the school counseling program, brochures developed to advertise specific services, evaluation forms designed to assess program functions, sample memos to teachers, and letters to parents.

Counselors also develop instructional and informational materials to use in classroom guidance, group counseling, and other services with students, parents, and teachers. These materials demonstrate a counselor's knowledge of developmental stages, understanding of

FORM 11.6   *School Counselor's Self-Assessment Sheet*

	Mostly True	Partially True	Not True
1. The school counseling program included a range of services this year—individual counseling, group counseling, parent and teacher consultation, referrals, large group guidance, and student appraisals.	____	____	____
2. I spent an adequate amount of time this year in individual helping relationships with students.	____	____	____
3. I led several group sessions with students each week.	____	____	____
4. I collaborated with teachers to plan classroom guidance lessons during the year.	____	____	____
5. I developed a written plan for the program this year.	____	____	____
6. The advisory committee assisted in developing the plan, designing needs assessments, and evaluating the program.	____	____	____
7. The school's testing program, clerical tasks, and administrative functions did not detract from my services to students, parents, and teachers.	____	____	____
8. I successfully facilitated large groups of students, parents, and teachers this year.	____	____	____
9. The time I spent in crisis intervention this year was sufficient.	____	____	____
10. I used appropriate assessment procedures to make decisions about professional services for students.	____	____	____
11. I attended workshops, conferences, or classes this year for my own professional development.	____	____	____
12. I was active in professional counseling associations this year.	____	____	____

how to use various media in different activities, and creativity in designing useful materials for presentations. Such materials could be included in the assessment process.

Consumer Feedback.   Asking students, parents, and teachers for feedback in evaluating specific functions and activities is important in the overall evaluation of the school counseling program. These observations are also valuable in helping counselors assess their performance. Figure 11.1, presented earlier, is an example of how student feedback can be used to assess a specific program function as well as a counselor's performance.

Sometimes consumer feedback is received incidentally by counseling supervisors, school principals, and counselors. These informal and often unsolicited comments and suggestions about a school counselor's performance are useful when they provide reliable information, are supported by documented evidence, and can be realistically acted on to bring about appropriate change. Comments that are heard infrequently or contradict other overwhelming evidence to the contrary are less useful. If supervisors and principals cannot validate and support incidental feedback with their own observations or other data, it is unwise to use such information in the performance appraisal process. Finally, if incidental feedback is used in counselor evaluation, the implication is that some action to remedy a negative situation or reward a positive report will be taken. If no action is possible, incidental feedback should not be included in the evaluation process.

Schedules and Records. The school counselor's role is described in a planned program that consists of varied activities to assist specific populations in achieving identified goals. If this is true, then part of an evaluation should include the plans that counselors write, the goals they set, the schedules they make, and the records they keep. Of all these evidences, records are ones that may be most difficult to include in the performance appraisal process. Because many of the relationships counselors form with clients are confidential, opening records to a supervisor or principal is inappropriate unless specific constraints are set and guidelines are followed.

Two types of records counselors can share as part of their performance appraisal process, if they take the necessary precautions, are records of decisions made regarding the type of services that counselors provided and records of outcomes. In all cases when counselors share these types of records, the client's identification must be deleted and the anonymity of the client maintained. The purpose of sharing these types of data is not to find out *who* has received services, but rather to assess *what* concerns have been addressed by the counselor, *why* the counselor chose certain services and techniques in assisting with these concerns, and *what* were the results of the services provided. By reviewing these kinds of records, a supervisor can advise and support the school counselor about clinical and program decisions he or she has made. It is through these evaluations that the counselor and supervisor are able to assess diagnostic skills and decision-making processes used to determine services for students, parents, and teachers.

Personnel Memos. Finally, other documents to include in a performance appraisal are memoranda used to cite specific instances where a counselor has not met a performance standard. Memoranda such as these are used when counselors perform in unsatisfactory ways and a plan for improvement must be established and carried out. In cases where a plan for improvement does not ultimately result in satisfactory performance, personnel action to terminate or reassign a counselor may be necessary. Memos of visits, conferences, and plans of action, as well as other documents filed during this phase of the performance appraisal process, are essential to protect the rights of the individual counselor, ensure the integrity of the school counseling program, and verify support offered by the supervisor and school system to remedy the situation.

Who Will Evaluate?

The last question to consider in designing a performance appraisal process for school counselors is who will do the evaluation? In most instances, school counselors report directly to building principals, who are ultimately responsible for the counselor's evaluation. This is a dilemma for both the counselor and principal, who want to create reliable and valid performance appraisal processes. Generally, school principals have little or no training in the practices and competencies that have been identified as major functions of professional school counselors. The "efficacy of counselor performance appraisals is jeopardized when critical functions cannot be adequately assessed so that strengths can be recognized and weaknesses remediated" (Schmidt, 1990, p. 91). Given this caveat, the challenge is to find ways in which counselors can receive appropriate supervision and accurate evaluation for the services they provide in schools.

A study by Roberts and Borders (1994) found "support for the administrative nature of existing school counselor supervision" (p. 155). At the same time, counselors reported a much lower incidence of supervision for the counseling function. The counselors in this sample expressed a need for less administrative supervision and more supervision for program development and direct services to students, parents, and teachers.

Among all the responsive services that counselors offer in school settings, most can be assessed by competent observers and evaluators who have little or no preparation in counseling processes and skills. A qualified principal who understands the broad purpose of student services, including counseling, is able to assess a counselor's ability to plan and lead a comprehensive program. At the same time, an effective administrator should be able to assess general employee behaviors such as punctuality, staff relationships, and communication skills, all of which are vital to effective programs. A school principal or other non-counselor may have difficulty assessing skills and competencies unique to the counseling profession. These skills include student assessment competencies particularly in the area of tests and measurement, counseling theory and techniques, and consulting processes. Occasionally, principals may have adequate preparation in some of these areas, but most graduate programs in educational administration are not oriented toward theories of human development and basic helping skills. For this reason, effective models of counselor performance appraisal should include observations, interviews, and other methods of collecting and analyzing data by appropriate supervisors of school counseling programs.

One way to create adequate and appropriate performance appraisal procedures is for principals and counseling supervisors to cooperate in the evaluation of school counselors. In such cooperative models, principals and supervisors jointly assess the counselor and combine their talents in offering sufficient program supervision. Schools that design a collaborative model of counselor evaluation ensure that administrative supervision by principals is adequate, and at the same time, they encourage appropriate clinical and technical supervision and support from qualified counseling supervisors.

In many school systems, the luxury of having a supervisor of counselors is unrealistic because of fiscal constraints. In such cases, other models of supervision could be explored. These models might include peer supervision approaches where "lead counselors" in a school district assume supervisory duties to help their peers assess clinical and technical performance. Other models include the use of counselor educators from neighboring colleges and universities to assist with counselor supervision or contracts with counselors in private practice who consult with school counselors and principals and help them design adequate performance appraisal processes. The goal in all these alternative approaches is to design evaluation processes that help counselors strengthen their program leadership and improve delivery of effective services.

All methods of gathering data to assess counselor performance have value when used for professional improvement and when they are collected and analyzed by competent evaluators. In part, the competency of the evaluator is either enhanced or diminished by the validity of the processes and instruments used in the assessment process.

Performance Appraisal Processes and Instruments

School counselors not only assist in the development of appropriate procedures for their performance appraisal, they also participate in designing adequate tools with which to do an accurate assessment. Specifically, the instruments designed to gather data for school counselor performance appraisal should relate to particular areas of counselor preparation and practice as well as job expectations. For example, an instrument created to evaluate a counselor's skill in group counseling is of little benefit if the school inhibits group procedures. Similarly, an instrument that is normally used to observe teachers in classroom instruction is useless in assessing individual counseling sessions. Instruments designed to evaluate counseling programs and responsive services relate to specific approaches and behaviors that are generally accepted as indicators of a particular professional practice.

The first step in designing adequate and appropriate instruments is to identify the functions and services expected of a school counselor. After this is done, the counselor, supervisor, principal, and other appropriate people list specific practices to observe in judging overall satisfactory performance. Earlier in this chapter, you learned about surveys and other methods to gather data for program evaluation. Similar instruments can be designed or adapted to gather information about a counselor's performance. Form 11.7 is a sample of an observation instrument designed to assess a counselor's group presentation skills in classroom guidance, parent education programs, or teacher in-service training. Implicit in this instrument is

---

FORM 11.7   *Counselor Observation Form for Group Presentations*

Large Group Observation Form

Instructions: Use this form to observe the school counselor when presenting group instructional or informational sessions. Record the counselor's behaviors during the presentation by using the observation code below and through any additional comments you may have.

Observation Code:	#	Appropriate use of practice
	+	Strong indication of practice
	−	Weak or negative use of practice
N/O		Not Observed

COMPETENCIES AND PRACTICES
  Observations

1. USE OF TIME
    1.1 Has all materials ready for presentation   _____
    1.2 Begins the presentation on time   _____
    1.3 Uses presentation time efficiently   _____
    1.4 Ends the presentation on schedule   _____

Comments: _____

_____

_____

(continued)

FORM 11.7 *(Continued)*

2. **INSTRUCTIONAL PRESENTATION**
    2.1 States purpose and makes goals clear to group
    2.2 Gives clear instructions and directions
    2.3 Speaks clearly
    2.4 Listens to group members' comments and opinions
    2.5 Uses appropriate group skills (e.g., questioning, structuring, linking, etc.)
    2.6 Remains open to comments and suggestions from group members
    2.7 Uses appropriate media and instructional methods
    2.8 Summarizes main points of presentation

    Comments: _____
    _____
    _____

3. **GROUP BEHAVIOR AND MANAGEMENT**
    3.1 Encourages participation of all group members
    3.2 Maintains participants' attention
    3.3 Demonstrates appropriate group management skills
    3.4 Respects the individuality of participants

    Comments:_____
    _____
    _____

4. **LEADER RESPONSES**
    4.1 Affirms group members
    4.2 Reinforces participants' willingness to share
    4.3 Answers questions clearly and concisely
    4.4 Gives feedback to all participants when appropriate

    Comments: _____
    _____
    _____

5. **GROUP OUTCOMES**
    5.1 Asks participants for feedback during presentation
    5.2 Uses evaluation measures and methods to assess outcomes

    Comments: _____
    _____
    _____

Source: Adapted from the *Counselor Group Presentation Observation Instrument* developed by John J. Schmidt, Ed.D., for the North Carolina State Department of Public Instruction, Raleigh, NC, 1988.

the understanding that the observer/evaluator who uses the instrument is knowledgeable and skilled in these instructional methods and facilitative practices.

Although some counseling functions are more difficult to assess by observation, with client permission, it is possible to do so and appropriate instruments can be designed. The interview method described earlier is one way to avoid the difficulties of observing confidential relationships. A knowledgeable supervisor of counseling programs, for example, could plan a structured interview with a counselor about individual counseling services in the program. By using a series of short, structured interviews, the supervisor could give constructive feedback about the counselor's use of assessment and diagnostic procedures, knowledge of counseling approaches, and understanding of the helping process. Although such interviews do not assess specific counseling skills and techniques, they do provide information about the counselor's knowledge and use of specific approaches to counseling. From such an assessment, a supervisor may decide whether specific counseling skills need to be evaluated more thoroughly. Form 11.8 is a sample questionnaire designed to assess a counselor's use of individual counseling.

When counselors in schools evaluate comprehensive programs and services, many methods are available to formulate goals, plan new strategies, and refocus their programs.

FORM 11.8   *Structured Interview of Counseling Relationship*

Interview with Counselor

Instructions: This structured interview form may be used to ask the counselor about specific individual counseling relationships. Ideally, the questionnaire should be used in a series of interviews about the same case.

1. Understanding of client's concerns and appropriate use of diagnostic methods and procedures.

   Question: Tell me about the concerns of the student you are seeing. How does the student perceive the main issues, problems, and areas of concern?

   Question: Describe the assessment procedures you have used and how the results of these methods led you to choose the intervention(s) you selected for this student.

2. Understanding of the helping process and the stages of a counseling relationship.

   Question: Where are you and the student in your relationship at this point? Relate the progress you have made to the phases of a helping relationship.

   Question: Given the nature of the student's concerns, are you satisfied with where the helping relationship is at this point?

3. Knowledge of counseling approaches and techniques.

   Question: Tell me about specific techniques, strategies, and interventions that you have used in this counseling relationship.

   Question: What was the rationale for choosing these approaches?

4. Use of evaluation methods to assess progress.

   Question: How much longer do you expect to be seeing this student?

   Question: What are your goals for the remainder of the counseling relationship?

   Question: What methods do you plan to use to evaluate the overall success of this intervention?

No single method of assessment is adequate to gather data for making these critical decisions. In performance appraisal of school counselors, this caution is even more critical. Because the instruments and processes to evaluate counselor performance are primitive at best, successful supervisors take great care to avoid forming firm conclusions without ample evidence. School counselor performance appraisal, ethically and legally, must provide the best reasonable processes and instruments to judge a counselor's effectiveness. The school counselor who is being evaluated shares this responsibility with the building principal, the counseling supervisor, and any other person involved in the process. By ensuring adequate evaluation of school counseling programs and of the competencies demonstrated, school counselors and those responsible for their supervision behave in professionally ethical and responsible ways. Ethical behaviors and legal issues surrounding the practice of counseling in school settings are the topics addressed in the next chapter of this text.

Additional Readings

Lusky, M. B., & Hayes, R. L. (2001). Collaborative Consultation and Program Evaluation, *Journal of Counseling and Development, 79,* 26–38.
In this article, the authors call for new methods and models of evaluating school counseling programs. They promote a collaborative model and present a case example.

Stone, C. B., & Dahir, C. A. (2004). *School Counselor Accountability: A Measure of Student Success* (Upper Saddle River, NJ: Merrill/Prentice Hall).
A practical guide to accountability that reflects the changing role of school counselors as emphasized by the transformation movement and the ASCA National Model.

Website

CAREI Research and Evaluation
www.education.umn.edu/carei

Exercises

1. In a small group, discuss a time when you were evaluated for your performance. Share your feelings about this experience and talk about aspects of the evaluation that could have been changed to make it a more positive event. What aspects did you control that could have been adjusted to make the evaluation more helpful?

2. Pretend you are a school counselor. Your principal has indicated that he or she wants you to document the effectiveness of your counseling relationships. What would you do in planning such documentation? Create the documents you would use and share them in class.

3. Visit and interview a school counselor about evaluation methods he or she uses in assessing program effectiveness. If the counselor has any forms to share, bring them back to class and compare them with other forms your classmates obtain in their visits. Use these visits to stimulate discussion about what counselors are, or are not, doing to be accountable in their schools.

4. As a way of comparing what counselors in non-school settings do for accountability, visit a counselor in an agency or higher education setting and ask the same questions you used for exercise 3 above.

5. In a small group, brainstorm with classmates and list measures that already exist in most schools that could be used as outcomes of a comprehensive school counseling program.

12

Professional Ethics and Legal Issues

School counselors practice according to standards, regulations, laws, and codes that have been established by professional associations, state and federal governmental bodies, the courts, and other institutions. They make decisions about correct services and proper conduct based on current literature, research findings, preparation standards, certification and licensing criteria, federal and state laws, local school board policies, administrative regulations, and professional ethics. The ethical guidelines followed by most school counselors are the *Ethical Standards for School Counselors* adopted by the American School Counselor Association (2004) (see Appendix) and the *Ethical Standards of the American Counseling Association* (ACA, 2005).

By themselves, ethical standards do not always provide clear choices for counselors to avoid conflict, to make the best decisions for all involved, and to maintain freedom from legal entanglement. They are, as their name implies, guides to professional practice, which counselors must apply to individual situations using their own personal and professional judgment. Ethical standards serve as a broad framework within which counselors interpret situations, understand legal and professional implications, and make reasonably sound judgments in assisting clients. As such, "Codes do not hold the answers to our specific ethical problems, but coupled with help from our professional colleagues, the codes do provide guidance" (Stone & Dahir, 2006, p. 300). For this reason, it is essential that school counselors have a clear understanding of their professional standards; acquire knowledge of local, state, and federal policies; and stay abreast of legislation that governs schools and counseling practices. In their study of school counselors' awareness of ethical and legal aspects of counseling, Davis and Mickelson (1994) found that counselors tended to be aware more of their ethical standards than federal and state laws.

In this chapter, we examine the ethical standards developed by the American School Counselor Association and consider legal issues related to the ethical practice of school counseling. In some respects, counselors today face ethical dilemmas similar to those of their predecessors years ago. Confidentiality, testing procedures, use of school records, and appropriate referral processes remain important issues for counselors today, just as they were decades ago. For example, contemporary school counselors struggle with the challenge of how to maintain helpful, trusting relationships with students who exhibit antisocial behaviors, while at the same time they attempt to serve school and society. They balance the goal of helping students with the understandable need for parents to be involved in educational decisions regarding their children. Counselors in schools are also concerned about maintaining professional relationships with community agencies, classroom teachers, and others who have a vested interest in the education of children and adolescents.

Today's ethical issues are complicated by ever-changing social structures and a technologically advancing society. So, while broad topics are similar to those of years past, contemporary school counselors experience increasingly complex issues when dealing with ethical and legal questions. As one illustration, changing family structures make parents' rights difficult to ascertain. In a blended family, for example, where stepparents have custodial responsibilities and natural parents share legal custody, decisions about who has access to school records, who can see a child at school, and what permissions schools need to talk to family members about a child's progress are not easily defined.

The explosion of computer technology has also added a new dimension to ethical practice (Bloom & Walz, 2000; Guillot-Miller & Partin, 2003). Increased accessibility to students' records, use of computer-assisted instructional programs, and the need for adequate preparation of counselors in the use of computer technology are a few areas of concern. Counselors who use computers to maintain records, present computer-assisted instruction, administer computer-scored inventories, correspond by electronic mail, and manage data for a comprehensive school counseling program must be knowledgeable about ethical guidelines and aware of legal parameters within which to use this expanding technology. There is no end to computer applications envisioned for the future. As a result, knowledge of ethical standards and legal precedent will continue to be a necessary condition of professional practice. School counselors want to keep abreast of ethical standards for online counseling developed by the National Board of Certified Counselors (NBCC) and the American Counseling Association (ACA). They should also follow standards that have been developed by professional organizations such as the National Career Development Association (NCDA) (Bloom & Walz, 2000) for using the Internet as a resource for counseling students.

With these present and future considerations, the first step for school counselors is to understand their ethical responsibilities and learn about how these obligations influence daily practice. As mentioned earlier, school counselors generally are guided by the ethical standards of the American Counseling Association (ACA, 2005) and, specifically, by the standards of the American School Counselor Association (ASCA, 2004). For the purposes of this text, the ASCA standards are presented as the foundation and framework for the ethical practice of school counseling.

Ethical Standards for School Counselors

Ethical standards provide the framework for professional practice and responsible behavior, and at the same time contribute to the identity of the profession that is governed by these measures of conduct. The standards for school counselors are not absolute guides for every decision counselors must make in their daily practice. Instead, they are guidelines that enable counselors to establish a foundation of ethical behavior. In serving clients, assessing needs, sharing information, and performing the wide array of responsive services expected of them, counselors search for additional guidance to complement their knowledge and understanding of ethical guides and legal restraints. Several years ago, Mabe and Rollin (1986) cautioned, "A responsible member of the counseling profession must look to various sources for guidance. We fear that many professions may see a code of ethics as the sole basis for explicating responsibility for its members" (p. 294). Their admonition continues as sound advice for today's counselors in schools.

Although an ethical code of conduct plays a central role in defining a professional's responsibilities, it is not a sufficient guide. Part of a school counselor's responsibilities is to understand the limits of the profession's standards and supplement one's knowledge of sound ethical and legal practices with information from many resources and learning activities. Counselors have a responsibility to use sources available to assist them in acquiring this understanding, including workshops, conferences, and publications.

In addition to serving the three major populations of students, parents, and teachers, school counselors are responsible for carrying out assignments delegated to them by school principals and counseling supervisors. In performing these functions, school counselors work with other professionals, such as school social workers, nurses, and psychologists, as well as professionals in the community. The responsibilities associated with such a wide range of clients and professionals make it necessary to delineate ethical guidelines according to different areas of accountability and service. For this reason, the ethical standards put forth by ASCA are divided according to the counselor's responsibilities with students, parents, and other professionals; the school and community; the counseling profession; and oneself. By aligning these different responsibilities enumerated in the ASCA code with guidelines from the ethical standards of the American Counseling Association, school counselors develop a broader understanding of how their profession views ethical behavior and professional practice.

In the following sections, the responsibilities outlined by the ASCA ethical standards help to define and explain the ethical practice of school counselors. The appendix at the end of this text may serve as a reference while reading these sections. In addition, you may want to locate other professional codes of ethical conduct, such as those for school social workers and school psychologists, and compare them with the standards for school counselors. The first area of ethical behavior for school counselors addresses their responsibilities to students.

Responsibilities to Students

School counselors have primary responsibility for ensuring that their counseling services and the educational program of the school consider the total development of every student, including educational, vocational, personal, and social development. Counselors accept responsibility for informing students about the purposes and procedures involved in counseling relationships and use appropriate assessment and diagnostic techniques to determine which services to provide.

Ethical school counselors avoid imposing their values on students. Such counselors encourage students to explore their own values and beliefs in making decisions about educational plans and life goals. This responsibility is not an easy task. Counselors, too, have strong values and in dealing with young people, particularly minors in a school setting, these convictions are not easily ignored or disguised. Even if a counselor is successful in concealing his or her beliefs, such behavior may threaten the trust one would expect in a counseling relationship. The challenge for school counselors is to balance their views with the goals and purposes of the helping relationship as understood by the student. In this way, counselors may find it appropriate to express their views and allow students to consider these opinions while broadening their available options. There is a distinct difference between expressing one's views and imposing one's values. When a counselor's values and views are so strongly opposed to those of the student's that a healthy and helpful relationship is impossible, the counselor is obliged to assist the student in finding another professional with whom a beneficial relationship can be established. Ethically, the counselor assists with this referral.

The ethical standards stipulate that school counselors protect the confidentiality of students' records and information received from students in counseling relationships. In practice, the concept of confidentiality and its limitations are explained to students at the beginning of a helping relationship. Because of the ages of students they serve, school counselors are in a unique position regarding confidentiality. The courts have not always recognized that minors have the capacity to understand and establish confidential helping relationships (G. Corey & M. S. Corey, 2002). For this reason, school counselors not only need to be aware of their professional code of ethics, they also need to know their legal responsibilities regarding confidentiality. First, counselors need to know the difference between confidentiality and privileged communication.

The term *confidentiality* refers to an individual's right to privacy that is inherent in professional counseling relationships. The necessity for and appropriateness of confidentiality are expressed in ethical standards of conduct. By contrast, *privileged communication* is a legal term used to indicate that a person is protected from having confidential information revealed in a public hearing or court of law. As such, confidentiality is established in an agreement between the school counselor and student when they form a helping relationship. Privileged communication, on the other hand, is granted to students by states that have laws protecting the confidences students share in relationships with their school counselors.

In 1987, twenty states granted some form of privileged communication rights to students in school counseling relationships (Sheeley & Herlihy, 1987). The movement toward professional licensure for counselors in a majority of states may increase the number that provide privileged communication in the future. School counselors not only follow their ethical codes regarding confidentiality but also are aware of statutes granting students the right of privileged communication (McCarthy & Sorenson, 1993). Where statutes exist, counselors want to know the limitations of these laws and that it is the student, not the counselor, who is protected. For example, some statutes grant privileged communication to students except when a judge in court requires disclosure. At the same time, students may waive their right to privileged communication, in which case a counselor has no basis for withholding information that is requested. Some states provide for parental involvement in decisions of whether to waive privileged communication, so school counselors should be aware of what state law stipulates regarding parental permission. Other states, such as Idaho (Stone & Dahir, 2006) provide full privileged communication to students.

An additional note regarding confidentiality and privileged communication pertains to consulting relationships and group processes. Generally, courts have not recognized privileged communications beyond two people. Therefore, when a counselor shares information with a third party, or students self-disclose in group counseling, these confidences may or may not be protected by state statutes. When doubt exists, this issue will likely be resolved by a judge's ruling in a court of law.

A final consideration about confidential counseling relationships relates to situations that indicate a clear and imminent danger to a student or to others. When students share information indicating their intentions to harm themselves or others, or when they, themselves, are being abused, counselors cannot keep this information confidential. Sadly, sometimes children and adolescents are forced into abusive situations that include physical harm, sexual assault, emotional or physical neglect, and psychological harassment. Counselors are obligated to learn about laws and procedures governing the reporting of child abuse and neglect, and to fulfill their responsibilities as outlined by such statutes and regulations. In cases of abuse and neglect and instances of imminent danger to students, school counselors must break confidence and report to appropriate authorities. Protection of the student is imperative, so timely reports are essential, and, in cases of potential suicide, the security of students is paramount.

Other areas of ethical responsibility covered under this section of the ASCA standards are the development of appropriate counseling plans; the use of referrals when necessary; maintaining secure records in providing services; proper use of evaluation, assessment, and interpretation; screening prospective members for group counseling; and protection of group members from physical and psychological harm. In addition, school counselors are warned about establishing dual relationships that might diminish their objectivity. If a dual relationship is unavoidable (e.g., counseling a family relative in your school when you are the only counselor available), each counselor has a responsibility to take action that would address the potential for harm to the client.

Two additional areas of responsibility mentioned by the ethical standards are the appropriate use of technology and appropriate protection of students who participate in peer helper programs. As computer technology is increasingly used in schools, counselors have a responsibility to ensure that (1) students' individual needs are met by various programs, (2) the counselor has adequate understanding of the programs being used, (3) proper assistance is given to students, and (4) students have equitable access to computer technology and applications. In peer helper programs, counselors have a responsibility to protect the welfare of all students selected as helpers as well as those who seek services.

Responsibilities to Parents/Guardians

As indicated in Chapter 5, counselors sometimes form helping relationships with parents or guardians in either counseling or consulting roles. Most, if not all, of the guidelines in Section A, Responsibilities to Students, of the ASCA ethical standards can be adapted to these helping relationships. Informing parents of the purposes and procedures to be followed and maintaining confidences are practices that apply to helping relationships established with parents as well as with students.

Section B of the ASCA standards pertains specifically to counselors' responsibilities to inform parents about services available to students and involve parents when appropriate. Although the ethical responsibility for maintaining confidentiality between a counselor and student may be understood, the legal responsibility of counselors to involve parents in their helping relationships is not as clear. These differences between ethical practice and legal requirements sometimes confuse counselors and place them in the precarious position of deciding whether to protect children's rights or parents' rights (Stone & Dahir, 2006).

Generally, school counselors can avoid some of these entanglements by keeping parents informed of the services provided in their counseling programs, making program brochures available to parents, and using other media to advertise services and develop an open dialogue with parents. Counselors who open communications with parents and speak freely about the types of services they offer to students in schools are in a stronger position to win the confidence of parents and protect the privacy of students at the same time.

In school counseling, particularly at the primary and elementary school grades, parental involvement is essential. For this reason, school counselors encourage students in counseling relationships to give permission to involve their parents or guardians at an appropriate time. The success of child and adolescent counseling depends on the degree to which parents become involved, are able to alter their own behaviors, and assist their children in achieving educational, career, personal, and social goals. Typically, very young children do not have sufficient control of their lives to make decisions and take the necessary steps toward changing problematic situations. In these cases, parental support is imperative.

Encouraging parental involvement and seeking a student's permission to release information and facilitate this involvement is a delicate matter (Salo & Shumate, 1993). Counselors use caution to protect the welfare of students while respecting the rights of parents and guardians. Again, counselors search for a balance between their legal obligations and ethical responsibilities. There is no single guideline to direct counselors toward the correct path on every occasion. Each situation is unique because ethical guides are influenced by judgment and laws are subject to different interpretations. A key element that assists in making sense of counseling relationships and choosing a course of action that protects the student while facilitating communication between the home and school is for school counselors to weigh all aspects, including social and cultural issues, and make a decision. The counselor who most often falters is not the one who takes reasonable, responsible action and justifies his or her behavior based on ethical standards and legal precedent. Rather, the counselor who most likely errs is one who chooses to do nothing out of fear of making a mistake.

Finally, responsibilities to parents include the practice of providing accurate and objective information while following the Family Educational Rights and Privacy Act of 1973. By doing so, counselors share assessment data, school policies, and other information in an equitable and objective manner to strengthen parents' understanding of their children's needs and the services available to help students progress in school. Accordingly, counselors are obliged to share information about services in the school and community accurately and fairly without bias or discrimination.

Responsibilities to Colleagues and Professional Associates

Earlier chapters of this book presented information about the counselor's responsibilities in collaborating with other professionals in the school system and community. The ethical code of professional conduct addresses this area of school counseling by promoting the qualities of cooperation, fairness, respect, and objectivity. School counselors who function at a high level of ethical practice demonstrate regard and respect for the education profession and their teaching colleagues. A successful and effective school counseling program does not exist without cooperative relationships between and among teachers, administrators, and counselors.

In addition to the teachers and principals who assist in developing and delivering beneficial services for students and parents, other educational specialists also cooperate with school counselors. As mentioned before, these professionals include school nurses, social workers, psychologists, and special education teachers. The services offered by these specialists are further expanded and complemented by services provided in community agencies and by private practitioners. School counselors function in an ethical fashion when they are aware of the availability of these services, judge the effectiveness of these services accurately, and use appropriate resources for the benefit of students, parents, and teachers who need assistance beyond what the counselor is able to offer. By establishing collaborative relationships with a wide range of school and community specialists, school counselors avoid the possibility of overextending themselves and reduce the risk of delivering services beyond their level of competency.

Implied in this section of the ethical standards is the counselor's responsibility to be informed about the effectiveness of these additional sources of information and assistance. To achieve an informed level of practice, school counselors follow up the referrals they make to professionals in the school as well as to agencies in the community. Determining the level of success another professional has had with a student, parent, or teacher and assessing the client's degree of satisfaction are essential follow-up processes. They provide counselors with information to decide which professionals and agencies to use in the future.

Ethical counselors keep lines of communication open, and within the limits set by confidentiality and privileged communication guidelines, they share and receive information to assess services that have been provided. Through this continuous process of referral and evaluation, counselors locate referral sources, professionals, and agencies that are knowledgeable, competent, and effective with the cases they accept from the school.

Responsibilities to the School and Community

Because school counselors focus primarily on the educational development of students, they also have the responsibility of protecting the integrity of the curriculum and instructional program. Part of being a spokesperson for the welfare of students is accepting the role as an advocate for the educational mission of the school. When outside forces and special interests take students away from their primary purpose in school, counselors are among those who speak out against such infringement. Partly, this responsibility is fulfilled when counselors assess school climate and keep administrators and teachers informed of potential dangers to students' welfare, the instructional program, or the school environment. For example, a special program designed to offer remedial services to needy students may unintentionally isolate these students from the mainstream of school activity. Differentiating students to this degree may detract from the broader goal of assisting students with their total development. School counselors who are visible in the school, participate in supervisory duties when appropriate, offer services to all students, and communicate regularly with their principals and supervisors are in a position to make assessments and share pertinent information about the school environment and the impact of special programs.

This section of the school counselor's ethical standards also addresses the importance of defining and describing the counselor's role and functions in the school and performing systematic evaluation of these services. An additional note is that school counselors should notify principals and supervisors when conditions in the school inhibit their effectiveness in providing services. This standard addresses a problem that many school counselors encounter in attempting to develop comprehensive programs of services. Counselors are frequently told to perform tasks that take time away from direct services to students, parents, and teachers.

Because schools are inundated with tasks and expectations from the central office, state government, federal regulators, and other outside forces, school principals search for personnel to perform a variety of functions. Often these requests have little to do with the major roles for which these professionals were employed. For example, it is not uncommon to find classroom teachers collecting money, filing forms, or performing other duties that have nothing to do with their instructional role in the school. Likewise, principals occasionally assign counselors to clerical and administrative tasks that take them away from their primary functions of program leadership, counseling, and collaborating with students, parents, and teachers. According to the ASCA ethical code, it is the counselor who is responsible for raising these issues with appropriate school officials.

This section of the ethical standards also gives counselors responsibility for program development and evaluation, two areas addressed throughout this text. It also cautions counselors about accepting employment in positions for which they are not fully qualified.

A final word about responsibilities to the school and community pertains to the counselor's motives for cooperating with other professionals and agencies on behalf of students. School counselors establish relationships with other professionals and agencies for the benefit of students, parents, and teachers without regard for their own interests. Hence, counselors do not accept reward or payment beyond the contracts negotiated with their school systems for services, direct or indirect, provided to school populations.

Responsibilities to Self

When reviewing ethical standards, we sometimes forget the *person* who is expected to behave ethically. The school counselor's ethical guidelines address the need for counselors to behave within the boundary of their professional competencies and accept responsibility for the outcomes of their services. Counselors are obliged to choose approaches and use techniques for which they have adequate knowledge, training, and skill, including an understanding of cultural diversity. School counselors must also comprehend how their own cultural and social identity can affect the counseling relationship. To ensure this level of ethical practice, counselors keep abreast of issues and trends in counseling, attend conferences and workshops, return to graduate school, read professional journals, and choose other avenues to improve their performance and elevate their effectiveness.

A common dilemma for school counselors, which is related to this section of the standards, is deciding when to stop seeing a student in a counseling relationship and refer the student to another professional or agency. The ethical standards address this issue but give little guidance about how to refer to another source for assistance. There are no simple and clear answers to this question, but in setting their own guidelines counselors might ask themselves these questions (Schmidt, 2004, pp. 241–242):

1. Do I have the knowledge and skills to help this student explore concerns, examine alternatives, make appropriate decisions, and act accordingly?
2. Is another professional, who is more able to help than I am, available and accessible to the student or other person needing services?
3. Do I need to involve parents (or guardians) in this helping relationship?
4. By seeing this person on a regular basis, am I denying other vital functions in my role as a school counselor?
5. Am I making progress with this person, and can I show evidence of this progress?

Some students in schools need regular contact with a person in whom they can confide. In most of these instances, students do not require intensive counseling or therapy; they simply need a reliable relationship with someone who will listen and guide them toward appropriate decisions. School counselors who establish these relationships are careful to monitor students' progress in school. By the same token, counselors evaluate the time they allow for these services in comparison to other functions they perform.

Responsibilities to the Profession

School counselors who are members of the American School Counselor Association and follow the ASCA standards accept responsibility for behaving in an exemplary fashion on behalf of their colleagues and the profession they represent. These exemplary behaviors include the research that counselors perform; their participation in professional associations; their adherence to local, state, and federal regulations; and the distinction they make between privately held views and views they espouse as school counseling representatives.

Counselors are responsible for conducting research and reporting their results in an appropriate manner that conforms with acceptable practice in educational and psychological research. In Chapter 11, you learned about program evaluation. The research counselors perform as part of program evaluation, or through attempts to publish significant findings in professional journals, must be performed according to sound practices, and the results must be reported accurately.

Another area of professional responsibility is participation in counseling and educational associations. It is difficult for practicing school counselors to keep abreast of issues and trends in the profession without belonging to educational and counseling organizations. By belonging to and participating in these associations, counselors have access to current information through conferences, workshops, and professional publications. Counselors who participate in professional organizations, network with colleagues across the state or country, read current research about counseling practices, and assume leadership roles in counseling associations are in a stronger position to promote their profession and perform at a high level of ethical practice.

As mentioned earlier in this chapter, school counselors sometimes confront legal regulations that make ethical practice more difficult. On one hand, ethical standards require adherence to local, state, and federal laws, while on the other hand, counselors are expected to protect the best interests of their clients. This dilemma is most apparent when schools establish policies without the best interests of students in mind. For example, when the convenience of a few faculty members or the importance of school maintenance takes priority over student welfare, counselors should intervene. In these cases, it is the counselor's own values and judgments that become most important as he or she chooses and delivers services. Although legal statutes and ethical guidelines share some common ground, they are not equivalent terms. Sometimes there may be conflicts between the two, and when this happens, the values of the counselor become deciding factors.

One part of this section of the code addresses how counselors behave publicly, particularly when expressing their own personal and professional views. The standards require that counselors make a clear distinction between their own opinions and those expressed as representatives of the school counseling profession. Counselors should never make statements that portray their own views as being embraced by the profession of school counselors.

Maintenance of Standards

As members of a profession that adheres to a code of ethical standards, school counselors are responsible for seeing that the standards are followed, not only by themselves but also by their professional colleagues, their supervisors, and the institutions that hire them. For this reason, when school counselors are forced to work under conditions that clearly violate these standards, they must take the necessary action to educate their superiors about this conflict and make alterations as deemed appropriate. When no changes are forthcoming, school counselors face the difficult decision of whether to remain in their present position without violating ethical practice.

In instances when a counselor observes a violation of ethical standards, the guidelines encourage the use of available avenues within the school and school system to bring this problem to the attention of appropriate persons. If attempts to resolve the situation go unheeded or are rejected, the counselor's next step is to refer to an appropriate ethics committee in a school counselor association, first at the local level, then at the state level, and finally at the national association level. When school counselors receive information from a student, parent, or teacher about apparent unethical activity of a counseling colleague or other professional helper, they need to be clear about the nature of the complaint before determining a course of action. For example, a counselor who receives a criminal complaint about a colleague, such as selling drugs, should contact local law enforcement officials. By contrast, a parent who confides that another school counselor routinely breaks confidentiality by reporting private information to the school principal is encouraged to first confront the colleague to discuss the complaint and resolve the questionable practice. If such a resolution is not found, the counselor should use avenues established by the school and/or school system, and if still unresolved should make a report to the local counselor association. In most cases of reported violations, it is best for the person who has firsthand knowledge to make the report. In this way, school counselors need to support their clients in the reporting process.

While ethical standards are the guidelines for appropriate practice established by professional organizations, legal parameters are the policies and regulations set by governing agencies, statutes passed by legislatures, and ruling in courts of law. Ethical standards, as we have seen, seldom answer ethical dilemmas with specific recommendations. Professional codes of conduct are necessary guides for school counselors, but they do not replace knowledge and understanding of local, state, and federal laws and regulations. In the remaining sections of this chapter, we examine some legal aspects of school counseling practice.

The Nature of Law

Schools are vital institutions of society and reflect the legal standards demanded by the citizenry. In determining what these legal standards are, which ones apply to schools, and how they relate specifically to particular school programs and services, we first need to understand the nature of law.

The United States has a common-law tradition that exists beyond the simple declaration of specific codes of conduct. This tradition includes a continuous process of developing legislation at different levels of local, state, and national government; interpreting these statutes through legislative and judicial processes; and compiling legal rulings that are derived from specific court cases. The latter of these, known as judge made or case law and sometimes referred to as common law, evolves from the common thoughts and experiences of people in a society (Fischer & Sorenson, 1996). The sources of laws in our society include federal and state constitutions, statutes, case law, and common law. In addition, local school board policies and regulations, which must conform to state and federal laws, may also apply to the practice of school counseling. As local boards of education devise rules and regulations for their schools, they must do so according to the laws established by the legislature of their states (Alexander & Alexander, 1992, 2003).

The Law and Schools

Many factors relate to the interpretation and application of law as it pertains to education and schools. When considering a particular legal issue involving education, counselors review pertinent court cases, local school board policies, state and federal laws, government regulations, and constitutional questions. All of these are sources of law in U.S. society, and thus, they enable counselors to locate information and make appropriate decisions that are guided by current legal thinking. Because laws in U.S. society are created as the result of an evolving process, it is important that counselors consider all sources, not as absolute indications of what must be, but as origins of a particular law or guideline. By learning the background of law, counselors are better able to understand what needs to happen for law to change or be repealed.

It is noteworthy that one of the most renowned educators, John Dewey, had significant influence on judicial proceedings and the development of law in this country. Fischer and Sorenson (1996) were "particularly persuaded by his thoughtful, pragmatic description of law as a flexible and adaptable process, neither rigidly adhering to historically derived rules and principles nor ignoring their possible relevance and importance to current problems" (p. 3). As counselors practice in schools, they are continuously affected by past regulations, and when appropriate, they attempt to challenge and change these rules to meet the needs of students, parents, and teachers. At the same time, school counselors seek a balance between legal requirements of their school boards, state legislatures, and the federal government and the ethical standards of their profession. By having a clear understanding of the nature and history of law, counselors are in a stronger position to seek changes in regulations that conflict with ethical practice or, as the case may require, alter ethical guidelines to conform with legal precedent.

An initial source of legal information and understanding is the Constitution of the United States. Though no mention of education or counseling is found in this historic document, clearly as the "supreme law of the land" this document supersedes all other local and state regulations. As such, all rules, regulations, policies, and laws set by local school boards, school administrators, county commissioners, state legislatures, and other bodies must be congruent with the Constitution. When they are not, they are invalid (Fischer & Sorenson, 1996). Counselors who have basic knowledge of educational law can assist their schools in developing appropriate policies and regulations that are consistent with constitutional requirements. This is particularly important in areas of student services that make use of school records, honor the right to privacy, and protect against discrimination.

Other sources of information that help counselors learn about the law are state statutes, local policy manuals, websites, and legal briefs. School administrators, including principals, often subscribe to professional newsletters and other publications that summarize current legal rulings from court proceedings. In addition, general statutes pertaining to educational practice and schooling frequently are published by state governments as references for school personnel.

It is essential for school counselors to be fully aware of local policies and regulations, especially those that apply to counseling and other student services in the schools. Local school board policy manuals are typically found in every building of a school system. In some cases, counselors may have their own copy. Counselors want to be aware not only of written policies that may be in conflict with existing state or federal regulations, but also of policies that have been omitted from the school system's current manual, particularly those needed to protect students. An example of a policy that might be unknowingly omitted is a statement about the professional obligation and duty to report suspected child abuse. Although the definitions vary, all states have laws regarding the duty to report suspected child abuse, and school systems support this legislation by developing clear policies and procedures to facilitate accurate and proper reporting in cases where abuse is suspected.

School counselors also obtain legal information and support from professional associations and attorneys who specialize in educational law, including their school board's attorney. In some school systems, counseling supervisors assist in gathering information, planning workshops, and seeking legal guidance for counselors. As one example, school counselors occasionally testify in child custody hearings. Workshops to advise counselors about appropriate actions to take as court witnesses, including how to handle confidential information when testifying as a school counselor, can be helpful. Material and information presented in these workshops may differ from state to state because statutes regarding confidentiality and privileged communication vary, but the important point is that these types of workshops inform counselors about their legal responsibilities.

Having access to pertinent information and receiving preparation in appropriate aspects of law help counselors practice within legal boundaries and attain knowledge about laws that may be problematic for the school and school system. One area of preparation and information that strengthens a counselor's knowledge of the law is learning about the court system and how case law affects educational practices.

The Courts

The legal system in the United States consists of federal and state courts. Both levels of the legal system adjudicate criminal and civil cases, "but the jurisdiction of the federal courts is limited by the Constitution" (Fischer & Sorenson, 1996, p. 7). Federal courts hear only those cases pertaining to constitutional questions, such as equal protection under the law as granted by the Fourteenth Amendment of the Constitution. By contrast, state courts have broader responsibility for trying criminal and civil cases as well as those pertaining to federal and state constitutional issues.

When people raise legal questions regarding educational practice and regulation, these inquiries often involve federal issues. As a result, people may choose either the federal or state court system in which to initiate their cases. The plaintiffs and their counsel determine which court has jurisdiction over the matter to be litigated. Their selection of the appropriate court system is the first step in the judicial process.

State Courts.   The fifty state court systems typically consist of four levels or categories of jurisdiction (Alexander & Alexander, 1992). These levels include district (or circuit) courts, courts of special jurisdiction, small claims courts, and appellate courts. Courts of special jurisdiction include domestic relations courts, probate courts, and juvenile courts. District courts generally have jurisdiction over all cases except those reserved for special courts. Small claims courts handle lawsuits involving small amounts of money, and in some states these cases are handled by justice of the peace courts. Appellate courts handle appeals of decisions that are ruled in lower courts of general jurisdiction. These appellate courts are called Courts of Appeals or Supreme Courts, and, in some large states, both Courts of Appeals and state Supreme Courts are found. The names used for the appellate court are not uniform from state to state. As a result, in one state it may be called a Superior Court and in another the Court of Appeals. Furthermore, states with more than one appellate level are inconsistent in how they name these levels: "In New York State, for example, the lowest trial court of general jurisdiction is called the 'Supreme Court,' whereas the state's highest court is called the 'Court of Appeals'" (Fischer & Sorenson, 1996, p. 8).

Federal Courts.   The federal court system of the United States consists of nearly one hundred District Courts, Special Federal Courts, thirteen Courts of Appeals, and the Supreme Court. Eleven of the thirteen Courts of Appeals rule in the judicial circuit of the United States and its territories. One Court of Appeals deals with Washington, DC, and another handles special copyright and patent issues. Each state has at least one federal District Court, and the cases heard in these courts include issues between people from different states and litigation involving federal statutes or the Constitution (Alexander & Alexander, 1992). Special federal courts include courts in the District of Columbia, the Tax Court, the Customs Court, and the territorial courts, among others.

When cases are appealed, they move from the trial courts that make up the U.S. District Court System to the Court of Appeals in the respective judicial circuit, and then to the Supreme Court. In addition, a case in the state judicial system can move from the highest state court to the U.S. Supreme Court in the form of a *writ of certiorari.* When litigants lose their case at a state's highest level of appellate court, they may petition the U.S. Supreme Court to hear the case. If four of the nine Supreme Court justices vote to review, the Court will issue a *writ of certiorari* to have the case sent forward. This usually happens when the constitutional validity of a state statute or federal law is questioned. Most school law cases fall within this classification. Therefore, the *writ of certiorari* is the most common means of getting a school or education case before the Supreme Court (Alexander & Alexander, 1992).

School counselors who read about the case decisions of these various federal and state courts want to know the effect that particular decisions will have on their schools and the practice of counseling. Ultimately, the question is whether a particular decision will be binding on a particular state and school district. Decisions of lower federal courts are binding only on those states and territories within their own circuit. Similarly, decisions handed down by state courts are binding only on those specific states. Although they are not legally binding beyond the jurisdiction of the ruling court, many state and lower federal court decisions help set precedent and "are often considered persuasive in other jurisdictions" (Fischer & Sorenson, 1996, p. 9). Generally, the decisions of the U.S. Supreme Court are binding in every state and territory.

School Board Policies

School districts have broad responsibility for developing and implementing regulations that affect schools within the limitations and guidelines set by state statutes. As noted earlier, at no time does an individual school or school system have authority to legislate beyond the limits defined by the state. For example, if a state statute grants privileged communication to students in counseling relationships, a school system cannot deny that privilege through local policy unless such authority is expressly permitted by state law.

Although school counselors need to be aware of state and federal court rulings and legislation regarding schools and the practice of professional counseling, they are particularly concerned about specific policies and regulations passed by their local school boards and administrators. Practically speaking, these are the day-to-day regulations that guide a counselor's actions and occasionally contribute to ethical and legal dilemmas.

School counselors are responsible for being familiar with their local board policies and understanding how these regulations govern their programs of services for students, parents, and teachers. When policies seem to be in conflict with state laws, counselors are duty-bound to raise these issues. In most instances, the appropriate channels for such discussions begin with school principals, counseling supervisors, and officers of state counseling associations.

A review of school board policies may reveal several areas of potential conflict, but there are particular topics of concern for most school counselors. These include students' rights to privacy, parents' rights, issues of gender equity, the use of school records, child abuse reporting, potential liability, and rights of exceptional students. We consider each of these issues briefly in the next section.

Legal Issues for School Counselors

Many legal issues that arise in schools relate indirectly to the practice of counseling because school counselors, as discussed in this text, are responsible for a wide range of activities to serve all students. In this section, we review a few of the major topics involving legal issues and the practice of counseling in a school setting. Some of these issues are governed by local policies and others are regulated by state and federal laws. Counselors need to have appropriate background information about their school policies and district court rulings to make accurate decisions about these issues. Because court rulings frequently change current thinking and existing policies regarding these issues, counselors need access to accurate, up-to-date information. Timely textbooks on school law are excellent resources. In addition, legal references such as the *Journal of Law and Education* and *West's Education Law Reporter* are helpful resources on current court rulings.

Students' Rights

Many aspects of students' rights are related to schooling, and counselors should keep abreast of the latest rulings involving these issues. Some common issues include freedom of expression, the right to due process, appropriate/compensatory education, and the right to privacy. Of these, the most debated issue in the counseling profession is the student's right to privacy when involved in helping relationships with counselors. Earlier we considered the issue of confidentiality and its relationship to legal rights as granted by privileged communication statutes. School counselors need to know, from an ethical as well as legal perspective, what rights are granted students in their states and by their schools.

Privacy rights are influenced by the nature of the confidential relationship and the age of the student. For example, current law suggests that students who seek information and guidance about abortion in counseling can expect their request to remain confidential unless their state has a parental notification law, in which case, if the student is a minor, parental notification may be required. Some states require parental notification. In 1990, the U.S. Supreme Court upheld notification laws in two states (*Ohio v. Akron*) and Minnesota (*Hodgson v. Minnesota*) (Fischer & Sorenson, 1996). Stone and Dahir (2006) have presented several cases involving HIV and sexually active students, abortion counseling, sexual harassment, and other issues related to parental involvement and notification.

Students' rights to privacy also affect policies regarding educational records and student searches. The *Family Educational Rights and Privacy Act* of 1974 (FERPA) clarified students' and parents' rights regarding school records. This law is explained in great detail later under the section titled The Buckley Amendment. In another area related to students' privacy, courts have restricted unreasonable searches of students in schools as further protection of their constitutional rights. Counselors want to be fully aware of the legal ruling regarding this issue so they know what constitutes a justified search of students or their property in schools.

The legal rights of young children in schools are, at best, uncertain (Mitchell, Disque, & Robertson, 2002; Remley & Herlihy, 2007). This may be particularly true when considering the issue of privacy. Although school counselors have an ethical obligation of confidentiality with young students, they frequently need to involve adults in the concerns of students who are minors. Kaplan (1996) cautioned that "the legal rights of minors to provide consent to enter counseling or to release information . . . resides in the custodial parent or guardian as a matter of common law and state statutes" (p. 167). Therefore, students' understanding of and desire for confidentiality are sometimes offset by requirements to inform parents and guardians. In most instances, this is a judgment call by the counselor unless evidence of imminent danger or harm to the client exists. When counselors choose to inform parents and guardians or to involve them in helping relationships with students, it is advisable to tell students beforehand and include them in the process of notifying parents. Counselors must maintain a delicate balance between the duty to protect the rights of students and their ethical and legal responsibilities to respect the rights of parents and involve them in the education of their children.

Another area of students' rights, the right to due process, covers a range of issues from discipline to minimum competency testing (Fischer & Sorenson, 1996). Essentially, the intent of due process, as provided by the Fourteenth Amendment, is to protect students from actions and regulations that are inherently unfair. The Supreme Court case of *Goss v. Lopez* in 1975 set the precedent for defining due process and the types of procedures schools must include in their disciplinary codes to protect students' rights. Procedural due process has subsequently come to include three basic elements: (1) the student must have proper notice about the regulations that have been violated; (2) the student must be given an opportunity for a hearing; and (3) the hearing must be conducted fairly (Alexander & Alexander, 1992).

A second type of due process, called substantive due process, requires the state to demonstrate a valid objective, and reasonable means for reaching this objective, when imposing restrictions or punishments. Substantive due process "requires that state officials not impose punishments that are arbitrary, capricious, or unfair" to students in schools (Fischer & Sorenson, 1996, p. 5). For example, a school that deprives a student access to an educational service for which the student qualifies simply because the parents have not kept scheduled appointments with the school might be demonstrating denial of substantive due process. Students have no control over the behaviors of their parents and should not be unfairly penalized for actions over which they have no control.

Parents' Rights

Schools rely on cooperative relationships with parents to provide the most appropriate educational programs for children. For this reason, schools need to respect parents' rights in planning programs and making decisions for individual children and adolescents. Distinguishing the lines between students' rights, parents' rights, and the school's obligation to educate all children is not an easy task. This is particularly true when reviewing issues involving school counseling services. In their article about factors that affect school counselors' choices regarding confidentiality, Isaacs and Stone (1999) noted the inconsistent rules from state to state surrounding this issue. They also recognized that counselors have multiple responsibilities beyond the helping relationships formed with students. These responsibilities include respect for the rights of families, regard for teachers and other students in the school, and the duty to follow procedures and policies set by administrators and the school system.

Isaacs and Stone (1999) asserted that the courts, including the U.S. Supreme Court, have maintained the legal rights of parents to provide guidance to their children according to values and directions they choose. At the same time, these authors noted that legal authorities in counseling have not fully agreed on the extent of parental rights to have access to information revealed by students in counseling relationships (Fischer & Sorenson, 1996).

Counselors in today's schools face an array of childhood, juvenile, and adult problems that require special relationships beyond the scope of educational and career guidance decisions. Substance abuse, family violence, sexual orientation and activity, and pregnancy are among the difficult issues school counselors confront with students. Knowing when and how to involve parents requires knowledge of current laws and clear understanding of local and state policies. A parent's right to be involved varies from case to case and from situation to situation. For example, if a child is in imminent danger of being harmed by someone, the school and counselor have an obligation to inform the parents. This course of action would change, however, if the parent were the suspected perpetrator of abuse. In this and other cases of abuse, the school is obligated to report to the appropriate child protective services.

Athough the "Supreme Court guarantees minor children basic due process rights in juvenile court proceedings . . . and calls them 'persons' under the Constitution with fundamental rights . . . the constitutionality of parents' rights is not clear" (Kaplan, 1997, p. 337). As noted above, state rulings have been inconsistent and consequently confuse parents and schools alike. All the more reason for school counselors to work closely with parents, keeping them informed of program services, and educating them about developmental needs of their children.

State and federal courts have ruled that schools have the authority to design educational curriculum and require students to participate in instructional programs (Alexander & Alexander, 1992). In certain instances, parents may object to their children's participation in particular activities and, based on objections, such as religious grounds, may ask that their children be excluded. To date, no federal court rulings have specifically addressed guidance and counseling activities and parents' rights to determine the appropriateness of these services for their children. As a result, school counselors are guided by state mandates and local board policies that may or may not include counseling services as an integral part of the educational program and school curriculum. Because the courts have ruled that parents have no constitutional right to deprive their children of an education and, at the same time, have delegated to schools the responsibility of determining appropriate curriculum and educational services, access to school counseling services may fall within this broad area of students' rights. How future courts will perceive this issue remains to be seen, but for now a critical condition would seem to be whether school counseling services are considered essential to the educational program and if written documents verify this relationship in the state and local system.

Laws and court rulings have helped to clarify some areas of parents' rights in schools. These include access to students' records when children are under the age of 18 and involvement of parents in planning special education programs for their children. Each of these areas is considered in the next two sections.

The Buckley Amendment

In Chapter 5, you were introduced to the Family Educational Rights and Privacy Act (FERPA), also known as the *Buckley Amendment.* This legislation gives parents of minor students (and students 18 years of age or older) the right to review all official school records related to their children (or themselves in the case of eligible students). Included in these records are cumulative folders, academic reports, test data, attendance records, health information, family background, discipline records, and other pertinent information. In reviewing these records, parents and eligible students may challenge the accuracy of information. If schools reject the challenge and refuse to alter the questionable information, parents or eligible students may ask for a hearing. Eventually, if the school continues to refuse the request for change, parents (or eligible students) may add a statement of disagreement, which the school is obliged to disclose whenever the record is shared with another person or used by school personnel (Fischer & Sorenson, 1996).

FERPA also sets guidelines for disseminating educational records. In addition, schools are required to notify parents and students of their rights under the local policy regarding the use of educational records. Schools must ensure that procedures for disclosing educational records follow appropriate guidelines and that they obtain prior written consent of parents or eligible students before disclosing records.

Counselors in schools are aware of FERPA regulations, as well as their ethical standards and current court rulings, to guide their conduct in matters dealing with student records. Of particular concern is how counselors' private notes and files regarding confidential counseling sessions might be controlled by this law. Generally, the implementation of FERPA, subsequent interpretations by legislators, and court rulings seem to indicate that the law and its regulations do not necessarily require disclosure of private counseling notes. Once more, school counselors should be informed of interpretations and rulings regarding their services and activities as they are related to the Buckley Amendment. Services and activities of most concern to school counselors include but are not limited to

1. Letters of recommendation written on behalf of students
2. Taped recordings of counseling sessions
3. Correction of inaccurate information in educational records
4. Use of testing results
5. Records of students with handicaps
6. Destruction of outdated educational records
7. Development or revision of a school policy regarding educational records

Staying informed of current rulings about these and other types of counseling services helps practicing school counselors prevent litigation against themselves and their schools. Again, by participating in professional associations, attending workshops and conferences, and reading current resources such as those cited in this chapter, counselors keep abreast of these critical and timely issues.

Public Law 94-142

In Chapter 2, you learned of the Education For All Handicapped Children Act of 1975, commonly referred to as Public Law 94-142. As noted there, the 1990 amendment renamed this bill the Individuals with Disabilities Education Act (IDEA, Public Law 101-476). Although the role of counselors in this law is not spelled out, school counselors offer many vital services to exceptional students of all categories. Counselors confer with teachers and parents, help to develop the Individual Education Plan (IEP) for each student placed in a program, provide counseling services when stipulated in a student's IEP, and consult with parents to help them cope with the exceptionalities of their children.

As coordinators of student services within their schools, counselors also have responsibility for knowing how the federal law and its administrative regulations affect the school's financial obligations, student transfer policies, and referrals to outside agencies. Courts have ruled that the ultimate responsibility for costs related to the education of students with handicaps rests with the state (Fischer & Sorenson, 1996). This means that counselors, teachers, and other school personnel must be aware of local school board policies that govern how educational recommendations, which sometimes include a financial obligation, are made to parents and guardians of exceptional students.

Child Abuse

All states and the District of Columbia have passed legislation addressing child abuse and the obligation of school personnel to report suspected cases. Child abuse covers a range of behaviors that includes physical abuse, sexual abuse, general neglect, psychological and emotional torment, abandonment, and inadequate supervision. A majority of states stipulate a penalty for the failure to report suspected abuse, and all states require reporting by school personnel. This includes school counselors. As such, any provision of privileged communication for students is superseded by a state's desire to protect children from abuse.

Responsibility for investigating reported cases of child abuse and neglect rests with children's protective services as defined by specific state statutes. The school's role, and, accordingly, the school counselor's role, is to report instances of suspected abuse. As such, school personnel should cooperate with protective service investigators who need to prove whether abuse exists in the cases reported. School systems should have clear policies and procedures that guide personnel in the process of following state laws for child abuse reporting.

Counselor Liability

In serving a wide audience of students, parents, and teachers, school counselors occasionally become concerned about malpractice and professional liability. In 1985, Remley noted that most school counselors "are either immune from malpractice suits because they are employed by a governmental agency or are covered for malpractice damages by insurance purchased by their schools" (p. 187). More recently, Fischer and Sorenson (1996) listed these activities as "most likely to lead to legal problems":

> Administering drugs
>
> Giving birth control advice
>
> Giving abortion-related advice
>
> Making statements that might be defamatory
>
> Assisting in searches of students' lockers
>
> Violating confidentiality and the privacy of records (p. 51)

Counselors want to know what protection they have. In determining their liability coverage, school counselors should learn about insurance carried by their school systems and whether they, as counselors, are exempt from coverage under these policies. If counselors find they are not adequately covered by their school systems, they may want to buy an individual policy through a professional organization such as the American Counseling Association (ACA) or the American School Counselor Association (ASCA).

Malpractice suits against school counselors have been rare, but the changing climate of schools and the seriousness of concerns being raised by children, adolescents, and families today elevate the risks counselors take given the wide range of services they provide. Malpractice suits typically address two types of liability—civil liability and criminal liability. The first, civil liability, occurs when counselors behave in inappropriate or wrongful ways toward others or fail to act when situations require a dutiful response. For example, school counselors risk civil liability if they neglect to inform parents of a student's threat to commit suicide or if they disclose confidential information in violation of their ethical standards of conduct. These two examples illustrate harmful and inappropriate professional practice. By contrast, criminal liability occurs when counselors behave in unlawful ways, such as being an accessory to a crime, disobeying civil ordinances, and contributing to the delinquency of a minor (Anderson, 1996).

While proof of criminal wrongdoing rests with the prosecuting office of the county, state, or federal government, the proof of malpractice in civil liability lies with the plaintiff who brings suit against the counselor. To be successful, the suit must demonstrate that harm was done to someone as a direct result of a counselor's negligence or flagrant omission. Furthermore, the plaintiff must show evidence that other counselors in a similar situation would not have behaved the same way (Remley & Herlihy, 2007).

Reaching a judgment of malpractice is difficult when dealing with professional counseling. In part, this is because all states do not have licensing laws that control the practice of school counseling as they might for counselors in private practice or in other helping professions such as psychiatry and clinical psychology. If states are unclear about what responsibilities school counselors have and the level of standards for their professional practice, it is difficult for jurors and judges to find fault. Nevertheless, as noted above and throughout this chapter, the practice of counseling is becoming more visible, and standards of practice are being developed through various accreditation and certifying bodies. In the future, school counselors will want to know how to prevent legal action from being taken against them. Some preventive measures might include

1. *A clear description of the school counseling program and a counselor's job description that reflects a true accounting of daily functions.* School counselors should provide services advertised in program statements, school brochures, and school system manuals. When counselors stray beyond the scope of their program or job description in offering services to students, parents, and teachers, they open themselves up for possible litigation. By the same token, when they fail to offer services described in their job descriptions, they are also vulnerable.

2. *Reliance on other professionals for guidance and support in providing comprehensive service.* School counselors are highly trained professionals, but they cannot provide all the services that may be needed by the school population. Having appropriate referral sources and professionals with whom to consult is good practice for all helping professionals.

3. *Knowledge and understanding of professional standards of ethical practice.* Counselors are not protected by ignorance of the law or of their own ethical standards. Knowing about sound professional practices and behaving accordingly are essential conditions for preventing legal entanglements.

4. *Knowledge and information about legal rulings and ethical interpretations.* Legal and ethical issues evolve and change every day. Counselors who read about current cases, attend workshops about legal and ethical practice, and participate in their professional associations take preventive action to avoid misconduct.

As noted earlier the following behaviors and services present the most risk for school counselors:

1. *Administering drugs.* An increasing number of students come to school with prescription drugs to be taken during the school hours. In schools without nurses, clearly written policies help administrators delegate responsibility and require written instructions from the prescribing physician and written permission from parents (guardians) for the school to dispense medication. In most instances, school counselors are wise to resist accepting responsibility for administering drugs to students.

2. *Student searches.* Students are protected under the Fourth Amendment to the Constitution from unreasonable searches. In the 1985 case of *New Jersey v. T. L. O.,* the U.S. Supreme Court ruled that "Students' legitimate expectations of privacy . . . must be balanced against that need for the search" (Fischer & Sorenson, 1996, p. 177). Searches of students and their property must be carried out only when there is justification and reason to believe that a search will disclose a violation of school policy or law. Counselors who participate in unreasonable and unjustified searches may be liable.

3. *Birth control and abortion counseling.* Perhaps no areas of school counseling are more explosive and emotional in the responses they bring from counselors and lay people alike than the issues of birth control and abortion. As attitudes continue to change and new judicial appointments are made to state and federal courts, legal views and answers to these topics will again be altered. The pendulum of public opinion is forever moving one way or the other. At this time, minors are permitted to seek abortions, but as noted earlier, the Supreme Court has upheld state laws that require parent notification provided there is a judicial bypass option (Fischer & Sorenson, 1996). Local school boards may pass policies regarding birth control and abortion counseling, and school counselors should be informed of all current legislation, court rulings, and local policies regarding this area of counseling (Stone & Dahir, 2006).

4. *Use of student records and violation of privacy.* School counselors must adhere to local, state, and federal regulations regarding the use and dissemination of students' records. This area of practice, as we have seen, is guided by the Family Educational Rights and Privacy Act of 1974 (FERPA). Generally, the major concern for schools is who has the legal right to see students' records. Two areas seem most problematic: noncustodial parents' rights to see educational records and "special files" for school personnel only. Fischer and Sorenson (1996) clarified that both parents, custodial and noncustodial, in separated or divorced families have the legal right to see a child's records. The only exception would be by a judge's order. Regarding the second issue, the law disallows any special educational files being kept private for school personnel use only. Private notes kept by counselors, as indicated earlier, are not addressed by FERPA and, therefore, may be held in confidence if in the judgment of the counselor it is best to do so (Fischer & Sorenson, 1996).

5. *Defamation.* Related to the use of records and matters of student privacy, school counselors, as with other mental health professionals, must be judicious about the confidential information they share with others without consent of students. School counselors are sometimes asked to provide recommendations or evaluations of students. This may place them as risk of defamation, which is any published statement that injures or damages another person's reputation. Counselors who act in good faith and serve their clients in a consistent manner will generally be protected under the law when they provide negative comments or evaluations about students.

Title IX

The primary purpose of Title IX of the Education Amendments of 1972 is to protect students against discrimination on the basis of sex. This law states, "No person in the United States shall, on the basis of sex, be excluded from participation in, be denied the benefits of, or be subjected to discrimination under any education program or activity receiving Federal financial assistance." If schools violate this law, the penalty is loss of federal financial assistance.

Courts have applied Title IX to the concept of equal access for both girls and boys to join athletic teams and enroll in courses in the school's curriculum. This law has been used to guarantee equity for students' participation in all aspects of school life regardless of gender or marital status. Therefore, pregnant teenagers have the same rights to an education as all other students. In addition, Title IX and the Fourteenth Amendment have been used to help settle disputes over admissions policies that set different standards for girls than for boys.

School counselors at all levels of education should be aware of Title IX regulations and pertinent court rulings. As advocates of students, counselors are in an ideal position to monitor school policies and programs and protect against subtle and overt sex discrimination. In part, the counselor's role is to educate staff and administrators and guide them in developing policies and procedures that are free from discrimination.

Another way in which counselors prevent illegal action or stereotypical behavior is by helping schools select appropriate instructional materials and activities. Textbooks, media, and instructional activities that unintentionally or otherwise depict learning, career choices, or other aspects of student development in inequitable or stereotypical fashion must be avoided. Workshops for teachers and other school personnel about Title IX and sex discrimination, in general, are appropriate vehicles for school counselors to become positive forces in helping develop and implement appropriate programs, policies, and instruction for all students.

Title IX also regulates the professional relationships counselors form on behalf of students, parents, and teachers beyond the schoolhouse doors. Counselors cannot cooperate with community organizations or persons who discriminate against people on the basis of gender. Title IX includes criteria for exempting certain organizations such as Boy Scouts and Girls Scouts, but unless an organization is exempt, counselors should refer boys and girls alike. For example, if an employer is seeking weekend help from teenagers, a high school counselor is obliged to announce this opportunity to all students regardless of the nature of the work or the specific preferences expressed by the employer for either boys or girls to fill the positions.

With this chapter, we complete a summary of the school counseling profession today, including its brief history, a discussion of diversity issues related to school counseling practice, a description of comprehensive programs and responsive services, background about the professionals who are prepared and certified to be school counselors, and ethical and legal guidelines that assist these counselors in their professional practice. The information presented thus far describes where we have been and where we are in the profession of school counseling. The final chapter of this text explores questions about professional directions for school counseling in the future.

Additional Readings _____

Corey, G., & Corey, M. S. (2002). *Issues and Ethics in the Helping Professions* (6th ed.) (Pacific Grove, CA: Brooks/Cole).

This book is a contemporary guide to counselors in all professional settings. It presents typical cases with comments by the authors.

Fischer, L., & Sorenson, G. P. (1996). *School Law for Counselors, Psychologists, and Social Workers* (3rd ed.) (New York: Longman).

This text is a comprehensive guide to legal issues that confront school counselors and other student services professionals on a daily basis. Written in clear and understandable language, the book pre-sents each topic through a series of related questions and answers.

Remley, T. P., & Herlihy, B. (2007). *Ethical, Legal, and Professional Issues in Counseling* (2nd ed.) (Upper Saddle River, NJ: Prentice Hall).

Another comprehensive text on ethical and legal issues for professional counselors.

Stone, C. B., & Dahir, C. A. (2006). *The transformed school counselor* (Boston, MA: Lahaska/ Houghton Mifflin).

Chapter 11 of this contemporary text on school counseling offers several interesting cases and court decisions.

Website _____

EdLaw
www.edlaw.org

Note: See also the American Counseling Association, American School Counselor Association, and the National Board of Certified Counselors listed elsewhere in this text.

Exercises _____

1. Research recent court decisions and other legal sources to determine what rulings have been made regarding guidance activities for students in school. Look for decisions that affect students' rights, parents' rights, and the obligation of the school to provide a sound curriculum.

2. Interview a local attorney who concentrates on educational law and ask about the most important legal issues pertaining to the practice of school counsel-ing. Determine what the local perceptions and norms are about these issues.

3. Create a fictional situation in which a school counselor could find that ethical standards come in conflict with policies or regulations. Present your situation to the class for discussion.

13

School Counseling Today and Tomorrow

Although models of comprehensive school counseling programs have emerged as a result of conceptual development and action research, the role of school counselors has often taken its direction as a reaction to state, national, and world events. Throughout its development, the school counseling profession has been influenced by educational and social trends, both inside and outside the United States, and it has responded to these events by way of federal legislation, state initiatives, and changes within the profession itself. The early history of vocational guidance as a reaction to social ills and labor requirements of industrialization was the beginning. The demand for accurate assessment of military recruits in two world wars eventually led to the increased use of testing in schools by counselors. Likewise, public fear of Soviet domination in the late 1950s was reflected in national legislation to improve education, particularly in the areas of mathematics and science, which had historic impact on the training and employment of school counselors. Subsequent events, laws, and national reports from that time to the present day have shaped the direction and identity of the school counseling profession.

The work of Carl Rogers in the 1950s and 1960s on the counseling relationship and the helping process was the first notable influence that stemmed from a conceptual, theoretical perspective. His development of client-centered counseling, later to be called the person-centered approach, alerted counselors in schools and other settings of the need to view the entire person when establishing helping relationships, rather than dividing the individual's needs into compartments such as educational and vocational. This fresh approach, while itself a holistic and developmental perspective, began another series of reactions within the school counseling profession. Counselors and other educators began promoting the idea that counseling services were necessary earlier in students' lives. Thus, the profession expanded to the junior high school and later to the elementary level. It was common during this period to hear teachers and other people comment that counselors were needed in the "early grades rather than high schools" to help prevent problems before they began. Although complimentary toward the counseling profession, this conclusion offered a limited view of human development because it overlooked the need for counseling at all stages of life. Students at all levels of education face challenges and barriers to development. For this reason, it is appropriate to offer counseling services during all years of schooling and throughout the lifespan.

Today the counseling profession continues to react to social, economic, and political forces of the times, but it also has begun to establish for itself a direction and focus on the future. National counseling associations under the auspices of the parent organization, the American Counseling Association (ACA), have become strong forces in encouraging state and national legislation on a wide range of social and educational issues, on developing national certification standards for the practice of professional counseling, in creating the Council for Accrediting Counselor and Related Educational Programs (CACREP) to promote adequate training, and by giving counselors a unique identity and clear focus among other helping professions. With leadership from the American School Counselor Association (ASCA), one of the largest divisions of ACA, counselors in schools have benefited from these developments as well. This progress has occurred despite the fact that only a fraction of the counselors in the country belongs to ACA and its divisions. The efforts of ACA and ASCA have helped to chart a course for the future, but school counselors must do much more to establish themselves as a credible and valuable profession. The National Model created and promoted by ASCA (2003) is an attempt to transform the profession (Stone & Dahir, 2006). Time will tell if counselors in schools will embrace this model or other examples of comprehensive programs to give their profession clarity of purpose and direction in the future.

In this chapter, we examine what the future holds and how emerging trends and conditions might affect the practice of school counseling. It is risky business predicting the future, but counselors who are in the profession of helping others to prepare for the future must be ready to meet the challenges of a changing world. There are numerous factors to consider in looking at the future of school counseling, some positive and some negative. Each has a role in determining how counselors might practice in schools in the years to come. Futuristic projections for the school counseling profession include a wide spectrum of factors including programmatic issues, technological advances, an emerging global economy, and more (Baker & Gerler, 2004; Bloom & Walz, 2000; Sink, 2005; Stone & Dahir, 2006). This chapter highlights a few of these factors. In particular, we consider two primary elements because they incorporate all the others—the students and schools of tomorrow.

Students of Tomorrow

Who will be the students of the future and for what reasons will they seek assistance from school counselors? In its first century of development, the school counseling profession moved from a limited focus on vocational training and job placement to a wider vision encompassing a broad range of personal, social, educational, and career services for diverse student populations. Will students in the twenty-first century continue to need an array of counseling and other responsive services to optimize their educational development and ensure success in life? If present trends in the U.S. family and culture are any indication, the answer is an unequivocal "yes." Students today are facing difficult conditions in many aspects of their development, and there appears to be no sign of this pressure letting up in the future.

In serving students of tomorrow, school counselors will offer a range of responsive and related services that address developmental needs, prevent learning difficulties, and remedy existing conditions that inhibit growth and development. As with students today, students in the future will require services to develop skills, acquire information, and attain knowledge to make appropriate decisions about relationships, educational goals, and career aspirations. There is no reason to believe that these developmental goals will be any less appropriate for tomorrow's students than they are for today's students.

Similarly, because we cannot accurately forecast what the future holds, tomorrow's students have to be prepared to change their goals, make adjustments, and prevent major problems that block their progress. Both preventive and developmental goals are necessary for assisting students in the future, but it is unlikely that these objectives will be sufficient. Most likely, tomorrow's students will not be spared the challenges of human existence and the expected hardship of forging successful careers. For this reason, future school counselors will create expanded visions to meet the needs of a wide range of students by balancing the need to remedy existing concerns with opportunities for students to experience optimal learning and realize healthy futures. Viewing counseling relationships as simply a "remedy for conflict, anxiety, apathy, or personal misfortune seems to be an unnecessarily narrow definition," whereas "defining counseling in terms of self-fulfillment without considering barriers to development seems unrealistic" (Purkey & Schmidt, 1996, p. 158). We can expect future students to demand a broader context for services provided by school counselors, which will include comprehensive programs of various helping relationships to address problems as well as focus on prevention and development.

Remedial Concerns

The changing U.S. scene includes a continuing redefinition and restructuring of the family. Divorce, remarriage, cohabitation, dual careers, blended families, same-sex unions, and a host of other terms have come to describe the array of family structures and lifestyles in U.S. society. Each family with its own set of values and perspectives contributes in unique ways to the culture, attitudes, and beliefs that students bring to school. Accordingly, each family, regardless of how we define it, lays the foundation for educational success. As noted in Chapter 2, counselors in the future probably will experience increased diversity in the types of families and groups from which students come, and they will need knowledge and skill to help schools adapt programs and create services to meet these challenges.

In addition to the changing family structure, students of tomorrow might exhibit a range of personal, social, physical, and educational concerns emanating from serious ills of society. For example, the "war on drugs" in U.S. society continues to be waged with varied opinions about its success. Children born of drug-abusing parents enter preschools and elementary schools every day. Despite efforts to attend to this national crisis, students at alarmingly younger ages are becoming involved with drug and alcohol use and abuse. If the future holds no promise of turning this destructive behavior around, students will require additional services from counselors to handle family dysfunction, prevent substance abuse, and help them cope without drugs and alcohol. Unless a significant change in alcohol and drug abuse occurs soon, this condition will have a debilitating effect on students and schools in the years to come. Schools and counselors face a major challenge in designing programs and delivering services to help young people infected by addictions realize their human potential and succeed in life.

Violence is another phenomenon that, unless curtailed, will have a significant impact on schools and learning in the future. Too many students resort to aggressive behavior in attempting to save face and resolve conflicts at any cost (Fatum & Hoyle, 1996). At the same time, physical, sexual, and psychological child abuse is a disheartening characteristic of a society that prides itself on freedom, human worth, and dignity. If this society does not succeed in securing the rights of children and protecting them from abuse and neglect, professional counselors in the future can expect to serve more of these cases.

Added to the brutal violation of children's rights by some parents and adults is the growing number of students who resort to violent force as a means of addressing their own personal and social conflicts. Fights, homicides, and suicides are all too common among today's students. Simply passing policies to punish students for possessing weapons and fighting in school is not the answer. Helping students of tomorrow handle hostilities in appropriate ways while maintaining an acceptable level of assertiveness to protect their interests and enhance their welfare will be a necessary aspect of school life and the curriculum. Counselors will take a lead role in this effort.

Suicide is a private form of violence that illustrates a desperate attempt to free oneself from psychological and emotional pain, fear, and distress. Students who remain incapable of finding acceptable avenues to resolve social and personal crises will continue to be at risk of hurting themselves or others. Teachers and counselors in schools are often the first-line helpers for young people in distress and, therefore, need to be ready and skilled to assist in times of critical need.

Children and adolescents in the United States face many challenges that include traumatic experiences such as abuse, physical and mental disabilities, changing family structures, and social problems among others (Gladding, 2004). School counselors who ignore threatening and debilitating situations, and thereby focus services only on students who require information or instruction, neglect a significant portion of their schools' populations. One danger of programs that adopt a philosophy entirely of "developmental guidance" is that counselors may neglect or ignore students who need individual attention. Future counseling programs must maintain a balance of responsive and preventive services to meet the needs of a wide spectrum of students, including those with serious problems. Through either direct service or referral processes, school counselors can help these students alter behaviors, change environments, or enhance their situations in beneficial ways. At the same time, most other students will benefit from services that prevent problems as they progress through their school years.

Preventive Issues

It is difficult to forecast what personal and social issues will be most prominent for children and adolescents of the twenty-first century and beyond. For example, the alarming drug and alcohol problem pervasive in U.S. society during the past decades may escalate despite efforts to educate people and provide treatment. Teenage pregnancy, another devastating problem, continues despite the availability of birth control information and contraceptives. Helping youth establish healthy relationships and choose responsible behaviors will remain an important role of the school. In all likelihood, substance abuse, sexual activity, violence, and other issues will continue to concern students, parents, and teachers, who will expect school counselors to offer preventive services in addressing these topics.

Students in the immediate future will need the same information and education as today's students about how to prevent abuse, disease, pregnancy and other life-threatening and debilitating conditions. As new social issues develop, new preventive approaches will be needed. Similarly, as old issues are resolved, new challenges will emerge to take their place. This means that future school counselors, as in the present, must be prepared to assess the needs of students accurately and design services to enable students to make healthy, sound decisions about the challenges before them.

Preventive services of comprehensive school counseling programs in the coming century probably will retain many of the elements and characteristics of present-day approaches. As such, educational programs and counseling services will include assistance for helping students learn decision-making skills, acquire knowledge about sexual development, establish beneficial peer relationships, and develop coping behaviors to deal with the pressure of growing up in a complex, accelerated world. Adding to these direct services, future counselors will establish collaborative relationships with parents, teachers, and other professionals to ensure beneficial home and school environments for optimal learning and development.

One threat to student development in the future might be increased loneliness as society relies on more automation and offers fewer opportunities for social interaction. Other challenges include fears fueled by media information about the risk of nuclear war, the spread of AIDS, environmental catastrophes, bacterial contamination, global warming, and other natural or man-made disasters. More common, perhaps, will be the uncertainty of career choices in light of a rapidly advancing technology that will leave no area of vocational development untouched. The future will require students to expand career options and learn ways to deal with automation and other elements of our changing world. A first step is to identify the knowledge and skills necessary to be employable in the twenty-first century and beyond. The next step is to design curricula that enable students to attain this requisite knowledge and skill.

Schools and counselors that maintain a futuristic vision will constantly seek ways and create methods that encourage students to alter their goals, acquire new skills, cope with transitions, and adapt to emerging trends. In sum, prevention will continue to comprise services that help students address potential changes in their home, school, and vocational environments and learn behaviors and skills to handle these transformations and variations smoothly and productively.

Developmental Needs

The future will not ignore the developmental needs of students. Students of the next century will have the same biological, emotional, social, and educational expectations, as do students of today. The stages and elements of human development, as outlined and identified by theorists in the past, will most likely be relevant for future generations of schoolchildren and adolescents. There is no reason to believe that physical, social, and other transformations will occur so drastically that student development will be significantly altered. Although the general process of human development is expected to remain unchanged, the impact of a changing world will remarkably alter specific aspects and elements of that developmental process.

Automation and technology undoubtedly will have an effect on the developmental concerns of students, particularly regarding career exploration and decision-making. With the explosion of online learning, we have only to imagine what the impact will be on traditional teaching, curriculum, and the whole notion of "schooling" in American as well as worldwide education.

Other areas of students' lives also will be affected by technology and scientific discovery. Medical science, for example, is expected to make significant progress in enhancing an already ever-increasing lifespan. Although on one hand, we welcome this accomplishment, it raises questions of how to help families and children cope with terminal illnesses that no longer kill because advanced technology has given new meaning to the term *life-support system.* Counselors cannot view such issues in isolation, because they all relate to developmental aspects for tomorrow's students. Counselors and teachers will need to provide services, design activities, and plan instruction to help children and adolescents work through these added dimensions of their development.

A prominent theme for the twenty-first century focuses on the triumph of individualism complemented by a belief in personal responsibility. Simultaneously, the embrace of individual worth and responsibility is enhanced by a collectivistic philosophy—a spirit of togetherness and community, two other qualities that should be nurtured by school environments. Recognition of individual worth and value, combined with responsibility for one's own behaviors, means that individuals must come together and contribute to the betterment of all humankind. This notion of community is a familiar theme to school counselors.

Developmental guidance and counseling activities reflect the belief that students benefit from lessons and relationships designed to enhance their individual dignity and worth. At the same time, their goal is to teach responsible behaviors. Indeed, the works of Dreikurs, Dinkmeyer, Glasser, Purkey, and other counseling theorists who advocate self-responsibility are the forerunners of developmental services and activities we can expect to find in future schools with tomorrow's students.

In addition to the issues already presented, two other phenomena will have a tremendous impact on the students of tomorrow. The first, poverty, will have a serious, divisive consequence on education if not curtailed by future economic policies and progress. The second, diversity, as emphasized in Chapter 2, is an inevitable characteristic that will define students of tomorrow and challenge schools in the future.

Poverty

Social equality and individual responsibility are threatened by the disparity of wealth across segments of the U.S. population. Initiatives at local and national levels to move schools and students into the twenty-first century may be wasted unless we pay attention to the growing economic gap that divides this country. This gap is reflected in the "achievement gap" often cited in educational progress reports for the nation. U.S. Census figures reported in 2002 that almost 10 percent of all families lived in poverty. Although the percentage of citizens living in poverty has declined dramatically over the last forty years, too many subgroups suffer higher than average levels of poverty. For example, over 20 percent of African American and Hispanic families in 2002 were below the poverty level, while 7.8 percent of White families were (Schmidt, 2006). As a result of poverty, a high percentage of children suffer from poor nutrition, lack of heathcare services, and other deficiencies that inhibit their education and development.

According to the Joint Center for Poverty Research (2001), differences continued to emerge between rural and urban populations during the economic boom of the 1990s. Although poverty rates increased more in metropolitan areas (Institute for Research on Poverty, 2006), over 14 percent of the people who lived in nonmetropolitan areas were poor. Rural areas provided fewer job opportunities, unemployment rates for single-mother families were higher in rural areas, and rural communities accounted for only 3 percent of the nation's labor force while contributing 19 percent to the overall U.S. population. These findings have implications for schools and school counselors who work in both urban and rural areas. When one sociological factor, such as economic wealth, divides segments of a population, it compounds the challenge of bringing diverse groups together to work toward common goals like equal educational opportunities for all students.

If this economic wedge continues to separate and distinguish students in the future, the school counselor's role and responsibility must incorporate a posture of social activism to seek assistance for the disadvantaged. Such a role would include collaboration with social workers, nurses, and a host of other service providers in the school and community. If counselors assume this role, they will give developmental and preventive services for a majority of students a lower priority because of the demand for remedial services to meet the needs of impoverished students.

Poor students are handicapped in many ways because of the association of poverty with health, learning, familial, and neighborhood problems. As Howe explained in 1991, "Poverty is the parent of school failure, job failure, emotional imbalance, and social rejection" (p. 201). This perspective remains true today. The future of school counseling services will be significantly influenced by the success or failure of the United States to address this issue and turn around this gloomy economic forecast for students in the future.

Diversity

Some predictions are that the United States will more closely reflect the cultural and racial balance of the globe by the end of this century (Lee, 1995; Schmidt, 2006). Mitigating factors, such as immigration policies, worldwide economic depression, and unexpected changes in birthrates, may alter these forecasts. However, if these predictions come true and schools eventually reflect this balance, we can be assured that cultural diversity will become the norm. How schools and school counselors address the needs of culturally different populations and incorporate the concept of multiculturalism into the curriculum will determine their success in educating children and providing services to students, parents, and teachers. School counselors are in the vanguard of this movement, acting as advocates for all students, addressing issues of equity, designing appropriate services, and assisting teachers with educational curricula and instructional development.

Students of varied cultural backgrounds will require special attention to meet their individual needs and, at the same time, will benefit from learning about the multicultural community in which they live. Counselors in the future will play a pivotal role in helping teachers become aware of cultural differences and enabling schools to celebrate cultural diversity. Such celebrations will not be limited to a day, week, or month during the school year to recognize the backgrounds and heritage of different students. Rather, they will be embedded in the philosophy and mission of the school, and they will encompass all aspects of school life from policy development to curriculum planning.

As with other issues related to tomorrow's students, diversity will influence the role of future school counselors (Lee, 1995; Pedersen & Carey, 2003). Included in this role will be one of a sentinel for appropriate assessment and evaluation. As noted in Chapter 9, counselors must guard against the inappropriate use of testing and appraisal instruments and procedures that are culturally or socioeconomically biased. In addition, future counselors will incorporate multicultural activities and materials into their developmental guidance and counseling services to heighten students' and teachers' awareness. Again, because this progression toward multicultural diversity will parallel the emergence of individual worth in the context of community, the leadership role of the counselor as a consultant and collaborator with teachers and administrators to create beneficial learning environments for all students is imperative. We can expect that group work, both instructional and therapeutic, will increase for school counselors in effecting this change in school culture and environment. Coleman (1995) encouraged school counselors to constantly assess "the manner in which cultural realities are being created within their schools and their offices . . . to understand how each student makes sense of his or her situation and to help the student formulate effective strategies for managing the cultural challenges that face us all" (p. 185).

In summary, the future needs of students from diverse cultural and socioeconomic backgrounds will be addressed by a wide range of counseling and educational services that will encourage students to establish an identity and accept a beneficial role within the school community. To accomplish this, counselors will promote the celebration of diversity and broaden the focus of their services to students. Counseling services should help students adopt new behaviors that will facilitate their educational progress while allowing them to retain pride and respect for their heritage. In this process, counselors will continually examine their own awareness and acceptance of diversity, encourage cultural opportunities in the school and community, monitor school policies and programs for prejudicial aspects, become actively involved with different cultural groups, and develop counseling skills that accommodate all types of diversity (Lee, 1995; Pedersen & Carey, 2003).

Pedersen (1991) presented *multiculturalism* as a "fourth force" in professional counseling, "complementary to the other three forces of psychodynamic, behavioral, and humanistic explanations of human behavior" (p. 6). This view gives a broad definition to cultural diversity inclusive of demographic, socioeconomic, ethnic, religious, gender, and other variables that allow the construct of multiculturalism to be applied in all counseling relationships and processes. As such, school counselors in the future must be cognizant of all these cultural variables, as well as traditional theoretical perspectives, in attempting to explain student behaviors and design appropriate services to enhance learning and development.

Schools of Tomorrow

Schools are more than buildings, programs, and policies established by communities, organized by administrators, and implemented by teachers. Today and always schools will be defined and described by the students who enroll, attend, and in effect "become the school." As such, we can expect tomorrow's schools to reflect the diversity of U.S. society. This diversity will include all the aspects predicted earlier for the students of tomorrow: (1) a need to adapt to technological changes and advances; (2) the reality of an increasing lifespan that will simultaneously lengthen the dying process; (3) multiculturalism as an emerging significant force in education; (4) concern about healthcare and new diseases, such as new forms of viral infections that are resistant to current medication; (5) poverty as a divisive force in schools and society; (6) continued changes in employment trends and how the workweek is defined; and (7) increased violence and loss of security in U.S. communities.

Nearly two decades ago, Walz (1991) outlined nine trends that may affect the future of this country. Here, we adapt his predictions and add population forecasts and employment trends for counselors (Population Reference Bureau, 2006; U.S. Department of Labor, 2006). As with all social and economic forecasts, these trends should be considered with some caution. Nevertheless, they provide a stimulus and opportunity for dialogue about the future practice of school counseling.

1. Overall population in the United States is expected to grow at a rate of about forty percent over the next forty-five years (Population Reference Bureau, 2006). At the same time, a maturing population will complement this moderate growth. Although kindergarten through high school enrollments might be expected to stabilize, college populations will continue to grow as nontraditional, older students pursue formal education. U.S. businesses will continue to demand a better-educated work force. More accurately, they will require a work force educated in the applied sciences with technical knowledge and higher-order thinking skills. Demands on education will invite alternative education programs such as year-round schools and preschool programs. The counseling literature has begun to address this trend and the counselor's role in providing services to preschool populations (Hohenshil & Brown, 1991).

2. As noted earlier, cultural diversity is expected to expand significantly. With current U.S. immigration trends, the work force will reflect a multilingual, multicultural society. Schools will be expected to educate a diverse population of students, enabling them to adjust to a new society, become productive in the work force, and realize self-satisfaction in their lives.

3. Increased demands for services, including education, will put greater strain on already overstretched state and federal budgets. Private resources will be sought to respond to social and educational problems. As an example, the Gates Foundation (www.gates foundation.org/UnitedStates/Education, n.d.) has contributed millions to assist schools. We can expect businesses and government to cooperate in ventures that address many of these issues. Schools may see more involvement from business and industry, with the expectation that student outcomes become more clearly stated and measured.

4. Ever-changing information technology will have a continuous effect on communications and on how people work and live. Schools will require resources to keep up with technological advances as they become more important to instructional programs and student learning. Concerns about individual privacy will need to be addressed as new technology becomes available to gather more data on how people live. The opportunity to work at home will increase for many people as access to home computers and the Internet expands, and home learning will become a normal part of the educational process for many students. Distance learning as well as home-schooling programs might have an increasing impact on the way students are taught and learn.

5. The United States' role as an economic, industrial, and military leader will change as the world moves towards globalization. This process has already begun as a new world economy is emerging and global telecommunications and travel are rapidly expanding. At the same time, however, resistance to uniformity and a backlash towards asserting one's own culture and heritage is constantly evident. If this backlash persists, schools will feel the conflict firsthand. It has the potential to be a disruptive force in the future progress of our schools.

6. Medical developments and healthcare issues, on one hand, will improve the quality of life for many people and, on the other, will be criteria that separate people according to their ability to pay for services. Personal health concerns will be connected to responsible behaviors, such as with the spread of AIDS or bacterial contamination, and conflict between environmental responsibility and personal safety will increase. Communities will continue to struggle over where to locate hazardous waste disposal systems, garbage dumps, and power plants. As schools attempt to teach students about these social issues, it will be difficult to remain neutral amid emotional conflicts that pit neighbors against one another.

7. Economic, technological, and governmental changes in this and other countries will facilitate a restructuring of business and industry worldwide. Consumer markets will change with an aging, multicultural population comprising the major buyers. These and other changes will have an impact on career choices for the students of tomorrow. Schools of the future will have to implement learning programs that enable students to be flexible in their career development and vocational choices. More important, schools will need to realign curricula to teach the content and skills needed by workers in a technologically and scientifically sophisticated world.

8. The family unit will be a stabilizing factor amid all this change. Yet, the family itself will continue to take on new characteristics. Divorce is expected to decline, but two-income families may continue to grow in number. New technology and high-tech consumer services will alter traditional family behaviors such as meal times, television viewing, housecleaning, and other family chores and activities. Childcare will be an increasing concern, and schools will become more involved in preschool programs for younger students. Future school counselors will need the knowledge and skills to work with younger populations.

9. To a degree, social issues will replace concerns about economic growth and development that dominated most recent decades. As the nation becomes more involved in global issues, local communities will paradoxically pay attention to violence, homelessness, poverty, terrorism, and other debilitating concerns. Schools will become central units of communication and education, much as they were in many communities at the beginning of the twentieth century, helping citizens to address and solve local issues.

10. The demand for counselors to meet the needs of growing and diverse populations that require higher levels of formal and technical education is predicted. The U.S. Department of Labor anticipates that the employment of professional counselors is expected to "grow faster than average for all occupations through 2014" (2006). However, budgetary constraints may dampen the number of actual jobs in the future. More important, if the demand for school counselors increases, but schools and school systems fail to use counselors to lead comprehensive programs of services for students, parents, and teachers through the development and implementation of comprehensive programs, counselors may not continue in these positions. Some research suggests that newly hired counselors might be leaving their positions after a few years because school systems are not using them in roles advocated by the profession through comprehensive school counseling programs (Schmidt, Weaver, & Aldredge, 2001).

If these predictions come true, schools of the future will change in many ways. They will not be isolated from the concerns and needs of the community and society. Neither will schools remain autonomous organizations that ignore parents or discourage involvement of business and industry in matters of education. The restructuring of tomorrow's schools includes involvement of many aspects of society, cooperation with a multitude of community agencies and institutions of higher education, alternative programs to meet the needs of diverse populations, and shared governance among administrators, teachers, and parents. Elements of school restructuring that will have particular importance for school counselors in the future are technology, parental involvement, teacher collaboration, school-based community services, and youth service.

Technology

As noted earlier in this text, expanded electronic and computer technology will be used in the broad context of learning for all students. As such, new and expanded technology will influence every aspect of learning and communication, including guidance activities and counseling services (Baker & Gerler, 2004; Hohenshil, 2000; Sink, 2005). School counselors will be actively involved in planning and using new technology to deliver services to a wide range of students, parents, and teachers. Just as schools of tomorrow must adapt technology in restructuring learning environments and processes, counselors too must integrate new systems and services into their programs. As schools restructure for the future, it is inevitable that the programs within schools, such as counseling and related services, will need to change.

The future use of technology by school counselors depends on how counselors view the potential value of these tools. If viewed as a means of facilitating learning and involvement rather than diminishing human interaction, technology can become an asset. The difference may be as simple as the language counselors choose in adapting various technologies. Counselors who discover and use a positive language to describe innovative services will be able to transform their role in schools and integrate advanced technology with helping relationships and learning processes to benefit students.

Equally important as the language they choose to describe the use of technology in delivering services will be counselors' ethical understanding regarding the appropriate and inappropriate application of these advances (Guillot-Miller & Partin, 2003). Future counselors must understand the ethical implications of using computers and other electronic technology to provide counseling services, locate resource information, and assess students' interests and abilities. Such ethical understanding will be guided by professional associations and certifying organizations such as the American Counseling Association, its divisions, and the National Board of Certified Counselors.

Parental Involvement

Much educational research and literature in past years emphasized the importance of parental involvement in education (Stone & Dahir, 2006). Overall, research shows that successful students are blessed with strong support from parents and guardians at home, and this support is complemented by appropriate instructional programs at school. Supportive relationships between the home and school will continue as a requisite for the educational success of students in the years to come.

In the future, school counselors will play a significant role in establishing communication and strengthening relationships between parents and schools. This role will include the collaborative, consultative, instructional, and counseling services described here as components of a comprehensive school counseling program. Consequently, counselors will help schools assess parents' needs, set goals for increasing parental involvement, and design strategies to develop beneficial partnerships by encouraging parental involvement in a wide range of activities. These activities include inviting parents to sit on advisory committees for school governance, recruiting parents as tutors in the instructional program, involving parents in fundraising and school development projects, and enrolling parents in educational programs to strengthen parenting skills and learn about child and adolescent development. In addition, future school counselors will continue to provide counseling and consulting services to parents as clients who are facing temporary barriers in their family life.

Some of the predicted changes in family lifestyles, including dual career roles and at-home work schedules for parents will alter relationships between the home and school. In the next century, more students may stay at home, at least part of the "school day," learning through interactive media and with their parents also at home working. Such arrangements will require more collaboration and cooperation between teachers in the school and parents as the at-home instructional supervisors. Tomorrow's counselors might have a role in facilitating and nurturing these relationships between the home and school.

Teacher Collaboration

In addition to working more closely with parents, teachers in the future will collaborate with each other to ensure that all students have an opportunity to receive adequate instruction and achieve accordingly in their academic pursuits. Again, advanced technology, alternative school programs, flexible schedules, and home instruction are factors that will influence how teachers work together to create effective programs and design responsive learning environments.

To succeed in this cooperative venture, teachers will need relationship skills and support from the school community. School counselors are in an ideal position and have the background to assist teachers with these needs. Helping teachers focus on their combined efforts with each other to meet the needs of *all* students will be a major challenge for future school counselors. By planning teacher workshops and leading support groups, counselors contribute to this collaborative process. The skills that teachers perfect for establishing strong working relationships with each other will also benefit their relationships with parents.

If, as predicted, parental involvement becomes an essential ingredient of future schools, teachers will be front-line collaborators with parents. To be successful in this role, teachers will need communication skills and an empathic understanding of the parent's perspective of the school, the child, and the learning process. No longer will teachers be the sole experts in educating students. Instead, they will become leaders among a group of experts, including parents, who strive to design appropriate learning programs for children and adolescents, enabling students to take charge of their futures. Of all the trends predicted, this partnership has the most potential for improving schools and education in the twenty-first century.

School-Based Services

One collaborative relationship that could emerge in future years is a closer union between school counselors and other helping professionals in local communities. In past years, school counselors have assumed the role of referral agents, helping students and families locate and receive appropriate services to address an array of challenges. As a result, a multitude of public and private agencies has offered a wide range of services from social welfare to psychiatric care for students and their parents. As noted previously, there is little reason to believe that extensive social, medical, and other services will be needed any less in the years to come. What may change, however, is the way these many services are coordinated and delivered by counselors, physicians, and other professionals.

Currently, most of these services are provided outside the school setting. This arrangement requires considerable coordination and follow-up by the school to be certain that appointments are kept, evaluations are performed, and services are received. With divergent student populations and the likelihood that additional and expanded services for these students and their families will be needed, school-based service models may provide an efficient and effective alternative to outside referrals. If such service-delivery models emerge, school counselors will have ready access to medical and social interventions for students and parents. In school-based approaches to comprehensive student services, physicians, physicians' assistants, nurses, social workers, mental-health counselors, and other helping professions will be scheduled at school to provide direct services to identified students and their families. Such models have the potential to greatly improve referral and follow-up processes.

School-based services would allow counselors to retain their leadership roles in comprehensive programs. Counselors would also continue to offer all the developmental, preventive, and remedial services extended in the past, but when additional services were indicated, other professionals would be readily available to students and families.

Youth Service

Another trend in U.S. schools involves programs that combine classroom instruction with social service and activism. Known collectively as youth service or service-learning programs, many of these are already implemented in schools across the country. They cover a range of projects from performing environmental cleanup to operating day-care programs (Kleiner & Chapman, 2000). In states across the country, youth service programs have been implemented and evaluated (Carter, 1998; Veale & Morley, 1997; Warren & Fanscali, 1999). Outcomes have shown a relationship between youth services and dropout prevention and nonacademic needs of students. At the same time, findings suggest when youth service programs expect to have an effect on academic development, they must include a strong educational component (Warren & Fanscali, 1999).

The idea of combining education with service is not new. Civic education, social studies, and other curricular areas have long proposed that students should actively participate in community service and government projects to learn firsthand about social responsibility. Since World War I, a number of government initiatives, university reports, and educational books have encouraged the incorporation of youth service into the schooling process (Boyer, 1983; Conrad & Hedin, 1991; Goodlad, 1984). Youth services advocates have periodically promoted these activities under the premise that "schools should inculcate the values of social reform and teach the attitudes, knowledge, and skills necessary to accomplish it" (Conrad & Hedin, 1991, p. 744).

In some respects, youth service has been reflected in peer helper programs presented and promoted in the school counseling literature of recent years (Myrick, 2003). As with youth service programs, peer helper services are founded in part on the belief that such experiences raise social consciousness, develop understanding for fellow human beings, and create a learning atmosphere that enhances the overall development of students. As Lewis (1991) noted in her book for children on social activism, students who reach out to others in caring and socially active ways "learn to take charge" of their own lives (p. 2). They gain confidence in what they are able to accomplish regarding critical life tasks that encompass aspects of educational, social, and career development.

If social service has the potential to improve learning and foster student development to the extent that advocates assume, future school counselors will want to propose such programs. By establishing peer helper programs, encouraging community service, and recognizing students who contribute and participate in such endeavors, counselors participate in and contribute to youth service initiatives. As with guidance activities in general, youth service is most effective when integrated into the curriculum as part of an ongoing educational program for all students.

The preceding description of schools of tomorrow merely scratches the surface of myriad ways that the role of school counselors might be influenced by future trends. Technology, parental involvement, teacher collaboration, school-based services, and youth service are among many ideas that have the potential to expand, and in some ways redefine, the counselor's role in school. Whether counselors are prepared to meet these expanded demands or readjust their programs to include broader dimensions will, in part, determine the future of school counseling.

The Future of School Counseling

As students and schools move through the twenty-first century and confront the range of changes and challenges predicted for the future, counselors in schools must be ready to assist. Comprehensive programs and responsive services established and delivered by school counselors in the past need to be evaluated in light of the future. Traditional guidance and counseling services will no longer meet the needs of future students and families. School counselors at all levels—elementary, middle, and high school—can be expected to adjust their goals, create expanded services, develop new skills, and serve broader populations in the years to come. To meet these challenges, future counselors will

1. *Develop a broader knowledge of human development throughout the lifespan.* Clearly, counselors in schools will work with a wide audience of parents and teachers in helping students become successful. For this reason, communication skills and knowledge of adult learning and development will be required to establish beneficial collaborative relationships.

2. *Adapt to new technology.* The counseling profession will be affected as dramatically as other professions by the technology explosion of recent years. Computer-assisted learning, interactive media, voice-to-print capability, cybercounseling over the Internet, and other innovations will have a tremendous impact on all types of counseling services from information dissemination to therapeutic interactions. At the same time, counselors will monitor the ethical implications of such advances on their professional role and functions in schools.

3. *Increase the use of group processes.* Parental involvement, teacher collaboration, and youth services will require additional group methods and processes by school counselors. Similarly, diverse student populations of future schools will demand services that bring individuals together in groups to increase understanding and facilitate helping relationships.

4. *Expand their professional development.* Counselor preparation programs will reflect the emerging trends and future needs of school populations. By ensuring closer collaboration with other professions, counselors will become better informed and more skilled at assessing needs, selecting interventions, and referring clients to other resources when appropriate. As noted above, technology will play an increasingly important role in assisting counselors with these functions.

5. *Measure the outcome of their services.* The school counseling profession can no longer rely on its legacy for survival. With so many demands placed on public funds and costs straining the fiscal limits of all schools, counselors will be required to demonstrate their value to the overall education, welfare, and development of students. This means that counselors must demonstrate how they serve students, parents, and teachers and whether these services make a difference in people's lives. The issue of measuring outcomes not only addresses the effectiveness of particular counseling services, but more important, it also elevates the efficacy of the profession.

6. *Become professionally and perhaps politically active through state and national counseling associations to ensure the integrity of the school counseling profession.* At the same time that the profession has attempted to give clarity and value to the role of school counselors, we have seen a diminished emphasis on program leadership and direct services to students, replaced by testing coordination, administration of special education procedures, routine clerical tasks, and other functions. School counselors in the future will need to be more visible, assertive, and persuasive in reclaiming the roles for which they have prepared and are promoted by their professional associations.

With this chapter, we finish our journey through the past, present, and future of the school counseling profession. As a student of counseling who plans to assume the role of a school counselor, you will join the ranks of thousands before you who helped to establish this profession, as well as contemporary colleagues who with you are beginning to create the future. It is a noble challenge. I have been fortunate to spend over thirty-five years in the school counseling profession. In that time as a counselor, supervisor, and counselor educator, I have witnessed the benefits of having highly skilled counselors in schools. I commend you on your choice of career and welcome you in this venture of providing beneficial school counseling programs and services for students, parents, and teachers in the future. You have my best wishes for success as a professional counselor.

Additional Readings

Baker, S. B., & Gerler, E. R. (2004). *School Counseling for the Twenty-First Century* (4th ed.) (Upper Saddle River, NJ: Prentice Hall).
  Chapter 14 in this text gives an excellent overview of the transition that young counselors will make when moving from their graduate study to the role of a school counselor.

Paisley, P. O., & Borders, L. D. (1995). School Counseling: An Evolving Specialty, *Journal of Counseling and Development, 74*(2), 150–153.
  This article reviews school counseling as a professional specialty and discusses its historical development, standards of preparation and certification, and future trends and issues for counselors to consider.

Pedersen, P., & Carey, J. C. (Eds.) (2003). *Multicultural Counseling in Schools* (2nd ed.) (Boston: Allyn and Bacon).
  This edited volume consists of several interesting chapters about how counselors can enhance multicultural awareness in their schools. The chapters are written by different authors and cover a range of topics from dropout prevention strategies to family-based approaches.

Websites

Center for the Study and Prevention of Violence
  www.colorado.edu/cspv
Institute for Research on Poverty
  www.irp.wisc.edu
National Center for Children in Poverty
  www.nccp.org
National Multicultural Institute
  www.nmci.org

Southeastern Equity Center
  www.southeastequity.org
U.S. Office of Migrant Education
  www.ed.gov/programs/mep
Youth Service
  www.ysa.org

Exercises

1. Visit a school and ask a small group of students to design a school of the future. In helping with their designs you might suggest that they consider what school buildings of the future might be like, what elements classrooms will have that are not here today, and what students will be like.

2. In this chapter, we have predicted some possibilities for school counseling in the future. What does your future hold? Brainstorm and list ten things that will be different about your life in the future. Share this list with a classmate. How many things on both of your lists will you control? How many things will be inevitable? What will these changes mean for you as a professional counselor?

Appendix

Ethical Standards for School Counselors

Revised June 26, 2004
Ethical Standards for School Counselors was adopted by the ASCA Delegate Assembly, March 19, 1984, revised March 27, 1992, June 25, 1998, and June 26, 2004.

Preamble

The American School Counselor Association (ASCA) is a professional organization whose members are certified/licensed in school counseling with unique qualifications and skills to address the academic, personal/social and career development needs of all students. Professional school counselors are advocates, leaders, collaborators and consultants who create opportunities for equity in access and success in educational opportunities by connecting their programs to the mission of schools and subscribing to the following tenets of professional responsibility:

- Each person has the right to be respected, be treated with dignity and have access to a comprehensive school counseling program that advocates for and affirms all students from diverse populations regardless of ethnic/racial status, age, economic status, special needs, English as a second language or other language group, immigration status, sexual orientation, gender, gender identity/expression, family type, religious/spiritual identity and appearance.
- Each person has the right to receive the information and support needed to move toward self-direction and self-development and affirmation within one's group identities, with special care being given to students who have historically not received adequate educational services: students of color, low socio-economic students, students with disabilities and students with nondominant language backgrounds.
- Each person has the right to understand the full magnitude and meaning of his/her educational choices and how those choices will affect future opportunities.
- Each person has the right to privacy and thereby the right to expect the counselor-student relationship to comply with all laws, policies, and ethical standards pertaining to confidentiality in the school setting.

In this document, ASCA specifies the principles of ethical behavior necessary to maintain the high standards of integrity, leadership and professionalism among its members. The

Ethical Standards for School Counselors were developed to clarify the nature of ethical responsibilities held in common by school counseling professionals. The purposes of this document are to:

- Serve as a guide for the ethical practices of all professional school counselors regardless of level, area, population served or membership in this professional association;
- Provide self-appraisal and peer evaluations regarding counselor responsibilities to students, parents/guardians, colleagues and professional associates, schools, communities and the counseling profession; and
- Inform those served by the school counselor of acceptable counselor practices and expected professional behavior.

A. *Responsibilities to Students*

A.1. *Responsibilities to Students*

The professional school counselor:

a. Has a primary obligation to the student, who is to be treated with respect as a unique individual.
b. Is concerned with the educational, academic, career, personal and social needs and encourages the maximum development of every student.
c. Respects the student's values and beliefs and does not impose the counselor's personal values.
d. Is knowledgeable of laws, regulations, and policies relating to students and strives to protect and inform students regarding their rights.

A.2. *Confidentiality*

The professional school counselor:

a. Informs students of the purposes, goals, techniques and rules of procedure under which they may receive counseling at or before the time when the counseling relationship is entered. Disclosure notice includes the limits of confidentiality such as the possible necessity for consulting with other professionals, privileged communication, and legal or authoritative restraints. The meaning and limits of confidentiality are defined in developmentally appropriate terms to students.
b. Keeps information confidential unless disclosure is required to prevent clear and imminent danger to the student or others or when legal requirements demand that confidential information be revealed. Counselors will consult with appropriate professionals when in doubt as to the validity of an exception.
c. In absence of state legislation expressly forbidding disclosure, considers the ethical responsibility to provide information to an identified third party who, by his/her relationship with the student, is at a high risk of contracting a disease that is commonly known to be communicable and fatal. Disclosure requires satisfaction of all of the following conditions:

- Student identifies partner or the partner is highly identifiable
- Counselor recommends the student notify partner and refrain from further high-risk behavior
- Student refuses
- Counselor informs the student of the intent to notify the partner
- Counselor seeks legal consultation as to the legalities of informing the partner

d. Requests of the court that disclosure not be required when the release of confidential information may potentially harm a student or the counseling relationship.

e. Protects the confidentiality of students' records and releases personal data in accordance with prescribed laws and school policies. Student information stored and transmitted electronically is treated with the same care as traditional student records.

f. Protects the confidentiality of information received in the counseling relationship as specified by federal and state laws, written policies and applicable ethical standards. Such information is only to be revealed to others with the informed consent of the student, consistent with the counselor's ethical obligation.

g. Recognizes his/her primary obligation for confidentiality is to the student but balances that obligation with an understanding of the legal and inherent rights of parents/ guardians to be the guiding voice in their children's lives.

A.3. Counseling Plans

The professional school counselor:

a. Provides students with a comprehensive school counseling program that includes a strong emphasis on working jointly with all students to develop academic and career goals.

b. Advocates for counseling plans supporting students' right to choose from the wide array of options when they leave secondary education. Such plans will be regularly reviewed to update students regarding critical information they need to make informed decisions.

A.4. Dual Relationships

The professional school counselor:

a. Avoids dual relationships that might impair his/her objectivity and increase the risk of harm to the student (e.g., counseling one's family members, close friends, or associates). If a dual relationship is unavoidable, the counselor is responsible for taking action to eliminate or reduce the potential for harm. Such safeguards might include informed consent, consultation, supervision and documentation.

b. Avoids dual relationships with school personnel that might infringe on the integrity of the counselor/student relationship

A.5. Appropriate Referrals

The professional school counselor:

a. Makes referrals when necessary or appropriate to outside resources. Appropriate referrals may necessitate informing both parents/guardians and students of applicable resources and making proper plans for transitions with minimal interruption of services. Students retain the right to discontinue the counseling relationship at any time.

A.6. Group Work

The professional school counselor:

a. Screens prospective group members and maintains an awareness of participants' needs and goals in relation to the goals of the group. The counselor takes reasonable precautions to protect members from physical and psychological harm resulting from interaction within the group.

b. Notifies parents/guardians and staff of group participation if the counselor deems it appropriate and if consistent with school board policy or practice.

c. Establishes clear expectations in the group setting and clearly states that confidentiality in group counseling cannot be guaranteed. Given the developmental and chronological ages of minors in schools, the counselor recognizes the tenuous nature of confidentiality for minors renders some topics inappropriate for group work in a school setting.

d. Follows up with group members and documents proceedings as appropriate.

A.7. Danger to Self or Others

The professional school counselor:

a. Informs parents/guardians or appropriate authorities when the student's condition indicates a clear and imminent danger to the student or others. This is to be done after careful deliberation and, where possible, after consultation with other counseling professionals.

b. Will attempt to minimize threat to a student and may choose to 1) inform the student of actions to be taken, 2) involve the student in a three-way communication with parents/guardians when breaching confidentiality or 3) allow the student to have input as to how and to whom the breach will be made.

A.8. Student Records

The professional school counselor:

a. Maintains and secures records necessary for rendering professional services to the student as required by laws, regulations, institutional procedures and confidentiality guidelines.

b. Keeps sole-possession records separate from students' educational records in keeping with state laws.

c. Recognizes the limits of sole-possession records and understands these records are a memory aid for the creator and in absence of privilege communication may be subpoenaed and may become educational records when they 1) are shared with others in verbal or written form, 2) include information other than professional opinion or personal observations and/or 3) are made accessible to others.

d. Establishes a reasonable timeline for purging sole-possession records or case notes. Suggested guidelines include shredding sole-possession records when the student transitions to the next level, transfers to another school or graduates. Careful discretion and deliberation should be applied before destroying sole-possession records that may be needed by a court of law such as notes on child abuse, suicide, sexual harassment or violence.

A.9. *Evaluation, Assessment and Interpretation*

The professional school counselor:

    a. Adheres to all professional standards regarding selecting, administering, and interpreting assessment measures and only utilizes assessment measures that are within the scope of practice for school counselors.

    b. Seeks specialized training regarding the use of electronically-based testing programs in administering, scoring and interpreting that may differ from that required in more traditional assessments.

    c. Considers confidentiality issues when utilizing evaluative or assessment instruments and electronically based programs.

    d. Provides interpretation of the nature, purposes, results and potential impact of assessment/evaluation measures in language the student(s) can understand.

    e. Monitors the use of assessment results and interpretations, and takes reasonable steps to prevent others from misusing the information.

    f. Uses caution when utilizing assessment techniques, making evaluations and interpreting the performance of populations not represented in the norm group on which an instrument is standardized.

    g. Assesses the effectiveness of his/her program in having an impact on students' academic, career and personal/social development through accountability measures especially examining efforts to close achievement, opportunity and attainment gaps.

A.10. *Technology*

The professional school counselor:

    a. Promotes the benefits of and clarifies the limitations of various appropriate technological applications. The counselor promotes technological applications (1) that are appropriate for the student's individual needs, (2) that the student understands how to use and (3) for which follow-up counseling assistance is provided.

    b. Advocates for equal access to technology for all students, especially those historically underserved.

    c. Takes appropriate and reasonable measures for maintaining confidentiality of student information and educational records stored or transmitted over electronic media including although not limited to fax, electronic mail and instant messaging.

    d. While working with students on a computer or similar technology, takes reasonable and appropriate measures to protect students from objectionable and/or harmful online material.

    e. Who is engaged in the delivery of services involving technologies such as the telephone, videoconferencing and the Internet takes responsible steps to protect students and others from harm.

A.11. Student Peer Support Program

The professional school counselor:

Has unique responsibilities when working with student-assistance programs. The school counselor is responsible for the welfare of students participating in peer-to-peer programs under his/her direction.

B. Responsibilities to Parents/Guardians

B.1. Parent Rights and Responsibilities

The professional school counselor:

    a. Respects the rights and responsibilities of parents/guardians for their children and endeavors to establish, as appropriate, a collaborative relationship with parents/guardians to facilitate the student's maximum development.

    b. Adheres to laws, local guidelines and ethical standards of practice when assisting parents/guardians experiencing family difficulties that interfere with the student's effectiveness and welfare.

    c. Respects the confidentiality of parents/guardians.

    d. Is sensitive to diversity among families and recognizes that all parents/guardians, custodial and noncustodial, are vested with certain rights and responsibilities for the welfare of their children by virtue of their role and according to law.

B.2. Parents/Guardians and Confidentiality

The professional school counselor:

    a. Informs parents/guardians of the counselor's role with emphasis on the confidential nature of the counseling relationship between the counselor and student.

    b. Recognizes that working with minors in a school setting may require counselors to collaborate with students' parents/guardians.

    c. Provides parents/guardians with accurate, comprehensive and relevant information in an objective and caring manner, as is appropriate and consistent with ethical responsibilities to the student.

    d. Makes reasonable efforts to honor the wishes of parents/guardians concerning information regarding the student, and in cases of divorce or separation exercises a good-faith effort to keep both parents informed with regard to critical information with the exception of a court order.

C. *Responsibilities to Colleagues and Professional Associates*

C.1. *Professional Relationships*

The professional school counselor:

a. Establishes and maintains professional relationships with faculty, staff and administration to facilitate an optimum counseling program.
b. Treats colleagues with professional respect, courtesy and fairness. The qualifications, views and findings of colleagues are represented to accurately reflect the image of competent professionals.
c. Is aware of and utilizes related professionals, organizations and other resources to whom the student may be referred.

C.2. *Sharing Information with Other Professionals*

The professional school counselor:

a. Promotes awareness and adherence to appropriate guidelines regarding confidentiality, the distinction between public and private information and staff consultation.
b. Provides professional personnel with accurate, objective, concise and meaningful data necessary to adequately evaluate, counsel and assist the student.
c. If a student is receiving services from another counselor or other mental health professional, the counselor, with student and/or parent/guardian consent, will inform the other professional and develop clear agreements to avoid confusion and conflict for the student.
d. Is knowledgeable about release of information and parental rights in sharing information.

D. *Responsibilities to the School and Community*

D.1. *Responsibilities to the School*

The professional school counselor:

a. Supports and protects the educational program against any infringement not in students' best interest.
b. Informs appropriate officials in accordance with school policy of conditions that may be potentially disruptive or damaging to the school's mission, personnel and property while honoring the confidentiality between the student and counselor.
c. Is knowledgeable and supportive of the school's mission and connects his/her program to the school's mission.
d. Delineates and promotes the counselor's role and function in meeting the needs of those served. Counselors will notify appropriate officials of conditions that may limit or curtail their effectiveness in providing programs and services.

    e. Accepts employment only for positions for which he/she is qualified by education, training, supervised experience, state and national professional credentials and appropriate professional experience.

    f. Advocates that administrators hire only qualified and competent individuals for professional counseling positions.

    g. Assists in developing: (1) curricular and environmental conditions appropriate for the school and community, (2) educational procedures and programs to meet students' developmental needs and (3) a systematic evaluation process for comprehensive, developmental, standards-based school counseling programs, services, and personnel. The counselor is guided by the findings of the evaluation data in planning programs and services.

D.2. Responsibility to the Community

The professional school counselor:

    a. Collaborates with agencies, organizations and individuals in the community in the best interest of students and without regard to personal reward or remuneration.

    b. Extends his/her influence and opportunity to deliver a comprehensive school counseling program to all students by collaborating with community resources for student success.

E. Responsibilities to Self

E.1. Professional Competence

The professional school counselor:

    a. Functions within the boundaries of individual professional competence and accepts responsibility for the consequences of his/her actions.

    b. Monitors personal well-being and effectiveness and does not participate in any activity that may lead to inadequate professional services or harm to a student.

    c. Strives through personal initiative to maintain professional competence including technological literacy and to keep abreast of professional information. Professional and personal growth are ongoing throughout the counselor's career.

E.2. Diversity

The professional school counselor:

    a. Affirms the diversity of students, staff and families.

    b. Expands and develops awareness of his/her own attitudes and beliefs affecting cultural values and biases and strives to attain cultural competence.

    c. Possesses knowledge and understanding about how oppression, racism, discrimination and stereotyping affects her/him personally and professionally.

    d. Acquires educational, consultation and training experiences to improve awareness, knowledge, skills and effectiveness in working with diverse populations: ethnic/racial status, age, economic status, special needs, ESL or ELL, immigration status, sexual orientation, gender, gender identity/expression, family type, religious/spiritual identity and appearance.

F. Responsibilities to the Profession

F.1. Professionalism

The professional school counselor:

a. Accepts the policies and procedures for handling ethical violations as a result of maintaining membership in the American School Counselor Association.
b. Conducts herself/himself in such a manner as to advance individual ethical practice and the profession.
c. Conducts appropriate research and report findings in a manner consistent with acceptable educational and psychological research practices. The counselor advocates for the protection of the individual student's identity when using data for research or program planning.
d. Adheres to ethical standards of the profession, other official policy statements, such as ASCA's position statements, role statement and the ASCA National Model, and relevant statutes established by federal, state and local governments, and when these are in conflict works responsibly for change.
e. Clearly distinguishes between statements and actions made as a private individual and those made as a representative of the school counseling profession.
f. Does not use his/her professional position to recruit or gain clients, consultees for his/her private practice or to seek and receive unjustified personal gains, unfair advantage, inappropriate relationships or unearned goods or services.

F.2. Contribution to the Profession

The professional school counselor:

a. Actively participates in local, state and national associations fostering the development and improvement of school counseling.
b. Contributes to the development of the profession through the sharing of skills, ideas and expertise with colleagues.
c. Provides support and mentoring to novice professionals.

G. Maintenance of Standards

Ethical behavior among professional school counselors, association members and non-members, is expected at all times. When there exists serious doubt as to the ethical behavior of colleagues or if counselors are forced to work in situations or abide by policies that do not reflect the standards as outlined in these Ethical Standards for School Counselors, the counselor is obligated to take appropriate action to rectify the condition. The following procedure may serve as a guide:

1. The counselor should consult confidentially with a professional colleague to discuss the nature of a complaint to see if the professional colleague views the situation as an ethical violation.
2. When feasible, the counselor should directly approach the colleague whose behavior is in question to discuss the complaint and seek resolution.
3. If resolution is not forthcoming at the personal level, the counselor shall utilize the channels established within the school, school district, the state school counseling association and ASCA's Ethics Committee.
4. If the matter still remains unresolved, referral for review and appropriate action should be made to the Ethics Committees in the following sequence:

   - State school counselor association
   - American School Counselor Association

5. The ASCA Ethics Committee is responsible for:

   - Educating and consulting with the membership regarding ethical standards
   - Periodically reviewing and recommending changes in code
   - Receiving and processing questions to clarify the application of such standards; questions must be submitted in writing to the ASCA Ethics chair.
   - Handling complaints of alleged violations of the ethical standards. At the national level, complaints should be submitted in writing to the ASCA Ethics Committee, c/o the Executive Director, American School Counselor Association, 1101 King St., Suite 625, Alexandria, VA 22314.

References

ACES-ASCA Joint Committee on the Elementary School Counselor. (1966). The Elementary School Counselor: Preliminary Statement, *Personnel and Guidance Journal, 44,* 658–661.

Alexander, K., & Alexander, M. D. (1992). *American Public School Law* (3rd ed.) (St. Paul, MN: West Publishing).

Alexander, K., & Alexander, M. D. (2003). *The Law of Schools, Students, Teachers* (3rd ed.) (St. Paul, MN: West—Thomson Learning).

Alexander, W. M., & George, P. S. (1981). *The Exemplary Middle School* (New York: Holt, Rinehart and Winston).

Allen, R. D. (1931). A Group Guidance Curriculum in the Senior High School, *Education, 52,* 189–194.

Amatea, E. S., & Fabrick, F. (1981). Family Systems Counseling: A Positive Alternative to Traditional Counseling, *Elementary School Guidance and Counseling, 15,* 223–236.

American Counseling Association. (1989). Responsibilities of Users of Standardized Tests, *Guidepost, 31*(6), 11, 16, 27–28.

American Counseling Association (ACA). (1995). *Code of Ethics and Standards of Practice* (Alexandria, VA: Author).

American Counseling Association. (2005). *ACA Code of Ethics* (Alexandria, VA: Author).

American Educational Research Association (AERA). (1985). *Standards for Educational and Psychological Testing* (Washington, DC: Author).

American Psychiatric Association (APA). (2000). *Diagnostic and Statistical Manual of Mental Disorders* (4th ed.) (DSM-IV-TR) (Washington, DC: Author).

American Psychological Association. (1988). *Code of Fair Testing Practices* (Washington, DC: Joint Committee on Testing Practices, American Psychological Association).

American School Counselor Association (ASCA). (1997). ASCA Publishes National Standards for School Counseling Programs, *The ASCA Counselor, 35*(1), 1, 7.

American School Counselor Association (ASCA). (1998). *Ethical Standards* (Alexandria, VA: Author).

American School Counselor Association. (2003). *American School Counselor Association National Model: A Framework for School Counseling Programs* (Alexandria, VA: Author).

American School Counselor Association. (2004). *Ethical Standards for School Counselors.* (Alexandria, VA: Author).

Anastasi, A. (1988). *Psychological Testing* (6th ed.) (New York: Macmillan).

Anderson, B. (1996). *The Counselor and the Law* (4th ed.) (Alexandria, VA: American Counseling Association).

Aponte, J. F., & Crouch, R. T. (2000). The Changing Ethnic Profile in the United States in the Twenty-first Century. In J. F. Aponte & J. Wohl (Eds.), *Psychological Intervention and Cultural Diversity* (2nd ed., pp. 1–17) (Boston: Allyn and Bacon).

Aponte, J. F., & Johnson, L. R. (2000). Ethnicity and supervision: Models, methods, processes, and issues. In J. F. Aponte & J. Wohl (Eds.), *Psychological Intervention and Cultural Diversity* (2nd ed., pp. 268–285) (Boston: Allyn and Bacon).

Arrendondo, P., Toporek, R., Brown, S. P., Jones, J., Locke, D. C., Sanchez, J., & Stadler, H. (1996). Operationalization of the Multicultural Competencies, *Journal of Multicultural Counseling & Development, 24,* 42–78.

Aubrey, R. F. (1978). Consultation, School Interventions, and the Elementary Counselor, *Personnel and Guidance Journal, 56,* 351–354.

Aubrey, R. F. (1982). Program Planning and Evaluation: Road Map of the 80s, *Elementary School Guidance and Counseling, 17,* 52–50.

Axline, V. M. (1947). Nondirective Therapy for Poor Readers, *Journal of Consulting Psychology, 11,* 61–69.

Baker, S. B. (1994). Mandatory Teaching Experience for School Counselors: An Impediment to Uniform Certification Standards for School Counselors, *Counselor Education and Supervision, 33,* 314–326.

Baker, S. B., & Gerler, E. R. (2004). *School Counseling for the Twenty-first Century* (4th ed.) (Upper Saddle River, NJ: Merrill/Prentice Hall).

Baruth, L. G., & Manning, M. L. (1999). *Multicultural Counseling and Psychotherapy: A Lifespan Perspective* (2nd ed.) (Upper Saddle River, NJ: Prentice Hall).

Baruth, L. G., & Robinson, E. H. (1987). *An Introduction to the Counseling Profession* (Englewood Cliffs, NJ: Prentice Hall).

Beers, C. (1908). *A Mind That Found Itself* (New York: Longmans Green. Republished by Doubleday, 1953).

Bemak, F., & Chung, R. C. (2000). Psychological Intervention with Immigrants and Refugees. In J. F. Aponte & J. Wohl (Eds.), *Psychological Intervention and Cultural Diversity* (2nd ed., pp. 200–213) (Boston: Allyn and Bacon).

Bergan, J. R. (1977). *Behavioral Consultation* (Columbus, OH: Merrill).

Berliner, D. C., & Biddle, B. J. (1995). *The Manufactured Crisis: Myths, Fraud, and the Attack on America's Public Schools* (Reading, MA: Addison-Wesley).

Blocher, D. H. (1966). *Developmental Counseling* (New York: Ronald Press).

Bloom, J. W., & Walz, G. R. (Eds.) (2000). *Cybercounseling and Cyberlearning: Strategies and Resources for the Millennium* (Alexandria, VA: American Counseling Association).

Bonnington, S. B. (1993). Solution-focused Brief Therapy: Helpful Interventions for School Counselors, *The School Counselor, 41,* 126–128.

Borders, L. D., & Drury, S. M. (1992). Comprehensive School Counseling Programs: A Review for Policymakers and Practitioners, *Journal of Counseling and Development, 70,* 487–498.

Boscardin, M. L., Brown-Chidsey, R., González-Martínez, J. C. (2003). Counseling Approaches to Working with Students with Disabilities from Diverse Backgrounds. In P. B. Pedersen and J. C. Carey (Eds.), *Multicultural Counseling in Schools: A Practical Handbook* (2nd ed., pp. 257–269) (Boston, MA: Allyn and Bacon).

Bowman, R. P. (1987). Small-Group Guidance and Counseling in Schools: A National Survey of School Counselors, *The School Counselor, 34,* 256–262.

Bowman, R. P., & Campbell, C. A. (1989). Positive Peer Influence: A Powerful Tool for Middle School Counselors, *American Middle School Education, 12*(3), 5–16.

Boyer, E. L. (1983). *High School: A Report on Secondary Education in America* (New York: Harper & Row).

Breckenridge, A. (1987). Performance Improvement Program Helps Administrators Assess Counselor Performance, *NASSP Bulletin, 71,* 23–26.

Brewer, J. M. (1932). *Education as Guidance: An Examination of the Possibilities of Curriculum in Terms of Life Activities in Elementary and Secondary Schools and Colleges* (New York: Macmillan).

Brown, D., Pryzwansky, W. B., & Shulte, A. C. (2006). *Psychological Consultation and Collaboration: Introduction to Theory and Practice* (6th ed.) (Boston: Allyn and Bacon).

Brown, D., & Srebalus, D. (1972). *Contemporary Guidance Concepts and Practices* (Dubuque, IA: William C. Brown Co.).

Brown, D., & Trusty, J. (2005). *Designing and Leading Comprehensive School Counseling Programs* (Belmont, CA: Brooks/Cole—Thomson Learning).

Bruce, M. A. (1995). Brief Counseling: An Effective Model for Change, *The School Counselor, 42,* 353–363.

Bruce, M. A., & Hooper, G. C. (1997). Brief Counseling versus Traditional Counseling: A Comparison of Effectiveness, *The School Counselor, 44,* 171–184.

Campbell, C. (2000). K–12 Peer Helper Programs. In J. Wittmer (Ed.), *Managing Your School Counseling Program: K-12 Developmental Strategies* (pp. 229– 241) (Minneapolis, MN: Education Media Corporation).

Campbell, C. A. (Ed.) (1993). Counseling through Play: An Overview, *Elementary School Guidance & Counseling, 28,* 2–75.

Campbell, C. A., & Dahir, C. A. (1997). *Sharing the Vision: The National Standards for School Counseling Programs* (Alexandria, VA: American School Counselor Association).

Caplan, G. (1970). *The Theory and Practice of Mental Health Consultation* (New York: Basic Books).

Caplan, G., & Caplan, R. B. (1999). *Mental Health Consultation and Collaboration* (Prospect Heights, IL: Waveland).

Carkhuff, R. R., & Berenson, B. G. (1967). *Beyond Counseling and Psychotherapy* (New York: Holt, Rinehart & Winston).

Carns, A. W., & Carns, M. R. (1991). Teaching Study Skills, Cognitive Strategies, and Metacognitive Skills through Self-diagnosed Learning Styles. *The School Counselor, 38,* 341–346.

Carter, K. G. (1998). *Hooking Out-of-School Youth through Service Learning: Linking Learning with Life* (Clemson, SC: National Dropout Prevention Center, Clemson University).

Casey, J. A. (1995). Developmental Issues for School Counselors Using Technology, *Elementary School Guidance and Counseling, 30,* 26–35.

Cassel, R. N. (1970). *Child Behavior Rating Scale* (Los Angeles: Western Psychological Services).

Cecil, J. H., & Comas, R. E. (1987). *Development of Strategies for the Preservation of School Counselor Preparation Programs,* Monograph (Alexandria, VA: American Association for Counseling and Development) (ERIC Document Reproduction Service No. ED 288 111).

Colbert, R. D. (1996). The Counselor's Role in Advancing School and Family Partnerships, *The School Counselor, 44,* 100–104.

Cole, C. (Ed.) (1990). Guidance in Rural and Small Schools, *The Rural Educator, 4*(2), 1–6.

Coleman, H. K. (1995). Cultural Factors and the Counseling Process: Implications for School Counselors, *The School Counselor, 42,* 180–185.

Combs, A. W. (Ed.) (1962). *Perceiving, Behaving, Becoming* (Washington, DC: Yearbook of the Association for Supervision and Curriculum Development).

Comer, J. P. (2005). A Missing Element in School Reform, *Phi Delta Kappan, 86,* 757–763.

Comstock, D. (Ed.) (2005). *Diversity and Development: Critical Contexts That Shape our Lives and Relationships* (Belmont, CA: Brooks/Cole).

Conrad, D., & Hedin, D. (1991). School-Based Community Service: What We Know from Research and Theory, *Phi Delta Kappan, 72*(10), 743–749.

Corey, G. (2001). *The Theory and Practice of Counseling and Psychotherapy* (6th ed.) (Pacific Grove, CA: Brooks/Cole).

Corey, G., & Corey, M. S. (2002). *Issues and Ethics in the Helping Professions* (6th ed.) (Pacific Grove, CA: Brooks/Cole).

Corey, M. S., & Corey, G. (2002). *Groups: Process and Practice* (6th ed.) (Pacific Grove, CA: Brooks/ Cole).

Crabbs, S. K., & Crabbs, M. A. (1977). Accountability: Who Does What to Whom When, Where, and How?, *The School Counselor, 25,* 104–109.

Cunningham, B., & Hare, J. (1989). Essential Elements of a Teacher In-Service Program on Child Bereavement, *Elementary School Guidance and Counseling, 23,* 175–182.

Dahir, C. A. (2001). The National Standards for School Counseling Programs: Development and Implementation, *Professional School Counseling, 4,* 320–327.

Dahir, C. A., Sheldon, C. B., & Valiga, M. J. (1998). *Vision into Action: Implementing the National Standards for School Counseling Programs* (Alexandria, VA: American School Counselor Association).

D'Andrea, M., & Daniels, J. (2004, January). Multicultural Competence and Social Justice: Some New Year's Resolutions, *Counseling Today, 46*(7), 24–25.

Davis, J. L., & Mickelson, D. J. (1994). School Counselors: Are You Aware of Ethical and Legal Aspects of Counseling?, *The School Counselor, 42,* 5–13.

Davis, T. E., & Osborn, C. J. (2000). *The Solution-Focused School Counselor: Shaping Professional Practice* (Philadelphia, PA: Accelerated Development).

De Luca, R. V., Hazen, A., & Cutler, J. (1993). Evaluation of a Group Counseling Program for Preadolescent Female Victims of Incest, *Elementary School Guidance & Counseling, 28,* 104–114.

de Shazer, S. (1985). *Keys to Solution in Brief Therapy* (New York: Norton).

de Shazer, S. (1991). *Putting Difference to Work* (New York: Norton).

Dettmer, P., Dyck, N., & Thurston, L. P. (1999). *Consultation, Collaboration and Team Work for Students with Special Needs* (Boston, MA: Allyn and Bacon).

DeVoss, J. A., & Andrews, M. F. (2006). *School Counselors as Educational Leaders* (Boston: Houghton Mifflin).

Dollarhide, C. T., & Lemberger, M. E. (2006). "No Child Left Behind": Implications for School Counselors, *Professional School Counseling, 9,* 295–304.

Driver, H. I. (1958). *Counseling and Learning through Small Group Discussion* (Madison, WI: Monona Publications).

Drummond, R. J. (2004). *Appraisal Procedures for Counselors and Helping Professionals* (5th ed.) (Upper Saddle River, NJ: Merrill/Prentice Hall).

Dugan, W. E. (Ed.) (1958). *Counseling Points of View.* Proceedings of the Minnesota Counselors Association Midwinter Conference, 1958 (Minneapolis: University of Minnesota Press).

Eckerson, L., & Smith, H. (1966). *Scope of Pupil Personnel Services* (Washington, DC: Office of Education, U.S. Department of Health, Education, and Welfare).

Edmonds, R. R. (1979). Effective Schools for the Urban Poor, *Educational Leadership, 37,* 15–24.

Education Trust. (1997). *Transforming School Counseling: Planning Grant Guidelines.* (Washington, DC: Author).

Education Trust. (1998). *Summary of Work being Undertaken for Transforming School Counseling Initiative.* (Washington, DC: Author).

Education Trust. (2003). *Transforming School Counseling Initiative.* Retrieved June 23, 2006, from www2.edtrust.org/EdTrust/Transforming+School+Counseling.

Elias, M. J., & Hoover, H. V. A. (1997). Computer-facilitated Counseling for At-risk Students in a Social Problem-solving "Lab," *Elementary School Guidance and Counseling, 31,* 293–310.

Erford, B. T. (Ed.) (2003). *Transforming the School Counseling Profession* (Upper Saddle River, NJ: Merrill/Prentice Hall).

Erford, B. T., House, R., & Martin, P. (2003). Transforming the School Counseling Profession. In B. T. Erford (Ed.), *Transforming the School Counseling Profession* (pp. 1–20) (Upper Saddle River, NJ: Merrill/Prentice Hall).

Erikson, E. H. (1963). *Childhood and Society.* New York: W. W. Norton.

Eysenck, H. J. (1961). The Effects of Psychotherapy. In H. J. Eysenck (Ed.), *Handbook of Abnormal Psychology* (New York: Basic Books).

Fairchild, T. N. (1986). Time Analysis: Accountability Tool for Counselors, *The School Counselor, 34,* 36–43.

Fatum, R. W., & Hoyle, J. C. (1996). Is It Violence? School Violence from the Student Perspective: Trends and Interventions, *The School Counselor, 44,* 28–34.

Faust, V. (1968a). *History of Elementary School Counseling: Overview and Critique* (Boston: Houghton Mifflin).

Faust, V. (1968b). *The Counselor-Consultant in the Elementary School* (Boston: Houghton Mifflin).

Ficklen, E. (1987). Why School Counselors Are So Tough to Manage and Evaluate, *The Executive Educator, 9,* 19–20.

Fischer, L., & Sorenson, G. P. (1996). *School Law for Counselors, Psychologists, and Social Workers* (3rd ed.) (New York: Longman).

Fishbaugh, M. S. (1997). *Models of Collaboration* (Boston: Allyn and Bacon).

Foster, C. M. (1967). The Elementary School Counselor: How Perceived? *Counselor Education and Supervision, 6,* 102–107.

Frazier, F., & Matthes, W. A. (1975). Parent Education: A Comparison of Adlerian and Behavioral Approaches, *Elementary School Guidance and Counseling, 19,* 31–38.

Froehle, T. C., & Rominger, R. L., III. (1993). Directions in Consultation Research: Bridging the Gap Between Science and Practice, *Journal of Counseling and Development, 71,* 693–699.

Fullmer, D. W., & Bernard, H. W. (1972). *The School Counselor-Consultant* (Boston: Houghton Mifflin).

Gallassi, J. P., & Gulledge, S. A. (1997). The Middle School Counselor and Teacher-Advisor Programs, *Professional School Counseling, 1(2),* 55–61.

Gates Foundation. (n.d.). *Education.* Retrieved October 17, 2006, from www.gatesfoundation.org/United States/Education.

Gazda, G. M. (1989). *Group Counseling: A Developmental Approach* (4th ed.) (Boston: Allyn and Bacon).

Gazda, G. M., Ginter, E. J., & Horne, A. M. (2001). *Group Counseling and Group Psychotherapy: Theory and Application* (Boston: Allyn and Bacon).

George, P. S. (1986). The Counselor and Modern Middle-Level Schools: New Roles in New Schools, *The School Counselor, 33,* 178–188.

George, R. L., & Cristiani, T. S. (1995). *Counseling Theory and Practice* (4th ed.) (Boston: Allyn and Bacon).

Gerler, E. R. (Ed.) (1990). Special Issue on Multimodal Theory, Research, and Practice, *Elementary School Guidance and Counseling, 24(4),* 242–317.

Gerler, E. R. (1995). Advancing Elementary and Middle School Counseling through Computer Technology, *Elementary School Guidance and Counseling, 30,* 8–16.

Gerler, E. R., & Anderson, R. F. (1986). The Effects of Classroom Guidance on Children's Success in School, *Journal of Counseling and Development, 65,* 78–81.

Geroski, A. M., Rodgers, K. A., & Breen, D. T. (1997). Using the DSM-IV to Enhance Collaboration among School Counselors, Clinical Counselors, and Primary Care Physicians, *Journal of Counseling & Development, 75,* 231–239.

Getson, R., & Schweid, R. (1976). School Counselors and the Buckley Amendment—Ethical Standards Squeeze, *The School Counselor, 24,* 56–58.

Giannotti, T. J., & Doyle, R. E. (1982). The Effectiveness of Parental Training on Learning Disabled Children and their Parents, *Elementary School Guidance and Counseling, 17,* 131–136.

Gibson, R. L. (1990). Teacher Opinions of High School Counseling and Guidance Programs: Then and Now, *The School Counselor, 37,* 248–255.

Gibson, R. L., & Mitchell, M. H. (1999). *Introduction to Counseling and Guidance* (4th ed.) (Upper Saddle River, NJ: Prentice Hall).

Gibson, R. L., Mitchell, M. H., & Basile, S. K. (1993). *Counseling in the Elementary School: A Comprehensive Approach* (Boston: Allyn and Bacon).

Gladding, S. T. (2002). *Family Therapy: History, Theory, and Practice* (3rd ed.) (Upper Saddle River, NJ: Prentice-Hall).

Gladding, S. T. (2003). *Group Work: A Counseling Specialty* (4th ed.) (Upper Saddle River, NJ: Merrill/Prentice Hall).

Gladding, S. T. (2004). *Counseling: A Comprehensive Profession* (4th ed.) (Upper Saddle River, NJ: Merrill/Prentice Hall).

Glasser, W. (1965). *Reality Therapy: A New Approach to Psychiatry* (New York: Harper & Row).

Glasser, W. (1984). Reality Therapy. In R. J. Corsini (Ed.), *Current Psychotherapies* (3rd ed., pp. 320–353) (Itasca, IL: F. E. Peacock).

Glasser, W. (2000). *Reality Therapy in Action* (New York: Harper Collins).

Golden, L. B. (1988). Quick Assessment of Family Functioning, *The School Counselor, 35,* 179–184.

Goldman, L. (1982). Assessment in Counseling: A Better Way, *Measurement and Evaluation in Guidance, 15,* 70–73.

Good, T. L., & Brophy, J. E. (1994). *Looking in Classrooms* (6th ed.) (New York: Harper Collins).

Goodlad, J. L. (1984). *A Place Called School* (New York: McGraw-Hill).

Green, A. G., Conley, J. A., & Barnett, K. (2005). Urban School Counseling: Implications for Practice and Training, *Professional School Counseling, 8,* 189–195.

Greene, K. (1967). Functions Performed and Preferred by Elementary School Counselors in the United States, *Dissertation Abstracts International, 28.* (University Microfilms No. 67-14 780).

Gronlund, N. E., & Linn, R. L. (1990). *Measurement and Evaluation in Teaching* (6th ed.) (New York: Macmillan).

Grummon, D. L., & John, E. S. (1954). Changes over Client-Centered Therapy Evaluated on Psychoanalytically Based Thematic Apperception Test Scales. In C. R. Rogers & R. F. Dymond (Eds.), *Psychotherapy and Personality Change* (Chicago: University of Chicago Press).

Guillot-Miller, L., & Partin, P. W. (2003). Web-Based Resources for Legal and Ethical Issues in School Counseling, *Professional School Counseling, 7,* 52–57.

Gysbers, N. C., & Henderson, P. (1988). *Developing and Managing Your School Guidance Program.* (Alexandria, VA: American Association for Counseling and Development).

Gysbers, N. C., & Henderson, P. (Eds.) (1997). *Comprehensive Guidance Programs That Work—II* (Greensboro, NC: ERIC/CASS).

Gysbers, N. C., & Henderson, P. (2000). *Developing and Managing your School Guidance Program* (3rd ed.) (Alexandria, VA: American Association for Counseling and Development).

Gysbers, N. C., & Henderson, P. (2001). Comprehensive Guidance and Counseling Programs: A Rich History and a Bright Future, *Professional School Counseling, 4,* 246–256.

Gysbers, N. C., Lapan, R. T., & Blair, M. (1999). Closing in on Statewide Implementation of a Comprehensive Guidance Program Model, *Professional School Counseling, 2,* 357–366.

Gysbers, N. C., & Moore, E. H. (1981). *Improving Guidance Programs* (Englewood Cliffs, NJ: Prentice Hall).

Haas, C. (2000, January). Entangled in the Net: Online Counseling Can Turn "You've got mail" into "You've got help," *Counseling Today, 42*(7), 26–27.

Hadley, H. R. (1988). Improving Reading Scores through a Self-esteem Intervention Program, *Elementary School Guidance and Counseling, 22,* 248–252.

Hansen, J. C., Himes, B. S., & Meier, S. (1990). *Consultation: Concepts and Practices* (Englewood Cliffs, NJ: Prentice Hall).

Hare, J., & Cunningham, B. (1988). Effects of Child Bereavement Training Program for Teachers, *Death Studies, 12,* 345–353.

Harrison, T. (2000). Brief Counseling in the K–12 Developmental Guidance Program. In J. Wittmer (Ed.), *Managing Your School Counseling Program: K–12*

Developmental Strategies (pp. 85–94) (Minneapolis, MN: Educational Media Corporation).

Helms, J. E., & Cook, D. A. (1999). *Using Race and Culture in Counseling and Psychotherapy* (Boston: Allyn and Bacon).

Henderson, P. A. (1987). Effects of Planned Parental Involvement in Affective Education," *The School Counselor, 35,* 22–27.

Henderson, P. A., Kelby, T. J., & Engebretson, K. M. (1992). Effects of a Stress-Control Program on Children's Locus of Control, Self-Concept, and Coping Behavior, *The School Counselor, 40,* 125–130.

Herr, E. L. (1986). The Relevant Counselor, *The School Counselor, 34,* 7–13.

Herr, E. L., Cramer, S. H., & Niles, S. G. (2004). *Career Guidance and Counseling through the Lifespan: Systemic Approaches* (6th ed.) (Boston: Allyn and Bacon).

Herring, R. D. (1999). Experiencing a Lack of Money and Appropriate Skin Color: A Personal Narrative, *Journal of Counseling and Development, 77,* 25–27.

Hetherington, E. M., & Kelly, J. (2002). *For Better or for Worse: Divorce Reconsidered* (New York: Norton).

Hill, G., & Luckey, E. (1969). *Guidance for Children in Elementary Schools* (New York: Appleton-Century-Crofts).

Hinkle, J. S. (1993). Training School Counselors to Do Family Counseling, *Elementary School Guidance and Counseling, 27,* 252–257.

Hitchner, K. W., & Tifft-Hitchner, A. (1987). *A Survival Guide for the Secondary School Counselor* (West Nyack, NY: The Center for Applied Research in Education).

Hitchner, K. W., & Tifft-Hitchner, A. (1996). *Counseling Today's Secondary Students: Practical Strategies, Techniques & Materials for the School Counselor* (Englewood Cliffs, NJ: Prentice Hall).

Hobbs, B. B., & Collison, B. B. (1995). School-Community Agency Collaboration: Implications for School Counselors, *School Counselor, 43,* 58–65.

Hohenshil, T. H. (1981). The Future of the Counseling Profession: Three Issues, *Personnel and Guidance Journal, 60,* 133–134.

Hohenshil, T. H. (2000). High Tech Counseling, *Journal of Counseling and Development, 78,* 365–368.

Hohenshil, T. H., & Brown, M. B. (1991). Public School Counseling Services for Prekindergarten Children, *Elementary School Guidance and Counseling, 26,* 4–11.

Holcomb-McCoy, C. (1998). *School Counselor Preparation in Urban Settings.* ERIC Clearinghouse on Urban Education. (ERIC Document Reproduction Service No. ED 418 343)

Holcomb-McCoy, C. (2003). Multicultural Competence. In B. T. Erford (Ed.), *Transforming the School Counseling Profession* (pp. 317–330) (Upper Saddle River, NJ: Merrill/Prentice Hall).

Holcomb-McCoy, C., & Mitchell, N. (2005). A Descriptive Study of Urban School Counseling Programs, *Professional School Counseling, 8,* 203–218.

Holland, J. L. (1985). *Making Vocational Choices: A Theory of Careers* (2nd ed.) (Englewood Cliffs, NJ: Prentice Hall).

House, A. E. (1999). *DSM-IV: Diagnosis in the Schools* (New York: Guilford).

Housley, W. F., McDaniel, L. C., & Underwood, J. R. (1990). Mandated Assessment of Counselors in Mississippi, *The School Counselor, 37,* 294–302.

Houston, P. D. (2005). NCLB: Dreams and Nightmares, *Phi Delta Kappan, 86,* 469–470.

Howe, H., II (1991). America 2000: A Bumpy Ride on Four Trains, *Phi Delta Kappan, 73,* 192–203.

Hoy, W. K., Tarter, C. J., & Kottkamp, R. B. (1991). *Open Schools/Healthy Schools* (Newbury, CA: Sage Publications).

Humes, C. W., & Hohenshil, T. H. (1987). Elementary Counselors, School Psychologists, School Social Workers: Who Does What?, *Elementary School Guidance and Counseling, 22,* 37–45.

Hutchinson, R. L., Barrick, A. L., & Groves, M. (1986). Functions of Secondary School Counselors in the Public Schools: Ideal and Actual, *The School Counselor, 34,* 87–91.

Hutchinson, R. L., & Bottorff, R. L. (1986). Selected High School Counseling Services: Student Assessment, *The School Counselor, 33,* 350–354.

Ibrahim, F., Helms, B., & Thompson, D. (1983), Counselor Role and Function: An Appraisal by Consumers and Counselors, *The Personnel and Guidance Journal, 61* 597–60.

Institute for Research on Poverty. (2006). *Who was Poor in 2004?* (Madison: University of Wisconsin). Retrieved July 29, 2006, from www.irp.wisc.edu/faqs/faq3.htm.

Isaacs, M. L., & Stone, C. (1999). School Counselors and Confidentiality: Factors Affecting Professional Choices, *Professional School Counseling, 2,* 258–266.

Isaacson, L. E., & Brown, D. (2000). *Career Information, Career Counseling, and Career Development* (7th ed.) (Boston: Allyn and Bacon).

Ivey, A. E. (1986). *Developmental Therapy.* (San Francisco, CA: Jossey-Bass).

Ivey, A. E. (2000). *Developmental Therapy: Theory into Practice.* (North Amherst, MA: Mirotraining Associates).

Ivey, A. E., & Ivey, M. B. (2003). *Intentional Interviewing and Counseling: Facilitating Development in a Multicultural Society* (5th ed.). (Pacific Grove, CA: Brooks/Cole).

Ivey, A. E., Pedersen, P. B., & Ivey, M. B. (2001). *Intentional Group Counseling: A Microskills Approach.* (Pacific Grove, CA: Brooks/Cole).

Jackson, M. D., & Brown, D. (1986). Use of Systematic Training for Effective Parenting (STEP) with Elementary School Parents, *The School Counselor, 34,* 100–104.

Jackson, M. L., & Vontress, C. E. (2003, July) Where has Culture in Counseling Gone?, *Counseling Today, 46*(1), 7, 10.

Jacobs, E. E., Masson, R. L., & Harvill, R. L. (2002). *Group Counseling: Strategies and Skills* (4th ed.) (Pacific Grove, CA: Brooks/Cole—Thomson Learning).

Johnson, C. (Ed.) (1983). *Microcomputers and the School Counselor* (Alexandria, VA: American School Counselor Association).

Johnson, D. W., & Johnson, F. P. (2000). *Joining Together: Group Theory and Group Skills* (7th ed.) (Boston: Allyn and Bacon).

Johnson, L. S. (2000). Promoting Professional Identity in an Era of Educational Reform, *Professional School Counseling, 4,* 31–40.

Joint Center for Poverty Research (2001). *Rural Dimensions of Welfare Reform* (Chicago, IL: Northwestern University/University of Chicago). Retrieved January 3, 2001, from www.jcpr.org/conference/ruralbriefing.html#selectfindings.

Jourard, S. M. (1964). *The Transparent Self: Self-Disclosure and Well-Being* (Princeton, NJ: Van Nostrand).

Kameen, M. C., Robinson, E. H., & Rotter, J. C. (1985). Coordination Activities: A Study of Perceptions of Elementary and Middle School Counselors, *Elementary School Guidance and Counseling, 20,* 97–104.

Kaplan, L. S. (1996). Outrageous or Legitimate Concerns: What Some Parents are Saying about School Counseling, *The School Counselor, 43,* 165–170.

Kaplan, L. S. (1997). Parents' Rights: Are School Counselors at Risk?, *The School Counselor, 44,* 334–343.

Keys, S. G., & Bemak, F. (1997). School-Family-Community Linked Services: A School Counseling Role for Changing Times, *The School Counselor, 44,* 255–263.

Kimura, D. (2002, May). Sex differences in the brain. *Scientific American.* Retrieved July 23, 2006, from www.sciam.com/article.cfm?articleID=00018E9D-879D-1D06-8E49809EC588EEDF.

Kirk, S. A., Gallagher, J. J., & Anastasiow, N. J. (1996). *Educating Exceptional Children* (8th ed.) (Boston: Houghton Mifflin).

Kleiner, B., & Chapman, C. (2000). *Youth Service-Learning and Community Service among 6th- through 12th-Grade Students in the United States: 1996 and 1999*

(Washington, DC: National Center for Education Statistics). (ERIC Document Reproduction Service No. ED 439 086)

Kohn, A. (1991). Caring Kids: The Role of the Schools, *Phi Delta Kappan, 72*(7), 496–506.

Kottler, J. A. (2001). *Learning Group Leadership: An Experiential Approach* (Boston: Allyn and Bacon).

Kreeger, K. Y. (2002, February). Sex-Based Differences Continue to Mount, *The Scientist, 16*(4). Retrieved July 23, 2006, from www.the-scientist.com/yr2002/feb/research_020218.html.

Krumboltz, J. D. (1974). An Accountability Model for Counselors, *Personnel and Guidance Journal, 52,* 639–646.

Kurpius, D. (1978). Consultation Theory and Process: An Integrated Model, *Personnel and Guidance Journal, 56*(6), 335–338.

Kurpius, D. J., & Brown, D. (Eds.) (1985). Consultation (Special Issue), *The Counseling Psychologist, 13,* 333–476.

Kurpius, D. J., & Brown, D. (Eds.) (1988). *Handbook of Consultation: An Intervention for Advocacy and Outreach* (Washington, DC: Association for Counselor Education and Supervision).

Kurpius, D. J., & Fuqua, D. R. (1993a). Fundamental Issues in Defining Consultation, *Journal of Counseling and Development, 71,* 598–600.

Kurpius, D. J., & Fuqua, D. R. (Eds.) (1993b). Special Issue: Consultation: A Paradigm for Helping, I, *Journal of Counseling & Development, 71,* 593–708.

Kurpius, D. J., & Fuqua, D. R. (Eds.) (1993c). Special Issue: Consultation: A Paradigm for Helping, II, *Journal of Counseling & Development, 72,* 113–198.

Kurpius, D. J., & Robinson, S. E. (1978). An Overview of Consultation, *Personnel and Guidance Journal, 56,* 320–323.

Lambie, G. W., & Williamson, L. L. (2004). The Challenge to Change from Guidance Counseling to Professional School Counseling: A Historical Proposition, *Professional School Counseling, 8,* 124–131.

Langston, D. (2001). Tired of Playing Monopoly? In M. L. Anderson & P. Hill Collins (Eds.), *Race, Class, and Gender: An Anthology* (4th ed., pp. 125–134) (Belmont, CA: Wadsworth/Thomson Learning).

Lapan, R. T., Gysbers, N. C., & Petroski, G. F. (2001). Helping Seventh Graders Be Safe and Successful: A Statewide Study of the Impact of Comprehensive Guidance and Counseling Programs, *Journal of Counseling & Development, 79,* 320–330.

Lee, C. C. (Ed.) (1995). *Counseling for Diversity: A Guide for School Counselors and Related Professionals* (Boston: Allyn and Bacon).

Lee, C. C. (2001). Culturally Responsive Schools Counselors and Programs: Addressing the Needs of all Students, *Professional School Counseling, 4,* 257–261.

Lee, C. C. (2005). Urban School Counseling: Context, Characteristics, and Competencies, *Professional School Counseling, 8,* 184–188.

Lee, R. S. (1993). Effects of Classroom Guidance on Student Achievement, *Elementary School Guidance and Counseling, 27,* 163–171.

Lewis, B. (1991). *The Kids' Guide to Social Action* (Minneapolis, MN: Free Spirit Publishing).

Lewis, M. W., & Lewis, A. C. (1996). Peer Helping Programs: Helper Role, Supervisor Training, and Suicidal Behavior, *Journal of Counseling and Development, 74,* 307–314.

Locke, D. C. (2003). Improving the Multicultural Competence of Educators. In P. B. Pedersen and J. C. Carey (Eds.), *Multicultural Counseling in Schools: A Practical Handbook* (2nd ed., pp. 171–189) (Boston: Allyn and Bacon).

Lockhart, E. J. (2003). Students with Disabilities. In B. T. Erford (Ed.), *Transforming the School Counseling Profession* (pp. 357–409) (Upper Saddle River, NJ: Merrill/Prentice Hall).

Lombana, J. H. (1985). Guidance Accountability: A New Look at an Old Problem, *The School Counselor, 32,* 340–346.

Lopez, F. G. (1985). Brief Therapy: A Model for Early Counselor Training, *Counselor Education and Supervision, 34,* 307–316.

Lusky, M. B., & Hayes, R. L. (2001). Collaborative Consultation and Program Evaluation, *Journal of Counseling and Development, 79,* 26–38.

Lyman, H. B. (1998). *Test Scores and What They Mean* (6th ed.) (Boston: Allyn and Bacon).

Mabe, A. R., & Rollin, S. A. (1986). The Role of Code of Ethical Standards in Counseling, *Journal of Counseling and Development, 64,* 294–297.

Manning, M. L., & Saddlemire, R. (1996). Implementing Middle School Concepts into High Schools, *Clearinghouse, 69,* 339–343.

Martinson, R. A., & Smallenburg, H. (1958). *Guidance in the Elementary Schools* (Englewood Cliffs, NJ: Prentice Hall).

Maslow, A. H. (1957). A Philosophy of Psychology: The Need for a Mature Science of Human Nature, *Main Currents in Modern Thought, 13,* 27–32.

May, R. (Ed.) (1966). *Existential Psychology* (New York: Random House).

McCarthy, M., & Sorenson, G. (1993). School Counselors and Consultants: Legal Duties and Liabilities, *Journal of Counseling and Development, 72,* 159–168.

McKellar, R. (1964). A Study of Concepts, Functions, and Organizational Characteristics of Guidance in the Elementary School as Reported by Selected Elementary School Guidance Personnel, *Dissertation Abstracts International, 24,* 4477 (University Microfilms No. 643601).

Meeks, A. R. (1968). *Guidance in Elementary Education* (New York: Ronald Press Co).

Michael, J. (1986). *Advisor-Advisee Programs* (Columbus, OH: National Middle School Association).

Miller, F. W. (1968). *Guidance: Principles and Services* (Columbus, OH: Merrill).

Miller, G. (1988). Counselor Functions in Excellent Schools: Elementary through Secondary, *The School Counselor, 36,* 88–93.

Mitchell, C. W., Disque, J. G., & Robertson, P. (2002). When Parents Want to Know: Responding to Parental Demands for Confidential Information, *Professional School Counseling, 6,* 156–161.

Molnar-Stickels, L. (1985). Effect of a Brief Instructional Unit in Death Education on the Death Attitudes of Prospective Elementary School Teachers, *Journal of School Health, 55,* 234–235.

Morrison, J. (1995). *DSM-IV Made Easy: The Clinician's Guide to Diagnosis* (New York: Guilford).

Morrissette, P. J. (1997). The Rural School Counselor: A Review and Synthesis of the Literature, *Guidance & Counseling, 13*(1), 19–23.

Morse, C. L., & Russell, T. (1988). How Elementary Counselors See Their Role, *Elementary School Guidance and Counseling, 23,* 54–62.

Mostert, M. P. (1998). *Interprofessional Collaboration in Schools* (Boston: Allyn and Bacon).

Muro, J. J., & Kottman, T. (1995). *Guidance and Counseling in the Elementary and Middle Schools* (Madison, WI: Brown and Benchmark).

Myrick, R. D. (1984). Beyond the Issues of School Counselor Accountability, *Measurement and Evaluation in Guidance, 16,* 218–222.

Myrick, R. D. (1993). *Developmental Guidance and Counseling: A Practical Approach.* (Minneapolis, MN: Educational Media).

Myrick, R. D. (2003). *Developmental Guidance and Counseling; A Practical Approach* (4th ed.) (Minneapolis, MN: Educational Media).

Myrick, R. D., & Dixon, R. W. (1985). Changing Student Attitudes and Behavior through Group Counseling, *The School Counselor, 32,* 325–330.

Myrick, R. D., Merhill, H., & Swanson, L. (1986). Changing Student Attitudes through Classroom Guidance, *The School Counselor, 33,* 244–252.

Myrick, R. D., & Moni, L. (1976). A Status Report of Elementary School Counseling, *Elementary School Guidance and Counseling, 10,* 156–164.

Myrick, R. D., & Myrick, L. S. (1990). *The Teacher-Advisor Program: An Innovative Approach to School Guidance* (Ann Arbor, MI: ERIC/CAPS).

National Center for Children in Poverty (1999). *Poverty and Brain Development in Early Childhood* (New York: Columbia University). Retrieved May 27, 2004, from www.nccp.org/pub_pdb99.html.

Nicoll, W. G. (1992). A Family Counseling and Consultation Model for School Counselors, *The School Counselor, 39,* 351–361.

Nugent, F. A. (2000). *Introduction to the Profession of Counseling* (3rd ed.) (Columbus, OH: Merrill).

Nystul, M. S. (1993). *The Art and Science of Counseling and Psychotherapy* (New York: Merrill).

Oakland, T. (1982). Nonbiased Assessment in Counseling: Issues and Guidelines, *Measurement and Evaluation in Guidance, 15,* 107–116.

O'Hanlon, W., & Weiner-Davis, M. (1989). *In Search of Solutions: A New Direction in Psychotherapy* (New York: Norton).

Omizo, M. M., Hershberger, J. M., & Omizo, S. A. (1988). Teaching Children to Cope with Anger, *Elementary School Guidance and Counseling, 22,* 241–245.

Omizo, M. M., & Omizo, S. A. (1987). Group Counseling with Children of Divorce: New Findings, *Elementary School Guidance and Counseling, 22,* 46–52.

Owen, D. J. (1999). Computer Utilization by School Counselors, *Professional School Counseling, 2,* 179–183.

Paisley, P. O. (2001). Maintaining and Enhancing the Developmental Focus in School Counseling Programs, *Professional School Counseling, 4,* 271–278.

Paisley, P. O., & Borders, L. D. (1995). School Counseling: An Evolving Specialty, *Journal of Counseling and Development, 74*(2), 150–153.

Paisley, P. O., & Hubbard, G. T. (1989). School Counseling: State Officials' Perceptions of Certification and Employment Trends, *Counselor Education and Supervision, 29,* 60–70.

Palmo, A. J., Lowry, L. A., Weldon, D. P., & Scioscia, T. M. (1984). Schools and Family: Future Perspectives for School Counselors, *The School Counselor, 31,* 272–278.

Parloff, M. B. (1976, February 21). Shopping for the Right Therapy, *Saturday Review,* 14–16.

Parsons, F. (1909). *Choosing a Vocation* (Boston: Houghton Mifflin).

Parsons, R. D., & Kahn, W. J. (2005). *The School Counselor as Consultant: An Integrated Model for School-based Consultation* (Belmont, CA: Brooks/Cole—Thomson Learning).

Patterson, C. H. (1962). *Counseling and Guidance in Schools* (New York: Harper and Brothers).

Pedersen, P. B. (1991). Multiculturalism as a Generic Approach to Counseling, *Journal of Counseling and Development, 70,* 6–12.

Pedersen, P. B. (2000). *Handbook for developing multicultural awareness* (3rd ed.). (Alexandria, VA: American Counseling Association).

Pedersen, P. B., & Carey, J. C. (Ed.) (2003). *Multicultural Counseling in Schools: A Practical Handbook* (2nd ed.) (Boston: Allyn and Bacon).

Perry, N. S. (2000). Reaching Out: Involving Parents and Community Members in the School Counseling Program. In J. Wittmer (Ed.), *Managing Your School Counseling Program: K–12 Developmental Strategies* (pp. 264–272) (Minneapolis, MN: Educational Media Corporation).

Pérusse, R., & Goodnough, G. E. (2004). *Leadership, Advocacy, and Direct Service Strategies for Professional School Counselors* (Belmont, CA: Brooks/Cole—Thomson Learning).

Peterson, J. S., Goodman, R., Keller, T., & McCauley, A. (2004). Teachers and Non-teachers as School Counselors: Reflections on the Internship Experience, *Professional School Counseling, 7,* 246–255.

Population Reference Bureau (2006). *World Data Sheet.* Retrieved October 3, 2006, from www.prb.org/pdf06/06WorldDataSheet.pdf.

Post-Krammer, P. (1988). Effectiveness of Parents Anonymous in Reducing Child Abuse, *The School Counselor, 35,* 337–342.

Potts, B. (Summer, 1999). National Board for Professional Teaching Standards, *The ASCA Counselor, 36*(5), 3.

Purkey, S. C., & Smith, M. S. (1983). Effective Schools: A Review, *The Elementary School Journal, 83,* 427–452.

Purkey, W. W. (1970). *Self-concept and School Achievement.* (Englewood Cliffs, NJ: Prentice-Hall).

Purkey, W. W. (2000). *What Students Say to Themselves: Internal Dialogue and School Success* (Thousand Oaks, CA: Corwin Press).

Purkey, W. W., & Novak, J. (1996). *Inviting School Success* (3rd ed.) (Belmont, CA: Wadsworth).

Purkey, W. W., & Schmidt, J. J. (1990). *Invitational Learning for Counseling and Development* (Ann Arbor, MI: ERIC/CAPS).

Purkey, W. W., & Schmidt, J. J. (1996). *Invitational Counseling: A Self-Concept Approach to Professional Practice* (Pacific Grove, CA: Brooks/Cole).

Randolph, D. L., & Masker, T. (1997). Teacher Certification and the Counselor: A Follow-up Survey of School Counselor Certification Requirements, *ACES Spectrum, 57*(4), 6–8.

Rappaport, N. (2002, Fall). Increasing Teachers' Caring Potential through Advising, *Middle Matters,* 4–6.

Remley, T. P., Jr. (1985). The Law and Ethical Practice in Elementary and Middle Schools, *Elementary School Guidance and Counseling, 19,* 181–189.

Remley, T. P., & Herlihy, B. (2007). *Ethical, Legal, and Professional Issues in Counseling* (2nd ed.) (Upper Saddle River, NJ: Prentice Hall).

Reynolds, J. (2005). Familial and Relational Transitions Across the Life Span. In D. Comstock (Ed.), *Diversity and Development: Critical Contexts that Shape our Lives and Relationships* (pp. 269–298) (Belmont, CA: Brooks/Cole).

Riddle, J., Bergin, J. J., & Douzenis, C. (1997). Effects of Group Counseling on the Self-Concept of Children of Alcoholics, *Elementary School Guidance and Counseling, 31,* 192–203.

Roberts, E. B., & Borders, L. D. (1994). Supervision of School Counselors: Administrative, Program, and Counseling, *The School Counselor, 41,* 149–157.

Robinson, T. L. (2005). *The Convergence of Race, Ethnicity, and Gender: Multiple Identities in Counseling* (2nd ed.) (Upper Saddle River, NJ: Prentice Hall).

Roeber, E. C. (1963). *The School Counselor* (Washington, DC: The Center for Applied Research in Education).

Rogers, C. R. (1942). *Counseling and Psychotherapy: New Concepts in Practice* (Boston: Houghton Mifflin).

Rogers, C. R. (1951). *Client-Centered Therapy: Its Current Practice, Implications, and Theory* (Boston: Houghton Mifflin).

Rogers, C. R., Gendlin, E. T., Kiessler, D., & Truax, C. B. (1967). *The Therapeutic Relationship and Its Impact: A Study of Psychotherapy and Schizophrenics* (Madison: University of Wisconsin Press).

Rose, S. R. (1987). Social Skill Training in Middle Childhood: A Structured Group Research, *Journal for Specialists in Group Work, 12,* 144–149.

Roysircar, G. (2003). Understanding Immigrants: Acculturation Theory and Research. In F. D. Harper & J. McFadden (Eds.), *Culture and Counseling: New Approaches* (pp. 164–195) (Boston: Allyn and Bacon).

Rust, E. B. (1995). Applications of the International Computer Network for Elementary and Middle School Counseling, *Elementary School Guidance and Counseling, 30,* 16–26.

Ryan, K., & Cooper, J. M. (1988). *Those Who Can Teach* (5th ed.) (Boston: Houghton Mifflin).

Rychlak, J. F. (1985). Eclecticism in Psychological Theorizing: Good and Bad, *Journal of Counseling and Development, 63,* 351–353.

Sabella, R., & Booker, B. (2003). Using Technology to Promote Your Guidance and Counseling Program Among Stake Holders, *Professional School Counseling, 6*(3), 206–213.

Sabella, R. A. (1996). School Counselors and Computers: Specific Time-Saving Tips, *Elementary School Guidance and Counseling, 31,* 83–95.

Salo, M. M., & Shumate, S. G. (1993). *Counseling Minor Clients* (Alexandria, VA: American Counseling Association).

Scarborough, J. L. (1997). The SOS Club: A Practical Peer Helper Program, *Professional School Counseling, 1*(2), 25–29.

Schlossberg, S. M., Morris, J. D., & Lieberman, M. G. (2001). The Effects of a Counselor-Led Guidance Intervention on Students' Behaviors and Attitudes, *Professional School Counseling, 4,* 156–164.

Schmidt, J. J. (1986). Becoming an "Able" Counselor, *Elementary School Guidance and Counseling, 21,* 16–22.

Schmidt, J. J. (1987). Parental Objections to Counseling Services: An Analysis, *The School Counselor, 34,* 387–391.

Schmidt, J. J. (1990). Critical Issues for Counselor Performance Appraisal and Supervision, *The School Counselor, 38,* 86–94.

Schmidt, J. J. (1991). *A Survival Guide for the Elementary/Middle School Counselor* (West Nyack, NY: The Center for Applied Research in Education).

Schmidt, J. J. (1993a). *A Review of School Counseling Programs, K–12.* Unpublished manuscript, Chapel-Hill Carrboro City Schools, Chapel Hill, NC.

Schmidt, J. J. (1993b). *Counseling in Schools: Essential Services and Comprehensive Programs.* (Boston: Allyn and Bacon).

Schmidt, J. J. (1994). *School Counseling Program Review.* Unpublished manuscript, Washington County Schools, Plymouth, NC.

Schmidt, J. J. (1995). *School Counseling Program Review.* Unpublished manuscript, Pitt County Schools, Greenville, NC.

Schmidt, J. J. (1996). Assessing School Counseling Programs through External Reviews, *The School Counselor, 43*(2), 114–123.

Schmidt, J. J. (2000). Counselor Accountability: Justifying Your Time and Measuring Your Worth. In J. Wittmer (Ed.), *Managing Your School Counseling Program: K–12 Developmental Strategies* (2nd ed., pp. 275–291). Minneapolis, MN: Educational Media Corporation.

Schmidt, J. J. (2002). *Intentional Helping: A Philosophy for Proficient Caring Relationships* (Upper Saddle River, NJ: Merrill/Prentice Hall).

Schmidt, J. J. (2003a). *Counseling in Schools: Essential Services and Comprehensive Programs* (4th ed.) (Boston: Allyn and Bacon).

Schmidt, J. J. (2003b). *Assessment of School Counseling Programs.* Unpublished manuscript, Jones County Schools, Trenton, NC.

Schmidt, J. J. (2004). *A Survival Guide for the Elementary/Middle School Counselor* (2nd ed.) (San Francisco, CA: Jossey-Bass).

Schmidt, J. J. (2006). *Social and Cultural Foundations of Counseling and Human Services: Multiple Influences on Self-concept Development* (Boston: Allyn and Bacon).

Schmidt, J. J., & Ciechalski, J. C. (2001). School Counseling Standards: A Summary and Comparison with Other Student Services' Standards, *Professional School Counseling, 4,* 328–333.

Schmidt, J. J., & Medl, W. A. (1983). Six Magic Steps of Consulting, *The School Counselor, 30,* 212–216.

Schmidt, J. J., & Osborne, W. L. (1981). Counseling and Consulting: Separate Processes or the Same? *Personnel and Guidance Journal, 60,*168–171.

Schmidt, J. J., Weaver, F. S., & Aldredge, A. (2001). *Perceptions of School Counselor's Role and Satisfaction by Newly Hired Counselors and Principals in Eastern North Carolina.* Unpublished manuscript, East Carolina University School of Education, Greenville, NC.

Sciarra, D. T. (2004). *School Counseling: Foundations and Contemporary Issues* (Belmont, CA: Brooks/Cole—Thomson Learning).

Sexton, T. L. (1999). Evidence-Based Counseling: Implications for Counseling Practice, Preparation, and Professionalism, *ERIC Digest* (Greensboro, NC: ERIC Clearinghouse on Counseling and Student Services).

Sexton, T. L., & Whiston, S. C. (1991). A Review of the Empirical Basis for Counseling: Implications for Practice and Training, *Counselor Education and Supervision, 30,* 330–354.

Sheeley, V. L., & Herlihy, B. (1987). Privileged Communication in School Counseling: Status Update, *The School Counselor, 34,* 268–272.

Shertzer, B., & Stone, S. C. (1966). *Fundamentals of Guidance* (Boston: Houghton Mifflin).

Shertzer, B., & Stone, S. C. (1981). *Fundamentals of Guidance* (4th ed.) (Boston: Houghton Mifflin).

Shilling, L. E. (1984). *Perspective on Counseling Theories* (Englewood Cliffs, NJ: Prentice Hall).

Sink, C. A. (2001). Comprehensive Guidance and Counseling Programs and the Development of Multicultural Student-Citizens, *Professional School Counseling, 6,* 130–137.

Sink, C. A. (2004). Spirituality and Comprehensive School Counseling Programs, *Professional School Counseling, 7,* 309–317.

Sink, C. A. (2005). *Contemporary School Counseling: Theory, Research, and Practice* (Boston: Lahaska Press).

Sink, C. A., & Yillik-Downer, A. (2001). School Counselors' Perceptions of Comprehensive Guidance and

Counseling Programs: A National Survey, *Professional School Counseling, 4,* 278–288.

Stamm, M. L., & Nissman, B. S. (1979). *Improving Middle School Guidance* (Boston: Allyn and Bacon).

Stefflre, B., & Grant, W. H. (1972). *Theories of Counseling* (2nd ed.) (New York: McGraw-Hill).

Stickel, S. A. (1990). Using Multimodal Social-Skills Groups with Kindergarten Children, *Elementary School Guidance and Counseling, 24,* 281–288.

Stone, C. B., & Dahir, C. A. (2004). *School Counselor Accountability: A Measure of Student Success* (Upper Saddle River, NJ: Merrill/Prentice Hall).

Stone, C. B., & Dahir, C. A. (2006). *The Transformed School Counselor* (Boston: Lahaska/Houghton Mifflin).

Studer, J. R. (2005). *The professional school counselor: An Advocate for Students* (Belmont, CA: Brooks/Cole—Thomson Learning).

Super, D. E., Savickas, M. L., & Super, C. M. (1996). A Life-Span, Life-Space Approach to Careers. In D. Brown, L. Brooks, & Associates (Eds.), *Career Choice and Development* (2nd ed., pp. 121–178) (San Francisco, CA: Jossey-Bass).

Sussman, R. J. (2000). *Counseling over the Internet: Benefits and Challenges in the Use of New Technologies* (Greensboro: University of North Carolina, ERIC-CASS). Retrieved November 1, 2000, from www.cybercounsel.uncg.edu/manuscripts/internet counseling.htm.

Sutton, J. M., Jr., & Southworth, R. S. (1990). The Effect of the Rural Setting on School Counselors, *The School Counselor, 37,* 173–178.

Sweeney, T. J. (1998). *Adlerian Counseling: A Practitioner's Approach* (4th ed.) (Philadelphia: Accelerated Development).

Tedder, S. L., Scherman, A., & Wantz, R. A. (1987). Effectiveness of a Support Group for Children of Divorce, *Elementary School Guidance and Counseling, 22,* 102–109.

Tennyson, W. W., Miller, G. D., Skovholt, T. G., & Williams, R. D. (1989). Secondary School Counselors: What Do They Do? What Is Important?, *The School Counselor, 36,* 253–259.

Thetford, W. N. (1952). An Objective Measure of Frustration Toleration in Evaluating Psychotherapy. In W. Wolff (Ed.), *Success in Psychotherapy* (New York: Grune & Stratton).

Thomas, J. (2005, January). Calling a Cab for Oregon Students, *Phi Delta Kappan, 86,* 385–395.

Thompson, C. E. (2004). Awareness and Identity: Foundational Principles of Multicultural Practice. In T. B. Smith (Ed.), *Practicing Multiculturalism: Affirming Diversity in Counseling and Psychology* (pp. 35–56) (Boston: Allyn and Bacon).

Thompson, C. L., Rudolph, L. B., & Henderson, D. (2004). *Counseling Children* (6th ed.) (Belmont, CA: Brooks/Cole—Thomson Learning).

Thornburg, H. D. (1979). *The Bubblegum Years: Sticking with Kids from 9 to 13* (Tucson, AZ: HELP Books).

Thornburg, H. D. (1986). The Counselor's Impact on Middle-Grade Students, *The School Counselor, 33,* 170–177.

Toseland, R. W., & Rivas, R. F. (2001). *An Introduction to Group Work Practice* (4th ed.) (Boston: Allyn and Bacon).

Truax, C. B., & Carkhuff, R. R. (1967). *Towards Effective Counseling and Psychotherapy* (Chicago: Aldine).

Umansky, D. L., & Holloway, E. L. (1984). The Counselor as Consultant: From Model to Practice, *The School Counselor, 31,* 329–338.

U.S. Bureau of the Census (2003). *Population Projections.* (Washington, DC: U.S. Department of Commerce).

U.S. Department of Education (2002). *No Child Left Behind Act of 2001.* Retrieved June 27, 2006, from http://ed.gov/policy/elsec/leg/esea02/index.html.

U.S. Department of Labor (2006). *Occupational Outlook Handbook.* Retrieved October 3, 2006, from www.bls.gov/oco/ocos067.htm#outlook.

Vacc, N. A., & Loesch, L. C. (2000). *Counseling as a Profession* (3rd ed.) (Muncie, IN: Accelerated Development).

Vacc, N. A., Rhyne-Winkler, M. C., & Poidevant, J. M. (1993). Evaluation and Accountability of Counseling Services: Possible Implications for a Midsize School District, *The School Counselor, 40,* 260–266.

Van Hoose, W. H., & Vafakas, C. M. (1968). Status of Guidance and Counseling in the Elementary School, *Personnel and Guidance Journal, 46,* 536–539.

Van Horn, S. M., & Myrick, R. D. (2001). Computer Technology and the 21st Century School Counselor, *Professional School Counseling, 5,* 124–130.

VanZandt, C. E., & Hayslip, J. B. (1994). *Your Comprehensive School Guidance and Counseling Program* (New York: Longman).

Veale, J. R., & Morley, R. E. (1997). SBYSP: *School-Based Youth Services Program. 1996 Year-End Report. Executive Summary* (Des Moines: Iowa Department of Education) (ERIC Document Reproduction Service No. ED 419 051).

Vernon. A. (Ed.) (2004). *Counseling Children and Adolescents* (3rd ed.) (Denver, CO: Love).

Wachtel, S. S. (Ed.) (1994). *Molecular Genetics of Sex Determination* (San Diego, CA: Academic Press).

Walker, H. M. (1962). *Walker Problem Behavior Identification Checklist* (Los Angeles: Western Psychological Services).

Walsh, F. (2003). Changing Families in a Changing World. In F. Walsh (Ed.), *Normal Family Processes:*

Growing Diversity and Complexity (pp. 3–26) (New York: Guilford).

Walz, G. R. (1991). Nine Trends Which Will Affect the Future of the United States. In G. R. Gazda, & B. Shertzer (Eds.), *Counseling Futures* (pp. 61–69) (Ann Arbor, MI: ERIC/CAPS).

Warren, C., & Fanscali, C. (1999, April). *A Service-Based Approach to Addressing Educational and Social Outcomes for Youth: Lessons from the Evaluation of New Jersey's School-Based Youth Services Program.* Paper presented at the annual meeting of the American Educational Research Association, Montreal, Quebec, Canada.

Weathers, L. R., & Liberman, R. P. (1975). The Contingency Contracting Exercise, *Journal of Behavior Therapy and Experimental Psychiatry, 6,* 208–214.

Wheeler, P. T., & Loesch, L. (1981). Program Evaluation and Counseling: Yesterday, Today and Tomorrow, *Personnel and Guidance Journal, 59,* 573–578.

Whiston, S. C., & Sexton, T. L. (1998). A Review of School Counseling Outcome Research: Implications for Practice, *Journal of Counseling & Development, 76,* 412–426.

Wiggins, J. D. (1993). A 10-Year Follow-up of Counselors Rated High, Average, or Low in Effectiveness, *The School Counselor, 40,* 380–383.

Williams, G. T., Robinson, F. F., & Smaby, M. H. (1988). School Counselors Using Group Counseling with Family-School Problems, *The School Counselor, 35,* 169–178.

Williams, R. E., Omizo, M. M., & Abrams, B. C. (1984). Effects of STEP on Parental Attitudes and Locus of Control of their Learning Disabled Children, *The School Counselor, 32,* 126–133.

Williamson, E. G. (1939). *How to Counsel Students* (New York: McGraw-Hill).

Williamson, E. G. (1950). *Counseling Adolescents* (New York: McGraw-Hill).

Wittmer, J., & Clark, M. A. (Eds.) (2007). *Managing Your School Counseling Program: K–12 Developmental Strategies* (Minneapolis, MN: Educational Media).

Wrenn, C. G. (1962). *The Counselor in a Changing World* (Washington, DC: American Personnel and Guidance Association).

Wrenn, C. G. (1973). *The World of the Contemporary Counselor* (Boston: Houghton).

Zunker, V. G. (2002). *Career Counseling: Applied Concepts of Life Planning* (6th ed.) (Pacific Grove, CA: Brooks/Cole).

Zytowski, D. G. (1972). Four Hundred Years Before Parsons, *Personnel and Guidance Journal, 50,* 443–50.

Author Index

Subject Index